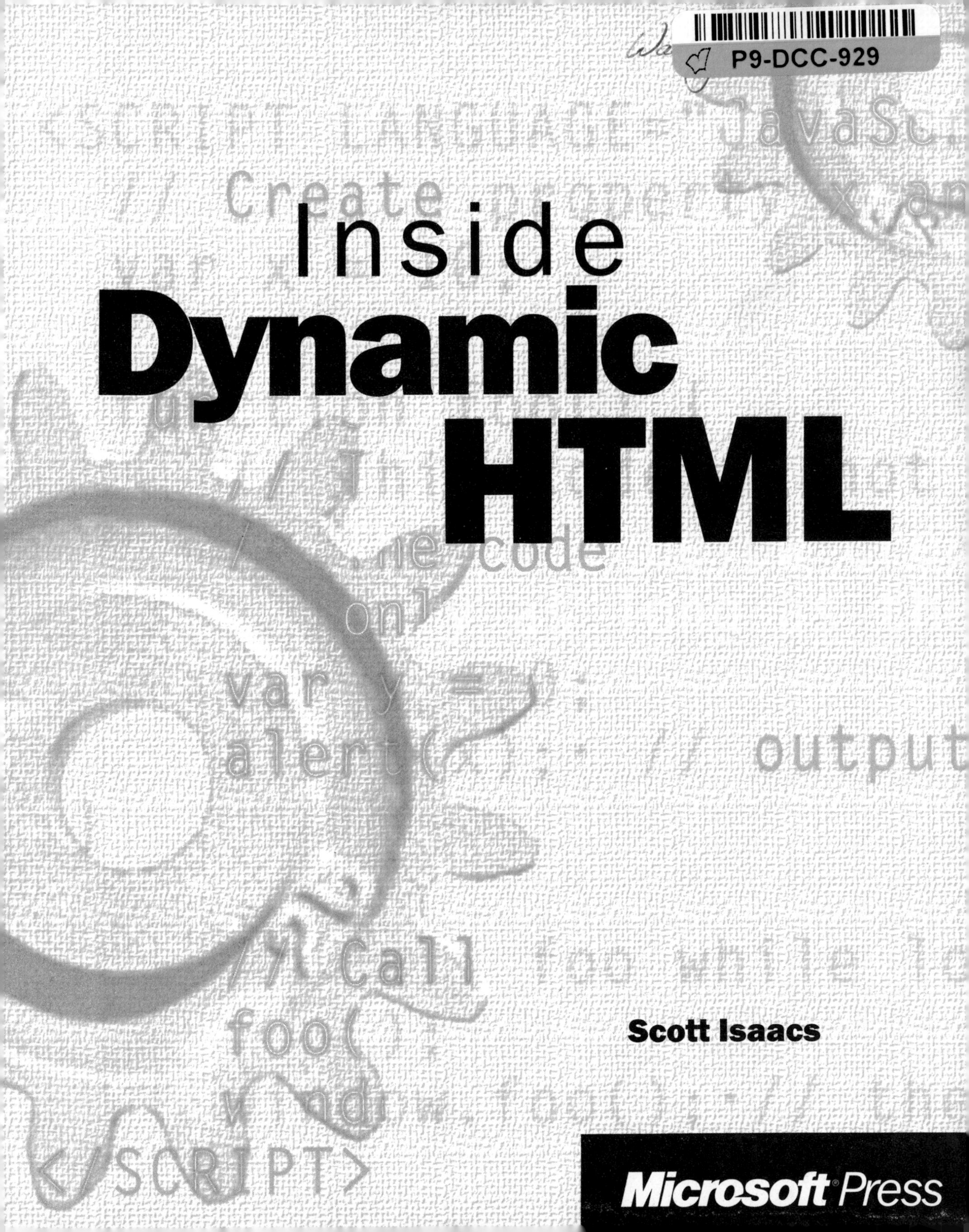

Inside
Dynamic
HTML
Scott Isaacs
Microsoft Press

PUBLISHED BY
Microsoft Press
A Division of Microsoft Corporation
One Microsoft Way
Redmond, Washington 98052-6399

Library of Congress Cataloging-in-Publication Data
Isaacs, Scott, 1971-
Inside Dynamic HTML / Scott Isaacs.
p. cm.
Includes index.
ISBN 1-57231-686-1
1. HTML (Document markup language) I. Title.
QA76.76.H94I83 1997
005.7'2--dc21 97-33678
CIP

Printed and bound in the United States of America.

1 2 3 4 5 6 7 8 9 QMQM 2 1 0 9 8 7

Distributed to the book trade in Canada by Macmillan of Canada, a division of Canada Publishing Corporation.

A CIP catalogue record for this book is available from the British Library.

Microsoft Press books are available through booksellers and distributors worldwide. For further information about international editions, contact your local Microsoft Corporation office. Or contact Microsoft Press International directly at fax (425) 936-7329. Visit our Web site at mspress.microsoft.com.

Acquisitions Editor: Eric Stroo
Project Editor: Patricia Draher
Manuscript Editor: Jennifer Harris
Technical Editors: Gary Nelson and Kurt Meyer

((parseInt(navigator.ap
(navigator.appVersion.

CONTENTS

CHAPTER NINE

Scripting Individual Elements **207**

CHAPTER TEN

Forms and Intrinsic Controls **251**

PART III: DOCUMENT STYLE AND ANIMATION

CHAPTER ELEVEN

Dynamic Styles **287**

CHAPTER TWELVE

Dynamic Positioning **329**

PART IV: DOCUMENT CONTENTS AND DATA BINDING

ACKNOWLEDGMENTS

The foundations for this book were built from presentations I've made on Dynamic HTML. The issues and questions raised served as the basis for this book's organization and samples. To everyone who has heard me speak and asked a question, thank you.

To the entire Microsoft Internet Explorer 4.0 team—especially the Trident team—without your hard work, the vision of Dynamic HTML would never have been achieved. Thanks to all the individuals at Microsoft, too numerous to list, who previewed and helped improve the book.

To Richard Rollman, a special thanks for all his help with the chapter "Data Binding with HTML." My thanks also go to the Microsoft Press team for producing the book and the companion CD.

And finally, thanks to my wonderful wife, Jocelyn. Without her patience and support, this book would never have been written or finished.

INTRODUCTION

The World Wide Web ignited a computer revolution by enabling anyone to publish HTML documents. Until recently, the information in these documents was mostly static, requiring the server to respond to user interactions. With the introduction of Dynamic HTML, the Web paradigm has shifted away from requiring server interactions to creating interactive Web sites and Web applications. Because Dynamic HTML allows HTML documents to interact with the user and change completely on the client, you can create rich Web applications.

Dynamic HTML is built on an object model that extends the traditional static HTML document. This book introduces you, the Web developer, to Dynamic HTML and teaches you how to create pages that are live and interactive on the client. This book assumes a working knowledge of HTML and basic programming principles. It does not teach you HTML or show you how to program in JavaScript, JScript, or VBScript; instead, these languages are used as tools for dynamically manipulating the page.

Near the end of this introduction, you'll find a description of the four parts of this book. Before continuing, read this overview to get a feel for how Dynamic HTML will be presented here through a series of building blocks. By the end of this book, all the pieces for creating live and interactive Web pages will be in place.

Creating Interactive Pages

The concept of creating interactive Web pages is not new—Microsoft and Netscape initially defined a simple object model that was presented as a way of creating interactive pages. On closer inspection, the object model was found to be efficient only for basic form validation. Dynamic documents were mostly a myth prior to Microsoft Internet Explorer 4.0 because the only time a page could change was during its creation. Interactive documents were simulated by completely reloading the page or by embedding objects in the page. Many of these Java applets, ActiveX controls, and even animated GIFs were designed to perform textlike manipulation, which provided a way to work around the static nature of HTML. However, using objects as a replacement for style and contents control is a poor solution.

After examining many of the scenarios for these objects and animated GIFs, Internet Explorer developers realized the need for a more powerful API (application programming interface) for manipulating documents. With an object model that provides full access to the document, authors can take advantage of the layout abilities built into HTML and CSS (Cascading Style Sheets). This object model greatly improves performance by reducing the need for downloading large animated GIFs and applets. Information becomes instantaneously accessible because it is no longer hidden within images or objects.

Dynamic HTML provides the API necessary for complete control over the HTML document. No longer does a page need to be defined while it is loading. After loading, any portion of the page can be dynamically and immediately changed. For example, you can create an application that has expanding and collapsing outlines. When the user expands or collapses the outline, the contents are displayed or hidden instantaneously. Imagine being able to create pages that can automatically change and tailor themselves to the user. All this and more is possible with Dynamic HTML.

The ability to modify a document and have the document automatically reflow itself is the underlying innovation used throughout Dynamic HTML. Traditional browsers were basically document navigation tools that displayed a document and then waited for the user to point to a new document. When a change to the document was needed, either a request was sent to the server for a new page or an entire new page was generated on the client.

Programming Languages

A programming language is used to manipulate the Dynamic HTML object model, but Dynamic HTML is designed to be platform independent and language neutral. Therefore, JavaScript, JScript, VBScript, C++, Java, or any other programming language can be used as the language of choice.

This book uses primarily JScript for accessing the document object model. JScript is Microsoft's implementation of the ECMA262 (European Computer Manufacturers Association) standard designed by Microsoft, Netscape, and other organizations. This standard formalizes the language constructs of JavaScript and JScript so that interoperable implementations can be created. It is important to remember that this standard defines only the constructs of the language. Even though the language is often associated with the object model, this standard does not define the object model. Therefore, when you are determining whether a browser supports a version of JavaScript or JScript, you must be careful to distinguish whether an object model or a language feature is being discussed. The JScript in Internet Explorer 4.0 is compliant with the ECMA standard, but the implementation of JavaScript 1.2 in Netscape 4.0 is not.

NOTE: The terms *JavaScript* and *JScript* can generally be used interchangeably to refer to the programming language. *JavaScript* is used throughout this book because it is more widely recognized.

Applets and objects on the page can also communicate with the page. For example, in Internet Explorer, an object written in Java, C++, or some other language can communicate with the page through the object model. The technique for creating applets that use Dynamic HTML is beyond the scope of this book. However, this book does provide a foundation for understanding the Dynamic HTML capabilities available to such objects.

If you are familiar with the existing JavaScript language and existing object model, you'll find that the extensions for the Dynamic HTML object model are a fully compatible superset. Any pages written for past versions of Internet Explorer or for Netscape Navigator 3.0 will continue to run in Internet Explorer 4.0. This compatibility allows Web developers to take advantage of their existing skills as they learn about these new innovations. If you are new to JavaScript, learning how to program the HTML page allows you to extend and enhance your pages and your users' experience in ways never before possible.

New Features

Dynamic HTML removes all restrictions on access to the document. Dynamic HTML in Internet Explorer 4.0 empowers developers with a number of new features, which are discussed in the following sections.

- **HTML 4.0 and advanced CSS support** Internet Explorer 4.0 supports the latest HTML 4.0 standard, CSS1, and many of the new CSS enhancements. These HTML and CSS standards define what is exposed by the Dynamic HTML object model.
- **Full access to the document's structure** All elements in the document are available through the Dynamic HTML object model. You are no longer limited to scripting the form elements. The style and contents of any element can be dynamically changed, and these changes will be immediately reflected in the document.

  In addition, the intrinsic controls have been enhanced to better support HTML and CSS, which allows the Web author to manipulate the appearance of these controls—including setting the text color, background color, and font—on buttons and text controls. The object model behind the intrinsic controls is similar to the object model behind the document and allows easy access to the style and contents.

- **Dynamic style** The document's CSS style sheets can be changed at any time. The document does not need to reload from the cache or communicate with the server. The object model is designed to allow a page to display any changes immediately. For example, the appearance of an element can change as the user moves the mouse or clicks on it.
- **Dynamic contents** The object model allows the contents of the document to be accessed and changed. Again, no server communications are involved, and the response is intended to be instantaneous. For example, you can write a ticking clock utility in standard HTML. You no longer need Java applets or ActiveX controls to change contents.
- **Instant user response** Dynamic HTML provides a powerful new event model that exposes all user actions to the page. Scripts in a document can respond to all the user's actions within the browser. Based on the user's actions, any aspect of the document's contents or style can be dynamically changed.
- **Client/server web pages** Internet Explorer 4.0 adds extensions to HTML elements to create data-bound tables and single-record forms and reports. Data is asynchronously downloaded and rendered in the document using a few basic HTML extensions. The data can be cached locally, allowing client-side searching and sorting without requiring assistance from the server. For example, search engines don't need to provide only a few matches at a time. Instead, a search engine can send responses to the client, where they are rendered as they are received. The user can immediately sort and further filter the data entirely on the client, without sending subsequent requests to the server.
- **Multimedia and animation effects** Internet Explorer 4.0 tightly integrates multimedia and animation effects with the document's contents. These effects include filters that can simulate light sources and shadows and other effects that operate directly on text or controls. Transition effects between images and text, and even between pages, can also be added.

All of these features are based on current discussion within the working groups of the W3C (World Wide Web Consortium). The Dynamic HTML object model is being reviewed by the Document Object Model working group. The goal of this group is to define an object model that is language independent and platform neutral and that meets a set of requirements for structured documents. The object model defined in Internet Explorer 4.0 meets most of the requirements outlined by the Document Object Model working group.

Defining an HTML Document

HTML is an application SGML (Standard Generalized Markup Language). In an SGML/HTML document, tags add structure to the document's contents. A traditional SGML document has three distinct aspects: structure, style, and contents. With the introduction of Dynamic HTML, HTML now includes a fourth component: behavior. The term *behavior* refers to the interaction between the HTML page and the user. This book's primary focus is on creating HTML-based applications by manipulating the different components of the document. Structure is exposed through a set of element collections; style is exposed on each element and through a style sheets collection; and contents are exposed through each element and through a *TextRange* object. Scripts manipulate structure, style, and contents in response to events to produce a document's behavior.

Structure and Style

Structure provides context for the information contained within a document. For example, the Header elements H1 through H6 are meant to define various headers and their relative importance. An H1 element might be followed by another H1 or an H2 but should not be followed by an H3 element. As HTML quickly evolved, however, the separation between structure and presentation was often ignored. Authors used HTML tags not as a way to provide structure but as a way to define style. The H1 element was often used to mean big, bold text rather than to indicate top-level headers. As a further deviation from SGML, stylistic tags were invented. For example, the <B> and <I> tags were introduced to mark bold and italic text.

When viewing a page, the user (and many times the author) usually does not care about structure. The author's goal is to create an interesting page that will hopefully increase the number of hits, or visits, the Web site receives. This desire for originality was the justification for many of the stylistic tags that were created.

Abusing style does have consequences, however. For one, tools become less powerful. If an author correctly uses structure, an indexing tool can more intelligently index the document's contents. If the <STRONG> tag is used to indicate that a word is of importance, an index tool can assign a greater weight. However, many authors use <STRONG> simply to display words in boldface, rather than to indicate they have greater importance, invalidating the usefulness of the tag.

A more important reason for properly structuring your page is to improve accessibility to the underlying information. Imagine a browser that speaks the information rather than displays it—perhaps a browser for visually impaired users or even a voice-based browser in your car. This browser needs to be able to extract various connotations from the text. Strong words should be spoken with greater emphasis, and headers should provide an outline of information on the page. If a document used markup for presentation only, the voice-based browser would not be able to properly deliver the document.

HTML also defines a set of rules representing the proper structure of the document. A DTD (document type definition) describes which elements can be contained within other elements. It is important to understand that not all HTML elements should be included anywhere within a document. Usually, when a Web page renders poorly across browsers, it is due to HTML that fails to conform to the DTD. Unfortunately, many of the pages on the Web do not conform to any HTML DTD, and rather than force users to define correct documents, browsers have evolved a lax set of rules for parsing the document that attempt to interpret the author's intent—often with less than ideal results.

Until mid-1996, style in HTML was controlled quite simply by using tags and stylistic attributes, such as ALIGN. Under these conditions, HTML was failing to be a true SGML language, in which structure and style are defined separately. In a true SGML language, a document can have an associated style sheet that defines how the structural elements are rendered. SGML provides a number of languages for defining a style sheet.

In mid-1996, a new language named Cascading Style Sheets was introduced for specifying style in HTML. The CSS specification was coauthored by Bert Bos and Håkon Lie of the W3C, with input from many W3C members, and has been adopted by the major browser implementations. Basically, with CSS a Strong element (and even a Bold element, for that matter) no longer indicates boldface text. Instead, the Strong element retains its traditional purpose, to indicate an important word. A style sheet now specifies that Strong element text should be rendered in boldface:

```
STRONG {font-weight:bold}
```

To take full advantage of Dynamic HTML, your document should properly separate the contents and structure from the presentation. Dynamic HTML is easier to use and works more predictably with valid HTML documents. And as the following chapters will show, manipulating invalid HTML is more difficult and might create unpredictable behavior.

The Organization of This Book

Learning to program interactive pages is a cumulative process. This book begins by explaining basic concepts and then builds on these concepts to teach you how to access the different components of the browser and the document. The following sections provide an outline of the four parts of this book.

Part I: HTML and Scripting

Chapters 1 through 5 introduce the relationship between scripting and the HTML document, describe the browser window, and show you how to use the Dynamic HTML event model. This book assumes a working knowledge of HTML and programming in either JavaScript or VBScript.

Part I introduces the object hierarchy, which exposes the four aspects of the document: structure, style, contents, and behavior. These aspects are discussed in detail in Parts II through IV, and since these areas are closely related, the explanations overlap somewhat.

Part II: Document Structure

In Dynamic HTML, all elements and their attributes are available programmatically. Part II shows you how to access and take advantage of the document element collections and how to manipulate the individual elements within the document. This part also demonstrates how to create rich, interactive forms that can process information on the client without requiring round-trips to the server.

Part III: Document Style and Animation

Tightly coupled with individual elements is the concept of style, the topic of Part III. Using style sheets, the Web author can specify the document's appearance, spacing, colors, and so on.

Part III also shows you how to add basic animation to an HTML page. Dynamic HTML exposes a set of member functions that enable an HTML element to float and move over the HTML page, allowing the creation of simple presentation-like effects. In addition, Dynamic HTML includes a set of powerful extensions that let you add real multimedia animation and transition effects to your Web page. With these enhancements, the HTML contents can be animated using only a few lines of code.

Part IV: Document Contents and Data Binding

Part IV demonstrates how Dynamic HTML allows pages to dynamically reshape themselves. The contents are exposed through properties on each element and through a text object model. With dynamic contents, HTML text and unformatted text can be easily accessed and changed.

Chapter 15, "Data Binding with HTML," shows you how to use Dynamic HTML to create client/server Web pages, including binding an HTML table to a set of data that can be locally manipulated. This feature allows you to create high-speed data-aware pages that can be sorted, filtered, and bulk-edited—all on the client.

Companion CD

The companion CD includes the sample code from the book, together with an indexing page that contains links to all the samples and can sort and filter the links to help you find particular programs quickly.

Also on the CD are copies of Microsoft Internet Explorer 4.0 and the Microsoft Internet Client Software Development Kit. The documentation in the SDK includes a complete reference to Dynamic HTML as well as other helpful information.

The author's personal Web site (www.insideDHTML.com) is a great source for additional information about Dynamic HTML. Microsoft maintains several Web sites related to Dynamic HTML, including the Site Builder (www.microsoft.com/sitebuilder) and JScript (www.microsoft.com/JScript) sites.

Support

Every effort has been made to ensure the accuracy of this book and the contents of the companion CD. Microsoft Press provides corrections for books through the World Wide Web at mspress.microsoft.com/mspress/support/. If you have comments, questions, or ideas regarding this book or the companion CD, please send them to Microsoft Press using postal mail or e-mail:

Microsoft Press
Attn: Inside Dynamic HTML Editor
One Microsoft Way
Redmond, WA 98052-6399
MSPINPUT@MICROSOFT.COM

Please note that product support is not offered through the above mail addresses.

P A R T I

HTML AND SCRIPTING

<SCRIPT LANGUAGE="JavaSc
// Create property x an
var x = 10;
function foo() {
// This code is not
// The code
var y =
alert(
// output
// Call foo while lo
foo();
window.foo(); // the
</SCRIPT>

CHAPTER ONE

Overview of HTML and CSS

HTML (Hypertext Markup Language) is continually evolving. Within the past year and a half, two major innovations have extended HTML: an entirely new language for controlling style, and an object model for adding behavior and dynamism to documents. Dynamic HTML in Microsoft Internet Explorer 4.0 encompasses not only the object model for manipulating the document, but also many of the latest HTML and CSS (Cascading Style Sheets) recommendations and working drafts from the W3C (World Wide Web Consortium).

This chapter introduces some of the recent innovations to HTML and CSS supported by Microsoft Internet Explorer 4.0. The combination of existing HTML features and these new innovations with the Dynamic HTML object model allows you to create interactive Web pages and Web applications. This chapter is not a comprehensive review of HTML and CSS—the effective use of HTML and CSS is a topic for an entire book. Rather, this chapter lets you, the Web author, familiarize yourself with the latest work in these areas.

The following topics are covered in this chapter:

- **New HTML features** This section introduces some of the new features that will be included in the next version of HTML. This next version of HTML, HTML 4.0, is being designed by the W3C and its members. By the time you read this book, the HTML 4.0 recommendation by W3C will probably be final. This section also introduces HTML features supported by Internet Explorer 4.0 that go beyond HTML 4.0.
- **Cascading Style Sheets** The intent of SGML (Standard Generalized Markup Language), and therefore of HTML, is to separate contents from presentation. This separation was not possible before the introduction of CSS, when tags such as <B> and <FONT> were incorporated in HTML to indicate how content was to be presented. These tags violate the fundamentals of a structured document by allowing the presentation to be embedded in the contents.

This section introduces the CSS language and its relationship to the recent scripting additions. CSS is a static representation for adding style to a document, but through the object model extensions, that style can be dynamically changed. For example, the style of text can be changed based on the user's environment.

- **Examining an HTML DTD** HTML is a structured language with a formal definition. This section discusses the importance of the DTD (document type definition) that defines HTML. The HTML DTD is the SGML declaration of the HTML language. A DTD defines the supported set of elements and their attributes and specifies whether an element can contain other elements. Unfortunately, the majority of pages on the Web violate the HTML DTD. With the addition of an object model that exposes the entire page to scripting, ensuring consistent and rational behavior by creating properly structured documents takes on greater importance. In this section, you'll learn how to read a DTD and use it to create valid HTML documents.

New HTML Features

Internet Explorer 4.0 adds full support for HTML 4.0, the next version of HTML to be embodied as a W3C recommendation. This section introduces the features newly incorporated into HTML 4.0. (Some of these features were available in Internet Explorer 3.0 but are only now being incorporated into a W3C recommendation.) At the time this book was written, HTML 4.0 was to include the following new features:

- Frameset and IFrame elements
- Form and accessibility enhancements
- Table enhancements for headers, footers, and columns
- Object element for embedding custom objects
- Script element for embedding scripts
- File upload capabilities for submitting files to the server
- Enhanced set of named entities

Framesets and IFrames, table enhancements, and the Object and Script elements have all been supported since Internet Explorer 3.0. Internet

Explorer 4.0 expands on the earlier version by providing support for the rest of the features in the preceding list. For information about HTML 4.0 and these features, check out the W3C Web site (www.w3.org) and Microsoft's Web site (www.microsoft.com). The scripting of these new elements and attributes is discussed throughout this book.

The rest of this section introduces the HTML syntax for the Object element, form and accessibility enhancements, and a few other HTML features supported by Internet Explorer 4.0 that go beyond HTML 4.0.

Chapter 2, "Fundamentals of HTML Scripting," focuses on the Script element, the primary mechanism for embedding scripts in the document. Framesets are introduced in Chapter 5, "Window and Frame Management."

The table enhancements are not discussed in detail in this book. These enhancements include specifying table headers, footers, and bodies as well as providing greater control over columns. More information about the table enhancements can be found at the Microsoft Web site.

A named entity consists of predefined characters that can be embedded in the document using *&name;*. For example, a commonly used named entity is the nonbreaking space (* *), which inserts a space that won't wrap at a line break in the document.

Embedding Custom Objects

The Object element is used to embed custom objects in an HTML document. This element was initially supported in Internet Explorer 3.0. The Object element is used to extend HTML by embedding Java applets, ActiveX controls, and supported MIME types in Internet Explorer. Supported MIME types include HTML files and the various image formats, such as GIF, JPEG, and PNG. The syntax for the Object element is generally as follows:

```
<OBJECT CLASSID="ActiveX UUID" WIDTH="pixels" HEIGHT="pixels">
    <PARAM NAME="property" VALUE="propertyValue">
</OBJECT>
```

In addition to specifying the CLASSID, an optional CODEBASE parameter can be specified to provide a location from which to download the object. Parameters can be specified through one or more Param elements contained within the Object element.

The only valid contents within an Object element are Param elements. Browsers that support the Object element ignore all other HTML within the

Object block. This feature can be used to provide contents for down-level browsers that do not support the Object element, as shown here:

```
<OBJECT CODE="myClass.class" WIDTH=200 HEIGHT=200>
   <PARAM NAME="color" VALUE="red">
   <PARAM NAME="background" VALUE="green">
   <P>Your browser does not support the Object element and
      cannot view the application.</P>
</OBJECT>
```

Form and Accessibility Enhancements

HTML forms were initially limited to requesting basic information from the user. The interface was limited to plain-text containers, radio buttons, and check boxes. Forms in HTML are evolving to provide more of the power and flexibility that existing form and database packages permit. In addition, many of the enhancements related to forms also greatly improve accessibility, allowing users with disabilities to better access a page with their browsers.

> NOTE: Throughout this book, the term *intrinsic controls* is used to refer to the built-in controls in HTML. Intrinsic controls include all elements the user directly interacts with for input and output, such as the image, text, button, and marquee controls.

The set of form enhancements in HTML 4.0 allows you to add labels and access keys, add advisory text to all elements, control tabbing order, disable controls, and group related controls. In addition, Internet Explorer 4.0 enhances the intrinsic form elements with support for style sheets and for default and cancel buttons. Buttons and text boxes can be created using different fonts and colors based on style sheets. The use of style sheets is introduced in the section "Cascading Style Sheets" later in this chapter.

Adding Labels and Access Keys

The new Label element is an inline text container that can associate contents with a specified control. Label elements are to controls what links are to bookmarks: just as links bring a bookmark into view, when the user clicks a label the associated control is brought into view and given the focus. For radio buttons and check boxes, clicking on the label also clicks the associated button, changing its value.

Just as the <A> tag that defines a link references a bookmark, the <LABEL> tag references an associated control element using a FOR attribute. The FOR attribute contains the unique ID of a control on the page. The following code creates labels for a check box and a text box:

```
<HTML>
   <HEAD>
      <TITLE>Label Demonstration</TITLE>
   </HEAD>
   <BODY>
      <H1>Label Demonstration</H1>
      <TABLE>
         <TR>
            <TD NOWRAP>
               <LABEL FOR="Info">Send Information: </LABEL>
            </TD>
            <TD>
               <INPUT TYPE=CHECKBOX ID="Info" VALUE="Information">
            </TD>
         </TR>
         <TR>
            <TD NOWRAP>
               <LABEL FOR="Email">E-Mail Address: </LABEL>
            </TD>
            <TD>
               <INPUT TYPE=TEXT ID="Email" SIZE=30>
            </TD>
         </TR>
      </TABLE>
   </BODY>
</HTML>
```

Figure 1-1 shows this label demonstration in action. When a buttonlike control is activated, its label is drawn with a dashed border around it. The label itself can also be clicked on to activate the control.

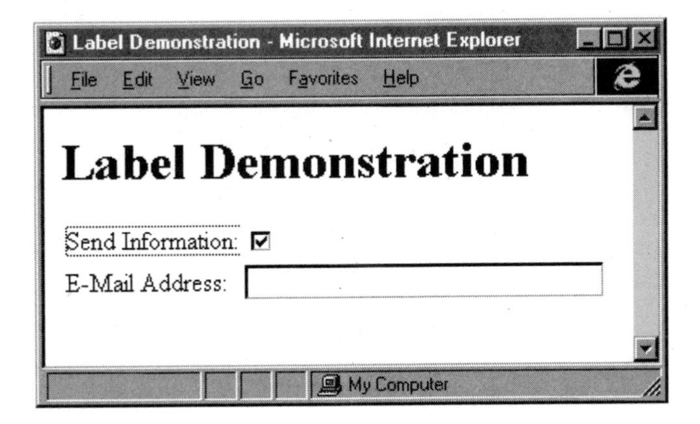

Figure 1-1.
The Label Demonstration Web page.

The Label element adds the capability to associate contents with a control. To help improve the accessibility of the Label element, HTML 4.0 also provides an ACCESSKEY attribute. The ACCESSKEY attribute contains a single character that can be used as a shortcut for referencing the control: pressing the Alt key followed by the access key character accesses the shortcut. (The access key is not case sensitive.)

The following code creates a label with an access key:

```
<!-- Label with an access key -->
<LABEL FOR="txt1" ACCESSKEY="U">
   <SPAN CLASS="accesskey">U</SPAN>ser Name:
</LABEL>
<INPUT TYPE=TEXT ID="txt1" SIZE=30>
```

The purpose of the <SPAN> tag in this example is to use a global style that defines how the access key in the label's text should be rendered. Microsoft Windows traditionally underlines access keys. This underlining can be accomplished in HTML by adding the following global style and wrapping the access key in the label's text with <SPAN> tags:

```
<STYLE TYPE="text/css">
   .accesskey {text-decoration:underline}
</STYLE>
```

The U element could be used as an alternative to the global style to force an underline. However, that technique does not provide the benefits of style sheets. Using a global style makes it easy to change the appearance of all access keys in the document.

Labels degrade gracefully in browsers that do not support them. Because the <LABEL> tag is ignored by down-level browsers, those browsers render the label as plain text. (Browsers that understand style sheets underline the access key letter.) The Label element significantly improves usability and accessibility and is highly recommended wherever controls are used.

Adding Advisory Text to an Element

All HTML elements now support the TITLE attribute, an advisory string that is rendered in Internet Explorer 4.0 as a ToolTip. A ToolTip is a small window of text that is displayed when the mouse pointer hovers over an element. A ToolTip can be associated with any element, allowing everything from a control to a heading to display extra information. Changing the input check box created earlier to include a TITLE attribute displays a ToolTip when the mouse pointer hovers over the check box:

```
<INPUT TYPE=CHECKBOX ID="Info" VALUE="Information"
   TITLE="Check here and enter your user name for more information.">
```

Figure 1-2 shows the ToolTip Demonstration application in action.

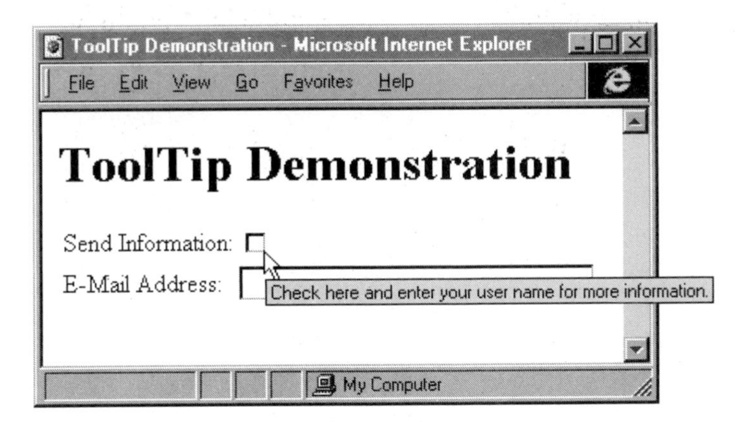

Figure 1-2.
The ToolTip Demonstration Web page.

As with the <LABEL> tag, the TITLE attribute raises no down-level browser issues because the attribute is ignored. Therefore, using this attribute is recommended when extra information might be helpful. The most common uses of the TITLE attribute are on links, for extra information about the link, and on controls, for information about the contents of the control.

Controlling Tabbing Order

A TABINDEX attribute was added in HTML 4.0 to all the input controls on the document. This attribute lets the Web author explicitly control the tabbing order. By default, the tabbing order of all elements on the page matches the order in which they are defined in the HTML source. The TABINDEX attribute lets the author control the tabbing order among elements, independent of the source order of the document. Supplying a negative TABINDEX value in an element causes the element to be skipped in the tabbing order.

While elements within a form belong to the form, the TABINDEX attribute applies to the entire document. Therefore, only one element in the document should have a tab index of a particular value. The source order resolves any conflicts in which multiple elements share the same tab index value.

Disabling Controls

Disabled controls are controls that cannot be activated or whose contents cannot be changed. In HTML 4.0, two attributes are exposed that prevent the contents from being edited: READONLY and DISABLED. The DISABLED attribute makes the element unable to receive the focus, and hence unable to receive any events. DISABLED should be used when a control is not applicable to the current context. For example, if prerequisite information must be entered before a control can be used, that control can be disabled until the correct information or state is reached. Disabling a control is a simple process:

```
<!-- Disabled Control -->
<INPUT TYPE=SUBMIT ID="btnSubmit" VALUE="Submit Data" DISABLED>
```

When appropriate data is entered that makes the submission valid, the Submit Data button can be enabled through a script. Examples of dynamically manipulating form elements with the object model are presented in Chapter 10, "Forms and Intrinsic Controls."

The READONLY attribute is used when the control is applicable to the context but the contents of the control are not editable. Unlike a disabled control, a read-only control can receive the focus and its contents can be selected. However, its contents cannot be changed. The READONLY attribute is applicable only for elements the user can enter data in. For example, Button elements are never editable, so supplying a READONLY attribute for a button control would be redundant.

A read-only control does not appear different from a control that is editable; a disabled control in Windows, however, appears grayed. The following code demonstrates how to make the E-Mail Address field from Figure 1-1 disabled:

```
<INPUT TYPE=TEXT ID="Email" SIZE=30 VALUE="UserName@com"
   TITLE="To enter an e-mail address, first check the Send
      Information check box."
   DISABLED>
```

Figure 1-3 demonstrates a disabled text box. A script can enable the text box when the user checks the Send Information check box.

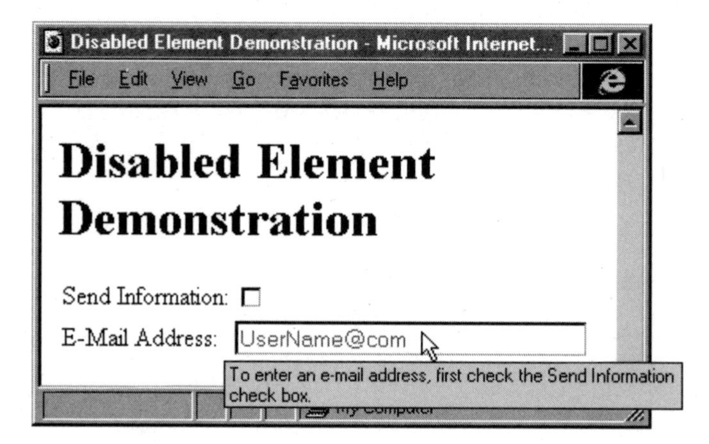

Figure 1-3.
The Disabled Element Demonstration Web page.

The New Button Element

HTML 4.0 provides a powerful new Button element that enables rich HTML contents to be displayed as a button. For instance, the following Button element can be added to the Label Demonstration example:

```
<!-- HTML-based button -->
<BUTTON STYLE="font-family:Arial; font-size:16pt; color:navy">
   Send Me
   <SPAN STYLE="font-style:italic; color:green">Information!</SPAN>
</BUTTON>
```

Figure 1-4 shows the Button Demonstration application in action.

Figure 1-4.
The Button Demonstration Web page.

Buttons can be created with all the flexibility available in HTML and style sheets. The only disadvantage to the Button element is that down-level browsers render the contents not as a button but as normal HTML text. Therefore, for down-level browsers, you must define another button within the Button element by using an <INPUT> tag:

```
<BUTTON STYLE="background:URL(cool.gif) yellow; font-weight:bold">
   <P ALIGN="Center">Calculate</P>
   <P ALIGN="Center" STYLE="font-style:italic">Now</P>
   <!-- The following button is for older browsers. -->
   <INPUT TYPE=BUTTON VALUE="Calculate Now">
</BUTTON>
```

In browsers that support the Button element, the <INPUT> tag is ignored, and in down-level browsers that do not support the Button element, the HTML is still rendered, plus a button is also displayed.

NOTE: This technique, in which the up-level browser ignores the alternative HTML, actually creates an invalid document because the DTD that defines HTML prohibits Input elements within a Button element. However, this technique is demonstrated here because it is currently the only way to use a Button element effectively with down-level browsers that do not support the <BUTTON> tag.

The Fieldset Element

The Fieldset element is used to group form controls, similar to the way <DIV> tags are used to group related HTML contents. The Fieldset element was designed mostly for accessibility, allowing pages to clearly group sets of controls. For example, an invoice form may contain three fieldsets: a shipping address, an order section, and billing information. If you specifically group the fields using a Fieldset element, a browser can easily distinguish the three groups. The Fieldset element is rendered by Internet Explorer 4.0 to look similar to group boxes in dialog boxes:

```
<!-- Grouping related controls -->
<FIELDSET>
   <LEGEND>Size</LEGEND>
   <INPUT TYPE=RADIO VALUE="Big" NAME="SIZE" ID="BIG">
   <LABEL FOR="BIG">Big</LABEL>
   <INPUT TYPE=RADIO VALUE="Small" NAME="SIZE" ID="SMALL">
   <LABEL FOR="SMALL">Small</LABEL>
</FIELDSET>
```

Figure 1-5 shows an example Fieldset element.

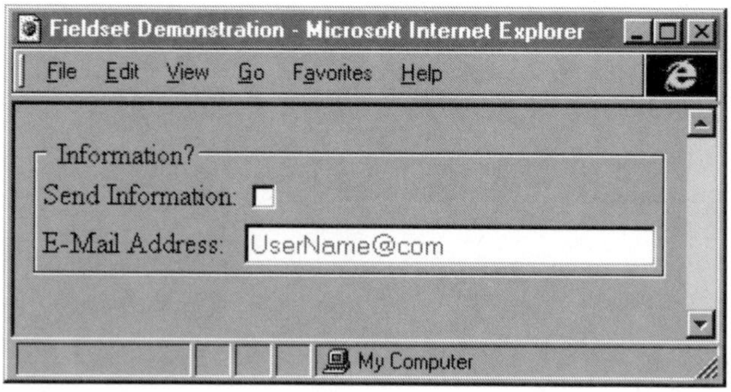

Figure 1-5.
Fieldset element containing a group of related controls.

The fieldset can contain a single legend displayed on the fieldset's border. The legend can be followed by any HTML contents. The fieldset works fairly well on down-level browsers and is recommended for grouping related fields, but <DIV> tags should still be used to group related HTML contents.

The Default and Cancel Buttons

Internet Explorer 4.0 adds two simple usability enhancements: The Submit button now acts as the default button for a form, meaning that the button is activated when the user presses Enter within a form. The Reset button acts as the cancel button for a form, meaning that the button is activated when the user presses Esc within a form.

The default and cancel buttons work within the scope of the currently active form. Therefore, if a document has multiple forms, the current default and cancel buttons depend on the form the user is interacting with. The Submit and Reset buttons can also work outside the scope of the form as the default and cancel buttons but without any default behavior. Outside a form, scripts are required to define a behavior for the buttons.

Figure 1-6 shows the default and cancel buttons. Default buttons specified using *TYPE=SUBMIT* have an extra border.

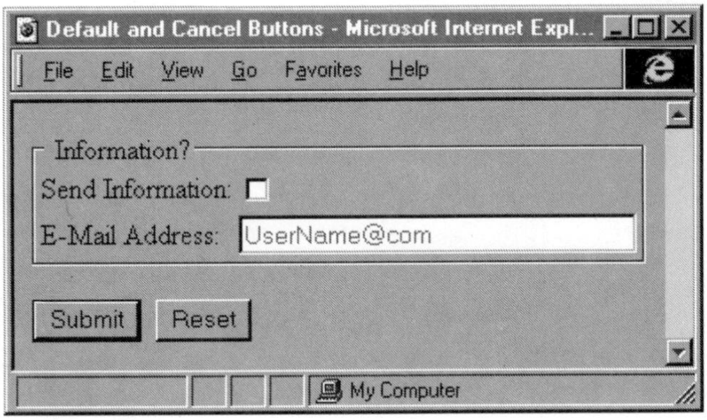

Figure 1-6.
The default and cancel buttons.

The Improved Marquee Element

The Marquee element is not new to Internet Explorer 4.0—it first shipped in Internet Explorer 3.0—but it is currently specific to Internet Explorer and is not a part of HTML 4.0. In Internet Explorer 4.0, the Marquee element has been extended to display HTML text and now includes the capability to scroll contents up and down in addition to left and right. The Marquee element is as rich as, and in some ways richer than, the Button element described earlier. Marquees can be created that contain controls and even tables, and all the event handlers for elements within a Marquee element fire appropriately. In addition, the marquee is now represented by a powerful object in the object model. Chapter 9, "Scripting Individual Elements," provides examples of using the Marquee element's object. The following code demonstrates an upward-scrolling marquee:

```
<!-- HTML marquee -->
<MARQUEE STYLE="height:150px" DIRECTION="Up">
   <TABLE>
      <CAPTION>Stock Ticker</CAPTION>
      <TR><TD>AAAA</TD><TD>100</TD></TR>
      <TR><TD>ZZFD</TD><TD>45</TD></TR>
   </TABLE>
</MARQUEE>
```

Data-Binding Enhancements

Internet Explorer 4.0 introduced the capability to bind an HTML page to a data source on the server and to bind different HTML elements to fields and data from that data source. When the page is loaded, the data is also sent from the server and asynchronously appears on the page. At a high level, this allows client/server Web pages to be created on which all the data is manipulated by the client. For example, a search engine can return a list of sites that can all be filtered and sorted by the client, without having to go back to the server. The data is instantly displayed on the page without reloading. The HTML data-binding enhancements are discussed in detail in Chapter 15, "Data Binding with HTML."

Cascading Style Sheets

CSS is a language with a set of properties for defining the appearance of a document. The CSS specification (CSS1) defines properties and a declarative language for associating those properties with elements in the document. Internet Explorer 3.0 provided initial support for CSS; this support has been expanded and improved in Internet Explorer 4.0. Understanding CSS is important for adding dynamic style to a page. (*Dynamic style* is the modification of the style sheet associated with the document through a script.) The W3C Web site (www.w3.org) contains the latest information about the innovations and features supported by CSS.

Style sheets are an abstraction in which the style of a document is defined separately from either the contents or the structure. There are essentially three techniques available to the Web author for adding style sheets to a document—in general, each level of complexity offers greater benefits while increasing the level of abstraction necessary. The first technique is to use an inline style sheet. Inline styles are simple: the style is defined directly on the element. The second technique is to use a global style sheet to define the style for a document at the beginning of the document. The third and most abstract and powerful technique is to use a linked style sheet to define the style separately in another document.

Inline styles are not much different from traditional HTML. With inline styles, the appearance of the document cannot be easily changed. The advantage is that the amount of markup is usually significantly reduced, and HTML can be used more appropriately to provide additional context rather than just presentation. Using a global style sheet better separates the presentation from the contents and allows the style and rendering of the document to be quickly and independently modified. Using a linked style sheet provides the greatest benefit by allowing the appearance of a set of pages or an entire Web site to be defined through a single file.

The term *cascading* in CSS refers to the ability to merge multiple style sheets to form a single style definition for an element or for the entire document. This feature allows the Web site's style sheet to be merged in a predictable way with the style sheet in the document, and even with an inline style.

Inline Styles

An inline style is basically a style sheet for a single instance of an element and is specified in line in the element's begin tag. The inline style sheet is defined using the STYLE attribute, and the data for the attribute is specified using the style sheet language. For example, the following code makes a paragraph's contents larger and centered on a yellow background:

```
<P STYLE="font-size:120%; text-align:center; background:yellow">
   This creates a yellow, centered paragraph with a larger font.
</P>
```

Inline styles can help you learn the style sheet language or quickly change a single instance of an element. However, inline styles are not in keeping with the true spirit of a structured document and do not work well when you are trying to change the appearance of a set of elements in a document where the presentation and contents are not completely separate. To separate the document's style from its structure, the style sheet should be specified either in the document's head or as a separate file that is linked to the document.

Global Style Sheets

The <STYLE> tag is used to add a global style sheet to a document and is usually contained within the document's header. Centralizing all the document's style in a single location makes it easy to modify how the document is rendered. The following style sheet defines the rendering for all paragraphs in a document. To change the rendering of all paragraphs, only this single entry needs to be modified. If inline styles were used, every paragraph in the document would need to be changed.

```
<HTML>
   <HEAD>
      <STYLE TYPE="text/css">
         P {font-size:120%; text-align:center; background:yellow}
      </STYLE>
   </HEAD>
   <BODY>
      <P>All paragraphs are now larger and centered on a yellow
         background.</P>
   </BODY>
</HTML>
```

The TYPE attribute of the <STYLE> tag defines the language for the style sheet as a MIME type. Internet Explorer 4.0 supports only CSS and therefore parses only style sheets of type *text/css.* If a different type is specified that is not supported by the browser, the contents of the style block are ignored. Omitting the TYPE attribute causes the language to default to *text/css.* Although setting the TYPE attribute is optional, doing so is still recommended to more clearly document your source code.

A *selector* is used to associate a style with a particular element. In the preceding example, a *simple selector* was created that associated a style with all paragraphs. More powerful *contextual selectors* can also be defined; these selectors are introduced in the section "Defining a Style Sheet" later in this chapter.

Linked Style Sheets

A linked style sheet is a style sheet that is supplied in an external file. The advantage of using a linked style sheet is that all the rules and styles can be defined and encapsulated in a single file that can be shared across multiple pages or even across the entire Web site. With a linked style sheet, the rendering of all the paragraphs on an entire Web site can be changed through a single document. A linked style sheet can also improve performance because it is cached locally on the client, separate from the document, so each document is smaller and the style information needs to be downloaded only once.

To define a linked style sheet, the <LINK> tag is used in the head of the document:

```
<HTML>
   <HEAD>
      <LINK REL="stylesheet" TYPE="text/css" HREF="fancy.css">
   </HEAD>
   <BODY>
      <P>This document uses the styles specified in fancy.css.</P>
   </BODY>
</HTML>
```

The REL attribute is used to specify that the linked file is a style sheet, and the TYPE attribute specifies the style sheet MIME type. The HREF attribute is a URL pointing to the external style sheet. The contents of a linked style sheet must be only contextual rules and style definitions and must not include any HTML.

Defining a Style Sheet

You use the same syntax to create a style sheet within the document that you use to create a linked style sheet. This section introduces the components of the CSS language. The CSS language consists of selectors and *presentation rules.* Selectors specify the elements that are associated with a particular rule, and presentation rules specify how those elements are to be rendered.

CSS provides two types of selectors: simple and contextual. The simple selector associates an element based on its attributes or type, without regard to its contextual position within other elements. Contextual selectors are more powerful in that they can associate a rule with a particular element's containership—for example, all <EM> tags inside <P> tags.

In its most basic form, a simple selector can be created that associates a particular element, class of elements, or ID with a specific style. The following code demonstrates a number of simple selectors and their presentation rules:

```
<STYLE TYPE="text/css">
   /* Change all H1s to red. */
   H1 {color:red}

   /* Make all elements with CLASS="special" boldface. */
   .special {font-weight:bold}

   /* Give the element with ID="special" a yellow background. */
   #special {background:yellow}

   /* Give the H1 elements with CLASS="cool" wider letter spacing. */
   H1.cool {letter-spacing:2px}
</STYLE>
```

Selectors can also be grouped in a comma-delimited list, which allows multiple selectors to share the same declaration:

```
/* Make all headers share the same rule. */
H1, H2, H3, H4, H5, H6 {color:red; background:yellow}
```

Contextual selectors specify a containership hierarchy with which to associate the style. The containership is specified by a space-delimited list. For example, the following code defines a rule for all EM elements contained in a P element:

```
P EM {color:blue}
```

Each selector can reference the CLASS, the ID, or the element type. Here is a more complex version of a contextual selector:

```
/* Any element of CLASS="cool" that is contained within an
   LI element of CLASS="special" and further contained within
   a UL element will get this style. */
UL LI.special .cool{font-weight:bolder; font-size:120%}
```

All elements of a contextual selector are case insensitive—for example, *.cool* is the same as *.cOoL.*

Pseudo-Classes

A *pseudo-class* consists of elements of a single type that meet a certain contextual criterion. For example, Anchor elements that have been visited constitute a pseudo-class named *visited*, and active anchors and unvisited anchors constitute the *active* and *link* pseudo-classes, respectively.

The pseudo-class is specified in a style sheet using a colon (:) as the delimiter:

```
A:link {color:green}
:link {color:green}
```

The second example omits the element name *(A)* because only anchors have a *link* pseudo-class. The pseudo-class can be used in the same manner as the class or ID specifier and is also case insensitive. CSS1 defines pseudo-elements, which are similar to pseudo-classes, for the first line and first letter in an element, but Internet Explorer 4.0 currently supports only the anchor pseudo-classes.

Cascading Order

More than one selector can refer to the same elements. CSS defines a cascading order that is used to resolve any selector and rule overlaps. The cascading order merges all the rules applicable to an element by sorting them based on their specificity. For example, a Strong element contained within an H1 element might have presentation rules defined by an H1 selector, by a STRONG selector, and by a contextual selector for Strong elements inside H1 elements. The cascading aspect of CSS defines how those three rules will be merged. In general, a rule for a more specific contextual selector overrides a less specific one, and rules defined later in the source of the style sheet or document have higher precedence.

CSS Features

This section provides a sampling of some of the interesting new features of CSS supported by Internet Explorer 4.0. Some of these features can be used to replace common layout tricks that are currently performed using tables to align contents. These features are mostly contained in supplemental working drafts and proposals, not in the core CSS1 specification.

Text Justification

Internet Explorer 4.0 provides full support for left, right, and full justification of text. Full justification is new to Internet Explorer 4.0 and allows contents to be aligned at both the left and right margins. Justification is specified using the CSS *text-align* property:

```
<P STYLE="text-align:justify">
   This paragraph is justified using the CSS text-align property.
</P>
```

Custom Bulleted Lists

Using the *list-style* property, you can override built-in bullets in lists by using custom bullets as specified by a GIF. Bullets can be specified for the list itself or for individual list items. This technique degrades well on down-level browsers, where the list will be displayed using the standard bullet rather than the custom bullet. The following code demonstrates how to replace the standard bullet:

```
<HTML>
   <HEAD>
      <TITLE>Custom Bulleted List</TITLE>
      <STYLE TYPE="text/css">
         /* Display cool.gif instead of default bullet symbol. */
         UL {list-style-image:URL(cool.gif)}
      </STYLE>
   </HEAD>
   <BODY>
      <UL>
         <LI>The bullet is replaced with cool.gif.</LI>
      </UL>
   </BODY>
<HTML>
```

Figure 1-7 shows a list using custom bullets.

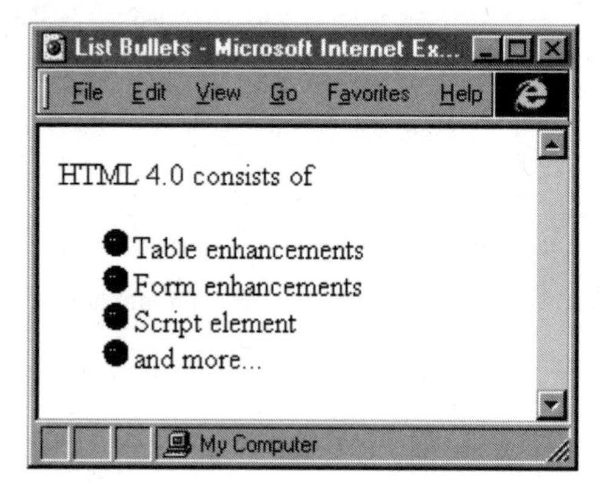

Figure 1-7.
A bulleted list using custom bullets.

Creating Sidebars

Sidebars were traditionally created using tables, but with the CSS *float* property, tables are no longer required. Text contents can be assigned a class by using a <SPAN> or <DIV> tag, and the *float* property can then be set in a style rule for that class. Using the *float* property, you can easily create two types of sidebars:

- Sidebars that are aligned along the left or right edge and that are surrounded by text, similar to images.
- Sidebars that appear outside the margins of the flow of the document. Creating this type of sidebar requires manipulating the margins of the element.

The following code demonstrates how to create these two types of sidebars:

```
<HTML>
   <HEAD>
      <TITLE>Sidebar Example</TITLE>
      <STYLE TYPE="text/css">
         BODY {margin-left:150pt; margin-right:0pt}
         .outflow, .inflow {float:left; width:150pt; color:navy}
         .outflow {margin-left:-150pt; width:150pt}
      </STYLE>
   </HEAD>
```

```
    <BODY>
        <H1>Sidebar Example</H1>
        <DIV CLASS="inflow">
            Notice that the text wraps around this sidebar.
        </DIV>
        <P>This example demonstrates a sidebar that exists within the
            flow of the document. The contents wrap around the sidebar
            and continue below it.
        </P>
        <DIV CLASS="outflow">
            This sidebar appears in the left margin of the document.
        </DIV>
        <P>This example demonstrates how to manipulate a document's
            margins to force a sidebar to float in the margin. By
            adjusting the margins, you can make the sidebar overlay the
            flow of the contents.
        </P>
    </BODY>
</HTML>
```

Figure 1-8 illustrates the two types of sidebars.

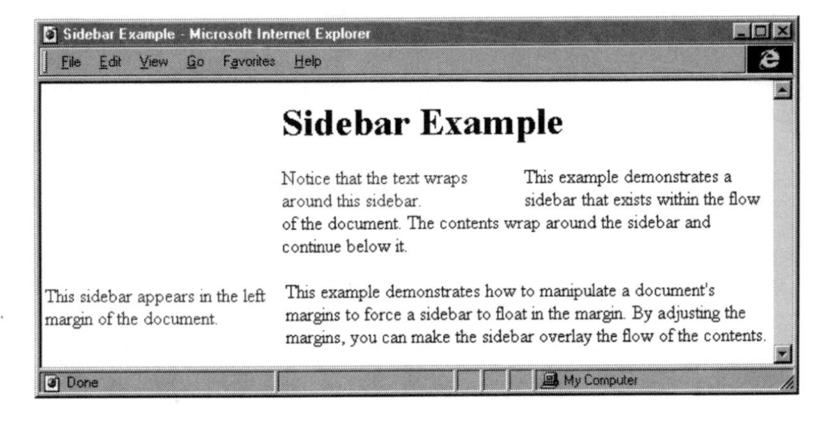

Figure 1-8.
A sidebar with text wrapping around it, and a sidebar set in the left margin.

The *visibility* Property vs. the *display* Property

The CSS1 specification defines the *display* property for removing elements from the presentation of the document. The working draft on CSS positioning exposes an additional property, *visibility,* that allows elements to become transparent in the document's flow. You use these two properties to achieve different presentation effects in the rendering and flow of the document. Setting the *visibility* property to *hidden* causes the contents to be rendered entirely transparently. The contents are still in position in the flow, but they are not visible. Setting the *display* property to *none* causes an element to be ignored by the rendering engine, as if the element never appeared in the document.

Figure 1-9 shows the effects of the *visibility* and *display* properties. The right column shows the contents either with *visibility:hidden* or *display:none*, and the left column shows the contents fully displayed. With *display:none*, the contents that are not displayed take up no space in the document's flow.

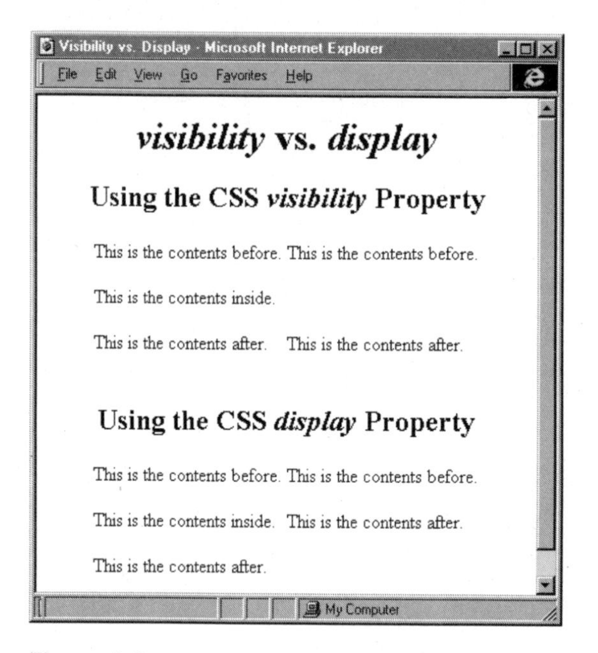

Figure 1-9.
The effects of setting the visibility *and* display *properties.*

Controlling the Cursor

The CSS *cursor* property is used to customize the mouse pointer when the user moves the mouse over an element. This property is especially useful when traditional text elements have script associated with them. For example, using a traditional I-beam cursor with text that the user is supposed to click like a button will be confusing. Instead, an arrow or other relevant cursor should be used.

The following table lists the settings for the *cursor* property currently specified by CSS. Examples of these cursors can be found with the Chapter 1 examples on the companion CD.

Value	Description
auto	The browser determines which cursor to display based on the current context.
crosshair	Simple crosshair cursor.
default	Usually an arrow; the platform-dependent default cursor.
hand	Hand cursor; used to represent a region on the screen that is clickable.
text	Usually an I-beam; used to indicate editable text.
help	Usually a question mark or a balloon; indicates that help is available for the object under the cursor.
e-resize, ne-resize, nw-resize, n-resize, se-resize, sw-resize, s-resize, w-resize	Various arrow-shaped cursors; used to represent a resize operation—for example, when the user clicks on the border of a window to resize the window.
move	Used to indicate that the element can be moved.
wait	Usually a watch or an hourglass; indicates that the program is busy and the user should wait.

CSS Support for Intrinsic Controls

In Internet Explorer 4.0, the text, button, and marquee controls fully support style sheets. The Select element has limited support for style sheets. To prevent problems on earlier browser implementations, intrinsic controls do not inherit style sheets from parent elements. Instead, style rules must be associated with specific elements through their element type or their CLASS or ID attributes.

The following simple style sheet formats all Input elements in a class named *text* as green boldface text:

```
<STYLE TYPE="text/css">
   INPUT.text {color:green; font-weight:bold}
</STYLE>
<INPUT CLASS="text" TYPE=TEXT VALUE="Green Bold Text">
```

Using the CLASS attribute ensures that only Input elements marked with the *text* class are changed. This technique requires a little redundancy between the TYPE and CLASS attributes because the selector in CSS that associates elements with styles currently does not recognize arbitrary attributes; CSS is limited to associating styles with elements based only on the CLASS or ID attribute or the element type.

Embedding Custom Fonts

Before Internet Explorer 4.0, Web authors had to use the built-in fonts of the browser or guess what fonts might be available on the system. Internet Explorer 4.0 provides the Web author with the ability to specify fonts that are downloaded with the Web page, ensuring that the page is rendered correctly. The downloadable font is specified using enhancements to the CSS syntax. The syntax for specifying a downloadable font in a style sheet is shown here:

@font-face {font-family:*fontName*; src:url(*filename.eot*)}

The *fontName* value is a user-defined name that is later referenced by the *font-family* CSS property. Here is a complete example:

```
<STYLE TYPE="text/css">
   @font-face {
      font-family:demoFont;
      src:url(http://somewhere.com/coolFont.eot)}
   H1 {font-family:demoFont, Arial, sans-serif}
</STYLE>
<H1>This text is displayed using the downloaded demoFont.</H1>
```

Once a new font is specified, it can be used as a valid font name for *font-family*. The *font-family* property can take a list of fonts so that if the first font could not be downloaded, the browser can try a different font or a different font family until one works. In this example, the last font specified is *sans-serif,* which allows the browser to use any sans serif font to render the element.

User Settings

Internet Explorer 4.0 supports the ability to create Web pages that automatically adapt to the look and feel of the user's system. A set of new color and font keywords is available for specifying the user's system settings. A demo page that displays text formatted with your system settings is included with the Chapter 1 examples on the companion CD.

Table 1-1 lists the set of new color keywords available in Internet Explorer 4.0. (Existing colors that can be specified for any CSS color attribute are not listed.) A complete list of named colors as well as a demo page that displays each of these colors can be found on the companion CD.

Table 1-2 on page 26 lists the font keywords that represent the current user system settings. These values can be used only for the *font* property; they cannot be used with the *font-family* property because the *font-family* property is already automatically based on the user's system settings.

Color Values

Keyword	Description
activeborder	Active window border color
activecaption	Active window caption color
appworkspace	Background color of multiple document interface (MDI) applications
background	Desktop background color
buttonface	Face color for buttons
buttonhighlight	Highlight color for buttons
buttonshadow	Shadow color for buttons
buttontext	Text color on buttons
captiontext	Text color in caption, the window sizing box, and scrollbar arrow buttons
graytext	Grayed (disabled) text color; set to *0* if the current display driver does not support a solid gray color
highlight	Color of item(s) selected in a control
highlighttext	Text color of item(s) selected in a control
inactiveborder	Inactive window border color
inactivecaption	Inactive window caption color
inactivecaptiontext	Text color in an inactive caption
infobackground	Background color for ToolTip
infotext	Text color for ToolTip
menu	Menu background color
menutext	Text color in menus
scrollbar	Color of scrollbar background
threeddarkshadow	Dark shadow color for three-dimensional display elements
threedface	Face color for three-dimensional display elements
threedhighlight	Highlight color for three-dimensional display elements
threedlightshadow	Light shadow color for three-dimensional display elements
threedshadow	Shadow color for three-dimensional display elements
window	Window background color
windowframe	Window frame color
windowtext	Text color in windows

Table 1-1.
New system color keywords in Internet Explorer 4.0.

Font Values

Keyword	Description
caption	Font used for captioned controls (buttons, drop-down lists, and so on)
icon	Font used to label icons
menu	Font used in menus
messagebox	Font used in dialog boxes
smallcaption	Font used for labeling small controls
statusbar	Font used in window status bars

Table 1-2.
New system font keywords in Internet Explorer 4.0.

CSS Positioning

Internet Explorer 4.0 also supports a new CSS draft, CSS-P, that provides greater control over the positioning of elements. Combining these new extensions with scripting allows elements to be animated and moved around on the page. This feature provides the Web author with complete control over the document's layout and the ability to control the position of and relationship between elements. Chapter 12, "Dynamic Positioning," introduces the syntax for positioning elements with CSS as well as the support for scripting positioned elements.

Filters and Transition Effects

Internet Explorer 4.0 also supports a set of filters and transitions that can be associated with the HTML contents. Filters can be directly applied to text in the document. Transitions allow presentation-like effects such as dissolves and slides to be added to the document or to elements in the document. For example, you can make text shadowed or semitransparent, and you can make pages fade in or out when the user enters or exits them. This functionality is supported through the new CSS *filter* property.

Examining an HTML DTD

HTML is an application of SGML, so it allows the creation of structured documents. Unfortunately, a recent scan of the Web shows that most Web pages are not true HTML documents. Browser implementations are partly to blame for this laxity because they are very lenient when parsing documents and often attempt to decipher the Web author's intent, rather than reject invalid documents.

With the introduction of Dynamic HTML and CSS, structure takes on greater importance. Pages that are properly structured will interact better and be more reliable across multiple browsers. Scripts will run much more predictably because there is no ambiguity in the document's description. The event architecture exposed by Dynamic HTML also relies heavily on the document's structure.

Understanding how to create a proper HTML document requires the ability to read a DTD (document type definition). The DTD defines the set of valid elements, identifies which elements can be properly contained by other elements, and specifies the valid attributes for each element. This section introduces you to the basics of reading and understanding a DTD; it is not intended to teach you how to author and create custom DTDs. Explaining all aspects of an SGML DTD would require an entire book—of which many are available.

Defining an Element

An element in the DTD is defined using the ELEMENT keyword. The element's definition specifies whether the element contains anything and whether the begin and end tags are optional or required. The following code demonstrates a prototype for defining an element:

```
<!ELEMENT elementName beginTag endTag contentModel>
```

The *beginTag* and *endTag* placeholders can be either a hyphen (-) or an *O*. A hyphen indicates that the tag is required, and an *O* indicates that the tag is optional. The *contentModel* placeholder can be *EMPTY*, which indicates that the element cannot contain anything, or it can be a specification of the valid contents for the element. The following code defines a Body element, in which the begin and end tags are optional:

```
<!ELEMENT BODY O O %body.content
   -- Begin and end tags are optional, containing body.content. -->
```

While there are many elements in HTML that support optional begin and end tags, it is still good practice to always explicitly provide them. Doing so helps make the document much more readable and reusable, especially to those who do not understand the intricacies of HTML. When these delimiters are not supplied, the browser will infer their location based on the contents.

The preceding Body element definition specifies that the element can contain *%body.content*. The *%* in this specifier indicates that the contents are defined through a macro (called an entity in SGML). The *<!ENTITY % body.content...>* definition specifies the elements that can be contained within a Body element. Such macros are useful because they allow contents models to be reused by multiple elements, making the DTD more compact and easier to use. Contents models can also be defined directly in line. For example, the code on the following page defines the Map element, which can contain only Area elements.

```
<!ELEMENT MAP - - (AREA)*>
```

The set of valid elements in the contents model is specified using a simple regular expression language. The * qualifier following the *(AREA)* tag indicates that any number of Area elements can be contained within a Map element.

Defining Attributes

Attributes are defined in a manner similar to elements. Attribute lists are defined using the !ATTLIST keyword. The attributes for the Body element are defined as follows:

```
<!ATTLIST BODY
   %attrs;                    -- id, class, style, lang, dir, events --
   %focus;
   background %URL #IMPLIED -- texture tile for document background --
   topmargin; CDATA #IMPLIED
   leftmargin; CDATA #IMPLIED
   %body-color-attrs;          -- bgcolor, text, link, vlink, alink --
   onLoad   %script  #IMPLIED -- intrinsic event --
   onUnload %script  #IMPLIED -- intrinsic event --
   >
```

The first tag following the !ATTLIST keyword specifies the element the attributes are associated with and is followed by the attribute list. Each attribute is either a macro pointing to another list of attributes or a definition of the data type that indicates whether the attribute is required or implied. A macro can be used to associate a group of attributes with the element or even to specify the data type.

Defining an Entity

An entity is a macro that can be reused elsewhere in the DTD. The *attrs* entity used by the Body element is shown below along with the *style* entity. Notice that the *attrs* entity points to additional entities: *style*, *i18n* (internationalization), and *events*.

```
<!ENTITY % attrs "%style %i18n %events">
<!ENTITY % style
  "id     ID      #IMPLIED  -- document-wide unique id --
   class  CDATA   #IMPLIED  -- comma list of class values --
   style  CDATA   #IMPLIED  -- associated style info --
   title  CDATA   #IMPLIED  -- advisory text --
   >
```

The *body.content* entity is also defined using other entities:

```
<!ENTITY % body.content "(%heading | %text | %block | ADDRESS)*">
```

This definition indicates that the body can contain any number of the elements specified by the *%heading*, *%text*, and *%block* entities and any number of Address elements.

One of the most complex elements in HTML is the Table element. Here is the definition for the Table element:

```
<!ELEMENT table     - -
   (caption?, (col*|colgroup*), thead?, tfoot?, tbody+)>
<!ELEMENT caption   - - (%text;)+>
<!ELEMENT thead     - O (tr+)>
<!ELEMENT tfoot     - O (tr+)>
<!ELEMENT tbody     O O (tr+)>
<!ELEMENT colgroup  - O (col*)>
<!ELEMENT col       - O EMPTY>
<!ELEMENT tr        - O (th|td)+>
<!ELEMENT (th|td)   - O %body.content>
```

The table's contents can begin with a single optional caption, followed by any number of Col or ColGroup elements, followed by a single optional THead element and an optional TFoot element, followed by one or more TBody elements. The comma delimiter defines the ordering of the elements. Therefore, the Caption element, if supplied, must be the first element contained within the table.

It may seem odd that the table does not allow a TR element to exist immediately below the table. This does not mean that almost all tables on the Web are invalid. The TBody element is defined as having an optional begin tag and an optional end tag. Therefore, a TR outside of a THead or TFoot implicitly falls into the TBody. This relationship is further maintained in the object model, where the TBody element is always *synthesized.* A synthesized element in the object model represents an element that implicitly belongs to all documents, regardless of whether it is explicitly defined. For example, all documents are considered to have HTML, Head, and Body elements exposed in the object model. Synthesized elements in the object model are discussed in greater detail in Chapter 7, "Document Element Collections."

This concludes your brief introduction into the world of SGML DTDs. You should now be able to read an HTML DTD and create valid HTML documents. For more information about HTML and to obtain valid DTDs for all versions of HTML, see the W3C Web site (www.w3.org). To see the DTD used in Internet Explorer 4.0, see the Microsoft Web site (www.microsoft.com).

<SCRIPT LANGUAGE="JavaSc
// Create property x an
var x = 10;
function foo() {
// This code is not
code
var y =
alert(; // output
// Call foo while lo
foo();
window.foo(); // the
</SCRIPT>

CHAPTER TWO

Fundamentals of HTML Scripting

The Dynamic HTML object model has evolved from the object models that were included in Microsoft Internet Explorer 3.0 and Netscape Navigator 3.0. This chapter provides a historical perspective, comparing the old object models with the one provided by Dynamic HTML and demonstrating the level of support provided by the different versions of the browsers.

Scripting languages have evolved alongside the HTML object models. By embedding scripts in your documents, you can access the HTML objects to manipulate the elements on your Web pages. This chapter introduces this powerful programming technique.

The following topics are covered in this chapter:

- **Dynamic HTML object hierarchy** The Dynamic HTML object hierarchy is the API for creating live and interactive pages. The objects in the hierarchy represent the browser and the elements of the HTML page. In this section, the object models supported by Internet Explorer 3.0 and Netscape Navigator 3.0 and 4.0 are discussed and compared to the Dynamic HTML object model supported by Internet Explorer 4.0.
- **Authoring scripts** The Dynamic HTML object model is accessed by writing scripts and associating them with the HTML document. A script is associated with the HTML document by using a Script element, which contains executable code in a specified language. The Script element can also be used to associate external script libraries with the document.

- **Choosing a scripting language: JavaScript vs. VBScript** The two primary programming languages used on the Web are JavaScript and VBScript. Both languages can fully manipulate the Dynamic HTML objects. This section helps you determine which language to use for specific circumstances.
- **Advanced JavaScript techniques** This section discusses some of the JavaScript techniques used throughout this book. It is not meant to provide a language tutorial, but rather to familiarize you with some of the interesting features of the JavaScript language and their relationship to Dynamic HTML.
- **Scripting and Web security** Security is a widespread concern on the Web. A programming language imposes limitations in order to ensure the clients' security, and a programmer must understand these limitations. This section introduces the security model for Dynamic HTML. Additional security issues are addressed throughout this book.

NOTE: This chapter uses elements of the Dynamic HTML object model to demonstrate various techniques. For each such use, you will find a reference to the chapter in which the feature is discussed in detail.

Dynamic HTML Object Hierarchy

A minimal HTML object model was first introduced as part of Netscape Navigator 2.0's JavaScript implementation. The original implementation exposed only a relatively small number of document aspects to manipulation by a scripting language. However, it did lay the groundwork for the object models that followed.

Internet Explorer 3.0 separated the original object model for describing the document from the language implementation. This laid the foundation for the language-independence requirement of Dynamic HTML. Internet Explorer 4.0 built on this object model to completely expose all aspects of the document.

Figure 2-1 shows the object model supported by Internet Explorer 4.0.

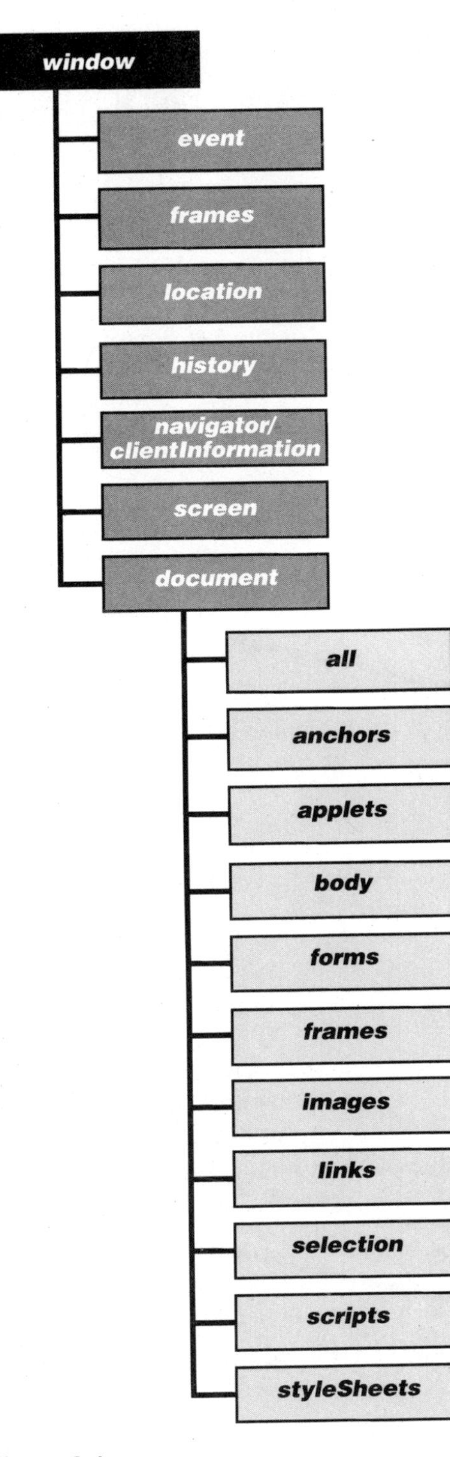

Figure 2-1.
The Internet Explorer 4.0 object model.

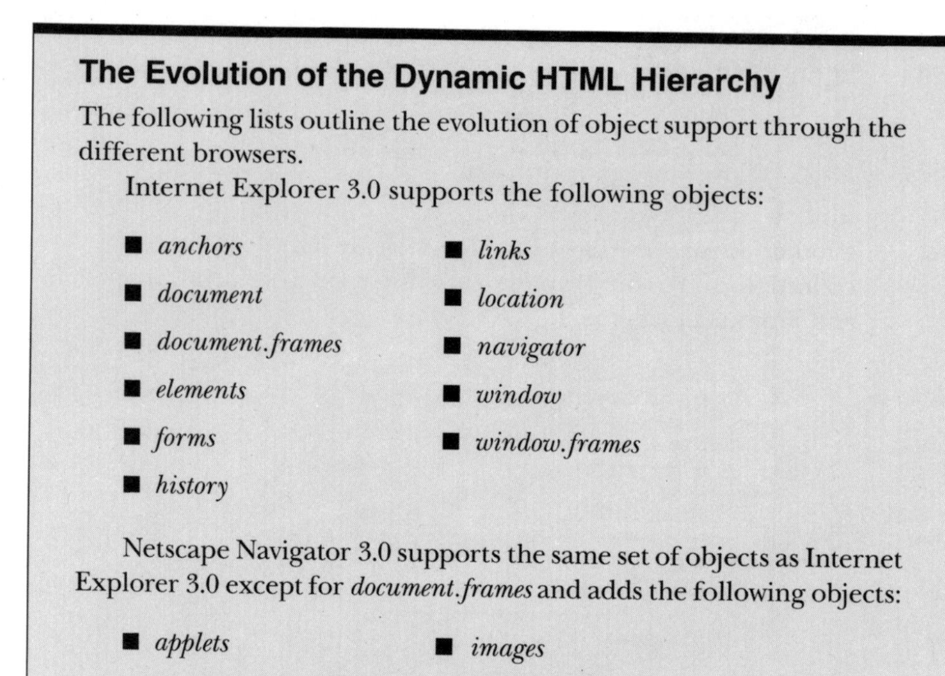

The Evolution of the Dynamic HTML Hierarchy

The following lists outline the evolution of object support through the different browsers.

Internet Explorer 3.0 supports the following objects:

- *anchors*
- *document*
- *document.frames*
- *elements*
- *forms*
- *history*
- *links*
- *location*
- *navigator*
- *window*
- *window.frames*

Netscape Navigator 3.0 supports the same set of objects as Internet Explorer 3.0 except for *document.frames* and adds the following objects:

- *applets*
- *images*

Internet Explorer 4.0 supports the same set of objects as Internet Explorer 3.0 and Netscape Navigator 3.0 and adds the following objects:

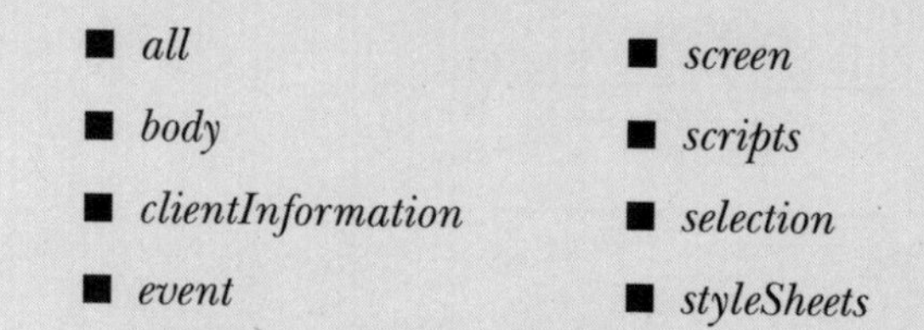

- *all*
- *body*
- *clientInformation*
- *event*
- *screen*
- *scripts*
- *selection*
- *styleSheets*

These lists are useful when you are comparing the level of functionality desired with the specified set of browsers. For Internet Explorer 3.0 compatibility, either your scripts must be limited to Internet Explorer 3.0 support or your code must conditionally check the version and brand of the browser to ensure graceful degradation.

The *window* object is the top-level object in the HTML object model. The *window* object is the frame for the *document* object. All interactions with the document occur through the window. The *window* object also exposes information about the current document's URL, previous URLs the client has visited, and the current document's type.

The window can contain different types of documents depending on the MIME type. There are two types of HTML documents: a traditional HTML document and an HTML frameset. For both types, the contents of the document are exposed through the *document* object. Because framesets divide the screen into multiple frames, each individual frame is also exposed through the window's *frames* collection. Each frame in this collection actually represents another *window* object—and potentially another document, or another *frames* collection, and so on. Framesets are discussed in detail in Chapter 5, "Window and Frame Management."

Dynamic HTML Evolution (or Revolution)

Netscape Navigator 2.0 and Internet Explorer 3.0 introduced basic object models for HTML documents. However, the level of support was mostly limited to conditional logic during page loading and form validation. No changes were permitted that would alter the shape or rendering of the document. Internet Explorer 4.0 has overcome this limitation by providing an object model that exposes the entire document.

Rather than define an entirely new object model, developers designed the Dynamic HTML object model as a superset of the existing model. In addition, the Dynamic HTML object model is consistent with current programming paradigms, allowing developers to leverage existing knowledge. If you are familiar with scripting for Internet Explorer 3.0 or Netscape Navigator 3.0, you already have the basis for learning Dynamic HTML.

Support for Older Browsers

While graceful degradation is intrinsic to HTML, it is not possible with scripting languages. When a parser does not recognize an HTML tag, it is supposed to ignore the tag. As a result, the presentation of the corresponding element's contents may be slightly different than intended. Ignoring statements is not feasible for scripts—ignoring a line in a script can be fatal to the rest of the code, as each line of code may create or change the existing state of the document. Therefore, when you are authoring scripts for multiple browsers and versions, degradation is not something that you can ignore; instead, you must carefully plan for it in the engineering and design of your page.

Dynamic HTML intrinsically provides power and flexibility not available in earlier versions of HTML. You can author your pages to use many of Dynamic HTML's features and still work well across all browsers. Throughout this book, techniques are provided to help you write code that can degrade gracefully.

In some cases, the code is merely providing a visual cue or effect, and degradation is usually trivial. In other cases, depending on the purpose of the script, the only solution is to create an alternative page that provides similar functionality in a different manner. In general, the more dynamic a page is, the more forethought is required to ensure that the page runs on down-level (less capable) browsers. Figure 2-2 shows a page enhanced for Dynamic HTML running in two browsers: Internet Explorer 3.0 on the left, and Internet Explorer 4.0 on the right. The Internet Explorer 3.0 version displays an expanded, flat table of contents pane, while the Internet Explorer 4.0 version contains an outline and a fancy table of contents.

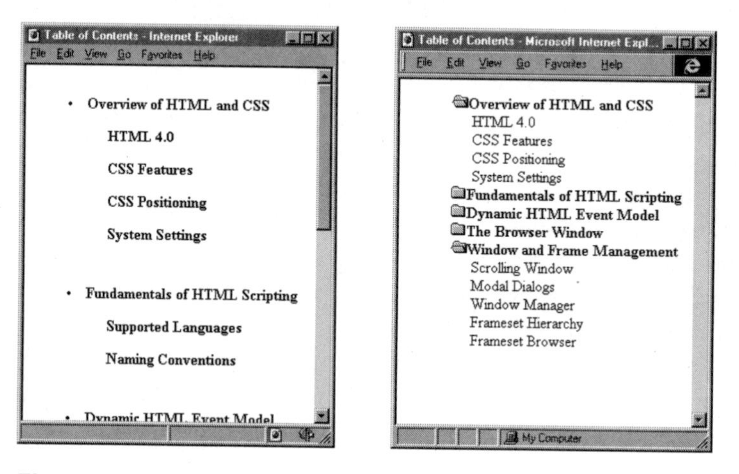

Figure 2-2.
A Dynamic HTML page as displayed by Internet Explorer 3.0 (on the left) and Internet Explorer 4.0.

Remember too that there may be bugs and inconsistencies in the existing implementations. Therefore, even if a page designed to run across browsers and versions uses a common set of objects and members (properties and methods), it should still be tested against all targeted platforms.

Dynamic Reflow

The ability to access and change any aspect of a page demonstrates one of the key innovations enabled by Dynamic HTML. Past browsers, while allowing some document changes, were not capable of causing the document to reflow itself without complicated scripts that reconstructed entirely new documents. Dynamic HTML breaks free from these restrictions. Whenever a script manipulates and changes an attribute of an element or a style sheet or modifies the contents, the document intelligently recalculates and repaints the page with the new information.

Dynamic HTML was designed to take advantage of the existing HTML and CSS (Cascading Style Sheets) recommendations and working drafts. Rather than require Web developers to learn a new model for representing a page, the Dynamic HTML object model exposes a reflection of the document to the scripting language. For example, a script can change the CLASS attribute of any HTML element. In the scripting language, the CLASS attribute, like all attributes, is exposed as a property of the element—in this case, the *className* property. Modifying any attribute is internally consistent with the user opening the file in an editor and changing the attribute in the source file. This model ensures that as HTML and CSS evolve, the object model naturally follows.

Authoring Scripts

Scripts are not the only way to access the Dynamic HTML object model; the Dynamic HTML object model can be accessed in the following three ways:

- Through scripts within or referenced by an HTML page. These scripts can access the contents of the current document or documents from the same domain in other frames or windows.
- Through embedded applets and controls that reside on the page.
- Through hosts that sit outside or alongside the browser. For example, the Find dialog box in Internet Explorer 4.0 was created using Dynamic HTML.

All three methods manipulate Dynamic HTML in similar ways. This book concentrates on the first approach, accessing the object model through scripts that are associated with an HTML document. However, all the concepts and techniques presented in this book can also be applied to the other two methods.

The Script Element

Scripts behind the page can be associated with the document using one of three techniques. The most common technique is to enclose code within a Script element. (The other two techniques are to put the code in a separate file and reference it with a <SCRIPT> tag or to put the code in an event attribute in another tag.) The Script element is a container for code written in a specific programming language. A Script element can either contain the code in line inside the document or refer to an external file. Scripts contained within a Script element can be associated with an element through code, through special attributes on the Script element, or through language-dependent mechanisms. Individual elements can have scripts associated directly with them through event attributes exposed in the element itself.

The syntax for the Script element is as follows:

```
<SCRIPT LANGUAGE="languageName" [TYPE="MIMEtype"]
        [SRC="optionalFile"] [DEFER]>
    Script statements
</SCRIPT>
```

The scripting language is specified using the LANGUAGE attribute. The following code demonstrates how to specify a script for both VBScript and JavaScript:

```
<SCRIPT LANGUAGE="VBScript">
   ' VBScript code
</SCRIPT>

<SCRIPT LANGUAGE="JavaScript">
   // JavaScript code
</SCRIPT>
```

> NOTE: In VBScript, comments are denoted by an apostrophe ('); in JavaScript, comments are denoted by either a // (which makes the rest of the line a comment) or /* *contents* */ (which makes *contents* a comment, even if it spans multiple lines). The scripting engine ignores all comment text.

For historical reasons, omitting a LANGUAGE attribute causes the script to be parsed as JavaScript. Rather than rely on the default language, you should always specify the LANGUAGE attribute in order to document the script's context.

> NOTE: The Script element's LANGUAGE attribute is deprecated in HTML 4.0 in favor of using the TYPE attribute. The TYPE attribute takes a MIME type for the language: for JavaScript you use *text/JavaScript,* and for VBScript you use *text/VBScript.* However, because down-level browsers will not recognize the TYPE attribute, we recommend that you continue to use LANGUAGE or use both LANGUAGE and TYPE. Note that specifying a TYPE attribute, when recognized, overrides any LANGUAGE setting.

With the introduction of Netscape Navigator 3.0, Netscape started to append a version number to the JavaScript language string. Therefore, to write code that executes only in Netscape Navigator 3.0 and Microsoft Internet Explorer 4.0 and later, set the LANGUAGE attribute to *JavaScript1.1*. This technique works because if the browser does not recognize the specified language, the code is not executed and the script block is skipped. For code that demonstrates how to determine what scripting languages the client supports without having to check the browser version or type, see the section "Multiple Scripting Languages" later in this chapter.

Scripts contained within a Script element can execute code in two contexts: during the parsing of the page and as the result of an event. The following script demonstrates both types of code. Code that is included directly in the Script element but not contained within a function is executed immediately when it is parsed. Code that is contained within a function can execute only when the function is called, either directly or because of an event. Events are notifications that occur when the user interacts with the page or when the state of the document changes—for example, when the user clicks on the document, or when the document is loaded. The event model is introduced in detail in Chapter 3, "Dynamic HTML Event Model."

```
<HTML>
   <HEAD>
      <TITLE>Execution of Code</TITLE>
      <SCRIPT LANGUAGE="JavaScript">
         // The following alert occurs while the page is being loaded.
         alert('Hello, World!');

         function helloWorld() {
            // This code executes only when the helloWorld function
            // is called.
            alert('Hello, World Too!');
         }
      </SCRIPT>
   </HEAD>
</HTML>
```

Script Libraries

Scripts may be contained in an external file and associated with any number of HTML documents. This arrangement serves several purposes, the most apparent of which is that it allows generic script libraries to be written that are shared by multiple pages. Depending on the browser, these script pages can become cached, thus increasing performance, as common functionality does not have to be written into every page. Another purpose depends on how pages are authored. If there are separate authors for scripts and contents, both do not need access to the same file simultaneously. Instead, the script author can write the scripts in one file, while the contents author writes the contents in another file. This is consistent with the separation of presentation and contents already available with style sheets.

Referencing of an external script is done using the SRC attribute, as in this example:

```
<SCRIPT LANGUAGE="JavaScript" SRC="genericFile.js">
   /* Optionally write code here for browsers that don't
      support the SRC attribute. */
   // The closing SCRIPT tag is always required.
</SCRIPT>
```

Even when the SRC attribute is supplied, the <SCRIPT> tag must still have an end tag. Browsers that support the SRC attribute ignore the contents of the Script element. Browsers that do not recognize the SRC attribute execute the contents of the Script element as the code.

External script file support is available only in Netscape Navigator 3.0 and Internet Explorer 4.0 and later. Therefore, if you use external script files, take care to make provisions for the prior versions of these browsers.

Immediately Executed Code

As mentioned, Dynamic HTML lets you create code that can execute during the parsing of a page. This code is written outside the scope of any event handler, subroutine, or function. Such code can serve two main purposes:

- Adding properties to the *window* object and initializing their state
- Outputting contents into the document's stream

The first purpose is similar to declaring what might normally be considered global variables. In all current scripting languages, variables that are scoped to the *window* object are added directly to the *window* object as properties. For example, here the variable *x* is added as a property to the window:

```
<SCRIPT LANGUAGE="JavaScript">
   var x = 0;          // Create property and initialize to 0.
   alert(window.x);  // Output 0, the value of x.
</SCRIPT>
```

To better understand the preceding code, consider the following, more elaborate example:

```
<SCRIPT LANGUAGE="JavaScript">
   // Create property x and initialize to 10.
   var x = 10;

   function foo() {
      // This code is not executed unless explicitly called.
      /* Create an instance variable, y, that lives only as
         long as the function is being executed. */
      var y = 0;
      alert(x);      // Output 10; x is a property of the window.
   }

   // Call foo while loading the page.
   foo();
   window.foo();     // Call the foo function again because the foo
                     // function is added to the window.
</SCRIPT>
```

This code demonstrates that immediately executed code and functions can be interspersed. Code that calls a function while the page is loading must have the function declared in advance.

The second purpose of code that executes when the page loads is to write contents into the document. This is done using the *document* object's *write* method. Here is a simple program that writes *Hello, World!* into the HTML document:

```
<HTML>
   <HEAD>
      <TITLE>Hello, World!</TITLE>
   </HEAD>
   <BODY>
      <SCRIPT LANGUAGE="JavaScript">
         // Write the string "Hello, World!" into the document.
         document.write("<H1>Hello, World!</H1>")
      </SCRIPT>
   </BODY>
</HTML>
```

The *write* method can be called only during the loading of the page, to insert contents into the parsing of the document. To manipulate and change the contents once the page is loaded, you must use a different technique.

Dynamically adding contents to the document during the loading process is discussed in Chapter 6, "The HTML Document," and manipulating the contents is discussed in Chapter 13, "Dynamic Contents."

Locations of Scripts in the Document

A document may contain any number of Script elements. A Script element can live in either the head or the body of the document. For most purposes, the location of the script is not important in relation to the design of the page. However, scripts that perform initialization are usually more convenient and more readable when placed in the document's head.

The location of a Script element is more important if the element is actually writing contents into the stream or is referencing an element in the document. Writing into the stream is done using the *write* or *writeln* method of the *document* object, as in the following example:

```
<HTML>
   <SCRIPT LANGUAGE="JavaScript">
      // Generate an entire document from this script.
      document.write("<HEAD><TITLE>My Document</TITLE></HEAD>");
      document.write("<BODY><H1>This is my page.</H1></BODY>");
   </SCRIPT>
</HTML>
```

This code creates and renders the following HTML:

```
<HTML>
   <HEAD>
      <TITLE>My Document</TITLE>
   </HEAD>
   <BODY>
      <H1>This is my page.</H1>
   </BODY>
</HTML>
```

If you are writing head contents, it is important to put the script within the head. For example, a script placed in the middle of the page should not output HTML text that sets the document's title. Any time the *write* methods are called, the contents are placed into the stream at the current location. For example, inserting a <TITLE> tag in the wrong place may violate the HTML DTD (document type definition) and have unpredictable results.

The use of the *write* methods is discussed in detail in Chapter 6, "The HTML Document." Generating pages using *document.write* is not always an ideal technique because it masks the contents from editing and indexing tools, which might not be able to interpret scripts. Without executing the script behind the page, the actual contents are unknown.

Object Availability

Scripts that execute during the parsing of the page and that reference elements on the page need to be positioned carefully. For these scripts, only the elements that have been previously loaded are available for scripting because no forward declarations of elements are possible. The same holds true for any functions or variables that may be called—they must always be specified prior to the call.

Attempting to access anything in the HTML source code that follows the Script element during immediately executing code will generate an error. For example, scripts that execute in the head of the document while the page is downloading cannot reference any of the forms or other elements that exist in the body.

This rule is true only for scripts that execute during the downloading of a page. Scripts that execute in response to events are not required to follow the referenced element. Once the document is entirely parsed, all aspects of the document are considered fully accessible. However, it is possible for event handlers to be called before the document is entirely loaded. Before referencing an element that might not yet be loaded, you should test for the existence of the element:

```
<SCRIPT FOR="document" EVENT="onclick()" LANGUAGE="JavaScript">
   // This code executes whenever the user clicks in the document.

   // Verify that the element exists.
   if (null != document.all.myElement) {
      // Do something.
   }
   else
      alert("The document is not entirely loaded yet!");
</SCRIPT>
```

Event binding is discussed in Chapter 3, "Dynamic HTML Event Model."

Deferring Script Execution

Internet Explorer 4.0 can provide improved performance for scripts that do not contain immediately executed code. If the Script element contains only function declarations, supplying the DEFER attribute in the <SCRIPT> tag notifies the browser that it does not have to wait for the entire script to be parsed and interpreted. Instead, the browser can continue to load and display the page. This attribute should be used only when the Script element contains nothing but function declarations and when any subsequent scripts that are immediately executed do not call these functions. Immediately executed code defined within a deferred Script element can react unpredictably. When used appropriately, the DEFER attribute has no adverse effect on browsers that do not recognize it. Those browsers ignore the attribute and perform the traditional blocking until the script is parsed.

Multiple Scripting Languages

Similar to its ability to specify multiple Script elements, a single document can also contain and execute multiple scripting languages. All currently available scripting languages will execute on the page, assuming that the browser supports them. For example, using Internet Explorer, a page can be authored containing both JavaScript and VBScript code. Furthermore, it is possible for one language to call the functions defined by another language, as demonstrated in the following code. Calling a function scripted in another language is possible because all functions and variables are added as methods and properties of the *window* object.

```
<SCRIPT LANGUAGE="VBScript">
   ' Simple subroutine that pops up a message box
   sub MyAlert(str)
      msgBox(str)
   end sub
</SCRIPT>

<SCRIPT LANGUAGE="JavaScript">
   // Call the VBScript subroutine, MyAlert, defined above.
   MyAlert("Hello, World!");
   window.MyAlert("MyAlert is a method of the window object.");
</SCRIPT>
```

The fact that multiple languages can be used together makes possible an easy technique to determine what languages the browser supports. The following code demonstrates this technique:

```
<SCRIPT LANGUAGE="JavaScript1.1">
<!--
   window.js11 = true;  // Set flag for JavaScript 1.1.
// -->
</SCRIPT>
```

```
<SCRIPT LANGUAGE="VBScript">
<!--
   vbSupport = True      ' Set flag for VBScript.
' -->
</SCRIPT>

<SCRIPT LANGUAGE="JavaScript">
<!-- --><H1>Your browser does not support scripting.</H1>
<!--
   /* In this example, JavaScript is considered the lowest common
      denominator. This example can be modified to use a different
      language for the final testing. */
   document.write("JavaScript is supported.<BR>");
   if (null != window.js11)
      document.write("JavaScript 1.1 is supported.<BR>");
   if (null != window.vbSupport)
      document.write("VBScript is supported.<BR>");
// -->
</SCRIPT>
```

Hiding Scripts from Down-Level Browsers

Unless you take some precautions, browsers that do not support scripting will render the script code as part of the document's contents. This occurs because the down-level browser will ignore the <SCRIPT> tag and process the contents as HTML text. This is consistent with how HTML handles unrecognized tags and is necessary in the evolution of HTML. To hide scripts from a down-level browser, create an HTML comment that wraps the code:

```
<SCRIPT LANGUAGE="VBScript">
<!--
   ' VBScript code
   ' The next line ends the HTML comment.
' -->
</SCRIPT>

<SCRIPT LANGUAGE="JavaScript">
<!--
   // JavaScript code
// -->
</SCRIPT>
```

Both languages interpret the opening HTML string for creating a comment, *<!- -*, as the beginning of a single-line comment, so the line is ignored by the language parser. The close comment must be preceded by the language-

specific comment delineator (' in VBScript, // in JavaScript). This causes all code within the Script element to be treated as a comment and not rendered by a down-level browser.

When using the commenting scheme, be careful not to output the opening or closing comment delimiter in any strings anywhere in the code. If outputting the string is necessary, be sure to break it into multiple parts:

```
<SCRIPT LANGUAGE="JavaScript">
<!--
   /* The close comment tag being written into the document
      is broken into two strings. */
   document.write("<" + "!-- This is a comment to write into the " +
      "stream. --" + ">");
// -->
</SCRIPT>
```

Using HTML comment tags inside a script hides the script from down-level browsers, but it does nothing to help warn the user that the page relies on scripting. Therefore, to supply text to a browser that does not support scripting, a special <NOSCRIPT> tag is exposed. The contents of a NoScript element are ignored by browsers that support scripting.

```
<!-- Contents for browsers without scripting support -->
<NOSCRIPT>
   <H1>This page requires scripting support.</H1>
   <H2>Please obtain the latest version of Internet Explorer
      to properly view this page.</H2>
</NOSCRIPT>
```

This technique works in a down-level browser because the down-level browser ignores the <NOSCRIPT> tag just as it ignores the <SCRIPT> tag and outputs the contents. A scriptable browser knows that when it encounters a <NOSCRIPT> tag, it should not render anything until after the </NOSCRIPT> tag ends the element.

The user of a scriptable browser can disable scripting support. When scripting support is disabled, the browser acts like a down-level browser and outputs the NoScript element's contents.

Internet Explorer 4.0 allows you to disable scripts through its security settings. Internet Explorer 4.0 has a powerful security model that can be customized for different "zones" of Web content; each zone represents the entire Web, the intranet, or a particular set of pages. The following steps disable scripting for a particular zone:

1. From the View menu, choose Internet Options to display an Internet Options dialog box.
2. Select the Security tab from the list of pages.
3. Select the zone to customize. Select Custom, and click the Settings button.
4. In the Scripting category, select the Disable option for Active Scripting.
5. Click OK or Apply to save these settings.

Netscape Navigator 2.0 does not support the <NOSCRIPT> tag. You must use another technique to warn the user that the page requires scripting. This involves writing a trivial script in the document that uses an enhancement of the commenting trick to force output on down-level clients:

```
<!-- Alternative technique for providing down-level contents -->
<SCRIPT LANGUAGE="JavaScript">
<!-- -->Your browser fails to recognize scripts. <!--
   // Write your code.
-->
</SCRIPT>
```

The commenting technique has the following disadvantage: when you disable scripts, the contents of the Script element are ignored, and the contents of the NoScript element are displayed. Therefore, the text for the comment is not displayed when scripting is disabled.

While the NoScript technique covers browsers that do not support scripting, it does nothing to differentiate vendor implementations. Different vendors will be implementing different versions of Dynamic HTML as it evolves. A script may or may not run on different browsers. There is unfortunately no easy solution to this problem. Some Web authors may choose to create multiple pages and send different pages based on the client's identity. This redirection can be done on the client. An example of this redirection is provided in the following section.

NOTE: In order to highlight the features of Dynamic HTML they demonstrate, most code samples in this book will not include any provisions for down-level browsers.

Client-Side Redirection

One method for handling different software versions is to redirect the user to different pages based on the client's browser, as shown in the following code. Client-side redirection occurs when a script behind the page conditionally switches the browser to a different document. By conditionally testing the version of the browser, an alternative version of the page can be loaded. When this technique is used, the base page should be the page that targets your most important audience because the redirection will have performance implications. When the redirection occurs, it will result in two pages being downloaded.

```
<SCRIPT LANGUAGE="JavaScript">
   var MS = navigator.appVersion.indexOf("MSIE");
   // Check whether this is IE4.
   window.isIE4 = (MS > 0) &&
      (parseInt(navigator.appVersion.substring(MS + 5, MS + 6)) >= 4);
   if (!isIE4) // If not IE4, get non-dynamic page.
      window.location="downlevelpage.htm";
</SCRIPT>
```

To avoid the performance implications of client-side redirection, you can perform the check on the server-side and send down only the correct page. However, depending on the server's privileges, this may not be a viable option.

Choosing a Scripting Language: JavaScript vs. VBScript

As mentioned, the Dynamic HTML object model is language neutral and can be scripted in any available programming language. Therefore, the choice of language depends on the preference of the Web author and the intended audience for the page.

There are currently two primary languages for scripting pages on the Web: JavaScript and VBScript. A committee of the ECMA (European Computer Manufacturers Association), with representatives from Netscape, Microsoft, and other vendors, has approved a standardization of the JavaScript language. Microsoft's JScript implementation in Internet Explorer 4.0 is fully compliant with the new standard.

For creating Web pages on the Internet for which maximum exposure is necessary, JavaScript provides the most potential, as it is currently supported by both Netscape's and Microsoft's browsers. (This also assumes that your code is targeting the set of features shared across the different implementations.)

In addition, the syntax for controlling program flow in JavaScript is very similar to the syntax in Java and C++, languages familiar to many Web authors.

Although both Microsoft and Netscape support JavaScript, the companies are at different stages of implementing the features in Dynamic HTML. Therefore, if you want cross-browser interoperability, exercise caution when you are authoring dynamic pages. Throughout this book, techniques will be offered to help you construct intelligent and interoperable pages.

For intranets in which only one type of browser is used, the scripting language becomes a secondary issue. In this case, the language choice should be based on what browser is the standard for the company and what knowledge the Web developers have. If the Web development staff is widely versed in Microsoft Visual Basic, and Microsoft Internet Explorer is the browser of choice, it may be cheaper to develop in VBScript than to retrain and use JavaScript.

This Book Uses JavaScript

This book separates the concept of the object model from the programming language. However, without a programming language Dynamic HTML would need to be presented very abstractly, so for the sake of clarity this book uses the JavaScript language for all examples.

Certain JavaScript objects are not a part of the Dynamic HTML object model and are specific to the language. For example, the date, math, number, and other data types are all specific to the language. It is up to the language implementation to expose compatible data types. For example, VBScript exposes a string data type, but in VBScript the string is not an object with its own interface. Instead, string manipulations are performed separately using functions. The following code compares a string manipulation of the *title* property using VBScript and JavaScript:

```
<!-- Simple comparison between VBScript and JavaScript
     string functions -->
<SCRIPT LANGUAGE="VBScript">
   dim s                       ' Declare the string variable.
   s = document.title          ' Initialize.
   msgBox(len(s))              ' Output the length of s.
   msgBox(left(s, 1))          ' Output the first character of s.
</SCRIPT>

<SCRIPT LANGUAGE="JavaScript">
   var s = document.title;   // Can initialize at declaration time.
   alert(s.length);          // Output the length of s.
   alert(s.charAt(0));       // Output the first character of s.
</SCRIPT>
```

Advanced JavaScript Techniques

This section introduces some of the advanced JavaScript concepts used throughout this book. This section is not meant to teach JavaScript, but rather to ensure familiarity with some of the more powerful but less common aspects of the language.

Adding Properties to Objects

Arrays and objects in JavaScript provide two techniques for accessing their contents: directly referencing the contents as a property using dot (.) notation, or referencing an index into the array using bracket ([*index*]) notation. An index into a JavaScript array can be a string value that represents the property name. Dot notation allows direct access to a property when the property name is known in advance. When the property being accessed needs to be a variable, it can be accessed late-bound using a string identifier:

```
<SCRIPT LANGUAGE="JavaScript">
   var prop = "title";
   alert(document.title); // Access the title using dot notation.
   alert(document[prop]); // Access the property referenced by
                          // the prop variable.

   // Arrays and built-in objects work alike.
   var ar = new Array;
   ar.myProperty = "Demo";
   alert(ar.myProperty);
   alert(ar["myProperty"]);
</SCRIPT>
```

Objects in JavaScript are unique in their ability to automatically expand. You can add a new property to an object simply by assigning it a value. This feature comes at the expense of making debugging more difficult.

JavaScript is case sensitive, as demonstrated here:

```
<SCRIPT LANGUAGE="JavaScript">
   alert(document.title);   // Output the title of the document.
   document.Title = "Not the real title"; // Add a Title property.
   alert(document.Title);   // Output the new Title property.
</SCRIPT>
```

In this example, the two alert statements are actually different. Furthermore, the second line generates no error; instead, *Title* is added as a property of *document.* Therefore, you must be careful when writing JavaScript code. Debugging a large amount of script may be quite difficult.

NOTE: Internet Explorer 3.0 did not enforce these case-sensitivity rules. Internet Explorer 4.0 and all Netscape Navigator releases enforce strict case sensitivity.

To help alleviate this debugging problem, Internet Explorer 4.0 exposes a property on the document, the *expando* property, that can be used to disable the implicit property addition feature of JavaScript, as shown in this code:

```
<SCRIPT LANGUAGE="JavaScript">
   /* Internet Explorer 4.0 supports the ability to turn off the
      associative array nature of built-in objects. */
   document.expando = false;
   document.Title = "Not the real title";  // Error--no such property
</SCRIPT>
```

The *expando* property does not disable the explicit addition of properties to the window through variable declarations, but it does disable the implicit addition, as in the following example:

```
<SCRIPT LANGUAGE="JavaScript">
   document.expando = false;
   var x = 0;          // No error
   alert(window.x);    // x explicitly added.
   window.y = 10;      // Error--no y property
</SCRIPT>
```

NOTE: Internet Explorer 4.0 is the first browser that supports the *expando* property to control the associative array characteristic of objects. Netscape Navigator 4.0 and earlier versions of Internet Explorer do not recognize this property. When the *expando* property is not recognized, referencing it will automatically cause it to be added to the *document* object.

Because any object may contain any number of properties, JavaScript exposes a convenient operator for accessing them. With a *for...in* loop, you can execute a statement for each exposed property in an object without knowing what the properties are. For example, the following code outputs all the properties exposed on the *window* object:

```
<SCRIPT LANGUAGE="JavaScript">
   // Display an alert with all the properties of the window and
   // their values.
   var sProps = "Window Properties\n";
   for (props in window)
      sProps += props + ": " + window[props] + "\n";
   alert(sProps);
</SCRIPT>
```

Function Pointers

Any function can be assigned to and manipulated as a property. This fact allows a function to be dynamically added as a method that can be invoked or to be dynamically associated with an event handler.

Function pointers are extremely powerful in that they let you reuse functions as methods of an object, as in this example:

```
<SCRIPT LANGUAGE="JavaScript">
   // Define a simple function named test.
   function test() {
      alert("Function has been invoked.");
   }

   // Assign the onclick handler to be test.
   // This causes the function test to be called when the document
   // is clicked.
   document.onclick = test;
</SCRIPT>
```

In addition, when a function is called, it has access to an *arguments* array containing any parameters that were passed into the function. JavaScript automatically populates the *arguments* array at the time the function is invoked. The following code demonstrates how a function can access the *arguments* array:

```
<SCRIPT LANGUAGE="JavaScript">
   function testArgs() {
      /* A function in JavaScript can access an arguments array.
         This array contains all parameters that were passed into the
         function. */
      alert(arguments.length + " arguments");  // Output the number of
                                               // arguments.
      // Output each argument.
      for (var i = 0; i < arguments.length; i++)
         alert("argument " + i + " - " + arguments[i]);
   }
   testArgs(1, 2, 3, 4);  // Call testArgs with four arguments.
</SCRIPT>
```

The *arguments* array allows a function to be written to which a variable number of arguments can be passed. Based on the arguments that were passed, different actions can occur. A simple demonstration of where to use this capability is a summation routine:

```
<SCRIPT LANGUAGE="JavaScript">
   function Sum() {
      // Sum up all the arguments passed in and return the result.
```

```
      var intSum = 0;
      for (var intLoop = 0; intLoop < arguments.length; intLoop++)
         intSum += arguments[intLoop];
      return intSum;
   }

   alert(Sum(1, 1, 1, 2)); // Add the four values.
</SCRIPT>
```

Functions can also be dynamically created using the *new* operator. The *new* operator allows a new function routine to be constructed on the fly. A function is created as follows:

var *functionname* = new Function(*args1*, ..., *argsn*, *body*);

Any number of *args* may be supplied, including 0. The last argument to the Function constructor is always the code to execute. For example, the following code creates a simple function that returns the difference between two numbers:

```
var Difference = new Function("x","y","return x - y;");
```

This example is contrived, as it would be simpler to either perform the operation directly or encapsulate the code in a real function. The value in this code is that a temporary function can be created and discarded, or the code provides a simple way to dynamically construct a function call. Creating functions to dynamically create event handlers is demonstrated in several examples in this book.

Checking for Support

JavaScript offers a flexible way to test whether a particular property or method is supported by the browser. This technique can be used to predetermine whether the code is going to succeed and possibly to run alternative code if the feature is unavailable. For example, the following code checks whether the *all* collection on the document is supported:

```
<SCRIPT LANGUAGE="JavaScript">
   if (null == document.all) {
      // The all collection is not supported; run alternative code.
   }
   else {
      // Do something with the all collection.
   }
</SCRIPT>
```

Property and Function Naming Conventions

The ability to add variables and functions to any object in JavaScript is very powerful. However, with this power comes risk as Dynamic HTML evolves. Every time a developer dynamically adds a property to an object, a potential conflict is created between that property and a future enhancement to the object model. Here are a few guidelines that can minimize the risk of future conflicts:

- Begin all variables with a capital letter, prefix them with the data type, or prefix them with an underscore (for example, *Counter*, *intCounter*, or *_counter*).
- Do not use the name of a tag as a variable name, regardless of how it is capitalized. This will prevent potential conflict with elements that use or may eventually use the *new* construct (for example, *new Image*).
- Do not prefix any variables or functions with *html*, *css*, or *style*. These prefixes may have more widespread use in the future.

Perhaps the best technique for avoiding any conflict is to add only a single member object to any built-in object and then add all the new custom members to this object. This technique isolates the potential conflict to a single property, but it requires a little forethought: you must predefine the single property to ensure that no syntax errors are generated in the code. Here is an example of this technique being used on the *window* object, in which all custom members are added to a property named *_Custom*:

```
<SCRIPT LANGUAGE="JavaScript">
   // Before using the _Custom object, initialize it as a property of
   // the window object.
   if (null == window._Custom)
      window._Custom = new Object;

   // Add properties to _Custom.
   window._Custom.special = true;
   window._Custom.top = self;
</SCRIPT>
```

The initializing statement is necessary before any properties can be added to the *_Custom* object because JavaScript can add only one member to an object at a time. If *_Custom* was not first initialized, an error would have occurred when the *special* property was accessed.

Scripting and Web Security

With the introduction of scripting, Internet security has become an extremely important issue. Currently, browsers create a *sandbox* around the scripted page so that it can access only a well-defined set of information. There is no way in Dynamic HTML to access the client's machine and hard disk beyond a very well-controlled mechanism known as *cookies*. Cookies are discussed in Chapter 6, "The HTML Document."

Even without accessing the user's machine, however, the ability to access the contents and manipulate a page could have been a security risk. For example, a page outside a firewall should not be able to access the contents of a page that is within the firewall. An unauthorized page could access the text of the page and send it back to the server. The sandbox model requires the pages to be from the same domain before permitting unlimited access to the contents. This restriction prevents a document in one frame from accessing a document in another frame if the documents come from different sites.

To further guarantee security, the object model is limited in a number of cases. For example, the file upload object allows a user to upload files to the server. To ensure that the page does not have access to the user's file system, the *value* property representing the file to be uploaded is read-only. The *history* object that allows Forward and Back buttons to be created does not expose any information about the URL that is about to be displayed. Additional security restrictions are pointed out throughout this book.

For those who are very concerned about security, the browser allows users to turn on and off different features, including Java applets and ActiveX controls, cookies, and even scripting. The object model can access limited information that helps it determine the state of the browser and react accordingly.

<SCRIPT LANGUAGE="JavaSc
// Create property x
var x = 10;
function foo() {
// This code is not
// The code
var y =
alert( ); // output
// Call foo while lo
foo();
foo(); // the
</SCRIPT>

CHAPTER THREE

Dynamic HTML Event Model

Events are notifications that occur as a result of user actions or state changes within a document or window. Dynamic HTML exposes a set of events that allows the Web author to respond to most interactions between the user and the document. By responding to events, the author can create completely interactive pages.

In this chapter, you'll be introduced to techniques for handling events. The chapter concludes by demonstrating an application that combines the built-in support features of Dynamic HTML with the power of JavaScript function pointers to create a customized event binding mechanism.

The following topics are covered in this chapter:

- **General event model** Dynamic HTML provides a powerful event model that is closely related to the document's underlying structure. By understanding and taking advantage of this model, you can write efficient, maintainable code. The Dynamic HTML event model is based on two powerful new features for controlling the document's behavior: *event bubbling* and *default actions.*

  Event bubbling is the event model feature that observes the document's structural hierarchy in the processing of event notifications. All events can be responded to by each parent element in the containership hierarchy as well as by the element the event occurred within. In other words, every action occurs on the element, its parent element, and so on until the body and eventually the document itself receive the event notification. The event can be processed at each level, enabling you to write compact generic code.

  Default actions represent the browsers' built-in handling of the event. Many events allow the default action to be overridden for custom handling or to be augmented with complementary processing.

Understanding the event model is crucial to understanding how to harness the power of Dynamic HTML to create interactive documents. This section introduces the event architecture; later chapters will cover techniques and operations in detail.

- **Event binding** *Event binding* is the association of a script with an event on the document or window, or with an event on an element in the document. This section discusses the different techniques available in Dynamic HTML for binding scripts to events.
- **The *event* object** The *event* object exposes the information related to an event to the script. The *event* object is a language-independent mechanism for passing parameters and for controlling different aspects of the event model. For example, on a mouse event, the current mouse location and button state information are exposed through properties of the *event* object.
- **Programming standard user events** Standard user events include the mouse, keyboard, focus, and help events that are available on almost every element in the document. This section introduces the interactions between these events and the *event* object. Additional events are supported by certain elements and objects and are discussed throughout this book with their respective objects.
- **Event examples** The chapter concludes with two examples of event binding. The first example consists of an Event Tutor that can be used to learn about the event model. In this example, events on a document can be tracked individually or as a group. The second example, Event Broadcaster, is a powerful demonstration of JavaScript function pointers and events. In this example, you'll learn how to write a custom event-binding mechanism that allows multiple functions to be easily associated with a single event.

General Event Model

When the user interacts with the page or when the document's state is about to change, an event is fired. The user generates events by moving the mouse, clicking a mouse button, or typing on the keyboard within a document. Document state changes that can fire events include the loading of the document, images, or objects; the occurrence of an error on the page; and the changing of focus from one element to another.

Event Bubbling

HTML documents are structured documents with a defined containership hierarchy. Event bubbling is the generic capability for all actions to follow this structural hierarchy. When an event occurs, it fires first on the source element and then on the source's parent element, and it continues to fire on successive parent elements until it reaches the document element.

Event bubbling did not exist in earlier versions of the HTML object model because it was not necessary. In the past, browser implementers considered only a few elements interesting enough to fire events. With the introduction of Dynamic HTML, however, all elements now fire events. This means that now all elements on the page—every P, H1, and so on—can and do fire events. The extension of events to all elements could have made scripting a lot more complex. But with event bubbling, the reverse happens—scripts can be more powerful *and* better written.

In the following code, the body, the anchor, and the image all have events associated with them:

```
<HTML>
   <HEAD>
      <TITLE>Go Home!</TITLE>
   </HEAD>
   <BODY>
      <A HREF="home.htm"><IMG SRC="home.gif">Go Home</A>
   </BODY>
</HTML>
```

Without event bubbling, trying to write an event handler for all click events that occur on the anchor would be complex. The same event handler would need to be written twice, once for the image and once for the anchor. This redundancy would be necessary because if the user clicks on the image, the image receives the event, and if the user clicks on the following text, the anchor receives the event. Event bubbling solves this problem. With event bubbling, clicking on the image first fires the click event on the image. The event then automatically fires on the anchor. After the event fires on the anchor, it fires on the body and finally on the document. Event bubbling allows an event to be handled at any level of the containership hierarchy. In the preceding code, a single event handler for clicks on the anchor will also handle clicks on the image.

Default Actions

In addition to event bubbling, many events have default actions. A default action is what the browser normally does as a result of the event. For example, the default action of clicking on a link *<A HREF="...">* is to follow the specified HREF and load the page.

With the Dynamic HTML object model, it is possible to override an existing default action with custom behavior. If an event does not have a default action and custom behavior is being written, it still is a good idea to cancel the potential default action. This ensures that the code will continue to execute correctly if a default action is later supported by a browser.

The default action is not always defined by the source of the event—it may be defined by a parent element. In the preceding example, when the user clicks on the image the default action of following the link is defined by the Anchor element that contains the image. However, if the image cancels an event's default action, the default action of the anchor will no longer apply, because the default action can be canceled by any element during the event chain. Once an event handler specifies that it is canceling the default action, the default action for the entire event chain is canceled.

Event bubbling and default actions are different concepts and can be controlled independently. For example, if the image stopped the event from bubbling up to the anchor but did not cancel the default action, the anchor's default action would still apply to the event, and the link would still be followed. The reverse also holds true: if neither the anchor nor the image cancel the default action, but instead when the event reaches the Body element the default action is canceled, the link will not be followed. The properties for canceling the default action or stopping the event from bubbling are introduced in the section "The *event* Object" later in this chapter.

Event Binding

Event binding is the association between a specific event and a script. Dynamic HTML supports a number of language-independent ways to bind scripts to events. In addition, the scripting engines themselves can expose further custom ways to support event binding.

The language-independent mechanisms bind events through attributes on the Script element, through special HTML attributes associated directly with a specific element, and through the object model itself. VBScript also offers the Visual Basic–style binding mechanism, which involves naming the handler subroutines in a specific way.

Event Attributes

In Dynamic HTML, all the elements within the document have been extended to support keyboard and mouse events. These events are exposed as attributes directly on each element, allowing a direct association between the element and the behavior. This association is similar to the one between an element and its inline style using the STYLE attribute. For example, you can bind the *onclick* event of a button to a function using an attribute as follows:

```
<!-- When the user clicks the button,
     the foo() function is called. -->
<INPUT TYPE=BUTTON VALUE="Click Here"
   ONCLICK="foo();" LANGUAGE="JavaScript">
```

The ONCLICK attribute can either call a function or immediately execute one or more lines of code. In this example, when the user clicks the button, the *foo* routine is called. The LANGUAGE attribute specifies in which language the inline code is written. Omitting the LANGUAGE attribute defaults to the language specified in the first script on the page, or to JavaScript in the absence of any prior scripts. The following example demonstrates two inline statements being executed when the user clicks the button:

```
<!-- When the button is clicked, display the alert and
     then call the function foo(). -->
<INPUT TYPE=BUTTON VALUE="Click Here"
   ONCLICK="alert('The user clicked here.'); foo();"
   LANGUAGE="JavaScript">
```

The button first outputs the alert box, and then it calls the *foo* function.

All HTML attributes are case insensitive, so case sensitivity is not an issue when you use attributes such as ONCLICK to bind handlers to events. Case sensitivity can be important when you use other event-binding mechanisms, however. Event binding with HTML attributes is convenient, but it has a number of disadvantages. The first is that the HTML language needs to be extended every time a new event is invented. For example, the preceding *onclick* event requires the DTD (document type definition) for the <INPUT> tag to be extended to include an ONCLICK attribute. This makes it much more difficult to add events in a standard way because HTML evolves slowly. Furthermore, objects or applications that expose arbitrary events also need to extend the language or expose their own custom event-binding techniques. Therefore, this approach is used only for a small set of built-in events. If an arbitrary object is embedded on the page, its events are exposed in a more generic way.

Generic Event Support

A second binding mechanism overcomes these disadvantages. It uses a few Script element extensions—namely, a FOR attribute and an EVENT attribute—to bind functions to events. The EVENT attribute refers to the event and any parameters that may be passed in, and the FOR attribute specifies the name or ID of the element the event is being written for. For example, an *onmousemove* event is exposed on the document. You can use the following <SCRIPT> tag to bind to this event:

```
<SCRIPT FOR="document" EVENT="onmousemove()" LANGUAGE="JavaScript">
   // This event handler is called whenever the mouse moves on the
   // document.
</SCRIPT>
```

> NOTE: JavaScript is case sensitive for both the EVENT and the FOR attribute values on the <SCRIPT> tag. Be careful to ensure that all event names are supplied in lowercase for built-in events and in the appropriate case for any embedded objects. Also, if you specify an ID in the FOR attribute, you must type it exactly as it appears in the ID attribute of the element itself. Whenever an event appears to not be firing, always verify that the spelling and case are correct in the <SCRIPT> tag.

There is one caveat to the preceding syntax. Netscape Navigator ignores the FOR and EVENT attributes and will attempt to execute the code immediately. Here's a potential trick for working around this restriction:

```
<SCRIPT LANGUAGE="JavaScript">
   // Assume that the browser supports the FOR attribute.
   var ForSupport = true;
</SCRIPT>

<SCRIPT FOR="fakeObject" EVENT="foo" LANGUAGE="JavaScript">
   // This event does not exist.
   // If FOR and EVENT are supported, this code will never execute.
   ForSupport = false;
</SCRIPT>

<SCRIPT FOR="document" EVENT="onmousemove" LANGUAGE="JavaScript">
   if (ForSupport) {
      // Write actual event handler.
   }
   else
      alert("Your browser does not support the required event
         syntax.");
</SCRIPT>
```

Another way to ensure that the script code is not executed is to specify the language as *JScript.* JScript is Microsoft's implementation of JavaScript. Because Microsoft Internet Explorer is the only browser that supports JScript, the script does not require an *if* statement in order to be ignored by Netscape.

```
<SCRIPT FOR="document" EVENT="onmousemove()" LANGUAGE="JScript">
   // This event handler is called whenever the mouse moves over
   // the document if the browser supports the JScript language
   // engine.
</SCRIPT>
```

NOTE: When you specify the event name, the parentheses are optional. For example, the above event could have been specified as *EVENT="onmousemove"*.

Visual Basic–Style Event Binding

In addition to the techniques already discussed, VBScript also supports the Visual Basic–style mechanism for binding scripts to events. Visual Basic traditionally binds code to an event using a specially named subroutine. If the subroutine is written in the Visual Basic–style format, the Visual Basic engine knows which event to bind the script to. For example, the following code binds to an *onmousemove* event and an *onclick* event on the document:

```
<SCRIPT LANGUAGE="VBScript">
   Sub document_onMouseMove()
      ' Event handler for the mouse moving over the document
   End Sub

   Sub document_onClick()
      ' Event handler for the user clicking on the document
   End Sub
</SCRIPT>
```

NOTE: Microsoft Internet Explorer 3.0 also supported the preceding syntax in JScript, but this syntax is not supported by Netscape Navigator or by Internet Explorer 4.0. Therefore, this technique should not be used with JavaScript.

In VBScript, an advantage to using this model is that multiple event handlers can be written within a single script block. The major disadvantage is that external tools cannot easily determine what events have event handlers written for them. Using the Script element's FOR and EVENT attributes syntax or the inline HTML event attribute syntax allows a tool to easily scan a document and determine what events have code associated with them. The Visual Basic–style event-binding model won't be understood by any tool that is not specially written.

It is possible to bind to the same event in multiple languages. In this case, the event will fire in each language when it occurs, but the order is undefined. In general, avoid using this approach, as the results may be unpredictable.

Specifying Scripting Languages in Event Attributes

You can specify different languages for each inline HTML event attribute. The LANGUAGE attribute used with the inline HTML event attributes specifies the default language for interpreting the code. This default can be overridden by specifying a language identifier in the event attribute value. The format is as follows:

<Element EventName="Language:Code">

Language is a case-insensitive string that specifies the scripting language for the *Code* that follows. The languages supported by Internet Explorer 4.0 are JScript, JavaScript, JavaScript 1.1, and VBScript. JScript, JavaScript, and JavaScript 1.1 run the same language engine. The *onclick* handler and the *onmousedown* handler in the following <BODY> tag are specified in different scripting languages:

```
<BODY ONCLICK="JavaScript:dothis(this);"
   ONMOUSEDOWN="VBScript:dothat(me)">
```

Netscape Navigator does not support specifying languages within the event attribute value. Netscape Navigator and Internet Explorer both support specifying a language on the HREF attribute of anchors, which allows you to create JavaScript or VBScript code that will run when the user clicks on an anchor. However, Netscape Navigator recognizes only JavaScript and will attempt to navigate to an invalid page if any other language is specified.

Events as Properties

All events are also exposed as properties in the Dynamic HTML object model. The property names are entirely in lowercase and begin with the prefix *on*. The purpose of exposing both events and event properties is to enable events to be dynamically bound to functions at run time. All event properties can be assigned a function pointer.

Whether function pointers are supported depends on the scripting language. JavaScript supports function pointers, but VBScript does not. Therefore, VBScript cannot generate an event handler dynamically. (However, you can use VBScript code to assign a JavaScript function to an event.) When the event occurs, the function specified by the property is invoked.

```
<HTML>
   <HEAD>
      <TITLE>Function Pointer Example</TITLE>
   </HEAD>
   <BODY>
      <INPUT TYPE=BUTTON ID="myButton" VALUE="Click here">
      <SCRIPT LANGUAGE="JavaScript">
         // Attach a function pointer to myButton.
         // When myButton is clicked, an alert box is displayed.
         document.all.myButton.onclick =
            new Function("alert('Hello');");
      </SCRIPT>
   </BODY>
</HTML>
```

To assign a function pointer, assign the name of the function directly to the property.

```
<HTML>
   <HEAD>
      <TITLE>Function Pointer Assignment</TITLE>
      <SCRIPT LANGUAGE="JavaScript">
         // Define a function named clicked.
         function clicked() {
            alert("Clicked");
         }
      </SCRIPT>
   </HEAD>
   <BODY>
      <INPUT TYPE=BUTTON ID="myButton" VALUE="Click here">
      <SCRIPT LANGUAGE="JavaScript">
         // Assign the clicked function to the onclick handler.
         document.all.myButton.onclick = clicked;
      </SCRIPT>
   </BODY>
</HTML>
```

NOTE: When assigning a function pointer, use only the name of the function. Do not supply parentheses or specify any parameters. Doing so will cause the function to be executed, resulting in the function's return value, rather than a pointer to the function itself, being assigned to the property.

Timing of Event Binding

The point at which event handlers are bound to elements depends on the scripting language. JavaScript hooks up events asynchronously while the page is being loaded. Each Script element and event attribute is hooked up as it is parsed from the document. VBScript, on the other hand, does not bind events until the entire page is parsed, all external scripts are downloaded, and embedded objects have begun loading.

For JavaScript, this means that events can start firing in response to user or other actions before the page is entirely downloaded. Therefore, you should take care that your event handlers don't try to access any elements that might not have downloaded yet.

You can write code that first checks for the presence of the element or, more generically, simply checks whether the entire page is parsed. Checking whether the page is completely parsed is the simplest method and should be compatible across scripting languages and browsers:

```
<HTML>
   <HEAD>
      <TITLE>Parsing Example</TITLE>
      <SCRIPT LANGUAGE="JavaScript">
         function doClick() {
            if (isLoaded) {
               // Run event handler.
            }
            else {
               alert("Please wait for the document to finish
                  loading.");
            }
         }
      </SCRIPT>
   </HEAD>
   <BODY>
      <INPUT TYPE=BUTTON ID="myInput" VALUE="Click here"
         ONCLICK="doClick()">
      <SCRIPT LANGUAGE="JavaScript">
         // This should be the last element parsed in the document.
         isLoaded = true;
      </SCRIPT>
   </BODY>
</HTML>
```

You can also use an event handler to check whether the entire page has been parsed. Two events can be used for this purpose: the *onload* event on the window, and the *onreadystatechange* event on the document. The *onload* event fires when the entire document is parsed and all elements are loaded. The more powerful *onreadystatechange* event on the document, which is supported only in Internet Explorer 4.0, fires several times as the document passes through several loading states and fires for the last time when the document is fully loaded. The *onload* and *onreadystatechange* events are discussed in detail in Chapter 4, "The Browser Window," and Chapter 6, "The HTML Document."

Scoping of Scripts

All event handlers are scoped to the element to which the handler is bound. This element is exposed to the scripting language in JavaScript using the *this* property and in VBScript using the *me* property.

The event's scope is not necessarily the element that *first* fired the event. The element that first fired the event is exposed through the *srcElement* property on the *event* object. The *event* object is discussed in more detail in the section "The *event* Object" later in this chapter.

Controlling the *this* Pointer

The following code demonstrates the three different ways you can bind a handler to an event. All three handlers are effectively equivalent to each other.

```
<INPUT NAME="myBtn" TYPE=BUTTON VALUE="My Button"
   ONCLICK="alert(this.name);" LANGUAGE="JavaScript">
```

or

```
<SCRIPT FOR="myBtn" EVENT="onclick()" LANGUAGE="JavaScript">
   alert(this.name);
</SCRIPT>
```

or

```
<SCRIPT LANGUAGE="JavaScript">
   myBtn.onclick = new Function("alert(this.name)");
</SCRIPT>
```

In these three examples, *this.name* returns *myBtn* because the element is referenced directly in the inline code or script. If you want to reference the element in a subroutine called by an event handler, you need to pass the element to the subroutine using the *this* keyword. For example, the following code will display an empty string rather than the text *myBtn* because the *this* pointer in the *foo* function refers to the function itself instead of the element that generated the event:

```
<SCRIPT LANGUAGE="JavaScript">
   function foo() {
```

(continued)

```
      // The this pointer does not refer to the button.
      alert(this.name);
   }
</SCRIPT>
<INPUT TYPE=BUTTON NAME="myBtn" VALUE="My Button"
   ONCLICK="foo();" LANGUAGE="JavaScript">
```

Instead, you should pass a reference to the *myBtn* element to the *foo* function using the *this* keyword:

```
<SCRIPT LANGUAGE="JavaScript">
   function foo(b) {
      // The b argument refers to the button because it was passed in
      // by the event handler.
      alert(b.name);
   }
</SCRIPT>
<INPUT TYPE=BUTTON NAME="myBtn" VALUE="My Button"
   ONCLICK="foo(this);" LANGUAGE="JavaScript">
```

The *this* pointer is also automatically set when an event handler is assigned as a function pointer:

```
<H1 ID="myH1">This is a header.</H1>
<SCRIPT LANGUAGE="JavaScript">
   function clickHandler() {
      // The this property points to the element
      // to which the handler is bound.
      alert(this.tagName)
   }
   // Function pointer assignments do not need to pass the
   // this pointer.
   document.all.myH1.onclick = clickHandler;
</SCRIPT>
```

Names in inline code are resolved by searching members of the object model in the following order:

1. All properties of the current element
2. All elements exposed for the name space—for example, in a form, the controls on the form
3. The properties of the element containing the name space—for example, the form's properties for elements within the form
4. The properties on the document

Shared Event Handlers

JavaScript supports the creation of a shared event handler. In JavaScript, any elements that share the same name can also share the same event handlers by using the Script element's FOR and EVENT attributes syntax:

```
<SCRIPT FOR="gender" EVENT="onclick()" LANGUAGE="JavaScript">
   // This event handler executes whenever any element with the name
   // or ID "gender" is clicked.
</SCRIPT>
<INPUT TYPE=RADIO NAME="gender" VALUE="Male">
<INPUT TYPE=RADIO NAME="gender" VALUE="Female">
```

This technique works only in JavaScript. VBScript can fire an event handler this way only on the basis of an element's unique ID, not its NAME. If this code were rewritten in VBScript, the radio buttons would need to be supplied with unique ID values, and separate handlers would need to be written for each one.

An alternative for VBScript that also works for any scripting language is to use event bubbling and track the event from a parent container:

```
<SCRIPT FOR="GenderGroup" EVENT="onclick()" LANGUAGE="VBScript">
   ' This event handler executes whenever any element within
   ' the GenderGroup block is clicked.
   If "gender" = window.event.srcElement.name Then
      ' User clicked a radio button.
   End If
</SCRIPT>
<DIV ID="GenderGroup">
   <INPUT TYPE=RADIO NAME="gender" VALUE="Male">
   <INPUT TYPE=RADIO NAME="gender" VALUE="Female">
</DIV>
```

The *event* Object

Most events by themselves are not very interesting without some additional information. For example, the *onmousedown* event is not very useful unless you know which mouse buttons are pressed and possibly where the mouse is positioned. Keyboard events are useless unless you know which key is pressed.

Dynamic HTML exposes a language-independent mechanism for accessing information related to an event and controlling whether the event bubbles and whether the default action occurs. This information is exposed through an *event* object, which is a property of the *window* object.

Before an event is fired, this *event* object is initialized with the current state of the keyboard and mouse. The *event* object gives access to the event parameters and provides control over event bubbling and the default action. The *event* object always exposes at minimum the following set of properties for identifying the element that originated the event sequence and for controlling event bubbling and the default action:

- *event.srcElement*
- *event.cancelBubble*
- *event.returnValue*

The *srcElement* property returns the element that first generated the event. For example, when you click on the home.gif image in the HTML sample at the beginning of this chapter, the image is the *srcElement* property while the event bubbles through the anchor, the body, and the document.

The *cancelBubble* property is used to stop an event from bubbling up the hierarchy. By default, this property is *false* and the event bubbles up. Assigning *true* to this property stops the current event from bubbling. Setting this property to *true* stops only the current instance of the event from bubbling, however; it does not prevent future events from bubbling.

The *returnValue* property is used primarily to override the default action of an event. Not all events have default actions. However, if you write code that adds behavior because of an event, always cancel the default so that if a default action is added to the event in the future, the page's behavior will not change. To cancel the default action, this property should be set to *false.*

The *returnValue* property is used most often to override the default action of the event, but some events use the *returnValue* property differently. This again reinforces the separation of event bubbling and default actions.

> NOTE: JavaScript supports returning values directly to an event handler using the *return* keyword. The *return* keyword updates the *returnValue* property of the *event* object when the event handler returns control to the browser.

The *event* object is established at each event sequence. Therefore, any assignments to the *event* object apply only to that instance of the event sequence. The next time an event occurs, the *event* object is reset. Canceling a default action, for example, cancels only the default action for the current event, not for all subsequent events. For this reason, an event handler—not the code that immediately executes during the download of the page—should access the *event* object.

Determining the Event

The *event* object exposes the type of the event through the *type* property. The *type* property returns the event name in all lowercase without the *on* prefix. For example, *onmousedown* is returned as *mousedown*, *onclick* as *click*, and so on. The advantage in knowing the type of event is that a single event handler can distinguish among and process multiple events:

```
function handleEvent() {
   // Run common event handler.
   switch (event.type) {
   case "click":
      // Handle onclick event.
      break;
   case "mousedown":
      // Handle onmousedown event.
      break;
   }
}
// Hook up events to handleEvent event handler.
document.onclick = handleEvent;
document.onmousedown = handleEvent;
```

Accessing Parameters Through the *event* Object

The *event* object exposes all parameters of the built-in events as properties. For example, information about the current mouse pointer position is available to all events. Some information is available only during a particular event. Mouse events also provide access to the current state of the mouse buttons. These parameters are initialized and updated prior to the firing of the event. This example shows how to access event parameters:

```
<SCRIPT FOR="document" EVENT="onmousedown()" LANGUAGE="JavaScript">
   // Output the state of the mouse button whenever it is pressed.
   alert("x:" + event.clientX);
   alert("y:" + event.clientY);
   alert("button:" + event.button);
   alert("Source Element:" + event.srcElement.tagName);
</SCRIPT>
```

Mouse Coordinates

The *event* object exposes properties that represent the mouse pointer location based on different coordinate systems. The following table lists these mouse event properties.

Property	Description
clientX, clientY	The horizontal and vertical coordinates of the mouse pointer relative to the client area of the window.
offsetX, offsetY	The horizontal and vertical coordinates of the mouse pointer relative to the rendering context.
screenX, screenY	The horizontal and vertical coordinates of the mouse pointer relative to the screen.

Figure 3-1 illustrates the relationship between the different coordinates. The creation of coordinate systems and rendering contexts is discussed in Chapter 12, "Dynamic Positioning." The values of these properties are constant through any event firing sequence, and these coordinates are established for all events, not just mouse events.

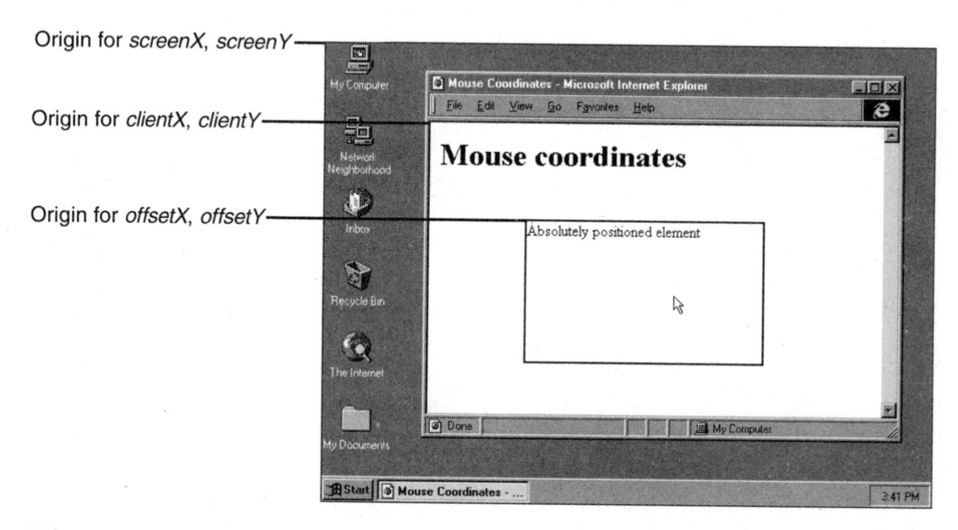

Figure 3-1.
Coordinate system origins for the event *object's mouse position properties.*

Key and Button Information

The *event* object also exposes properties that represent the current keys and mouse buttons that are pressed at the time of the event.

Parameter	Value
button	The current set of mouse buttons pressed: *0* No buttons pressed *1* Left button pressed *2* Right button pressed *4* Middle button pressed The *button* parameter represents the combined state of all the mouse buttons. For example, if the right and the left buttons are pressed, *button* returns *3*.
ctrlKey	A Boolean value that indicates whether the Ctrl key is pressed.
altKey	A Boolean value that indicates whether the Alt key is pressed.
shiftKey	A Boolean value that indicates whether the Shift key is pressed.

These properties are useful when you are writing a global event handler for the document. Using the mouse coordinates with the *elementFromPoint* or *rangeFromPoint* method on the document, you can check whether the mouse pointer is on a specific element or text:

```
<SCRIPT EVENT="onkeypress()" FOR="document" LANGUAGE="JavaScript">
   // Determine the element the mouse is on when a key is pressed.
   // The fromPoint methods are based on client coordinates.
   var e = document.elementFromPoint(event.clientX, event.clientY);
   if ("H1" == e.tagName) {
      // Do something when a key is pressed while the mouse pointer
      // is on an H1 element.
   }
</SCRIPT>
```

Programming Standard User Events

Standard user events are the set of events shared by all elements in response to user interactions. These are events for tracking the mouse and the keyboard, focusing elements, and scrolling any scrollable region. Many elements expose events specific to the purpose of the element. For example, form elements have *onsubmit* and *onreset* events. These additional events are discussed with their respective elements in Chapters 8 through 10.

Mouse Events

The Dynamic HTML object model exposes events for tracking the different states of the mouse, including every time the mouse is moved into and out of elements, as well as when mouse buttons are pressed. The following table lists the mouse events.

Event	Description
onmousedown	Mouse button was pressed.
onmousemove	Mouse was moved or is being moved.
onmouseup	Mouse button was released.
onclick	Left mouse button was clicked, or the default action of an element was invoked.
ondblclick	Left mouse button was double-clicked.
onmouseover	Mouse pointer entered the scope of an element.
onmouseout	Mouse pointer exited the scope of an element.
ondragstart	A drag-and-drop operation was initiated.
onselectstart	A new selection was initiated over an element using the mouse.
onselect	A selection is occurring.

The *onclick* and *ondblclick* Events

The *onclick* event is more a semantic event than a physical event. While an *onclick* event usually occurs when the left mouse button is pressed and released, it can also occur as the result of an action that simulates a click. For example, the *onclick* event fires when the user presses the Enter key while a buttonlike control has the focus. The *ondblclick* event fires when the user clicks the left mouse button twice within a system-defined amount of time.

When an element is clicked, the *onclick* event is fired after the *onmousedown* and *onmouseup* events fire. The *onclick* event is not required to fire on the same element the *onmousedown* and *onmouseup* events occurred on. Suppose, for example, that you have the following HTML code:

```
<HTML>
   <HEAD>
      <TITLE>Click Rules</TITLE>
   </HEAD>
   <BODY>
      <H1>Welcome to My Home Page</H1>
      <H2>Providing the Latest Dynamic HTML Information</H2>
   </BODY>
</HTML>
```

If the mouse button is pressed and released on the H1 element, the *onmousedown, onmouseup,* and *onclick* events are all fired on that element. If the mouse button is pressed on the H1 element and released on the H2 element, however, the *onmousedown* event is fired on the H1 element and the *onmouseup* event is fired on the H2 element. The *onclick* event is fired on the body, as is any subsequent *ondblclick* event that may fire as part of this sequence, because the body is the common element the mouse pointer is on when the mouse button is released. The *onmouseup* event is fired on the H2 element and not on the H1 element because the mouse is not captured by any textual contents.

HTML elements that accept user input do capture the mouse event. If the mouse button is pressed on a user input element and released on a textual element, the *onmousedown* event is fired on the user input element, the *onmouseup* event is fired on the textual element, but no *onclick* event is fired on any element. The *onclick* event occurs on a user input element only when the mouse button is pressed and released on the same element.

Because *onclick* and *ondblclick* can be fired on the element that is common to the elements on which the mouse button is pressed and released, these two events can initiate on elements that are not *leaf nodes* in the document's tree. Leaf nodes are the deepest nodes of the document and actually contain the contents. The *onclick* and *ondblclick* events are unusual among user events. With a few exceptions introduced in later chapters, all the other mouse and keyboard events always start at a leaf node and bubble upward through the hierarchy.

Here is the event-ordering relationship between the *onmouse* and *onclick* events:

1. *onmousedown*
2. *onmouseup*
3. *onclick*

If a double click occurs, the event sequence continues as follows:

4. *onmouseup*
5. *ondblclick*

The *onmouseover* and *onmouseout* Events

The *onmouseover* and *onmouseout* events occur when the mouse pointer enters or leaves an element on the page. These mouse events expose the same parameters as the *onmousedown* and *onmouseup* events. They fire only once on the leaf nodes of the document and bubble upward, rather than firing on every boundary crossing. For example, suppose you have the following HTML code:

```
<HTML>
   <HEAD>
      <TITLE>Over and Out Boundaries</TITLE>
   </HEAD>
   <BODY>
      <H1>This is a header.</H1>
      <DIV>
         <P><B>Welcome</B> to my page.</P>
      </DIV>
   </BODY>
</HTML>
```

In this HTML page, when the mouse moves from the body into the boldface text in the paragraph, a single *onmouseout* event is fired on the Body element and an *onmouseover* event is fired on the B element. Because the event bubbles, all elements whose boundaries are crossed receive an event notification.

When the mouse crosses from the boldface text into the nonboldface text in the paragraph, an *onmouseout* event is fired on the element and bubbles through the paragraph. This is important to note because the paragraph may receive an *onmouseout* event even while the mouse pointer is still contained within it.

To accurately test whether the mouse was moved off an element, use the element's *contains* method along with the *toElement* property of the *onmouseout* event, which indicates the new element to which the mouse has moved. The *contains* method indicates whether one element is contained within another element. With some simple code, you can test the destination element to see whether it is contained within the element on which the event fired. If it is, the mouse pointer is still on the firing element. In this example of an *onmouseout* event handler, the event handler would be attached to the *onmouseout* event of an element to test whether the mouse pointer is still within it:

```
<SCRIPT LANGUAGE="JavaScript">
   function testexit(src) {
      // Test whether the mouse really left an element.
      if (!src.contains(event.toElement)) {
         // Mouse exited the element.
      }
   }
</SCRIPT>
<H1 ONMOUSEOUT="testexit(this);">Some <EM>text</EM></H1>
```

In this example, the *this* pointer, which represents the element on which the event was fired, must be passed in. The *srcElement* property of the *event* object cannot be used instead; it might be a child element. For example, when the mouse moves over the emphasized text in the preceding header, the emphasized text, not the H1 itself, would be the *srcElement.*

The same method works when the mouse is entering an element—almost identical code works for the *onmouseover* event. The only change is that the *fromElement* property needs to be tested using the *contains* method:

```
function testenter(src) {
   if (!src.contains(event.fromElement)) {
      // Mouse entered the element.
   }
}
```

The *onmouseover* event fires when the mouse pointer is first moved over an element. The event-ordering relationship between the *onmouseover, onmousemove,* and *onmouseout* events when the mouse pointer crosses a boundary is as follows:

1. *onmouseout*
2. *onmousemove* (may occur many times)
3. *onmouseover*

The *ondragstart* Event

Currently, Dynamic HTML offers limited built-in support for implementing drag-and-drop operations. A single drag-related event is exposed in the object model for overriding the default drag behavior of the browser. When the user clicks and holds down the mouse button and drags over certain elements on the document such as images and anchors, those elements take part in a drag-and-drop operation.

There may be times when this behavior will interfere with the author's intentions. To prevent the built-in dragging behavior from being initiated, the *ondragstart* event is exposed. This event essentially serves the single purpose of allowing the developer to cancel the event by returning a value of *false.*

There is a close relationship between canceling the *onmousemove* event and the *ondragstart* event. To prevent a user from initiating a built-in drag-and-drop operation on an element, cancel the *ondragstart* event. To author your own drag operation on an element, you usually need to also cancel the *onmousemove* event.

An example in Chapter 12, "Dynamic Positioning," simulates drag-and-drop behavior by using the *onmousemove* event to move positioned elements around the screen. This technique works well for providing drag-and-drop support *within* a page. Dynamic HTML does not yet allow you to program generic drag-and-drop behavior across frames or across windows.

The *onselectstart* and *onselect* Events

Dynamic HTML exposes two events for completely tracking the user's selection anywhere in the document: *onselectstart* and *onselect,* fired in that order.

Similar to the *ondragstart* event, an *onselectstart* event is fired only when a selection is about to be initiated, usually by the user clicking on some contents in a document. The purpose of this event is to allow you to prevent a region of the document from being selected. It is important to recognize that this only prevents the initiation of the selection. For example, in the following document if the user clicks on the text *Scott's Page* and tries to make a selection, no selection occurs:

```
<HTML>
   <HEAD>
      <TITLE>onselectstart Example</TITLE>
   </HEAD>
   <BODY>
      <H1>Welcome to
         <EM STYLE="cursor:hand"
            ONSELECTSTART="event.returnValue=false;">Scott's Page
         </EM>
      </H1>
   </BODY>
</HTML>
```

However, if the user clicks on the text outside of *Scott's Page* and drags the mouse across *Scott's Page,* the text will be selected because only the initiation of the selection can be canceled.

The CSS *cursor* property is used to change the mouse pointer to a hand icon to signify that the contents can be clicked. By adding an *onclick* event handler, you can specify a custom action to take place when the user clicks on *Scott's Page.* The combination of the *cursor* property and the *onselectstart* event handler provides the same level of control as is available by default with anchors.

The *onselectstart* event bubbles up through the document. Therefore, it is possible to catch this event on the document and always return *false*. Doing so prevents the user from selecting any text in the document. The *onselectstart* event should be limited to situations in which the built-in text selection might cause problems with the intended user interface of the page.

The *onselect* event follows the *onselectstart* event and occurs while the selection is being made. It fires multiple times as the user extends or collapses the selection. The *onselect* event does not bubble. Instead, it occurs on the section of the document the selection is occurring within: either the document's Body element for textual contents or the input controls.

Keyboard Events

Dynamic HTML provides three events for tracking the user's keystrokes: *onkeydown*, *onkeyup*, and *onkeypress*, fired in that order. The *onkeydown* and *onkeyup* events fire whenever any key on the keyboard is pressed and released. The *onkeypress* event fires after any ANSI key is pressed.

The *event* object exposes four properties for determining the state of the keyboard when these events occur. The *shiftKey*, *altKey*, and *ctrlKey* properties are the same as those exposed for the mouse events.

Property	Value
keyCode	The ASCII value of the key pressed. Setting this property to *0* in an *onkeypress* event handler cancels the event. Setting it to a positive value replaces the key pressed with a different ASCII key.
shiftKey	State of the Shift key (*true/false*).
altKey	State of the Alt key (*true/false*).
ctrlKey	State of the Ctrl key (*true/false*).

Scroll Event

The Body element, as well as many other elements, can have scrollbars. Whenever one of these elements or its scrollbar is scrolled, the *onscroll* event fires. Scrolling occurs when the user explicitly scrolls the scrollbar or implicitly scrolls the element through another action. For example, clicking on a link to a bookmark fires the *onscroll* event if the document needs to scroll to bring the element into view. The *onscroll* event cannot cancel the scrolling because it is fired after the scrolling is complete. This event occurs only on the scrolled element (for example, the Body element) and does not bubble.

Focus Events

Dynamic HTML provides two events related to focus: *onfocus* and *onblur*. The *onfocus* event is fired when an element is activated either by clicking on it or through the keyboard. The element the user has just left receives an *onblur* event. Only user input elements and the body can receive the focus. Therefore, clicking on HTML contents causes the body to receive the *onfocus* event, not the actual contents.

The *onblur* event is also fired whenever another application or window is activated over the current frame or application. Therefore, when you switch windows, the current element fires an *onblur* event. When you return to the window, the *onfocus* event is fired on that element.

The timing of these events in relationship to the window has some complexities that are introduced in Chapter 5, "Window and Frame Management."

Help Event

The document exposes an *onhelp* event that fires whenever the user requests a help file for the document using the Microsoft Windows keyboard shortcut (F1). This event does not fire when the user selects Help from the Help menu. The *onhelp* event first occurs on the element with the focus and bubbles upward. The default action for this event is to display the built-in help file, but this event can be overridden to display a custom help file.

The *onhelp* event also fires in modal dialog boxes that support context-sensitive help through a Help icon available on the title bar. By clicking the Help icon, the user can change the cursor to a special help cursor. When the user clicks on an element using this cursor, an *onhelp* event fires on the element and then bubbles to each parent element.

An event handler for the *onhelp* event typically displays a custom help file. The handler can call the *showHelp* method to display a Windows help (HLP) file or the *open* method to display an HTML file. *showHelp* and *open* are both methods of the *window* object. The *showHelp* method can also display HTML files, but the *open* method is supported by more browsers and offers more control over the display window. Chapter 5, "Window and Frame Management," describes the *open* method.

Event Examples

The two sample programs in this section illustrate the power of the event architecture explained in this chapter. With the first example, the Event Tutor, you can test any page and see the events that fire when you interact with it.

Code in the second example, the Event Broadcaster, provides a general mechanism for hooking up several handlers to each event.

Event Tutor

To help you learn more about *event bubbling*, the Chapter 3 samples on the companion CD include an HTML document named tutor.htm that can report all events as they occur on a page. Figure 3-2 shows the Event Tutor application.

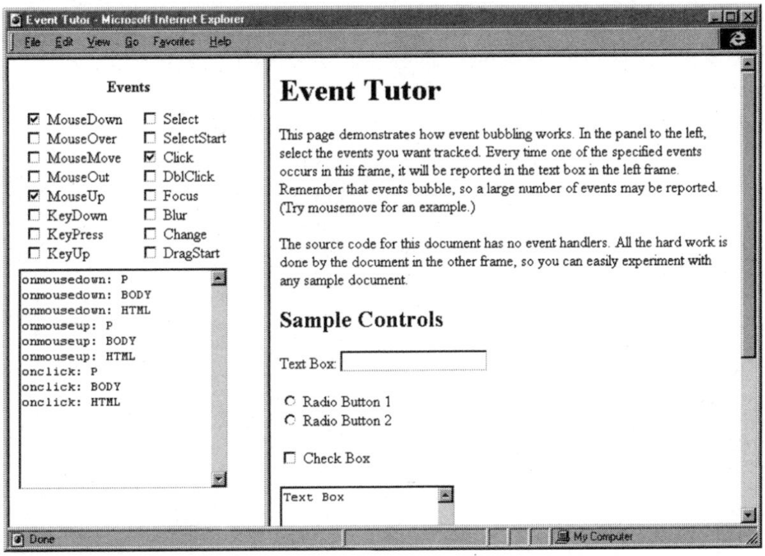

Figure 3-2.
The Event Tutor application.

This example allows you to select which events to track in the document contained within the right frame. When a selected event occurs on any element in the right frame, it is reported in the text box in the left frame. Playing with this example will clearly demonstrate for you how events bubble up through the hierarchy.

Following is the source code from events.htm used to create the Event Tutor. This code demonstrates tracking events across frames—a technique discussed in detail in Chapter 5, "Window and Frame Management." This code also takes advantage of JavaScript's model for exposing objects as associative arrays and the ability to create custom functions.

```
<HTML>
   <HEAD>
      <TITLE>Event Tutor</TITLE>
      <STYLE TYPE="text/css">
         caption {font-weight:bolder; color:navy}
      </STYLE>
      <SCRIPT LANGUAGE="JavaScript">
         function outputEvent(src, eventName) {
            // Append event name to text area control.
            document.all.txtEvents.value += eventName + ": " +
               src.tagName + "\n";
         }

         function setupEvents() {
            // The user clicked on a check box.
            // Hook up or remove event handlers.
            if ("checkbox" == event.srcElement.type) {
               var handler = event.srcElement.checked ?
                  new Function("outputEvent(this, '" +
                     event.srcElement.id + "')") :
                  null;
               var allSample = parent.frames.sample.document.all;
               // Add custom event handler to all elements in
               // the other frame.
               for (var intLoop=0; intLoop < allSample.length;
                     intLoop++) {
                  // Accesses the event property that matches
                  // the ID of the check box that was clicked.
                  allSample[intLoop][event.srcElement.id] = handler;
               }
            }
         }
      </SCRIPT>
   </HEAD>
   <BODY>
      <FORM NAME="EVENTS">
         <TABLE WIDTH=100% ONCLICK="setupEvents()" CELLPADDING=4>
            <CAPTION>Events</CAPTION>
            <TR VALIGN="Top"><TD NOWRAP>
               <!-- Notice the naming convention used below.
                    To add more events, the ID should specify
                    the event name. -->
               <INPUT TYPE=CHECKBOX ID=onmousedown>
               <LABEL FOR=onmousedown>MouseDown</LABEL><BR>
               <INPUT TYPE=CHECKBOX ID=onmouseover>
```

```
                <LABEL FOR=onmouseover>MouseOver</LABEL><BR>
                <INPUT TYPE=CHECKBOX ID=onmousemove>
                <LABEL FOR=onmousemove>MouseMove</LABEL><BR>
                <INPUT TYPE=CHECKBOX ID=onmouseout>
                <LABEL FOR=onmouseout>MouseOut</LABEL><BR>
                <INPUT TYPE=CHECKBOX ID=onmouseup>
                <LABEL FOR=onmouseup>MouseUp</LABEL><BR>
                <INPUT TYPE=CHECKBOX ID=onkeydown>
                <LABEL FOR=onkeydown>KeyDown</LABEL><BR>
                <INPUT TYPE=CHECKBOX ID=onkeypress>
                <LABEL FOR=onkeypress>KeyPress</LABEL><BR>
                <INPUT TYPE=CHECKBOX ID=onkeyup>
                <LABEL FOR=onkeyup>KeyUp</LABEL>
            </TD><TD NOWRAP>
                <INPUT TYPE=CHECKBOX ID=onselect>
                <LABEL FOR=onselect>Select</LABEL><BR>
                <INPUT TYPE=CHECKBOX ID=onselectstart>
                <LABEL FOR=onselectstart>SelectStart</LABEL><BR>
                <INPUT TYPE=CHECKBOX ID=onclick>
                <LABEL FOR=onclick>Click</LABEL><BR>
                <INPUT TYPE=CHECKBOX ID=ondblclick>
                <LABEL FOR=ondblclick>DblClick</LABEL><BR>
                <INPUT TYPE=CHECKBOX ID=onfocus>
                <LABEL FOR=onfocus>Focus</LABEL><BR>
                <INPUT TYPE=CHECKBOX ID=onblur>
                <LABEL FOR=onblur>Blur</LABEL><BR>
                <INPUT TYPE=CHECKBOX ID=onchange>
                <LABEL FOR=onchange>Change</LABEL><BR>
                <INPUT TYPE=CHECKBOX ID=ondragstart>
                <LABEL FOR=ondragstart>DragStart</LABEL>
            </TD></TR>
         </TABLE>
         <!-- TextArea to output event sequence -->
         <TEXTAREA ID="txtEvents" STYLE="width:95%" ROWS=14>
         </TEXTAREA>
      </FORM>
   </BODY>
</HTML>
```

You can experiment with this code on any document by copying it from the CD to your hard drive. Replace the sample.htm file with any file of your choosing. You can also run the example on the CD by opening the tutor.htm file, which uses both the sample.htm and the events.htm files.

Event Broadcaster

The event model exposed by Dynamic HTML is generally limited to a one-to-one relationship between event and event handler. However, as is demonstrated throughout this book, there will be many times when you need to associate multiple actions with a single event. This association can be accomplished by writing a routine for the event that calls each action in sequence, or this whole process can be automated by taking advantage of JavaScript's function pointers.

The Event Broadcaster generalizes the event binding used by Dynamic HTML to support a registration mechanism that can be used to bind multiple actions to a single event. This program provides a small, reusable set of functions that allow multiple actions to be bound to each event. Each of these actions can also execute conditionally.

By taking advantage of this code, you can write reusable event handlers that can be easily plugged into any Web page without having to rewire any other code. This technique works by using a registering model to allow functionality to register an element with a particular action. The registry takes the place of the developer manually hooking up event code.

While this mechanism greatly simplifies the writing of reusable code snippets, you must still be careful that multiple actions on a single event handler or document do not collide. There is no algorithmic way for you to provide this protection other than to be careful when adding new functionality. To be most effective, interactions between registered functions for the same event should be avoided.

The following code represents the entirety of the Event Broadcaster registry. This code can be written only in languages that support the dynamic creation of functions—therefore, this functionality cannot be implemented in VBScript. However, this code does not prevent you from supplying an action and registering an event handler written in VBScript.

```
<SCRIPT LANGUAGE="JavaScript">
   // Event Broadcaster Registry Code
   // This code generically binds multiple event handlers to
   // a single event.

   function runHandler(eventName, eventSrc) {
      // This is a generic event handler. For any event, this function
      // validates the condition and runs the appropriate code.

      var src = event.srcElement;
```

```
   // First check the srcElement property.
   for (var intLoop = 0;
         intLoop < eventSrc.manager[eventName].length; intLoop++)
      if (eventSrc.manager[eventName][intLoop].condition(src))
         eventSrc.manager[eventName][intLoop].doAction(src);

   src = src.parentElement;
   // Walk the tree; stop at the source element for the event.
   // tagName is null for the document; walk up entire tree.
   var top = (this.tagName == null) ? "HTML" : this.tagName;
   while (top != src.tagName) {
      for (var intLoop = 0;
            intLoop < eventSrc.manager[eventName].length;
            intLoop++)
         if (eventSrc.manager[eventName][intLoop].condition(src) &&
               eventSrc.manager[eventName][intLoop].doTree)
            eventSrc.manager[eventName][intLoop].doAction(src);
      src = src.parentElement;
   }
}

function setupHandler(eventName, eventSrc) {
   // Create a new function handler for the event.
   eventSrc[eventName] =
      new Function("runHandler('" + eventName + "', this);");
}

function alwaysTrue() {
   // Use this function when you don't want to check any condition.
   return true;
}

function register(eventName, action) {
   // This is the generic routine to register the event.
   // Parameters (in order):
   //  eventName             - Event to bind to
   //  action                - Code to run when the event occurs
   //  condition (optional) - Condition to test to perform the
   //                          action; defaults to true
   //  doTree (optional)     - Determines whether to walk up all
   //                          nodes of the tree; defaults to false
   //  eventSrc (optional)  - Element the event is associated with;
   //                          defaults to the document

   // Determine the source element.
   var eventSrc = (null != arguments[4]) ?
      document.all[arguments[4]] : document;
```

(continued)

```
      // Check whether an event manager exists on the object.
      if (null == eventSrc.manager)
         eventSrc.manager = new Object;
      // Check whether an event manager exists for the specific event.
      if (null == eventSrc.manager[eventName]) {
         eventSrc.manager[eventName] = new Object;
         eventSrc.manager[eventName].length = 0;
         setupHandler(eventName, eventSrc);
      }

      // Add the event handler.
      var ct = eventSrc.manager[eventName].length++;
      eventSrc.manager[eventName][ct] = new Object;
      eventSrc.manager[eventName][ct].doAction = action;
      // Check whether condition is supplied. If not, use alwaysTrue.
      eventSrc.manager[eventName][ct].condition =
         (null != arguments[2]) ? arguments[2] : alwaysTrue;
      // Check whether the tree is to be walked. Default to false.
      eventSrc.manager[eventName][ct].doTree =
         (null != arguments[3]) ? arguments[3] : false;
   }

   function hookupEvents() {
      var bindings = document.all.tags("BINDEVENT");
      for (var intLoop = 0; intLoop < bindings.length; intLoop++) {
         var bind = bindings[intLoop];
         if ((null != bind.getAttribute("event")) &&
               (null != bind.getAttribute("action"))) {
            var bEvent = bind.getAttribute("event");
            var bAction = new Function("return " +
               bind.getAttribute("action") +
               "(arguments[0])");
            var bCondition =
               (null == bind.getAttribute("condition")) ?
                  null :
                  new Function("return " +
                     bind.getAttribute("condition") +
                     "(arguments[0])");
            var bTree = ("walk" == bind.getAttribute("tree"));
            var bSrc = bind.getAttribute("for");
            register(bEvent, bAction, bCondition, bTree, bSrc);
         }
      }
   }

   window.onload = hookupEvents;
</SCRIPT>
```

This code takes advantage of many of the features of Dynamic HTML and JavaScript. All the techniques used in this example are covered in later chapters. For example, HTML does not define or support the <BINDEVENT> tag. Instead, Dynamic HTML exposes unrecognized elements in the object model. You can use this feature to associate information and extend scripts without having to modify any code.

To use this code, write an action function and register it with an event of a particular object on the page. The following code demonstrates how dynamic effects can be added to and registered in the preceding binding service. Dynamically changing the style of an element is discussed in Chapter 11, "Dynamic Styles."

```
<SCRIPT LANGUAGE="JavaScript">
   // Dynamic style mouseover effect

   function swapEffects(src) {
      // If an effect is supplied, swap it with className.
      if (null != src.getAttribute("effect")) {
         var tempClass = src.className;
         src.className = src.getAttribute("effect");
         src.setAttribute("effect", tempClass);
      }
   }

   function checkEffect(src) {
      // Condition to check for before swapping the effect
      return (src.getAttribute("effect") != null);
   }
</SCRIPT>
```

This script defines the action and condition for swapping effects with the class attribute. The following HTML binds this code to the *onmouseover* and *onmouseout* events of the document:

```
<BINDEVENT event="onmouseover" action="swapEffects"
   condition="checkEffect" tree="walk">
<BINDEVENT event="onmouseout" action="swapEffects"
   condition="checkEffect" tree="walk">
```

The custom event binding is powerful in that the author does not need to understand how to hook up code. Instead, the author can simply paste the code into the page. With easy-to-use HTML, the code can be associated with any event of any object. The real power of this model is revealed if the user tries to hook up another action to the *onmouseover* or *onmouseout* event. Normally, this would require writing custom *onmousemove* or *onmouseout* event handlers to call the different actions in sequence. With the method demonstrated here, all that is necessary is to paste the new function to be executed into the document and to hook it up to the event using another <BINDEVENT> tag. The registry code automatically manages the correct sets of event handlers and ensures that they are fired for each event.

An extra *for* attribute is supported on the <BINDEVENT> tag for associating the event directly with a specific element. By default, the event is attached to the document. The *for* attribute takes the ID of the element that the event is being bound to.

CHAPTER FOUR

The Browser Window

In this chapter, you'll learn how to program the browser window, the top-level object in the Dynamic HTML object model. Through the *window* object, information about the browser and the contained document can be accessed. Two types of HTML documents can be displayed inside a window: a frameset document and a standard HTML document. Frameset documents partition a single window into multiple, independently accessible frames. Chapter 5, "Window and Frame Management," and Chapter 6, "The HTML Document," discuss the two types of documents in detail.

The *window* object exposes document information (including information about the frames on the page and the URL for the current document) and provides access to information about the browser itself (including the client brand, version, and features supported, through a *navigator* object), access to event information, and most important, access to the *document* object that exposes the HTML document itself. The *window* object also lets you move forward and backward through the history, customize the browser's appearance, and move and relocate the window.

This chapter and Chapter 5 teach you how to manipulate the browser and the contained document using the *window* object. This chapter focuses on the members for manipulating the current window; Chapter 5 continues the discussion by showing you how to manipulate framesets and multiple browser instances.

The following topics are covered in this chapter:

- **The *window* object** This section provides a brief introduction to the *window* object and its relationship to other objects, including its unique relationship to global variables, which act as public members of the *window* object.
- **The window environment** This section shows you how to manipulate the browser environment—including the browser's status bar, the location of the document, the history list, and the user's screen resolution.

- **Window events** The *window* object exposes changes in the document's state through several events. For example, these events can help you determine when the document has finished loading and whether the document is currently active.
- **Timer events** The *window* object also exposes methods for creating timers. Timers are events that execute code after a specified amount of time.
- **The *clientInformation* or *navigator* property** The *navigator* object exposes specific information about the client. This information includes the brand, version, and user options, allowing scripts to determine the capabilities of the client and to adjust the page accordingly.

The *window* Object

As mentioned, the *window* object is the top-level object in Dynamic HTML. The easiest way to understand the *window* object is to think of it as a container for a document or for other windows. A window containing other windows is the basis of a frameset. Figure 4-1 shows the *window* object hierarchy.

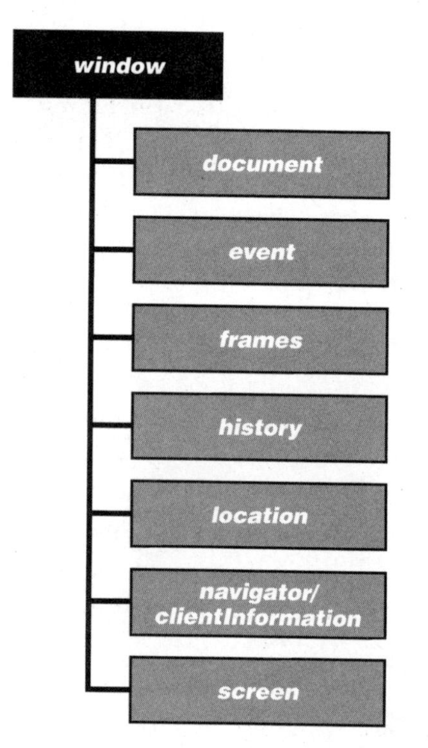

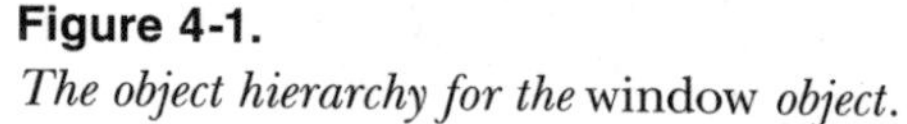

Figure 4-1.
The object hierarchy for the window *object.*

The *window* object maintains information about the browser and exists as long as the browser's application window exists. This means that as the user browses from page to page, the *window* object remains available, even though the current document changes.

Referencing the *window* Object

Because the *window* object is the top-level object in the HTML object model, it does not have to be explicitly referenced when you are accessing the properties of the window. For example, the following two lines of code are effectively the same:

```
window.location.URL  // Explicitly reference the window object.
location.URL         // The window object is implicitly referenced.
```

In addition, the *window* object exposes a *self* property that actually returns the window. Therefore, the following five lines of code reference the same *name* property:

```
name
self.name
window.self.name
window.self.window.name
window.window.name
```

Implicit window references work only for code that references the current window. To reference other, noncurrent windows or frames, the particular *window* objects must be explicitly referenced.

The *document* and *event* Properties

The *document* property returns a *document* object representing the page contained within the window. Through the *document* property, the style, structure, and contents of the contained document can be accessed.

As mentioned in Chapter 3, "Dynamic HTML Event Model," the *event* property of the *window* object returns an *event* object, which provides information about the current event. The *event* object is accessible only during an event sequence and returns *null* at all other times. It is possible to respond to events that occur in other windows or documents; Chapter 5, "Window and Frame Management," explains how.

Global Variables and User-Defined Properties

As mentioned in Chapter 2, "Fundamentals of HTML Scripting," no global variables are available when you are scripting in Dynamic HTML. Instead, all variables declared outside the scope of a function or an event handler are automatically added as user-defined properties of the *window* object. When the user exits a page, variables that were added by the page are removed from the window. This is done for a number of reasons: so that a new page can be certain that no properties yet exist on the page, and for security purposes, so that another page does not come along and attempt to read the state of the prior page.

Therefore, the lifetime of the user-defined properties of the *window* object is the same as the lifetime of the script, even though the *window* object exists until the application window is destroyed. When a new page is loaded, the only exposed *window* object properties are the built-in properties defined by Dynamic HTML.

Naming the Window

Each window is created without a name. You can name a window by assigning a string to its *name* property. You can supply a name for a frame when you create it as part of a frameset.

The *name* property designates the target for a link anchor or form results. By default, all pages are targeted to the current frame or to the frame or window specified by the <BASE TARGET=*windowName*> tag. You can override this target by supplying a TARGET attribute to a link anchor or Form element, specifying which named window the document should appear in.

The *window* object's *name* property is retained by the browser as the user navigates to a page in order to ensure that frame targeting is maintained.

Evaluating Strings as Code

The *window* object exposes an *eval* method that can evaluate a passed-in string as code and return the result. The code is executed in the context of the currently executing scripting language.

The Window Environment

This section discusses how to manipulate the browser's window and surrounding environment. The browser window consists of a number of areas that can be controlled through scripting, including the location of the currently displayed document, status bar text, history, and screen resolution. Figure 4-2 shows the various window features.

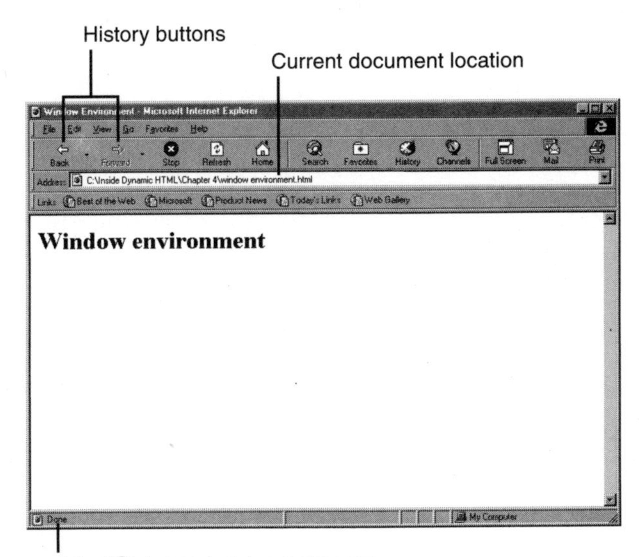

Figure 4-2.
The window features that can be controlled by the window *object.*

Status Bar

The status bar text is usually displayed along the bottom of the browser. Access to the message is available through two properties: *defaultStatus* and *status*. Both properties are read/write strings. The difference is that the *status* property is used for a message that is displayed temporarily, and the *defaultStatus* property displays a message until the *defaultStatus* property is changed or the user exits the browser window, as shown here:

```
<HTML>
   <HEAD>
      <TITLE>Status Text</TITLE>
      <SCRIPT LANGUAGE="JavaScript">
         function setStatus() {
            // Status message to display
            window.defaultStatus = "Default status";
            // Temporary message to display
            window.status = "Temporary status";
         }
      </SCRIPT>
   </HEAD>
```

(continued)

```
    <BODY>
      <FORM>
        <INPUT TYPE=BUTTON VALUE="Change Status"
          ONCLICK="setStatus();">
      </FORM>
    </BODY>
</HTML>
```

When the Change Status button is clicked, the status bar displays the string *Temporary status.* Once the mouse is moved, the message will change to *Default status.* When the user exits a page, the status bar text is reset to the browser's default message.

By using the *onmouseover* and *onmouseout* events on an element, you can very easily display a special status message when the mouse pointer is on the element:

```
<A ONMOUSEOVER="window.status='Go Home'" ONMOUSEOUT="window.status=''"
      HREF="home.htm">
   Top Page
</A>
```

Sample code for creating scrolling status bar text that takes advantage of the *status* property and timers is presented in the section "Scrolling Status Bar Text" later in this chapter.

History Buttons

Dynamic HTML provides methods for creating custom history buttons. Although accessing the actual URLs visited by the user is not possible, the *history* object exposes three methods that simulate clicking the history buttons on the toolbar: the *go*, *forward*, and *back* methods. The *length* property exposes the number of elements in the history list. The following code creates simple Back and Forward buttons:

```
<HTML>
   <HEAD>
      <TITLE>History Buttons</TITLE>
   </HEAD>
   <BODY>
      <FORM NAME="Browse">
         <INPUT TYPE=BUTTON VALUE="Back"
            ONCLICK="history.back();">
         <INPUT TYPE=BUTTON VALUE="Forward"
            ONCLICK="history.forward();">
      </FORM>
   </BODY>
</HTML>
```

Window Location

The address of the page in the window is exposed through the *location* property, which references an object that identifies the URL, parsed into easy-to-use properties. These components make the URL easier to retrieve and manipulate.

The *location* Object Properties

Most of the properties of the *location* object break the URL into easy-to-use components. The properties that relate to the URL are listed here:

protocol://hostname:port/pathname?search#hash

Almost all URLs have a *protocol*, a *hostname*, and a *pathname*. The *port*, *search*, and *hash* properties might not have values associated with them. The *search* property represents the search string usually supplied for server-side CGI (Common Gateway Interface) scripts. The *hash* property represents the bookmark on the page.

In addition, the *location* object exposes a few extra properties that concatenate the properties mentioned. For example, the *host* property simply returns the *hostname* followed by a colon and the *port*. The *href* property is the entire URL exposed as a single string.

Assigning a value to any of these properties causes the browser to immediately try to navigate to the new page. For most operations, the *href* property is the one you should set to load a new page; you can also use the *replace* method, discussed next.

The *location* Object Methods

Two of the methods exposed on the *location* object are *reload*([*force*]) and *replace*(*url*). Calling the *reload* method is analogous to clicking the Refresh button on the browser—both actions force the entire page to reload if it has changed. By supplying *true* as the *force* parameter, you can force the page to reload, even if the server claims that the page has not changed.

The *replace* method navigates to a new page. It works similar to assigning a value to the *href* property, except that the *replace* method does not add the current page to the history list. The *replace* method is useful for client-side URL redirection, as shown in the following example:

```
<HTML>
   <HEAD>
      <TITLE>Browser Detection</TITLE>
      <SCRIPT LANGUAGE="JavaScript">
```

(continued)

```
            // Load a different version of the page for Netscape users.
            if ("Netscape" == navigator.appName)
               location.replace("nsversion.htm");
         </SCRIPT>
      </HEAD>
      <BODY>
         <!-- Page for other browsers -->
      </BODY>
   </HTML>
```

Screen Information

The *screen* object exposes information about the current user's display, including the screen resolution and color depth. This information lets your code analyze the user's visual support and update the display accordingly. The following table lists the properties available on the *screen* object.

Property	Description
width	Horizontal resolution of the screen in pixels
height	Vertical resolution of the screen in pixels
colorDepth	Bits per pixel used by the display or buffer
availHeight	Screen height inside docked windows
availWidth	Screen width inside docked windows

The *availHeight* and *availWidth* properties give the dimensions of the portion of the user's screen that is available for windows—that is, the space not taken up by any docked tool bars.

This information can also be used at load time to determine how the document should be presented: either different style sheets can be applied, or an entirely different document can be loaded. The following code demonstrates how to redirect users with low-resolution screens to an alternative document and how to disable a style sheet intended only for users with a specific color depth:

```
<HTML>
   <HEAD>
      <TITLE>Screen-Based Pages</TITLE>
      <LINK REL="styleSheet" TYPE="text/css" HREF="256color.css">
      <SCRIPT LANGUAGE="JavaScript">
         if ((640 >= screen.width) || (480 >= screen.height))
            window.location.replace("lowres.htm");
         document.styleSheets[0].disabled = (screen.colorDepth < 8);
```

```
    </SCRIPT>
  </HEAD>
  <BODY>
    <!-- Document's contents -->
  </BODY>
</HTML>
```

Window Events

The *window* object exposes events that allow control over the current state of the window. These events are useful for determining whether the document is loaded and for responding when it receives or loses the focus or when an error occurs.

Document State Events

Events are available for tracking the loading and unloading of a document. Handlers for these events should always be written in the document's head to ensure that they are hooked up as early as possible in the document's loading process. If the events are written in the middle of the document's contents, the code might never run if, for example, the user leaves the document before the unloading code is even parsed.

Load Events

The two events related to the loading of the document are *onload* and *onreadystatechange*. Both events help you determine when the entire document has been parsed and all elements have been loaded. The *onreadystatechange* event is a new event that occurs on the document, not on the window; *onreadystatechange* is discussed in detail in Chapter 6, "The HTML Document."

The *onload* event fires when the entire document is parsed but does not necessarily signal that all objects on the document are completely downloaded. This event is also supported by the Netscape Navigator 3.0 and Microsoft Internet Explorer 3.0 object models.

Unload Events

Two events relate to the unloading of the document: *onbeforeunload* and *onunload.* The *onbeforeunload* event is fired immediately before the *onunload* event. The *onbeforeunload* event gives the Web author a chance to verify that the user really wants to exit the document. This confirmation is useful when exiting the document would cause information to be lost because the user failed to submit data to the server. For example, in a data-binding scenario in which the user batches many changes on the client, exiting the document without submitting the data would cause the changes to be unintentionally lost. (Data binding is covered in detail in Chapter 15, "Data Binding with HTML.")

The *onbeforeunload* event can display a predefined dialog box that presents the developer's text and asks whether the user wants to exit the document. To display this query, set the *returnValue* property to a string, as shown in the following code. If you don't set the *returnValue* property using a string value, the window simply unloads the document without displaying a dialog box.

```
<SCRIPT LANGUAGE="JavaScript" EVENT="onbeforeunload()" FOR="window">
   event.returnValue = "Your input will be lost if you leave.";
</SCRIPT>
```

Figure 4-3 shows this custom message displayed by Internet Explorer 4.0 in response to the *onbeforeunload* event.

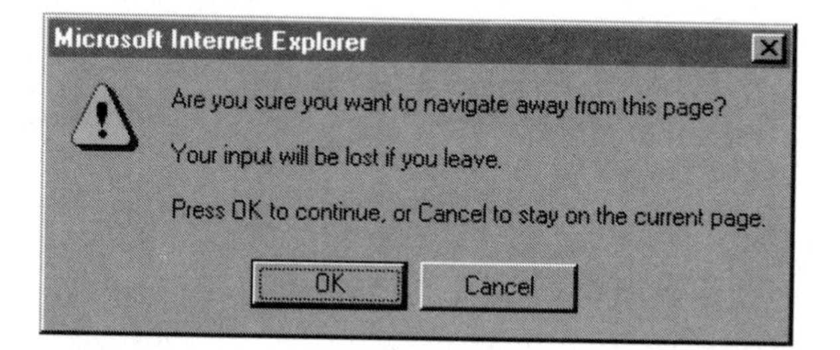

Figure 4-3.
Custom message displayed in a special dialog box by the onbeforeunload *event.*

For security reasons, a document cannot prevent the window from unloading it without the user's intervention. This restriction prevents a document from locking the system and requiring the user to either end the browser application or reboot.

Immediately before the document is unloaded, the *onunload* event fires. At this point, there is no way to stop the process or ask the user not to leave the document. Rather, this is where any cleanup code for the document should be written—it is the last opportunity for scripts to access the document and its contents.

Focus Events

The term *focus* refers to the window or element that is active and receives user notifications such as keyboard and mouse events. To allow you to determine when the window receives and loses the focus, the window exposes the *onblur* and *onfocus* events. In general, the *onblur* event fires when the window loses the focus to an element within the window or to another window, and the *onfocus* event fires when the window receives the focus.

The document that is loaded by the browser initially has the focus but does not fire an *onfocus* event. When the window has the focus, every user interaction with the window will cause the *onblur* and *onfocus* event sequence to occur. For example, clicking on the focusable window's document fires the *onblur* event on the window, followed by the *onfocus* event, even if the window already has the focus.

If the initial document is a frameset, the frameset itself has the initial focus. As with traditional HTML documents, loading the frameset does not fire an initial *onfocus* event. However, once the user clicks on or navigates to an instance of a frame in the frameset, an *onblur* event fires on the frameset and an *onfocus* event fires on the corresponding frame. This leads to the first rule of focus events:

- In any browser instance, only one item can have the focus at a time.

This one item can be a *window* object, a frameset, or an element within the document such as an input control or embedded object. Whenever the focus changes, an *onblur* event fires on a window or an element and an *onfocus* event fires on some other element.

A document may contain any number of focusable elements, including the input controls that take part in a form, embedded controls, and applets. Whenever one of these elements receives the focus, an *onblur* event fires on the prior window or element and an *onfocus* event fires on the focusable element. This leads to the second rule of focus events:

- Every change in focus occurs symmetrically, with an *onblur* event firing on the element losing the focus and an *onfocus* event firing on the element receiving the focus.

The *focus* and *blur* Methods

You can force a window or an element to receive or lose the focus by calling its *focus* or *blur* method. Calling one of these methods causes the associated event handler to be executed only if a change of state is required. For example, a window that already has the focus will not fire the *onfocus* event if its *focus* method is called. However, if the window does not have the focus and then receives the focus through the *focus* method, the *onfocus* event will be fired. This distinction is important to recognize because you cannot rely on code being executed in response to all *focus* or *blur* method calls.

Error Handling

The *window* object exposes an *onerror* event that is fired whenever a scripting error occurs on the page. When errors occur in a script, the user is usually presented with a cryptic message and the page fails to execute. Using an *onerror* event handler, the page can override the built-in dialog box and display a more explanatory message.

The *onerror* event also makes it possible to override the built-in dialog box and fail silently, as shown in the following code. While this is easy to accomplish, it is probably not advisable. If a scripting error occurs on the page, the page might enter an unpredictable state, causing the document to no longer function.

```
<SCRIPT LANGUAGE="JavaScript">
   function stopAllErrors() {
      // No scripting errors will ever display a message.
      return true;  // A value of true prevents the dialog box
                    // from appearing.
   }

   window.onerror = stopAllErrors;  // Hook up onerror event handler.
   thisBadCode.WillNot.GenerateAnError(); // Syntax error
</SCRIPT>
```

Unlike most events in the Dynamic HTML object model, returning *true* to the *onerror* event forces the dialog box to not appear. For all other events, returning *false* prevents the event from performing its default action. This difference is necessary in order to maintain compatibility with the *onerror* event in Netscape Navigator 3.0.

You can use the *onerror* event to gracefully handle errors in user input. In the following example, the user types a color name that is applied to the document's text box. If the user types an invalid color name, a custom dialog box warns the user that the color name is invalid.

```
<SCRIPT LANGUAGE="JavaScript">
   function doError() {
      if (arguments[0] == "runtime error 380") {
         alert("Invalid Color Name");
         return true;
      }
   }
   window.onerror = doError;
</SCRIPT>
Color:
<INPUT TYPE=TEXT ONCHANGE="this.style.color = this.value;"
   VALUE="Black">
```

The *onerror* event passes the event handler three arguments: an error description, the name of the file in which the error occurred, and the line number of the error. Error handlers should not use the line number parameter because if the source is edited, the line numbers will be updated and the error handlers will no longer work.

User Events

User events are events that fire when the user interacts with the window—for example, when the user resizes or scrolls the window. These events fire after the actions have been completed, so event handlers can't cancel the actions. Chapter 5, "Window and Frame Management," introduces methods that scripts can use to resize or scroll the window.

Using CSS (Cascading Style Sheets), you can create containers within the document that support scrolling and resizing. These actions fire the same events on the containers as they do on the window.

The *onresize* Event

Every time the user resizes a window, an *onresize* event fires on the window. This event lets you write code that rearranges the contents or even other windows in relation to the current size of the document.

The *onscroll* Event

The *onscroll* event is fired each time the document is scrolled, either by the user manually moving the scrollbar or by an action that results in the document being scrolled—for example, navigating to a bookmark or using the arrow keys. The properties for determining the current scrollbar's position are exposed through the *body* object on the document itself. Interacting with these properties is demonstrated in Chapter 5; a complete discussion of these properties is presented in Chapter 9, "Scripting Individual Elements."

Specifying Window Events

All the window events—including *onblur, onfocus, onload, onunload,* and *onbeforeunload*—can be specified as attributes of the <BODY> tag in an HTML page, which allows you to bind these events to a handler using attributes rather than scripts, as shown in the following code:

```
<HTML>
   <HEAD>
      <TITLE>Hooking Up Event Handlers</TITLE>
```

(continued)

```
      <SCRIPT LANGUAGE="JavaScript">
         function doLoad() {
            // Do something when document is loaded.
         }

         function doUnload() {
            // Do something when document is about to be unloaded.
         }
         window.onload = doLoad;  // Hook up event handler in script.
      </SCRIPT>
   </HEAD>
   <!-- Hook up event handler using a Body element attribute. -->
   <BODY ONUNLOAD="doUnload();">
   </BODY>
</HTML>
```

Timer Events

Timers fire events after a specified amount of time, rather than as the result of a user action. They are useful for animating objects in the browser or for forcing code to execute after a fixed amount of time. The *window* object can create two types of timers:

- Timers that execute the code once after the specified time elapses
- Timers that automatically cycle and execute the code each time the specified interval elapses

Timers can be added to the window only through code; they cannot be specified as attributes of any element. The *setTimeout* method creates a timer that executes only once, and the *setInterval* method creates a timer that repeatedly executes. Both methods take the same set of parameters:

var *timerRef* = window.setTimeout(*script, time*)
var *timerRef* = window.setInterval(*script, time*)

You can use a one-time timer to repeatedly execute a handler if you reset the timer in the handler, as shown here:

```
<SCRIPT LANGUAGE="JavaScript">
   var timeEvery100;
   function Every100() {
      // Write code to be executed here.
      // ...
      // Reset the timer.
      timeEvery100 = setTimeout("Every100();", 100);
   }
```

```
   // Make first call.
   timeEvery100 = setTimeout("Every100();", 100);

   // When user exits the page, remove timer.
   window.onunload = new Function("clearTimeout(timeEvery100);");
</SCRIPT>
```

If you use *setInterval* instead of *setTimeout*, you don't need to reset the timer in the handler.

> NOTE: The *setInterval* method was introduced in Netscape Navigator 4.0 and Internet Explorer 4.0 as a convenience. If you are writing code to run on down-level browsers, use the *setTimeout* method instead of the *setInterval* method.

You can pass parameters to the handler by building the function call string manually. The following code builds a function call with three parameters:

```
var tm = setTimeout("doThis(" + arg1 + ", 23, " + arg3 + ");", 100);
```

Timers are created using a *setTimeout* or *setInterval* method and can be removed at any point using the corresponding clear method: *clearTimeout* or *clearInterval*. Both clear methods take as a parameter the *timerRef* value returned by the set method. Therefore, when you are setting up a timer, the returned value should be saved in a variable.

In the preceding script example, the timer is cleared in the *onunload* event when the user exits the page. The *onunload* event is fired right when the page is about to be removed from memory. This step is optional, but it is good programming practice because it ensures that the browser releases the timer from memory.

Using Timers

This section provides three examples that use timers. The first example demonstrates a timer that navigates to a new page after a specified interval; it uses the *setTimeout* method because the code is intended to execute a finite number of times. The next two examples use the *setInterval* method. The second example creates scrolling status bar text using Dynamic HTML to improve on the typical implementation of this common device. The third example creates a ticking clock. Timers are used in many examples throughout this book to create interesting effects.

Automatic Page Navigation

The code on the following page demonstrates a simple timer that navigates to a new page after a specified amount of time. It also gives you a brief glimpse into dynamic contents by displaying an updated countdown.

```
<HTML>
   <HEAD>
      <TITLE>Countdown</TITLE>
      <SCRIPT LANGUAGE="JavaScript">
         var intLeft = 5;  // Seconds until navigation occurs

         function leavePage() {
            if (0 == intLeft)  // Time is up--navigate.
               document.location = "home.htm";
            else {
               // Count down and output updated time by
               // changing the contents of the element.
               intLeft -= 1;
               document.all.countdown.innerText = intLeft + " ";
               // Wait another second.
               setTimeout("leavePage()", 1000);
            }
         }
      </SCRIPT>
   </HEAD>
   <BODY ONLOAD="setTimeout('leavePage()', 1000)">
      Navigation to <A HREF="home.htm">home.htm</A> will occur in
      <SPAN ID="countdown">
         <!-- Output initial amount of time. -->
         <SCRIPT LANGUAGE="JavaScript">
            document.write(intLeft);
         </SCRIPT>
      </SPAN>
      seconds.
   </BODY>
</HTML>
```

The number of seconds the timer takes to navigate is controlled by the *intLeft* variable. Changing the initial value of the *intLeft* variable also automatically updates the initial value in the contents because of the simple script in the document's body.

Scrolling Status Bar Text

The following code creates status bar text that scrolls from right to left. This example will run only in Internet Explorer 4.0 because the Body element is customized with a user-defined attribute to store the message. This technique of adding attributes to elements to define new behavior is introduced in Chapter 8, "Scripts and Elements."

```
<HTML>
   <HEAD>
      <TITLE>Scrolling Status Bar Text</TITLE>
      <SCRIPT LANGUAGE="JavaScript">
         function spacer(pos) {
            // Simple routine to generate spaces
            var space = "";
            for (var i = 0; i < pos; i++)
               space += " ";
            return space;
         }

         function scrollStatus() {
            // Verify that there is a message to scroll.
            if (null != message) {
               with (message) {
                  // Restart message.
                  if (position < -text.length)
                     position = maxSpace;
                  // Scroll words off left edge.
                  if (position < 0) {
                     position--;
                     window.status = text.substring(-position);
                  }
                  else {
                  // Output preliminary spaces.
                  window.status = spacer(position--) + text;
                  }
               }
            }
         }

         function initMessage() {
         // Constructor for message object
         // Message to display is a required argument.
         this.text = document.body.getAttribute("message");
         // The speed is optional.
         if (null != arguments[0])
            this.speed = arguments[0];
         else
            this.speed = 10;
         // Initial number of prefix spaces
         this.maxSpace = 130;
         this.position = maxSpace;
         // Start timer.
         this.timer = setInterval("scrollStatus()", this.speed);
```

(continued)

```
            return this;
            }
         </SCRIPT>
      </HEAD>
      <BODY ONLOAD="message = initMessage(10);"
            message="Demo String to Scroll">
         Demo Message Page
      </BODY>
   </HTML>
```

Ticking Clock

Before Dynamic HTML, ticking clocks could be added to documents only through applets, images with complex code, or related tricks. This example demonstrates how to create a ticking clock that exists directly within the HTML document. The following code specifies that the output for the clock be placed inside a Span element with the ID *clock*. After each tick, the contents of the Span element are replaced with the new time.

```
<HTML>
   <HEAD>
      <TITLE>Ticking Clock</TITLE>
      <STYLE TYPE="text/css">
         #clock {color:blue; font-size:120%} /* Format the clock. */
      </STYLE>
      <SCRIPT LANGUAGE="JavaScript">
         // Check whether IE4 or later.
         var MS = navigator.appVersion.indexOf("MSIE");
         window.isIE4 = (MS > 0) &&
            (parseInt(navigator.appVersion.substring(MS + 5, MS + 6))
               >= 4);

         function lead0(val) {
            // Add leading 0s when necessary.
            return (val < 10) ? "0" + val.toString() : val;
         }

         function buildTime() {
            var time = new Date();
            var ampm = "AM";
            var h = time.getHours();
            // Fix military time and determine ampm.
            if (h > 12) {
               h = h - 12;
               ampm = " PM";
            }
            return lead0(h) + ":" + lead0(time.getMinutes()) + ":" +
               lead0(time.getSeconds()) + ampm;
```

```
         }

         function tick() {
            // Replace the clock's time with the current time.
            document.all.clock.innerText = buildTime();
         }
      </SCRIPT>
   </HEAD>
   <!-- Start up the timer only if the browser is IE4. -->
   <!-- When unloading, remove the timer if it exists. -->
   <BODY ONUNLOAD="if (null != window.tmr) clearInterval(window.tmr);"
         ONLOAD="if (window.isIE4)
            window.tmr = setInterval('tick()', 999);">
      <H1>Below is a live, ticking clock programmed entirely in HTML.
      </H1>
      <P>The current time is:
      <SPAN ID="clock">
         <SCRIPT LANGUAGE="JavaScript">
            // Down-level script support;
            // output an initial static time.
            document.write(buildTime());
         </SCRIPT>
      </SPAN>.
   </BODY>
</HTML>
```

This code runs acceptably on down-level browsers that support scripting. The trick here is the *document.write* method contained within the body of the document to output the current time in the appropriate position in the stream. In browsers that support Dynamic HTML, the clock will continue to be updated with the correct time. In nondynamic browsers, only the time at which the page was loaded is displayed.

Timer Precision

Timer events cannot be relied on to occur with precise regularity—a timer event designed to fire once per second may not actually do so. Depending on the operating system, the timer may not fire until another application or process yields to the browser.

Irregularity can be visible in a timer that is used for animation. The animation might appear to stop momentarily, rather than move smoothly. This hesitation is probably due to a delay in the timer's execution caused by some other process or by the browser itself.

The *clientInformation* or *navigator* Property

The *clientInformation* and *navigator* properties reference an object containing information about the client. The *clientInformation* property was added to Internet Explorer 4.0 as an alias for *navigator* to separate any implied relationship between the object model and a particular browser. However, because the *clientInformation* property is currently supported only by Internet Explorer 4.0, you should use the *navigator* property when you are targeting multiple browsers. Both properties return the same information, including the name and version of the client.

> NOTE: Throughout this section, the *clientInformation* and *navigator* properties and objects are used interchangeably. In all cases, both properties and objects provide exactly the same information.

Using the *clientInformation* or *navigator* object, code can be executed conditionally based on the browser brand or version number. If you are simply creating code to work around a bug or a small unsupported feature in one browser, client-side checking works well. But client-side negotiation that results in new pages being downloaded requires multiple hits to the server. If you want to provide different pages for each brand of browser, you can get better performance by transmitting the correct page initially, based on the header that is submitted.

Client Brand Information

The following four properties on the *navigator* object expose the client version and name:

- *appCodeName*
- *appName*
- *appVersion*
- *userAgent*

Both Internet Explorer and Netscape Navigator follow the same general format for the *appVersion* property. The *appVersion* property returns the version of the client in the following format:

clientVersion (*platform*; *information* [; *extraInformation*])

In Netscape Navigator, the *platform* field indicates which platform the browser is running on. In Internet Explorer versions 3.0 and 4.0, the string *compatible* is returned as the platform, and the actual platform is indicated in the *extraInformation* field.

In Netscape Navigator, the *information* field indicates the product's encryption level. For example, *I* is returned for the international release, which provides a weaker level of security than the U.S. version in order to comply with U.S. export restrictions. The U.S. release returns *U* in this field. Internet Explorer returns a version number in the *information* field.

The *extraInformation* field may return the platform or the build number of the required operating system. Internet Explorer uses this field to return detailed platform information. Depending on the platform, this field may or may not be used by Netscape Navigator.

In general, the fields in the *appVersion* property follow a consistent format. Your code can distinguish between the different clients by parsing the value of this property. The following table lists the values returned by Internet Explorer and Netscape Navigator on the Microsoft Windows platform for the *appCodeName*, *appName*, and *appVersion* properties.

Browser	*appCodeName*	*appName*	*appVersion*
Microsoft Internet Explorer 3.0	*Mozilla*	*Microsoft Internet Explorer*	*2.0 (compatible; MSIE 3.0A; Windows 95)*
Microsoft Internet Explorer 4.0	*Mozilla*	*Microsoft Internet Explorer*	*4.0 (compatible; MSIE 4.0; Windows 95)*
Netscape Navigator 2.01	*Mozilla*	*Netscape*	*2.01 (Win95; I)*
Netscape Navigator 3.0	*Mozilla*	*Netscape*	*3.0 (Win95; I)*
Netscape Navigator 4.0	*Mozilla*	*Netscape*	*4.0 (Win95; I)*

The *userAgent* property contains the HTTP (Hypertext Transfer Protocol) user-agent string that was specified in the HTTP request. The user-agent string is just the concatenation of the *appCodeName* property and the *appVersion* property, separated by a slash: *appCodeName/appVersion.*

Parsing *appVersion*

The code on the following page parses the *appVersion* property into its basic components. The individual elements of *appVersion* are then added to the *navigator* object as properties.

```
<HTML>
   <HEAD>
      <TITLE>Application Version</TITLE>
      <SCRIPT LANGUAGE="JavaScript">
         // Initialize version.
         function getVersionInfo() {
            var version = navigator.appVersion;

            // Locate the opening (.
            var iParen = version.indexOf("(", 0);

            // The client version is the string before the (.
            navigator.clientVersion =
               version.substring(0, iParen - 1);
            var information = new Array();

            // Automatically split the remaining values into an array.
            information = version.substring(iParen + 1,
               version.length - 1).split(";");

            // First value is the platform.
            navigator.platforminfo = information[0];

            // Second value is the information field.
            navigator.information = information[1];

            /* Third value is extra information, which may be null
               depending on the browser and platform. */
            navigator.extraInformation = information[2];
         }
         getVersionInfo();
      </SCRIPT>
   </HEAD>
   <BODY>
      <H1>Client Information</H1>
      <SCRIPT LANGUAGE="JavaScript">
         // Output the information.
         document.write("Platform: " + navigator.platforminfo +
            "<BR>");
         document.write("Client Version: " + navigator.clientVersion +
            "<BR>");
         document.write("Information: " + navigator.information +
            "<BR>");
         document.write("Extra Info: " + navigator.extraInformation +
            "<BR>");
      </SCRIPT>
   </BODY>
</HTML>
```

Multiple Windows and the *navigator* Object

The *navigator* object is not shared between all loaded instances of the window. Instead, each window has its own instance of the *navigator* object. While in almost all cases the information exposed by the *navigator* object is the same for each window, this isolation is important. For security reasons, if an instance of a page customizes the *navigator* object, only that instance is allowed to access it.

The preceding code parses the client information into multiple properties that are added directly to the *navigator* object. These properties are available only on the *navigator* object of the associated window. Referencing these user-defined properties of the *navigator* object on another window will return *undefined* values, as they do not exist.

User Settings

The *navigator* object provides access to information about whether Java and cookies are enabled or disabled on the user's browser.

Java Support

To determine whether Java is enabled on the client, the *navigator* object exposes a *javaEnabled* method. This method returns a Boolean value that specifies whether the client can display Java applets.

Using the *javaEnabled* method, you can write a script that either inserts the applet or displays a message to the user:

```
<SCRIPT LANGUAGE="JavaScript">
   if (navigator.javaEnabled())
      document.write("<APPLET NAME=demo CODE=demo.class " +
         "WIDTH=50 HEIGHT=50></APPLET>");
   else
      document.write("<B>This page cannot run with Java disabled." +
         "</B>");
</SCRIPT>
```

Cookie Support

Internet Explorer 4.0 exposes a property, *cookieEnabled*, that specifies whether the client supports cookies. Cookies allow a small piece of information that is associated with the current URL or domain to be retained on the client's machine. Some users do not want pages to retain any information on their hard drives and so disable this browser feature. The *cookieEnabled* property contains a Boolean value that indicates whether the user has deactivated this support. Using this property, you can write custom behavior that does not rely on the client-side cookie if it is unavailable.

Unfortunately, Internet Explorer 3.0 and Netscape Navigator 4.0 do not support the *cookieEnabled* property. Therefore, this method cannot always be relied on for determining whether cookies are enabled on the client machine.

New *navigator* Object Properties

The *navigator* object supports a number of new properties that you can use to adapt your document to different users. The following table summarizes these properties.

Property	Description
cpuClass	The type of CPU. The value for a Pentium machine is *x86.*
systemLanguage	The default language for the system. For American English the value is *en-us.*
userLanguage	The user's default language. For American English the value is *en-us.*
platform	The user's current operating system. For Microsoft Windows 95 the value is *win32.*
appMinorVersion	The minor version of the browser application. The value for Internet Explorer 4.0 is *0.*
onLine	A Boolean value indicating whether the user is reading the page online.

CHAPTER FIVE

Window and Frame Management

This chapter shows you how to create, manage, and navigate between multiple windows, modal dialog boxes, and framesets. With Dynamic HTML, your scripts can move, resize, and scroll windows. Your code can open HTML documents in their own windows in several different ways and manipulate the multiple browser instances created. It can also partition the window into multiple regions called frames and manipulate each frame as an independent window.

The following topics are covered in this chapter:

- **Manipulating the window** Chapter 4, "The Browser Window," introduced events that fire when the user interacts with the window. This section discusses the methods provided by the *window* object for moving, resizing, and scrolling the document.
- **Creating new windows** This section discusses how to write code to manipulate multiple windows. The *window* object can be used to create new instances of the browser window, thus creating new *window* objects. In addition, the *window* object exposes methods that let you display a variety of dialog boxes and HTML-based help windows. These dialog boxes are useful for providing notifications to the user, requesting simple strings, and asking yes/no questions. You can also create custom modal dialog boxes and help files whose contents are located in other HTML documents.
- **Manipulating framesets** This section presents the HTML code for creating a frameset and introduces the *frames* collection, which provides access to the individual frames. Each frame is an instance of the *window* object, so the object model for windows is also applicable to each frame. All the techniques available for manipulating windows can also be used for manipulating frames.

- **Special event considerations** This section introduces techniques for cross-frame and cross-window event handling and demonstrates how to write an event handler in one window that handles events in another window.

Manipulating the Window

The *window* object exposes methods for moving, resizing, and scrolling the window. All three operations can be performed relative to the current window state or to a new absolute position through a pair of methods for each operation. The following table lists these methods and their actions.

Method	Manipulates	Description
moveBy(offsetTop, offsetLeft)	Window	Moves the window by the specified offsets (measured in pixels)
moveTo(top, left)	Window	Moves the window so that its top left corner is at the specified location (measured in pixels)
resizeBy(offsetWidth, offsetHeight)	Window	Resizes the window by the specified offsets (measured in pixels)
resizeTo(width, height)	Window	Resizes the window to the specified size (in pixels)
scrollBy(offsetHorizontal, offsetVertical)	Document	Scrolls the document by the specified offsets (measured in pixels)
scrollTo(horizontal, vertical) or *scroll(horizontal, vertical)*	Document	Scrolls the document to the specified position (measured in pixels; *scrollTo* and *scroll* are aliases for each other)

The Manipulates column specifies whether the method applies to the physical window or to the current document. Normally, window methods called within a frame apply to the current frame, but the moving and resizing methods are exceptions. These methods always apply to the containing window. Therefore, an invocation of any of these four methods is the same as calling the method on the topmost window, as shown here:

```
top.methodName
```

The *top* property is described in the section "Manipulating Framesets" later in this chapter. This property of a *window* object always returns the topmost window in the document hierarchy. The moving and resizing methods have restrictions preventing them from moving the window off the screen or sizing it too small to be seen. The scrolling methods manipulate the document in the window the method is invoked on. The scrolling methods correspond to the *scrollTop* and *scrollLeft* properties exposed on the *body* property of the document, which are introduced in Chapter 9, "Scripting Individual Elements." Calling the *scrollTo* method is the same as assigning new pixel values to these properties.

Scrolling the Window

The *scroll* method (and the equivalent *scrollTo* method) can be used to scroll the document to a specified location using *xy*-coordinates. The *xy*-coordinates are specified in pixels relative to the document's top left corner—this means that *scroll(0, 0)* always scrolls the top left corner of the document onto the screen.

The *scroll* method will not scroll past the end of the document. If you pass a *vertical* argument that is too large, for example, the *scroll* method will not return an error; it will simply scroll the bottom of the document to the bottom of the screen. You cannot write code that will scroll the last line of the document off the screen.

Whenever the document is scrolled, an *onscroll* event is fired on the window. This event fires regardless of whether the scrolling is the result of the *scroll* method or the user manually scrolling the document.

In general, you should not write code that relies on the position of the scrollbar, even if the width and height of the document are taken into account, because different resolutions and different platforms may render fonts larger or smaller or calculate the size of the document differently. Instead, you should write more generic code that checks for specific state changes. For example, in response to the *onscroll* event, you can write code that directly checks whether an element is on the screen rather than trying to infer the location from the scroll position.

More browsers support the *scroll* method than the equivalent *scrollTo* method. The *scrollTo* method was introduced to allow naming consistency with the moving and resizing methods.

Creating an Auto-Scrolling Window

The following code shows you how to use a timer to create a document that automatically scrolls. This code demonstrates how to use the *scroll* method and take into account the document's size. This example produces scrolling text similar to that produced by the built-in Marquee element.

```
<HTML>
   <HEAD>
      <TITLE>Automatically Scrolling Window</TITLE>
      <SCRIPT LANGUAGE="JavaScript">
         var tScroll;
         var curPos = 0;

         function runTimer() {
            curPos = document.body.scrollTop + 3;
            window.scroll(0, curPos);
            // Start over when end of document is reached.
            if (curPos > document.body.scrollHeight -
                  document.body.clientHeight)
               window.scroll(0, 0);
            tScroll = window.setTimeout("runTimer();", 100);
         }

         window.onload = runTimer;
         window.onunload = new Function("clearTimeout(tScroll)");
      </SCRIPT>
   </HEAD>
   <!-- The margin-bottom style attribute adds white space
        following the last line of text. -->
   <BODY STYLE="margin-bottom:350pt">
      Contents to scroll
   </BODY>
</HTML>
```

Creating New Windows

Dynamic HTML exposes five methods on the window for creating different types of windows. These methods provide a set of predefined window types as well as custom HTML-based windows and dialog boxes.

The two styles of windows that can be created are modal and modeless. A modal window, normally a dialog box, is a window that the user must respond to before the application can continue. When a modal dialog box is displayed, the script in the original window stops and waits for the dialog box to be closed. Modeless windows are windows that operate independently of the current window; the code in modeless dialog boxes executes independently from the other windows. Using modeless windows you can create multiwindowed HTML applications.

The following table lists the methods available for creating modal and modeless windows.

Method	Description
alert(message)	Modal. Displays a simple modal dialog box containing a supplied message and a single OK button. The *alert* method should be reserved primarily for displaying error messages.
confirm(message)	Modal. Similar to *alert* but used to ask the user a question. This dialog box displays the text along with OK and Cancel buttons. Clicking OK returns *true*, and clicking Cancel returns *false.*
open([url [, name [, features [, replace]]]])	Modeless. Opens a new instance of the browser with the specified URL. The *open* method allows different window features to be turned on or off.
prompt(message [, defaultText])	Modal. Displays a dialog box that requests a string from the user. The optional *defaultText* parameter is used to provide a default value for the text box. If the user fails to enter a string and clicks OK, an empty string is returned. If the user clicks the Cancel button or the Close box, a value of *null* is returned.
showModalDialog (url [, arguments [, features]])	Modal. Similar to the *open* method but displays a modal dialog box containing the supplied URL. The script can pass arguments into the dialog box, and because modal dialog boxes block the flow of the creating script, the dialog box can specify a return value.

The following sections discuss the use of these methods in detail.

Modeless Windows

The *window* object exposes an *open* method that lets you create a new modeless window. The new window is simply another instance of the browser; it has its own history and it navigates independently of the creating window.

The *open* method has the following syntax:

[*windowObject* =] window.open([*url* [, *name* [, *features* [, *replace*]]]])

All parameters to the *open* method are optional. The *url* parameter specifies the initial page to load. Omitting this value opens an instance of the browser with a blank document, which is useful when the document is being generated from script.

The *name* parameter assigns a name to the window to be used when the window is a target for subsequent documents. Targeting indicates where a document will be displayed when the user follows a link. The TARGET attribute on the anchor can specify a window name. If no window exists for a specified target, the document is displayed in a new window. If no target is specified, the new document is displayed in the current window. The *name* parameter, and therefore the TARGET attribute, can contain only alphanumeric characters and underscores (_).

The *features* parameter consists of a string that specifies the window features to display in the newly created window, thereby turning on or off the menus, toolbars, and scrollbars and specifying an initial size for the window. These features are discussed in detail in the section "Window Features" later in this chapter.

The *replace* parameter specifies how the new URL will be handled in its window's history list. If you omit the *replace* parameter or pass a value of *false*, the URL will be added to the end of the list as usual. If you pass a value of *true*, the URL will replace the current URL in the list if there is one; otherwise, it will not be added at all. The *replace* parameter is useful primarily for windows that have already been opened.

Manipulating the New Window

The *open* method returns a reference to the newly created window. By assigning the return value to a variable, you can call methods on the window later in your code. If the supplied window name refers to a window that already exists, another window with the same name is not created; rather, the new URL is displayed in the existing window. If you do not assign the return value to a variable, you cannot call the new window's methods from code. You can, however, get a reference to the window later by reopening it, as shown in the following example:

```
// Open a new window, but do not save a reference to it.
window.open("myPlace.htm", "myPlace");

/* Load a new document in the window "myPlace"
   and save a reference to it. */
myPlace = window.open("myPlace2.htm", "myPlace");
```

This code creates only one new window instance. This technique is similar to targeting the window with a new document.

Modal and Custom HTML Dialog Boxes

As mentioned, modal dialog boxes require a response from the user before interaction with the browser can continue. The *window* object exposes four methods that let you prompt the user with a modal dialog box. Three methods display simple built-in dialog boxes, and the fourth method lets you create custom HTML dialog boxes. The companion CD contains a file that demonstrates how to create the different types of modal dialog boxes.

The methods for built-in dialog boxes—*alert*, *confirm*, and *prompt*—take *message* strings as arguments. In JavaScript, these strings can contain line breaks, indicated by the *\n* escape character. (VBScript uses *chr(13)* to specify line breaks.) Here is an example of a multiple-line *alert* message string:

```
alert("You entered invalid values on fields:\nName\nUser");
```

The *showModalDialog* method is used to create custom dialog boxes that can display HTML files. Inside the dialog box, the object model is slightly different from the traditional window object model because the dialog box is not a full instance of the browser, but rather a viewer for the HTML document. A modal dialog box differs from a standard browser window as follows:

- No navigation can occur. (Clicking a link will open the URL in a new instance of the browser.)
- The contents within the dialog box are not selectable.

Modal dialog boxes are intended for displaying messages that require a response and for requesting information from the user. Like the built-in *prompt* and *confirm* methods, custom modal dialog boxes can return information to the browser.

When you display a custom modal dialog box, you should always supply a close button. If you omit the close button, the dialog box can be dismissed only by clicking on the Close box in the upper right corner of the window. To create a close button, use the Submit button type so that the button acts as the default button. The following code creates an OK button that closes the dialog box:

```
<INPUT TYPE=SUBMIT VALUE="OK" STYLE="Width:5em"
   ONCLICK="window.close();">
```

Displaying Custom Dialog Boxes

The first and last arguments of the *showModalDialog* method are essentially the same as those of the *open* method. The first argument specifies the URL to display, and the last argument specifies the set of window features to display. The second argument is different. Rather than take a name, the second argument can take any variable, including an array, and pass it into the dialog box. This argument allows an application to pass information into the dialog box.

You can specify a return value for the *showModalDialog* method by setting a special property on the dialog box. This property can take any type of variable, which is returned to the calling application.

Passing Information to and from the Dialog Box

The information passed to and returned from the dialog box is exposed in the object model of the dialog box. A copy of the variable specified as the second argument of the *showModalDialog* method is exposed in the dialog box as the *dialogArguments* property. The *returnValue* property is exposed for passing information back to the calling application. When the dialog box is closed, the value of this property is used as the return value for the dialog box. The following code demonstrates how to access arguments passed into and return arguments from a dialog box:

```
<HTML>
   <HEAD>
      <TITLE>Passing Variables</TITLE>
   </HEAD>
   <!-- When the dialog box is unloaded,
        the value in the text box is returned. -->
   <BODY ONUNLOAD="window.returnValue = document.all.ret.value;">
      <P>You passed in the following value:</P>
      <P ALIGN=CENTER>
      <SCRIPT LANGUAGE="JavaScript">
         document.write(window.dialogArguments);
      </SCRIPT>
      <P>Enter a value to return to the application:</P>
      <P ALIGN=CENTER>
      <INPUT TYPE=TEXT ID="ret" VALUE="Return">
      <INPUT STYLE="width:5em" TYPE=SUBMIT VALUE="OK"
         ONCLICK="window.close()">
   </BODY>
</HTML>
```

This dialog box could be invoked using the following command:

```
showModalDialog("pass.htm", "Pass this string to the dialog box.");
```

Creating an About Dialog Box

With the *alert* method, you can create a simple About dialog box. With the *showModalDialog* method, you can create an HTML-enhanced About dialog box. The following code displays a custom About dialog box. The first document contains an About button to click to display the About dialog box.

```
<HTML>
   <HEAD>
      <TITLE>About Demo</TITLE>
      <SCRIPT LANGUAGE="JavaScript">
         function about() {
            // Display About dialog box.
            event.srcElement.blur();
            window.showModalDialog("about.htm", "",
               "dialogWidth:25em; dialogHeight:13em")
         }
      </SCRIPT>
   </HEAD>
   <BODY>
      <INPUT TYPE=BUTTON VALUE="About" ONCLICK="about();">
   </BODY>
</HTML>
```

The About dialog box code is in the file about.htm:

```
<HTML>
   <HEAD>
      <TITLE>About Inside Dynamic HTML</TITLE>
   </HEAD>
   <BODY STYLE="text-align:center; font-size:75%;
      background:lightgrey">
      <H2>Companion CD-ROM Version 1.0</H2>
      <H3>By Scott Isaacs</H3>
      <H4 STYLE="font-style:italic">
         Demonstrating the Power of Dynamic HTML!
      </H4>
      <!-- Submit button is the default button. -->
      <INPUT TYPE=SUBMIT STYLE="Width:5em" VALUE="OK"
         ONCLICK="window.close()">
   </BODY>
</HTML>
```

Creating Custom Input Dialog Boxes

The *prompt* method is useful for requesting simple information from the user. However, if multiple pieces of information are required, the *prompt* method is not sufficient. To pass multiple values back and forth between the dialog box and the creating window, you can use an array or an object. The following code demonstrates how to request multiple fields of information and pass the information back to the application:

```
<HTML>
   <HEAD>
      <TITLE>User Information</TITLE>
      <STYLE TYPE="text/css">
         BODY {margin-left:10pt; background:menu}
      </STYLE>
      <SCRIPT LANGUAGE="JavaScript">
         function saveValues() {
            // Build an array of return values.
            var retVal = new Array;
            for (var intLoop = 0; intLoop < document.UserInfo.length;
                  intLoop++)
               with (document.UserInfo[intLoop])
                  if (name != "")
                     retVal[name] = value;
            window.returnValue = retVal;
            event.returnValue = false;
            window.close();
         }
      </SCRIPT>
   </HEAD>
   <BODY>
      <!-- This form is used to group the contained controls in an
            easy-to-access array. -->
      <FORM NAME="UserInfo">
         <FIELDSET>
            <LEGEND>User Information</LEGEND>
            <P>User Name: <INPUT TYPE=TEXT NAME="User">
            <P>Address: <TEXTAREA ROWS="3" NAME="Address"></TEXTAREA>
         </FIELDSET>
      </FORM>
      <P STYLE="text-align:center">
      <INPUT TYPE=SUBMIT STYLE="width:5em" ONCLICK="saveValues();"
         VALUE="OK">
      <INPUT TYPE=RESET ONCLICK="window.close();" VALUE="Cancel">
   </BODY>
</HTML>
```

If the preceding code is in a file named UserInfo.htm, the following script will display the code in a modal dialog box and then loop through and report the return values:

```
<SCRIPT LANGUAGE="JavaScript">
   var vals = new Array();
   vals = window.showModalDialog("UserInfo.htm");
   if (vals != null) {
      strOut = "Returned values:";
      for (name in vals)
         strOut += "\n" + name + " = " + vals[name];
      alert(strOut);
   }
</SCRIPT>
```

The companion CD contains a complete set of these modal dialog box examples, listed together to allow easy comparison of the different dialog box types.

Size and Position of the Dialog Box

The size and position of the dialog box are exposed as four properties of the dialog box's window:

- *dialogLeft*
- *dialogTop*
- *dialogWidth*
- *dialogHeight*

These properties are specified in pixels and are read/write. In no case can the dialog box be sized smaller than 100-by-100 pixels or positioned off screen.

Creating Browsable Modal Dialog Boxes

A technique that can be used to work around the limitation that modal dialog boxes cannot be navigated is to display a quasidocument containing an IFrame element that references the real document to be displayed. The IFrame element creates a full instance of a browser. While this technique works, it should be used cautiously. It is not the purpose of a modal dialog box to permit the user to navigate out into the Web.

Window Features

When creating a new window using the *open* or *showModalDialog* method, you can specify a set of window features using the optional third parameter, *features*. The *features* string is a delimited list of values that turn on or off different aspects of the window. These values control the visual appearance of the window. The following two tables list the features available for these two methods.

The following features are available to the *window.open* method.

<table>
<tr><th>Feature</th><th>Values</th><th>Description</th></tr>
<tr><td>directories</td><td>[yes|no]|[1|0]</td><td>Displays a directories bar that provides quick links to various Web pages</td></tr>
<tr><td>height</td><td>pixels</td><td>Indicates the initial height of the browser window</td></tr>
<tr><td>left</td><td>pixels</td><td>Indicates the distance between the browser window and the left edge of the desktop</td></tr>
<tr><td>location</td><td>[yes|no]|[1|0]</td><td>Displays the address bar</td></tr>
<tr><td>menubar</td><td>[yes|no]|[1|0]</td><td>Displays the default menus (custom menus cannot currently be defined)</td></tr>
<tr><td>resizable</td><td>[yes|no]|[1|0]</td><td>Indicates whether the window is resizeable</td></tr>
<tr><td>scrollbars</td><td>[yes|no]|[1|0]</td><td>Displays the scrollbars for the document</td></tr>
<tr><td>status</td><td>[yes|no]|[1|0]</td><td>Displays the status bar at the bottom of the screen</td></tr>
<tr><td>toolbar</td><td>[yes|no]|[1|0]</td><td>Displays the toolbar</td></tr>
<tr><td>top</td><td>pixels</td><td>Indicates the distance between the browser window and the top of the desktop</td></tr>
<tr><td>width</td><td>pixels</td><td>Indicates the initial width of the browser window</td></tr>
</table>

The *window.showModalDialog* method supports a slightly different set of features for customizing the modal dialog box.

<table>
<tr><th>Feature</th><th>Values</th><th>Description</th></tr>
<tr><td>border</td><td>[thick|thin]</td><td>Specifies the thickness of the dialog box border</td></tr>
<tr><td>center</td><td>[yes|no]|[1|0]</td><td>Centers the dialog box</td></tr>
<tr><td>dialogHeight</td><td>CSS measurement</td><td>Indicates the initial height of the dialog box</td></tr>
<tr><td>dialogLeft</td><td>CSS measurement</td><td>Indicates the left position of the dialog box</td></tr>
<tr><td>dialogTop</td><td>CSS measurement</td><td>Indicates the top position of the dialog box</td></tr>
<tr><td>dialogWidth</td><td>CSS measurement</td><td>Indicates the initial width of the dialog box</td></tr>
</table>

(continued)

<table>
<tr><th>Feature</th><th>Values</th><th>Description</th></tr>
<tr><td>font</td><td>CSS font</td><td>Defines the default font for the dialog box</td></tr>
<tr><td>font-family</td><td>CSS font-family</td><td>Defines the default typeface for the dialog box</td></tr>
<tr><td>font-size</td><td>CSS font-size</td><td>Defines the default font size for the dialog box</td></tr>
<tr><td>font-style</td><td>CSS font-style</td><td>Defines the default font style for the dialog box</td></tr>
<tr><td>font-variant</td><td>CSS font-variant</td><td>Defines the default font variant for the dialog box</td></tr>
<tr><td>font-weight</td><td>CSS font-weight</td><td>Defines the default font weight for the dialog box</td></tr>
<tr><td>help</td><td>[yes|no]|[1|0]</td><td>Specifies whether to display a help icon on the title bar</td></tr>
<tr><td>maximize</td><td>[yes|no]|[1|0]</td><td>Specifies whether to display a maximize window button on the title bar</td></tr>
<tr><td>minimize</td><td>[yes|no]|[1|0]</td><td>Specifies whether to display a minimize window button on the title bar</td></tr>
</table>

Figure 5-1 illustrates some of the features available when you create a window using the *open* method.

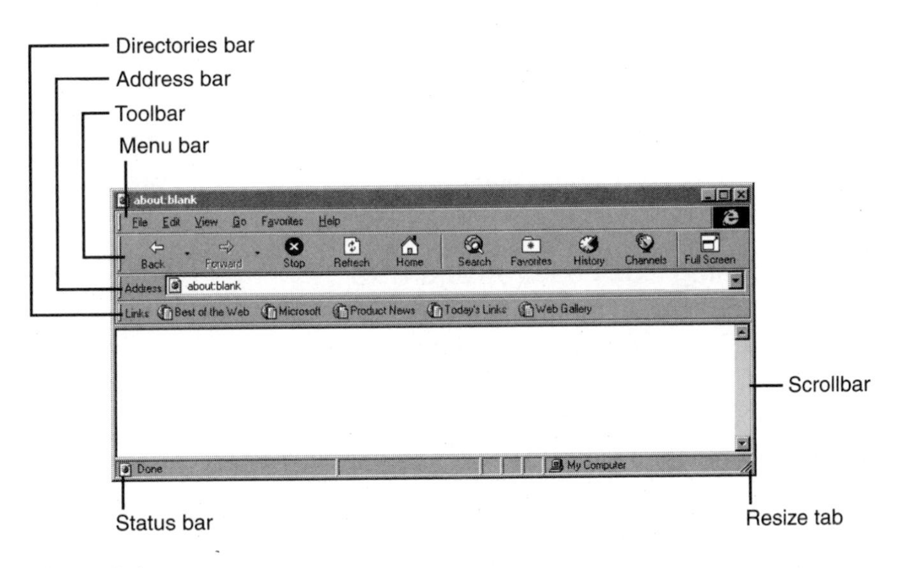

Figure 5-1.
Optional features of a window created using the open *method.*

The *features* String

Specifying a semicolon-delimited list of *feature-value* pairs creates the *features* string:

"[*feature* = *value* [; *feature2* = *value2*... [; *feature*n = *value*n]]]"

To create a window that does not display several of the browser features, use the following code:

```
window.open("example.htm", "example",
   "toolbar=no; location=no; menubar=no; status=no; directories=no");
```

For features that can be enabled or disabled, you can specify *yes* or *no* or *1* or *0,* or simply supply the parameter to turn on the feature. For example, all of the following statements turn on the *menubar* feature:

```
window.open("...", "...", "menubar=yes");
window.open("...", "...", "menubar=1");
window.open("...", "...", "menubar");
```

NOTE: If compatibility with existing browsers is required, use a comma-delimited list for the *open* method's *features* string. Semicolons are supported only by Internet Explorer 4.0.

Default Values

If you create a window with the *open* method but provide no *features* string, a default set of features is automatically provided. If you provide a *features* string that does not specify all of the features, unspecified features don't use the same defaults; rather, they use the settings on the original window. The *showModalDialog* method does not support any of the browser features such as toolbars and menu bars because the modal dialog box itself is not an instance of the browser. By default, modal dialog boxes are displayed with only a title bar, a status bar, a Close box, and a help icon.

Modal Dialog Box Features and CSS

Many of the features for the modal dialog box are closely related to CSS properties. This relationship is possible because a modal dialog box, unlike a modeless browser window, displays a single document that cannot be navigated.

The *font, font-size, font-weight, font-family, font-variant,* and *font-style* properties support the same values as the CSS properties of the same names. These properties and the dialog box position and size properties correspond directly to style sheet properties, and their values can be overridden by the document's style sheet.

For example, the size of the dialog box can be specified either by the page calling *showModalDialog* or by the HTML document displayed in the dialog box.

The page calling *showModalDialog* can use the *features* string to specify the size. The HTML document displayed in the dialog box can specify the size using the CSS *width* and *height* properties. This size overrides any size specified by the *showModalDialog* method. To create a dialog box that specifies its own size as 10-by-10 ems, use the style sheet shown in the following HTML page:

```
<HTML>
   <HEAD>
      <TITLE>10-by-10-Em Dialog Box</TITLE>
      <STYLE TYPE="text/css">
         HTML {width:10em; height:10em}
      </STYLE>
   </HEAD>
   <BODY>
      This example creates a 10-by-10-em dialog box. Ems are a
      relative unit that adapts well to different font sizes.
   </BODY>
</HTML>
```

The *opener* Property

When a window creates another window, the second window can access the first through its *opener* property. This property is read/write in Internet Explorer 4.0 and can be reassigned to another top-level window. This property was read-only in Internet Explorer 3.0. The *opener* property is useful for calling methods exposed by the window that created the new browser instance.

Closing a Window

Windows created using code can be closed using the object model. For security reasons, the user will be prompted if the code attempts to close the initial browser window. The *close* method is used to close the associated window:

```
window.close();  // Close the current window.
```

A user might close one window that is accessed or manipulated by a script in another window. For that reason, a closed window is not entirely destroyed; its *closed* property is still accessible to the user and to scripts. When you write code for one window that uses properties or methods of a second window, you should first check whether the second window still exists, as shown here:

```
// Check whether myWindow is closed.
if (!myWindow.closed) {
   // Code that executes if the window is open
}
else {
   // Error handler code if necessary
}
```

Creating a Window Manager

When a document in a browser creates another window, the only reference to the window is the variable returned by the *open* method. The object model does not expose a collection of open windows. Such a collection would be useful, for example, if you wanted to query for the existence of a particular window or to change the URL of a window.

The following code shows you how to implement your own *windows* collection containing references to all the windows your document has opened. This collection is analogous to the window's *frames* collection, which is discussed in the next section. However, due to the way variables work, the *windows* collection is accessible only for the lifetime of the document and is automatically cleared when the user navigates away from the page.

The code defines a method named *createWindow* that opens a window and adds a reference to it in the *windows* collection. Through this collection, you can query whether a window is open, change the contents, or close the window. When the document is unloaded, all windows created using *createWindow* are automatically closed.

```
<HTML>
   <HEAD>
      <TITLE>Window Manager</TITLE>
      <SCRIPT LANGUAGE="JavaScript">
         // Create an array to hold references to the child windows.
         /* Each member of this array will be a window object created
            using the createWindow method below. */
         var windows = new Array();

         function newWindow(url, wname) {
            // Constructor for the window
            /* This function should be called only by the createWindow
               function below. */
            var features = "";
            if (null != arguments[2])
               features = arguments[2];
            return window.open(url, wname, features);
         }

         function createWindow(url, wname) {
            // Add a window to the windows collection.
            var features = arguments[2] == null ? "" : arguments[2];
            windows[wname] = new newWindow(url, wname, features);
         }
```

```
      function closeWindows() {
         // Close all windows opened by addWindow.
         /* To close an individual window,
            its close method is called. */
         /* This function should be called during the onunload
            event to automatically close all open windows. */
         for (w in windows)
            if (!windows[w].closed)
               windows[w].close();
      }

      /* The following two functions demonstrate using the
         createWindow and closeWindows methods. */

      function listWindows() {
         // List the windows and their current states.
         var swin = "Window List\n";
         for (w in windows)
            swin += w + ":" +
               ((windows[w].closed) ? "Closed" : "Open") + "\n";
         alert(swin);
      }

      function openSampleWindows() {
         // Open two windows.
         createWindow("closeme.htm", "ChildWindow1");
         createWindow("closeme.htm", "ChildWindow2");
      }
   </SCRIPT>
</HEAD>
<BODY ONUNLOAD="closeWindows();">
   <H1>Window Manager</H1>
   <FORM>
      <INPUT TYPE=BUTTON ONCLICK="openSampleWindows();"
         VALUE="Add Windows">
      <INPUT TYPE=BUTTON ONCLICK="listWindows();"
         VALUE="List Windows">
      <INPUT TYPE=BUTTON ONCLICK="closeWindows();"
         VALUE="Close Windows">
   </FORM>
</BODY>
</HTML>
```

This window manager works well for named windows. If you create several windows using the *createWindow* method but pass empty strings for their names, the window manager will lose track of all but the most recently created window.

Manipulating Framesets

Framesets were first supported in Netscape Navigator 2.0 and Microsoft Internet Explorer 3.0. Framesets are a special type of HTML document used to divide a browser window into multiple regions called frames. Framesets are most commonly used to display a menu or other navigation mechanism in one frame and a document in another or to provide a nonscrollable header at the top of the page.

Figure 5-2 shows a frameset that displays four panes: a table of contents pane with information panes above and below it, and a document pane. The table of contents pane contains a list of anchors representing documents. When an anchor is clicked, the corresponding document is displayed in the right frame.

Figure 5-2.
Frameset with three frames on the left, including a table of contents, and a frame on the right containing a document.

This section first introduces the HTML elements for creating frameset documents and then describes the object model for manipulating them. Each frame is a distinct *window* object that can be accessed and referenced by other frames.

Authoring Framesets

The first step in creating a frameset is to determine the layout requirements. A frameset can divide a screen into any number of rectangular regions; each region contains its own HTML document.

The <FRAMESET> tag replaces the <BODY> tag in the HTML document and is used to split the screen. Within the Frameset element are <FRAME> tags that point each region to the individual document. Framesets can be nested to easily divide the screen into horizontal and vertical columns.

> NOTE: Internet Explorer 3.0 mixed the concepts of a frameset and a document with body contents even though these were intended to be independent concepts. In Internet Explorer 3.0, when a page consists of both a frameset and a body, the body is rendered as a frame behind the frameset. This behavior is no longer supported in Internet Explorer 4.0 and was never supported by Netscape Navigator and therefore should not be used.

The syntax for a frameset is shown here:

```
<FRAMESET COLS="..." ROWS="...">
    <FRAME SRC="..." NAME="...">
</FRAMESET>
```

The COLS and ROWS attributes take comma-delimited lists of measurements that are used to divide the screen. For example, the following frameset divides the screen into four equal regions:

```
<FRAMESET COLS="50%, 50%" ROWS="50%, 50%">
</FRAMESET>
```

When these measurements are not specified, the frameset contains one row and one column that take up the entire window.

To fill the regions with contents, the <FRAME> tag is used. The number of frames specified should be equal to the number of rows multiplied by the number of columns. In this example, the frameset should have four frames:

```
<FRAMESET COLS="50%, 50%" ROWS="50%, 50%">
   <FRAME SRC="f1.htm">
   <FRAME SRC="f2.htm">
   <FRAME SRC="f3.htm">
   <FRAME SRC="f4.htm">
</FRAMESET>
```

Frames in a frameset are populated across and then down. The preceding HTML code divides the browser into four regions containing HTML files, as shown in Figure 5-3.

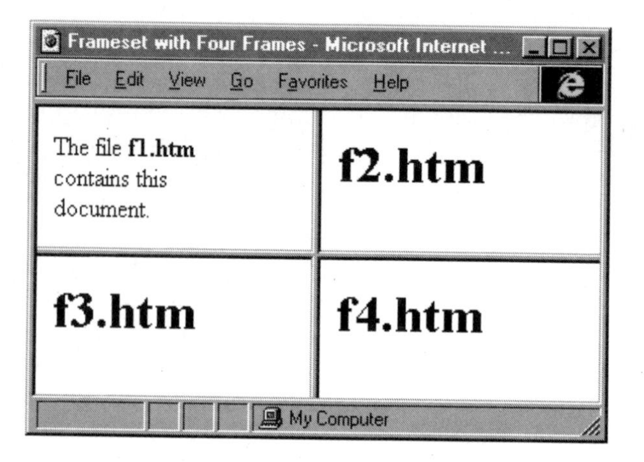

Figure 5-3.
Frameset with four frames.

There is no requirement that the number of frames match the specified number of rows and columns. If you provide too many Frame elements, the extra ones will be downloaded, but they will not be visible. If you provide too few Frame elements, some panes will appear without documents.

The following code demonstrates a technique that allows an extra frame to be supplied but not displayed. This frame can contain contents that are manipulated by custom code.

```
<FRAMESET COLS="50%, 50%">
   <FRAME SRC="f1.htm">
   <FRAME SRC="f2.htm">
   <FRAME SRC="hidden.htm">
</FRAMESET>
```

The frame containing hidden.htm is not displayed on the screen because the first two frames take up 100 percent of the screen real estate. Scripts or other contents that are being used for scripting purposes only might exist in hidden.htm.

Framesets can also be nested using two techniques: a single cell can be further subdivided into extra rows and columns by specifying another frameset, or a document loaded into a frame can itself contain a frameset that further divides the screen. To use the first technique in the example in Figure 5-3 to split the lower right region into two columns, create the following HTML code:

```
<FRAMESET COLS="50%, 50%" ROWS="50%, 50%">
   <FRAME SRC="f1.htm" NAME=f1>
   <FRAME SRC="f2.htm" NAME=f2>
   <FRAME SRC="f3.htm" NAME=f3>
   <FRAMESET COLS="50%, 50%">
      <FRAME SRC="f4.htm" NAME=f4>
      <FRAME SRC="f5.htm" NAME=f5>
   </FRAMESET>
</FRAMESET>
```

In this example, any one of the documents (f1.htm through f5.htm) can contain another frameset that further divides the window. When a document inside a frame contains another frameset, you can change the number and arrangement of your frames just by changing that document. This technique will be examined in more detail in the section "Targeting Frames" later in this chapter. With nested framesets, you can't change the arrangement of the frames as easily.

To create only rows or only columns, you need to supply only the ROWS or only the COLS attribute. More sophisticated control over the layout beyond percentage values for ROWS and COLS is also supported. The values supplied for each row or column can be a pixel measurement or an asterisk (*). The * is used to distribute the remaining space. To create a frameset in which the first column is 50 percent of the width of the screen, the second column is one-third of the remaining space, and the third column is the rest of the space, use the following code:

```
<FRAMESET COLS="50%, *, 2*">
   <FRAME SRC="f1.htm" NAME=f1>
   <FRAME SRC="f2.htm" NAME=f2>
   <FRAME SRC="f3.htm" NAME=f3>
</FRAMESET>
```

Fixing the Size and Scrollbars

By default, frames can be resized and have full support for scrolling. Two attributes can be added to a frame that fix the size and disable the scrollbars for the document: NORESIZE and SCROLLING. Specifying NORESIZE fixes the current size of the frame; SCROLLING has three valid values, as listed in the table on the following page.

Value	Description
auto	Displays scrollbars only if necessary
yes	Always displays scrollbars
no	Never displays scrollbars, even if the contents are clipped

The following code demonstrates a few of the different combinations available with the SCROLLING and NORESIZE attributes:

```
<FRAMESET COLS="50%, 50%" ROWS="50%, 50%">
   <FRAME SRC="f1.htm" NORESIZE>
   <FRAME SRC="f2.htm" SCROLLING="yes">
   <FRAME SRC="f3.htm" SCROLLING="no" NORESIZE>
   <FRAME SRC="f4.htm" SCROLLING="auto">
</FRAMESET>
```

Borderless Frames

Internet Explorer 3.0 and Netscape Navigator 3.0 introduced the ability to create borderless frames. Borderless frames seamlessly display multiple pages without any visual elements dividing the screen. This technique allows visually appealing documents to be easily constructed.

The BORDER attribute specifies the thickness of a border. Borderless frames are created by setting the BORDER attribute of the <FRAMESET> tag to *0* to make the borders invisible.

Three additional properties are available on the frameset that provide greater control over the borders. The FRAMEBORDER attribute specifies whether the border, if present, will be drawn as a three-dimensional frame. The FRAMESPACING attribute, like the BORDER attribute, sets the border thickness. The resulting border thickness will be the value of the FRAMESPACING attribute plus the thicknesses of the three-dimensional edges, if any. The BORDERCOLOR attribute defines the color of the frame border.

Supporting Down-Level Browsers

Browsers that do not support framesets will display an empty document when they attempt to load the page. To provide contents to an older client, HTML 4.0 defines the <NOFRAMES> tag. The NoFrames element can contain any valid body contents that will be ignored by frames-enabled browsers and displayed on any older clients. This technique works because the older clients do not understand the <FRAMESET>, <FRAME>, and <NOFRAMES> tags; they simply ignore these tags and display the contents of the NoFrames element.

Browsers that support framesets know to ignore the contents when they parse the NoFrames element. An example frameset document is shown here:

```
<HTML>
   <HEAD>
      <TITLE>Frameset Example</TITLE>
   </HEAD>
   <FRAMESET COLS="50%, 50%" ROWS="50%, 50%">
      <FRAME SRC="f1.htm">
      <FRAME SRC="f2.htm">
      <FRAME SRC="f3.htm">
      <FRAME SRC="f4.htm">
   </FRAMESET>
   <NOFRAMES>
      To view this Web site, please use a frames-enabled browser or
      click <A HREF="noframes.htm">here</A> for a no-frames version.
   </NOFRAMES>
</HTML>
```

It is a good idea to always provide no-frames comments in frameset documents. They can be as simple as the statement in the preceding code or as complex as an entire alternative Web page. The contents supplied in a NoFrames element can include anchors and any other valid HTML code. A minimal statement should be provided so that the user understands why the Web site is not working. Otherwise, a user with an older browser who sees no contents may choose to not come back to the Web site.

Another use of the NoFrames element is in the bodies of documents. For example, a frameset might provide a navigation bar next to a main document, but clients that do not support framesets will not display the bar when they display the main document. You can provide a simpler navigation bar in a NoFrames element in the main document, as shown in this example:

```
<HTML>
   <HEAD>
      <TITLE>Navigation Example</TITLE>
   </HEAD>
   <BODY>
      <NOFRAMES>
         <!-- These contents are displayed only in browsers without
              frameset support. Embed an alternative navigation bar
              below. -->
         <P>
            <A HREF="home.htm">Home Page</A>
            <A HREF="search.htm">Search Page</A>
         </P>
      </NOFRAMES>
```

(continued)

```
        Document's contents go here.
        <NOFRAMES>
           <!-- Add a message at the end of the document. -->
           <P>
              This page is best viewed with a frames-enabled browser.
        </NOFRAMES>
     </BODY>
</HTML>
```

This technique works correctly in Internet Explorer versions 3.0 and later. It does not work in Netscape Navigator because Navigator currently displays the contents of the NoFrames element when they exist in the body of the document.

Inline Frames

Internet Explorer versions 3.0 and later support the ability to create inline frames. An inline frame is contained within the body of a document instead of within a frameset and allows a single document to contain other, independent documents within the flow of the page. The inline frame is functionally similar to a frame in a frameset. It supports targeting and allows users to navigate within the frame, independent of the parent document.

Using an inline frame is similar to embedding an object using the <OBJECT> tag. The following two HTML statements both embed a document:

```
<IFRAME SRC="banner.htm" WIDTH=500 HEIGHT=500></IFRAME>
<OBJECT TYPE="text/html" DATA="banner.htm" WIDTH=500 HEIGHT=500>
   </OBJECT>
```

The primary difference between the two statements is that the IFrame element can later be targeted similar to a frame in a frameset. In general, the IFrame element should be used to define the navigable user interface within a page, and the Object element should be used to include contents. The two elements both embed banner.htm in the document, but only the IFrame element allows navigation within its own window.

The IFrame element is a container whose contents are ignored by browsers that support IFrame. Therefore, just as you can use the NoFrames element for non-frames-enabled browsers, you can specify alternative contents inside the IFrame element for browsers that do not support IFrame:

```
<IFRAME SRC="banner.htm" WIDTH=500 HEIGHT=500>
   <P>Your browser does not support IFrame.</P>
</IFRAME>
```

Adding Script Elements

Scripts in a frameset document must be defined in the Head element of the document prior to the first Frameset element, as shown below. Browsers may ignore scripts that appear within or after a Frameset element.

```
<HTML>
   <HEAD>
      <TITLE>With Framesets, Script Location Is Important</TITLE>
      <SCRIPT LANGUAGE="JavaScript">
         /* This script will execute because it occurs before the
            Frameset element. */
      </SCRIPT>
   </HEAD>
   <FRAMESET ROWS="*">
      <FRAME SRC="foo.htm">
      <SCRIPT LANGUAGE="JavaScript">
         // Scripts following the <FRAMESET> tag are ignored.
      </SCRIPT>
   </FRAMESET>
</HTML>
```

Targeting Frames

Naming a frame is similar to naming a window; the name is used to specify a target for a link. When an anchor targets a frame or window, it replaces the current contents of the frame or window with the new document. Only individual frames, including the frame containing the frameset itself, can be targeted. The replacement document can have any MIME type supported by the browser, including a frameset that further divides the screen. This provides a technique that gives the appearance that multiple frames are being updated simultaneously.

The simple frameset shown here divides the screen into two frames:

```
<HTML>
   <HEAD>
      <TITLE>Main Document</TITLE>
      <BASE TARGET="fContent">
   </HEAD>
   <FRAMESET COLS="300, *">
      <FRAME SRC="menu.htm" NAME="fMenu">
      <FRAME SRC="contents.htm" NAME="fContent">
   </FRAMESET>
</HTML>
```

The file contents.htm, shown next, appears in the right column and can itself be another frameset. When the user navigates, the right frame can be updated with a new document or an entirely new frameset definition.

```
<HTML>
   <HEAD>
      <TITLE>Contents</TITLE>
   </HEAD>
   <FRAMESET ROWS="20%, *">
      <FRAME SRC="welcome.htm">
      <FRAME SRC="home.htm">
   </FRAMESET>
</HTML>
```

Searching for a Targeted Frame

When you target a frameset, a specific algorithm is used to determine the resulting window for the document. This algorithm is important because multiple frames might share the same name. The location of a document with a specified target is determined by searching the set of named windows and frames.

If any of the predefined target keywords are specified, the document is displayed in that frame. For example, *_TOP* replaces the window with the new document, *_PARENT* replaces the parent frame, and *_SELF* replaces the current document. For any other target name, all frames, inline frames, and windows are searched in the following order:

1. The current frame
2. All subframes of the current frame, then all subframes of those subframes, and so on
3. The immediate parent of the current frame and then its subframes, the subframes of those subframes, and so on
4. The next immediate parent and all its subframes, and so on up the chain to the top-level window and its subframes
5. The named windows opened by the current window in an arbitrary order

If no match is found, a new window is opened as the target for the URL.

Scripting Framesets

Framesets are accessed and scripted through a *frames* collection that contains each frame defined by a frameset. The *frames* collection on a window contains all the child frames of the document. Each frame is a *window* object that exposes the same object model as a stand-alone window.

The *frames* collection is constructed based on the document hierarchy, not the visual hierarchy. Therefore, the visual hierarchy cannot be explicitly determined using the collection itself. For example, this HTML document divides the screen into two rows: the top row is a single frame, and the bottom row is divided into two columns.

```
<HTML>
   <HEAD>
      <TITLE>Nested Framesets in a Single Document</TITLE>
   </HEAD>
   <FRAMESET ROWS="50%, 50%">
      <FRAME SRC="top.htm" NAME="topRow">
      <FRAMESET COLS="50%, 50%">
         <FRAME SRC="bleft.htm" NAME="bottomLeft">
         <FRAME SRC="bright.htm" NAME="bottomRight">
      </FRAMESET>
   </FRAMESET>
</HTML>
```

The *frames* collection exposed for the window containing the preceding document orders the frames as follows:

topRow
bottomLeft
bottomRight

Even though the framesets are nested, the *frames* collection flattens them into source order.

If one of the documents referenced by a frameset contains another frameset, a document hierarchy results; each document defines its own children and each child window may further define more children. For example, suppose top.htm is a frameset document:

```
<HTML>
   <HEAD>
      <TITLE>Nested Document That Is a Frameset</TITLE>
   </HEAD>
   <FRAMESET COLS="40%, *">
      <FRAME SRC=tleft.htm NAME="nestLeft">
      <FRAME SRC=tright.htm NAME="nestRight">
   </FRAMESET>
</HTML>
```

The collections are now hierarchical because the document in the frame *topRow* contains a subsequent frameset that in turn contains two more documents:

topRow
  nestLeft
  nestRight
bottomLeft
bottomRight

The collection of the topmost document is still the same. However, drilling into the top frame returns a nested collection:

```
top.frames.length    // 3 frames: topRow, bottomLeft, bottomRight
top.frames["topRow"].frames.length // 2 frames: nestLeft and nestRight
top.frames["topRow"].frames["nestLeft"].length // 0: no children of
                                               // nestLeft
```

Frames as *window* Objects

Each frame in the *frames* collection is actually a *window* object. The set of properties exposed on each frame is the same as the set exposed by the top-level window. The *window* properties discussed in the rest of this section are therefore properties of frames.

Dynamic HTML exposes three related properties for referencing a window: *self*, *parent*, and *top*. The *self* property always returns the current window. The *parent* property returns the parent window in a frameset hierarchy. The *top* property returns a reference to the topmost window in the browser.

When the window is the topmost window, the *parent* property returns the current window. Therefore, when you write a loop that walks up the frameset hierarchy, the break case is when the current window equals the parent window, not when the parent window is *null*. The following code walks up the frameset hierarchy until the topmost window is reached:

```
var fParent = self;
while (fParent != fParent.parent) {
   fParent = fParent.parent;
}
```

Similar code determines whether the current window is the topmost window in the object hierarchy:

```
if (self == top) {
   // Top window; do something.
}
else {
   // Document is in a frameset; do something else.
}
```

The Implicit *frames* Collection

While the *frames* collection is exposed on the *window* object, it is not actually a distinct property. Instead, the *frames* object and the *window* object represent a single object. The existence of a *frames* property simplifies and helps disambiguate code.

The lack of distinction between objects is important. In JavaScript, whenever a property is added to the *window* object, it is also available through the *frames* collection and vice versa. Therefore, referencing the *frames* property is not required. For example, the following pairs of statements are equivalent:

```
// Specify number of frames.
window.length;
window.frames.length;

// Access the topRow frame.
window.topRow;
window.frames.topRow;

// Access the first frame in the collection.
window[0];
window.frames[0];
```

Although there is no real distinction between objects, it is good coding practice to use the *frames* collection when you explicitly refer to frame-related members and the *window* property when you are using properties on the current window. This practice helps self-document your code.

Defining Frame Contents

The contents of a frame are usually defined by a separate HTML document. The SRC attribute of a frame can contain literal HTML code. The advantage of putting HTML in a <FRAME> tag is that header frames can be defined inline, as shown here, without requiring an external URL. This technique is valuable in that it reduces the number of round-trips required to and from the server.

```
<HTML>
   <HEAD>
      <TITLE>JavaScript-Generated Frame</TITLE>
   </HEAD>
   <FRAMESET ROWS="80, *">
      <FRAME SRC="JavaScript:'<H1>Welcome to My Home Page</H1>'"
             NAME="header">
      <FRAME SRC="content.htm">
   </FRAMESET>
</HTML>
```

Supplying the initial contents for a frame has no effect on its ability to act as a target. This technique can be further generalized to most attributes that use an URL. For example, Chapter 9, "Scripting Individual Elements," demonstrates how to use JavaScript for the HREF attribute of an anchor. Alternatively, the *VBScript:* prefix can define the contents using VBScript.

Traversing the Frameset Hierarchy

The following code visually demonstrates the document hierarchy for any frameset. This code walks the window hierarchy in a specified browser instance and outputs the document containership hierarchy.

```
<HTML>
   <HEAD>
      <TITLE>Frameset Hierarchy</TITLE>
   </HEAD>
   <FRAMESET ROWS="60, *">
      <FRAME SRC="frames.htm">
      <FRAME SRC="anyDocument.htm" NAME="hierarchy">
   </FRAMESET>
</HTML>
```

The preceding file is a top-level frameset. In the bottom frame, it displays the document to be analyzed (anyDocument.htm, but you can substitute any document you want). In the top frame, it displays the document frames.htm, listed next, which consists of a button and JavaScript code. When you click the button, the code creates a separate window showing the document hierarchy. This example is included on the companion CD.

```
<HTML>
   <HEAD>
      <TITLE>Frameset Hierarchy Generator</TITLE>
      <SCRIPT LANGUAGE="JavaScript">
         function drillFrames(doc, w) {
            doc.write("<TR><TD>Name: " + w.name + "<BR>");
            doc.write("Location: " + w.location.href);
            for (var i = 0; i < w.frames.length; i++) {
               doc.write("<TABLE BORDER WIDTH=100% CELLPADDING=3>");
               drillFrames(doc, w.frames[i]);
               doc.write("</TABLE>");
            }
            doc.write("</TD></TR>");
         }

         function outputFrames() {
            var doc = window.open().document;
            doc.open();
            doc.write("<H1>Frameset Hierarchy</H1>");
            doc.write("<TABLE BORDER CELLPADDING=3>");
            // Start at the sibling frame in the hierarchy.
            drillFrames(doc, parent.hierarchy);
            doc.write("</TABLE>");
            doc.close();
         }
```

```
      </SCRIPT>
   </HEAD>
   <BODY>
      <FORM>
         <INPUT TYPE=BUTTON VALUE="Walk" ONCLICK="outputFrames();">
      </FORM>
   </BODY>
</HTML>
```

Determining the Layout of the Frameset

The *frames* collection exposes the document hierarchy in the browser; it does not expose the physical divisions of each frameset. This information is exposed through the *document* object. The *document* object has an *all* collection, which represents every element in the document. Using the *all* collection, you can determine the order of the framesets and frames. The *document* object and the *all* collection are discussed in Part II. Programming the Frameset element is discussed in Chapter 9, "Scripting Individual Elements."

Determining Whether All Frames Have Been Downloaded

Framesets also expose an *onload* event on the frameset window. The *onload* event occurs when all the frames within the frameset finish loading. Therefore, any initialization that requires communicating across the frames in the frameset should be written in this event handler.

In addition, the frameset document exposes a property that can be used to query the current state of each frame and window: *readyState.* While each frame is being loaded, this property's value is *interactive,* and when all the frames have been downloaded, its value is *complete.* The *readyState* property can be used as a flag to verify that all the frames have been downloaded. The *readyState* property and the related *onreadystatechange* event are discussed in detail in Chapter 6, "The HTML Document."

Simulating a Browser

The code in this section shows how to create a very simple browser using framesets. This HTML document sets up the frameset:

```
<HTML>
   <TITLE>Frameset Browser Demo</TITLE>
   <FRAMESET ROWS="60, *">
      <FRAME NAME="browser" SRC="browser.htm">
      <FRAME NAME="content" SRC="">
   </FRAMESET>
</HTML>
```

The following document represents the browser.htm file that is rendered in the top frame. The top frame contains Go and Refresh buttons and a text box in which the user types the URL. A Forward and a Back button are included for moving through the history list. These buttons simulate the same functionality found on most browsers' toolbars:

```
<HTML>
   <HEAD>
      <TITLE>Browser Bar</TITLE>
   </HEAD>
   <BODY>
      <FORM NAME="BrowseBar" ONSUBMIT="parent.content.location.href =
            this.txtGo.value; return false;">
         <INPUT TYPE=BUTTON VALUE="Back"
            ONCLICK="parent.content.history.back();">
         <INPUT TYPE=BUTTON VALUE="Forward"
            ONCLICK="parent.content.history.forward();">
         <INPUT TYPE=BUTTON VALUE="Refresh"
            ONCLICK="parent.content.location.reload();">
         <INPUT TYPE=SUBMIT VALUE="Go">
         <INPUT TYPE=TEXT NAME="txtGo">
      </FORM>
   </BODY>
</HTML>
```

NOTE: Browser security restrictions might prevent the Forward and Back buttons in this code from navigating if the documents involved are in different domains.

In this example, the controls are placed within a Form element to ensure compatibility with Netscape Navigator 2.0 and 3.0, which fail to render any controls that are not inside Form elements. Internet Explorer versions 3.0 and later do not have this limitation and can display and script controls even if they exist outside of forms.

Special Event Considerations

Using JavaScript function pointers, you can assign an event handler in one frame or a browser to an event property in another. This powerful technique allows easy sharing of code between documents; however, it also adds complexity.

The *event* object is tightly related to the window that fired the event. Therefore, even though an event handler might be located in a document in another frame, the *event* object of the frame that generated the event must be used, which requires walking the object hierarchy from the element that generated the event to the *event* object.

While this technique allows you to write flexible and powerful code, it is limited by the security model in the browser. For example, a page cannot assign event handlers to the events of a frame or browser window that contains a document from another domain. Without this restriction, a rogue page could hook the keyboard events and track the entry of confidential information. Furthermore, once the user navigates away from a page, all the event handlers are detached. This is consistent with the Dynamic HTML object model, in which a new page is always provided with an entirely fresh state.

The function assignment method is the most efficient way to hook events in another frame; it does not require the creation of an extra function handler. However, this technique allows access only to the element generating the event:

```
<SCRIPT LANGUAGE="JavaScript">
   function doClick() {
      /* This is the event handler for the click event of the
         document in window2. */
      /* The event object cannot be accessed directly using
         the current window's event object. Instead,
         window2's event object must be accessed.
         The this pointer passed in points to the document
         that generated the event. */
      with (this.document.parentWindow.event) {
         // Use the event object.
      }
   }

   var window2 = window.open("sample.htm");
   /* Bind the event handler of window2 to the
      doClick function in this document. */
   window2.body.onclick = doClick;
</SCRIPT>
```

Scripting events across frames is the basis of the Event Tutor example in Chapter 3, "Dynamic HTML Event Model." The Event Tutor works by dynamically hooking the events of the sample document and outputting strings in the current window.

// Create property x
var x = 10;
// This code is not
code
var y =
alert(
// output
// Call foo while
foo();
</SCRIPT>

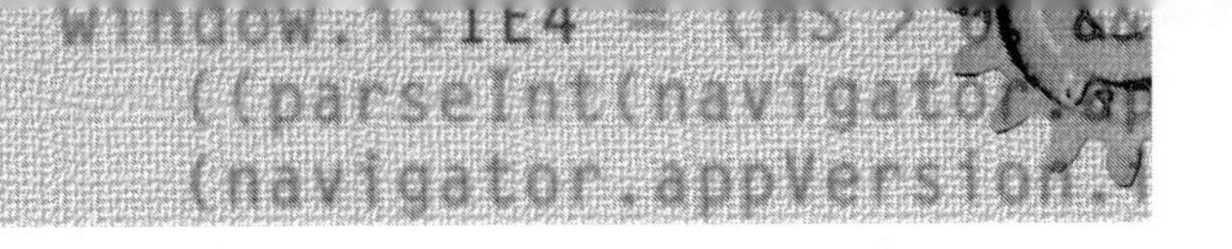

P A R T I I

DOCUMENT STRUCTURE

Create
code
output
// Call
foo();
</SCRIPT>

CHAPTER SIX

The HTML Document

The structure, contents, and style of an HTML document are exposed through the *document* property on the window. The *document* property references an object that encapsulates all the information about the document. The *document* object is the most important and powerful object of the Dynamic HTML object model. Through this object, all elements contained in the document can fire events and can be accessed and modified by scripts, allowing you to create a dynamic document.

The elements in the HTML document are exposed through the collections on the *document* object. The contents of the document are accessible through these elements and through a *TextRange* object. Both techniques allow you to access and change the contents. The style of the document is exposed through the *styleSheets* collection, which provides access to the global and linked style sheets associated with the document.

Our discussion of these issues will span several chapters. This chapter begins the discussion by covering the following topics:

- **Referencing the *document* object** The *document* object is a property of the window. This section shows you how to access the HTML document contained within the current window as well as documents displayed in other windows.
- **Changing the document's colors** The *document* object exposes properties for manipulating the color of the text and background on the page. These properties are compatible with the existing object model implementations in Netscape Navigator and Microsoft Internet Explorer 3.0.
- **Accessing meta information about the document** Information derived while the document is downloaded is exposed to the object model. This meta information includes the initial file size of the

document and the dates when the file was created and last modified. In addition, any cookies associated with the document can be retrieved or assigned.

- **Modifying the HTML stream** The *document* object exposes methods for manipulating the HTML stream while the page is loading. These methods work only while a page is rendering and are not used to modify a page once it is loaded—separate objects and methods are exposed for this purpose.

Figure 6-1 shows the *document* object and the collections it contains. Next to each collection is the tag for the HTML elements it contains.

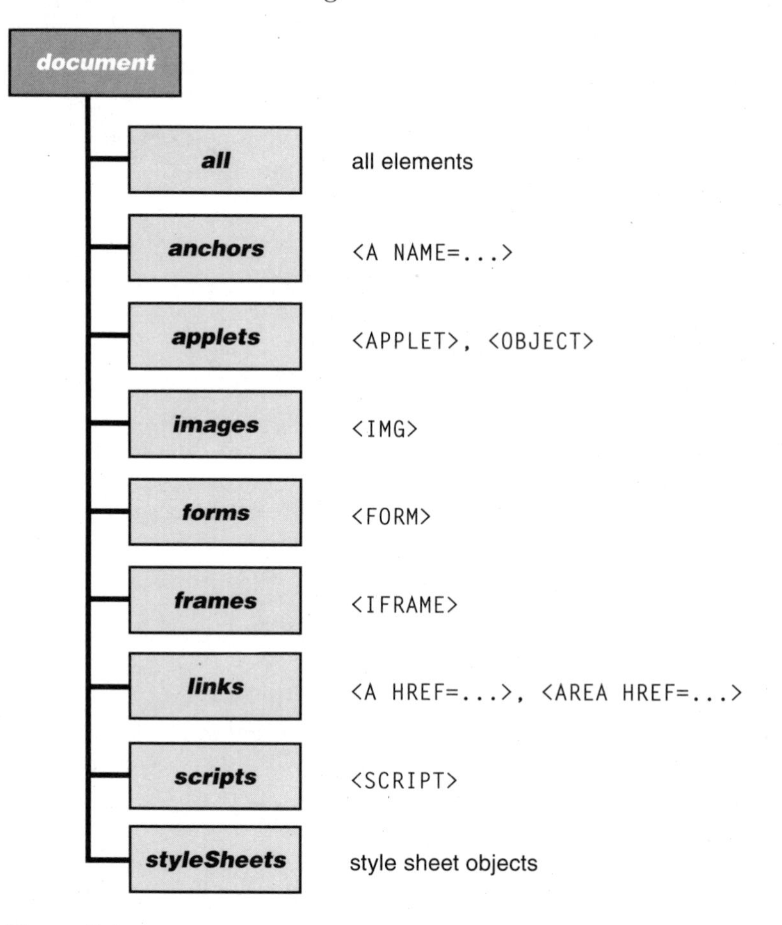

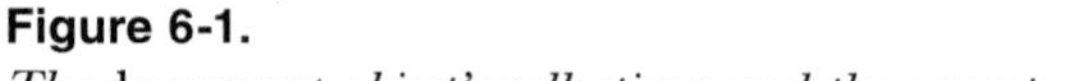

Figure 6-1.
The document *object's collections and the corresponding HTML elements.*

Referencing the *document* Object

The *document* object is referenced as a property of the *window* object. If you reference a document without specifying which window it is in, you get the current document. Each of the following examples references a document to get its title:

```
document.title          // Current document's title
window.document.title   // Same as above but explicitly references
                        // current window
myPlace.document.title  // Title of document in the window myPlace
```

The *myPlace* reference in this example must be a window reference returned by the *open* method or the name of a frame in the current frameset hierarchy.

Regardless of whether the current window contains a frameset or an HTML document, the *document* object is fully exposed. For security reasons, some properties may not be accessible across domains. For example, the contents of a document are accessible only to pages that share the document's domain.

Changing the Document's Colors

One of the simplest operations you can perform on a document is to change the colors of the background and the text. The *document* object exposes properties that define the colors of the background, the text, and the links.

The color properties available on the document are *alinkColor*, *bgColor*, *fgColor*, *linkColor*, and *vlinkColor*. The *bgColor* property controls the color of the document's background, and the *fgColor* property controls the default color of the text.

The three link color properties represent the colors of the active, visited, and unvisited links. *Link* is an ambiguous term—in this case, it refers to an Anchor element that has an HREF attribute set:

```
<A HREF="myPage.HTM">This is a link.</A>
```

The active link is the link that has the focus and is normally indicated by a change in color combined with a pale dotted border. A visited link is a link that the user has recently visited, and an unvisited link is a link that has not yet been followed.

Setting the document's properties directly is only one way to control the document's colors. You can also set the colors using attributes in the <BODY> tag or style sheets. If you use the <BODY> tag or style sheet attributes, your code will be more encapsulated, but the color properties on the *document* object are supported by more browsers.

The following table lists the color properties and their corresponding <BODY> tag attributes.

Property	Attribute
alinkColor	ALINK
bgColor	BGCOLOR
fgColor	TEXT
linkColor	LINK
vlinkColor	VLINK

Style sheets have a higher priority in setting colors than the document's properties or the <BODY> tag's attributes. The document's properties will always reflect the colors shown on the screen. If the color is set using a style sheet, assignments to the document's color properties will be ignored.

Valid Color Values

All the color properties, including those exposed on elements, take a literal string representing the color name or an RGB hex value. A list of the valid string names and their hexadecimal equivalents can be found on the companion CD. RGB hex values are specified in the following format:

```
#RRGGBB
```

R, *G*, and *B* stand for the red, green, and blue channels; each channel accepts a valid hexadecimal value in the range 0 through #FF.

When you access the value of one of these properties on the document or on an HTML element, you always get a hexadecimal number, even if you initially supplied a string. For example, a property set with the string *Red* returns *#FF0000*. However, the CSS (Cascading Style Sheets) properties retain values as supplied, so a style property set to *red* returns *red*.

Scenario: Color Selector

A large number of color names are now available in HTML. The colors that these names represent are often difficult to decipher, and determining what colors go well together can be a complex task. The following code helps by providing a color selector that sets the background and text colors. All aspects of the color selector are encapsulated in the Div element, so the color selector and its scripts can easily be moved and run unchanged in other HTML documents.

```
<HTML>
   <HEAD>
      <TITLE>HTML-Based Color Selector</TITLE>
      <STYLE TYPE="text/css">
         TABLE {background:white}
         /* Make all cells a uniform size. */
         TD {width:30pt; height:30pt; cursor:default}
      </STYLE>
   </HEAD>
   <BODY>
      <H1>Color Selector</H1>

      <!-- When the user clicks on the cell, the screen is redrawn
           with the corresponding background or text color. -->
      <DIV ONCLICK="colorSelector()">
         <SCRIPT LANGUAGE="JavaScript">
            function colorSelector() {
               // Based on the table, change to the correct color.
               // srcElement is the element the user clicked on.
               if ("TD" == event.srcElement.tagName)
                  if (document.all.Text.contains(event.srcElement))
                     document.fgColor = event.srcElement.bgColor;
                  else if (document.all.Background.contains(
                        event.srcElement))
                     document.bgColor = event.srcElement.bgColor;
            }
         </SCRIPT>

         <!-- To extend these tables, add cells to the background
              and/or the text color tables. Each cell consists of a
              background color only, set appropriately. -->
         <TABLE ID="Background" BORDER>
            <CAPTION>Background Color</CAPTION>
            <TR>
               <TD BGCOLOR=Black></TD><TD BGCOLOR=Red></TD>
               <TD BGCOLOR=Green></TD><TD BGCOLOR=LightBlue></TD>
               <TD BGCOLOR=Yellow></TD>
            </TR>
            <TR>
               <TD BGCOLOR=YellowGreen></TD><TD BGCOLOR=Orange></TD>
               <TD BGCOLOR=Navy></TD><TD BGCOLOR=Magenta></TD>
               <TD BGCOLOR=Brown></TD>
            </TR>
            <TR>
               <TD BGCOLOR=Black></TD><TD BGCOLOR=Blue></TD>
               <TD BGCOLOR=Burlywood></TD><TD BGCOLOR=Gold></TD>
               <TD BGCOLOR=Cyan></TD>
```

(continued)

```
            </TR>
         </TABLE>
         <TABLE ID="Text" BORDER>
            <CAPTION>Text Color</CAPTION>
            <TR>
               <TD BGCOLOR=Black></TD><TD BGCOLOR=Red></TD>
               <TD BGCOLOR=Green></TD><TD BGCOLOR=LightBlue></TD>
               <TD BGCOLOR=Brown></TD>
            </TR>
            <TR>
               <TD BGCOLOR=White></TD><TD BGCOLOR=Blue></TD>
               <TD BGCOLOR=Burlywood></TD><TD BGCOLOR=Gold></TD>
               <TD BGCOLOR=Cyan></TD>
            </TR>
         </TABLE>
      </DIV>
   </BODY>
</HTML>
```

The color selector works by enclosing the two tables in a DIV element and using event bubbling to detect all click events. When the user clicks in the DIV element, the click event handler checks whether the click occurred in a cell of one of the two tables. If the click occurred in a cell, the event handler first determines whether the cell is in the background table or text table and then changes the corresponding document color to match the color of the clicked cell.

The preceding code contains only a subset of the available colors, but the selection can easily be expanded by simply adding extra cells to either the background color or the text color table.

Reflecting HTML Attributes as Properties

The attributes of all HTML elements in a document are exposed as properties in the object model. You can set an attribute in an HTML tag, or you can set the corresponding property. If you do both, the assignment specified through script is the one that is displayed. For example, the script in the following code sets the background color to *Red*; subsequently setting the corresponding attribute in the <BODY> tag to *Blue* fails to change the color:

```
<HTML>
   <SCRIPT LANGUAGE="JavaScript">
      document.bgColor = "Red";
   </SCRIPT>
   <BODY BGCOLOR="Blue">
      The page background is red.
   </BODY>
</HTML>
```

Accessing Meta Information About the Document

In addition to providing access to the contents of the document, Dynamic HTML exposes information that is derived from the document while it is downloading. This meta information includes the initial file size of the document and the dates it was created, last modified, and last cached. Date information can be used to determine the age of the document to enable scripts to warn the user if the contents are out of date.

The document also exposes information about the client's cookies. Cookies are somewhat controversial because they allow a Web site to store a small piece of information on the client's machine that can later be referenced and updated by the site. This information is restricted in that the data can be accessed only by the Web sites that created the data.

While not really meta information, information about the state of any embedded object—including whether the downloading of the document or object is complete—is also exposed by the document. This information is essential when you are writing scripts that might execute before the page is completely available.

File Size

The document exposes a *fileSize* property that returns the initial size of the document in kilobytes. The returned value represents the number of bytes in the file that was downloaded and doesn't reflect any changes that scripts might have made to the document.

Title

The *title* property of the document is assigned a value in the HTML Head element as follows:

```
<HTML>
   <HEAD>
      <TITLE>Document Title</TITLE>
   </HEAD>
</HTML>
```

The title contains standard text; it cannot contain HTML. The document's *title* property returns the contents of the Title element as a string. You can assign a new value to this string to change the title displayed in the title bar. On windowed systems, the title is usually rendered as the window caption.

> NOTE: Netscape Navigator 3.0 and Internet Explorer 3.0 generate an error when a page attempts to assign a value to the *title* property. Internet Explorer 4.0 exposes this property as read/write.

Source Location

The document exposes two properties that represent the source location for the page: *location* and *URL*. The *location* property on the document is an alias for the window's *location* property—both return objects that expose the same set of properties. Chapter 4, "The Browser Window," discusses the window's *location* property in detail.

The document's *URL* property is an alias to the *href* property on the *location* object. It is exposed for compatibility with earlier browsers. The *location* property on the window or document is useful for determining and changing the currently displayed page.

Date

Three dates are relevant for any document: the date the document was initially created, the date the document was last updated by the author, and the date the document was last downloaded into the cache. This information is exposed through the following properties on the document:

- *fileCreatedDate*
- *fileModifiedDate* or *lastModified*
- *fileUpdatedDate*

The *fileCreatedDate* property is self-explanatory. The remaining properties are described in the sections that follow.

The *fileModifiedDate* and *lastModified* Properties

The *fileModifiedDate* and *lastModified* properties both contain the date the document was last modified. The value of either property can be combined with information stored in the *cookie* property to check whether the document has changed since the user's last visit. Internet Explorer 3.0 and Netscape Navigator support the *lastModified* property, but they do not support *fileModifiedDate*. Internet Explorer 4.0 supports the new variation to maintain name consistency with the other meta information that is newly exposed in Dynamic HTML.

The following code outputs the date a file was last modified:

```
<HTML>
   <HEAD>
      <TITLE>Last Modified Date</TITLE>
   </HEAD>
   <BODY>
      <P>Last Modified:
         <SCRIPT LANGUAGE="JavaScript">
            document.write(document.lastModified);
```

```
      </SCRIPT>
    </P>
  </BODY>
</HTML>
```

The *write* method is used to write into the stream of the document while the page is loaded. This technique is discussed in greater detail in the section "Writing HTML into the Stream" later in this chapter.

The *fileUpdatedDate* Property

During browsing, files may become cached on the local user's machine. The *fileUpdatedDate* property returns the date the file was last updated from the server. Using this property, you can write code that notifies the user if he or she is using a page that has existed in the cache for more than a specified amount of time:

```
<HTML>
  <HEAD>
    <TITLE>fileUpdatedDate Example</TITLE>
    <SCRIPT LANGUAGE="JavaScript">
      /* Number of days that can elapse before
         a new page is requested. */
      var intAge = 7;

      // Be sure there is an updated date.
      if ("" != document.fileUpdatedDate) {
         var dCreate = new Date(document.fileUpdatedDate);
         var dToday = new Date();
         /* Calculate number of days elapsed. getTime
            returns the number of milliseconds between
            midnight (GMT) on 1/1/1970 and the supplied
            date and time. */
         var intDays = Math.floor((dToday.getTime()
            - dCreate.getTime()) / (1000 * 60 * 60 * 24));
         if (intAge < intDays)
            if (confirm("Your cached page is " + intDays +
               " day(s) old.\n"
               + "Do you want to download a new page?"))
               // Force a reload from the server.
               location.reload(true);
      }
    </SCRIPT>
  </HEAD>
  <BODY>
    Document contents
  </BODY>
</HTML>
```

MIME Type

The *mimeType* property returns the document's MIME type. For all HTML documents (including framesets), the *mimeType* property returns the value *Internet Document (HTML).*

Cookies

An HTML page has the ability to save a small amount of information in a special file on the client's machine. This information is called a cookie. Many people consider cookies to be a potential security risk because cookies allow a page to write to the hard disk; browsers offer a way to disable this functionality. For this reason, no page should be written with the assumption that cookies are available. When they are supported, however, cookies are useful for maintaining state information used by multiple pages on the same site.

Assigning a value to a cookie is different from retrieving the value. This section shows you how to use cookies and provides helper functions for manipulating them. At the end of the section is a demonstration of using a cookie to create a client-side visit counter.

> NOTE: Internet Explorer 3.0 did not allow cookies to be modified when the page was accessed using the *file:* protocol. This limitation was removed in Internet Explorer 4.0.

Reading the Cookie

Multiple cookies can be associated with a single document or domain. When the *cookie* property is read, all the cookies associated with the document are returned as a semicolon-delimited list of name-value pairs. Therefore, a routine is needed that can parse a list of cookies. JavaScript exposes some useful methods for easily splitting delimited lists into arrays. The following function uses these methods to parse the cookie string and return it as an array of name-value pairs:

```
<SCRIPT LANGUAGE="JavaScript">
   function parseCookie() {
      // Separate each cookie.
      var cookieList = document.cookie.split("; ");
      // Array for each cookie in cookieList
      var cookieArray = new Array();
      for (var i = 0; i < cookieList.length; i++) {
         // Separate name-value pairs.
         var name = cookieList[i].split("=");
         // Decode and add to cookie array.
         cookieArray[unescape(name[0])] = unescape(name[1]);
      }
      return cookieArray;
```

```
   }
</SCRIPT>
```

The following code demonstrates how to use the cookie array that *parseCookie* returns:

```
var cookie;
var cookies = parseCookie();
// Output each cookie.
for (cookie in cookies)
   alert(cookie + "=" + cookies[cookie]);
// Check whether a cookie named foo exists.
if (null == cookies.foo) {
   // No cookie named foo
}
```

The name-value pairs you assign to cookies cannot contain white spaces, commas, or semicolons. Any such characters must be replaced with appropriate escape sequences. JavaScript provides two convenient functions that handle escape sequences for you: *escape*, for replacing characters by escape sequences in a string before assigning it to a cookie, and *unescape*, for reversing the operation when retrieving the cookie.

A stored cookie also contains expiration date, path, domain, and security information. You can supply this information when you create a cookie, but you can't retrieve it. This is one of the differences between assigning values to a cookie and retrieving the cookie.

Writing a Cookie

The *cookie* property takes a string value in the following format:

name=*value*; [expires=*date*; [path=*path*; [domain=*domain* [*secure*;]]]]

The name-value pair is the only required parameter when you assign information to the cookie. The name can be any valid string with which to associate a value. Supplying a name-value pair without any of the additional information creates a cookie that lasts only for the length of the current browser session. For example, the following code creates a simple cookie that stores the time and date a page was loaded:

```
<SCRIPT LANGUAGE="JavaScript">
   var strLoaded = new Date();
   document.cookie = "Loaded=" + escape(strLoaded);
</SCRIPT>
```

Assigning another value to the cookie does not necessarily overwrite the cookie—it overwrites the cookie only if you use the same name. In the preceding example, the name *Loaded* would be reused each time the page was loaded. In the following example, adding a new name adds a new entry to the cookie.

```
<SCRIPT LANGUAGE="JavaScript">
   document.cookie = "First=Hello;";
   document.cookie = "Second=Hello;";
   alert(document.cookie);    // First=Hello; Second=Hello
</SCRIPT>
```

To force a cookie to be deleted, you must specify an expiration date. To delete a cookie, create a new cookie using an existing name and any arbitrary value, but assign an expiration date that has already passed. When you use this technique, the cookie might not be immediately removed—it might remain until the current instance of the browser is shut down.

The expiration date must be specified in GMT in the following format:

wkd, day Mon Year hh:mm:ss GMT

For example, the following date has this format:

```
Sat, 28 Sep 1998 19:01:05 GMT
```

In JavaScript, the easiest way to convert to GMT is to use the *toGMTString* method exposed on the *Date* object.

If you set an expiration date in the future, the cookie will remain on the client's machine until it expires. There is no guarantee that supplying an expiration date will keep the cookie around because there is a limit to how many cookies the client can store and the user may at any time delete the cookie file.

By default, all cookies are saved with a path and domain, even if these settings are not specified explicitly. This is how security is maintained on the cookie. A cookie is accessible only to the path and domain that created it. Furthermore, when you create a cookie, you cannot specify an arbitrary domain. This restriction eliminates the possibility of secretly transferring information from one domain to another. However, multiple pages from the same domain can share a single cookie.

Using the Cookie

A cookie can be used to create custom pages for the user. The following code demonstrates how to use a cookie to count the number of times the user has visited a Web page. The code uses the *parseCookie* function introduced earlier.

```
<HTML>
   <HEAD>
      <TITLE>Cookie Counter</TITLE>
   </HEAD>
   <BODY>
      <SCRIPT LANGUAGE="JavaScript">
         // This code requires the parseCookie function.
```

```
      function setCookie(visits) {
         /* This routine sets up the cookie by setting its value
            to the number of visits and setting its expiration date
            to 1 year from now. */
         var expireDate = new Date();
         var today = new Date();
         // Set an expiration date in the future.
         expireDate.setDate(365 + expireDate.getDate());

         // Save the number of visits.
         document.cookie = "Visits=" + visits + "; expires=" +
            expireDate.toGMTString() + ";";

         // Save today's time and date as the last visit.
         document.cookie = "LastVisit=" +
            escape(today.toGMTString()) +
            "; expires=" + expireDate.toGMTString() + ";";
      }

      if ("" == document.cookie) {
         // Initialize the cookie.
         setCookie(1);
         document.write("<H2>This is your first visit to our " +
            "humble home page.</H2>");
      }
      else {
         // Parse the cookie.
         var cookies = parseCookie();

         // Output the Welcome Back message, and increment the
         // visit counter.
         document.write("<H2>Welcome Back! You have visited us " +
            cookies.Visits++ + " time(s)!</H2>");
         document.write("<H3>Your last visit was on " +
            cookies.LastVisit + ".</H3>");
         // Replace existing cookie with an updated one.
         setCookie(cookies.Visits);
      }
    </SCRIPT>
  </BODY>
</HTML>
```

Parent Window

Just as you can navigate from the window to the document, you can navigate from the document back to its containing window. The window containing the document is exposed through the *parentWindow* property. This property is useful for determining the containing object when only the *document* object is available.

Two additional properties are available for accessing the window from the document: *Script* and *frames*. The *Script* property is exposed for backward compatibility with Internet Explorer 3.0 and should no longer be used. The *frames* property returns a collection of inline frames in the document. This *frames* collection returns the window because it is an alias to the window's *frames* collection, which in turn is an alias to the *window* object. Manipulating collections is discussed in more detail in Chapter 7, "Document Element Collections." To clarify the relationships between these properties, the following code demonstrates several ways of returning the same *window* object:

```
window == self == window.frames == frames ==
   window.document.parentWindow == window.document.Script ==
   window.document.frames
```

Document Availability

As it loads, a document or an embedded object progresses through four states: uninitialized, loading, interactive, and complete. The object's *readyState* property contains the object's current state. When the object changes state, it fires an *onreadystatechange* event. By using these tools in your scripts, you can make your page behave appropriately for the states of the document and embedded objects and react to changes in states. Most important, your code can avoid accessing objects that haven't completely downloaded.

The following table describes the states that the document and embedded objects progress through.

State	Description
uninitialized	The page or object is not yet initialized. Once it starts loading, it immediately progresses to the loading state.
loading	The page or object is currently being loaded.
interactive	The user can interact with the page or object even though it is still loading—for example, anchors may be live and loaded elements may begin to fire events.
complete	The page or object is entirely loaded.

When the document begins loading, it immediately progresses to the loading state. It progresses to the interactive state when the browser encounters the first Script, Body, or Frameset element. The document progresses to the complete state when the entire document is parsed and all embedded objects are loaded.

The *readyState* Property

The document's *readyState* property contains the current state of the document as a string. Each embedded object has its own *readyState* property reflecting its own status.

Because a document will be in the interactive state before any of its scripts execute, the only *readyState* values its scripts will obtain are *interactive* and *complete*. A script in another frame or window might obtain a value of *loading*; this will happen if the script accesses the document's *readyState* property during the parsing of the document's Head element and before any scripts in the Head element have been encountered. Any script might obtain any of the four values as the *readyState* of an embedded object.

JavaScript event handlers are hooked up asynchronously during the parsing of the page. Such a handler might execute before the entire page is loaded. If the handler performs operations that require the page to be fully downloaded, it can test the document's *readyState* property before proceeding, as shown in the following example:

```
<SCRIPT LANGUAGE="JavaScript" EVENT="onclick" FOR="window">
   if ("complete" == document.readyState) {
      // Handle the event.
   }
   else
      alert("This action is not available until the document " +
         "finishes downloading.");
</SCRIPT>
```

Alternatively, the handler can test the *readyState* properties of only those elements it needs to access.

VBScript event handlers are hooked up as a last step before the document progresses to the complete state. Therefore, handlers written in VBScript don't need to test the document's *readyState*—except, of course, if a handler accesses elements in another document.

The *onreadystatechange* Event

The *onreadystatechange* event fires whenever the state of the document or of an embedded object changes. Each of these events can fire multiple times during the downloading of a document or an element.

If you bind a handler to the document's *onreadystatechange* event, the handler will not be hooked up until the document is already in the interactive state. Your handler will be called only once—namely, for the document's transition to the complete state. In this situation, the *onreadystatechange* event is essentially an alias for the window's *onload* event, and the two can be used interchangeably. Because Internet Explorer 4.0 is the only browser currently supporting *onreadystatechange*, you can use this event if you want to exclude other browsers; you can use the *onload* event if you want cross-browser execution.

Embedded objects in the document also fire the *onreadystatechange* event. For example, the Object and IMG elements have *onreadystatechange* events. For these elements, your code can receive the event for several state transitions, depending on when the event handler is hooked up. In general, however, you should not write code that depends on any state transition to occur other than the transition to the complete state.

Modifying the HTML Stream

Originally, the object model in Internet Explorer 3.0 did not allow the document contents to be changed once the page was rendered. Since then, a number of methods have been exposed for outputting HTML into the document's stream while the page is being loaded or for generating an entirely new HTML document in another frame or browser instance. The example earlier in this chapter that outputs the source file's last modified date illustrates how to add HTML to the stream of a downloading document. The example in Chapter 5, "Window and Frame Management," that creates a diagram of a document's frameset hierarchy shows how to generate complete documents.

The available methods for adding contents to an HTML stream as it is being parsed and for generating complete documents are as follows:

- *write*
- *writeln*
- *open*
- *close*

Even though the object model now provides access to the stream, these methods are still very useful for generating contents as the page loads. Your scripts can generate different HTML code in response to the different conditions they encounter.

> NOTE: One of the innovations in Dynamic HTML is the ability to modify the document's contents after the page is loaded. You can modify a document using properties and methods of the Body element and its child elements, or using a new object named *TextRange*. Modifying the contents of the document is discussed in detail in Part IV.

> **Marked Sections**
>
> If you are familiar with SGML marked sections, you will see that scripts that write to the HTML stream are similar to marked sections. Marked sections allow a browser to use different contents, depending on a specific condition. For example, a Java applet, a plug-in, or maybe an image can be output to the screen, depending on the feature support of the browser. However, generating contents through scripts has a significant disadvantage in that the contents of the document cannot be predetermined and indexed using tools without evaluating the scripts on the page.

Writing HTML into the Stream

The *write* and *writeln* methods allow you to write HTML into the current stream while the document is loading or into another stream that has been opened using the *open* method. The *write* method is used in quite a few examples in this book to output HTML into the stream while loading. Arguments passed to the *write* method are always converted to strings before they are output into the document.

The *writeln* method is similar to the *write* method, but it appends an end-of-line character to the end of the line. Whether you use *write* or *writeln* rarely matters because most end-of-line characters are ignored in the HTML stream. End-of-line characters and spaces are important in only three instances:

- PRE and XMP elements, in which end-of-line characters are retained
- Elements that do not contain HTML, such as Script and Style
- Streams to a MIME type other than HTML

You should not use the *write* and *writeln* methods on the current document after the document has finished loading unless you first call the *open* method, which clears the current document's window and erases all variables.

Creating Documents Using the *open* and *close* Methods

The document methods *open* and *close* allow you to create new documents in other frames or windows. These documents do not even have to be written in HTML because the *open* method takes a MIME-type identifier. Therefore, if you know the format for an image or other document type, the image or document type can be output directly into a window.

The following code demonstrates using the *open* and *close* methods to output document information for a specified window into another window:

```
function docInfo(win) {
   /* Create an About dialog box. */
   var aboutWindow = window.open("", "Info",
      "toolbar=no; location=no; directories=no; width=375; " +
      "height=250; status=no; menubar=no; resizable=no");
   var prop;
   // Open a stream on the new window.
   aboutWindow.document.open();

   // Output document information.
   aboutWindow.document.write("<H1>Document Information</H1>");
   for (prop in win.location)
      aboutWindow.document.write(prop + ": " + self.location[prop] +
         "<BR>");
   // Close the stream on the new window.
   aboutWindow.document.close();
}
```

> NOTE: The *clear* method was exposed in Internet Explorer 3.0 for clearing the document's contents. This method should no longer be used because its future support is questionable and it acts unpredictably on different browsers. Instead, the *open* and *close* methods are sufficient for clearing and generating new documents.

Writing Scripts into the Stream

Your script can insert additional scripts into the stream. When you use this technique, be careful how your script closes the Script element it is inserting. Your script must insert the </SCRIPT> tag as two strings to be concatenated, as shown in the following code. Otherwise, the HTML parser will assume that the tag ends the script you are writing rather than the script it is inserting.

```
<SCRIPT LANGUAGE="JavaScript">
   // Example of dynamically generating a script
   document.write("<SCRIPT LANGUAGE='JavaScript'> x = 0; <" +
      "/SCRIPT>");
</SCRIPT>
```

CHAPTER SEVEN

Document Element Collections

The Dynamic HTML object model represents the document's structure through a set of collections exposed on the *document* object. These collections provide access to all HTML elements contained within the document. Understanding how these collections relate to the HTML source code and how to access these collections is the first step to programming the HTML document. This chapter shows you how to manipulate the document element collections as well as how Microsoft Internet Explorer 4.0 parses the document.

Consider the following short HTML document:

```
<HTML>
   <HEAD>
      <TITLE>Document Structure</TITLE>
   </HEAD>
   <BODY>
      <H1>Overview</H1>
      <P>Examining an HTML document</P>
   </BODY>
</HTML>
```

The object model provides a way to access the HTML, Head, Title, Body, H1, and Paragraph elements and thereby modify their attributes. The markup, like all aspects of the document, is accessed using the *document* object introduced in Chapter 6, "The HTML Document." The *document* object exposes an *all* collection that represents every element in the document and several filtered collections that represent a subset of the document's elements. For example, the *forms* collection contains only the Form elements. In addition, developers can create their own custom collections of document elements.

The ability to access any element in the document is a key innovation in Dynamic HTML. Until Dynamic HTML, scripts could manipulate only the set of elements deemed interesting by vendors developing the browsers. Now Web developers have complete control over the page and can decide for themselves what is interesting. They can filter the *all* collection and manipulate any set of elements as a group, removing all limitations and providing universal access to the document.

The following topics are covered in this chapter:

- **Using the collections** Every collection in Dynamic HTML shares the same set of operations. This section shows you how to access the elements within each collection, as well as how to create custom collections of elements. Because every collection in the HTML object model follows the same rules, this section provides a solid basis for manipulating and using the collections. The rest of Part II builds on this information by showing you how to manipulate the individual elements within the collections.
- **The HTML structure and collections** This section describes how the HTML document is parsed and exposed by the underlying collections. This discussion also covers how invalid HTML documents are parsed and surfaced in the object model, which is important to understand when you are scripting generic pages in which control over the document's structure is not available.

Using the Collections

This section focuses on using the *all* collection to access the elements on the page. The *all* collection in the *document* object represents every element in the HTML file. It is manipulated using a set of properties and methods that all the element collections support. These properties and methods specify how many elements are in the collection, provide access to the individual elements, and provide the ability to filter the collection based on element type.

> NOTE: Because all the collections share a common set of properties and methods, all the members discussed here can be used with any element collection in the document.

Collection Size

The first and most fundamental operation on a collection is determining the number of elements in the collection. The number of elements is returned by the *length* property. For example, the sample document at the beginning of this chapter has six elements:

```
alert(document.all.length);    // 6 elements
```

Accessing Elements

Elements in collections are accessed using the *item* method. The *item* method takes either an ordinal position or a string identifier representing the *name* or *id* attribute of an element. When you are supplying an ordinal position, keep in mind that all collections are zero-based. Therefore, the following code enumerates the elements in the *all* collection:

```
// Display the tag name for each element.
for (var i = 0, i < document.all.length, i++)
   alert(document.all.item(i).tagName);
```

NOTE: In a loop like this that accesses the elements of a collection, the conditional expression must test that the index is less than the length of the collection. Because the collection is zero-based, it has no element whose index equals the collection's length.

In VBScript, *item* is the default method on collections; specifying the *item* method is optional when you are accessing elements. In JavaScript, default methods are not supported; however, all objects are associative arrays, allowing all named elements to be accessed using the array lookup notation. For collections, this means that all elements in the collection are also exposed as properties on the object, which allows the elements to be accessed by their ordinal position in the underlying array or by their string name or ID. The preceding code fragment can be rewritten as follows:

```
// Display the tag name for each element.
for (var i = 0, i < document.all.length, i++)
   alert(document.all[i].tagName);
```

NOTE: In JavaScript, referencing into an array is done using square brackets ([]). In VBScript, because the default method is used instead of an array, the reference uses parentheses:

```
msgbox(document.all(i).id)    ' VBScript
```

The *id* and *name* Attributes

Up to now, only referencing the item by ordinal position has been demonstrated. Referencing elements can also be done directly by using the *id* or *name* attribute. There are a few distinctions between *id* and *name*. The *id* attribute is supposed to uniquely identify an element within the document. The *name* attribute can be shared by multiple elements; it is exposed only by certain elements and usually has a specific meaning. For example, on an element in a form block, the *name* attribute is used as the submit name, and on multiple radio buttons, the *name* attribute is used to group the buttons.

When you are assigning names for programmatic access, the *id* attribute should be used. The *name* attribute should be reserved for its intended behavior based on the element's context. You may need to use *name* if you are writing code to run on Netscape Navigator, as it currently does not recognize the *id* attribute on any element other than elements positioned with CSS (Cascading Style Sheets) positioning. The *name* attribute is supported in Netscape Navigator to access the Form element, frames, and all built-in controls.

NOTE: To simplify terminology, from here on the term *named element* refers to an element that has either the *id* or *name* attribute set.

Referencing Named Elements

In JavaScript, you can use a *name* or an *id* to reference an element in three ways: using the collection's *item* method, directly as a property of the collection, or indirectly as an array lookup. The following examples illustrate the three ways to reference an element whose *name* or *id* is *myElement*:

```
document.all.item("myElement")
document.all.myElement
document.all["myElement"]
```

When you are referencing elements using the *item* method or an array index on the *all* collection, you can query for an element by passing a variable. This technique is useful because the *id* or *name* attribute does not have to be known in advance and hard-coded. You can write generic code with a variable that contains the *id* attribute, as shown here:

```
// Get the tag name for the element with the specified id.
var retValue = window.prompt("Enter an ID:");
if (retValue != null)
   alert(document.all[retValue].tagName);
```

Using the *item* Method to Return a Collection

An element's *name* does not have to be unique in a document. Radio buttons in a group typically share the same *name*, as in the following example:

```
<HTML>
   <HEAD>
      <TITLE>Radio Button Group</TITLE>
   </HEAD>
   <BODY>
      <FORM>
         Name: <INPUT TYPE=TEXT NAME="YourName"><BR>
         <INPUT TYPE=RADIO NAME="Gender" VALUE="Male">Male
```

```
            <INPUT TYPE=RADIO NAME="Gender" VALUE="Female">Female
        </FORM>
    </BODY>
</HTML>
```

Because *name* need not be unique, a *name* string you use to look up a collection element can match more than one element. When more than one element matches, the result of the lookup is a new subcollection containing all the elements with the given *name*. The following examples access named elements in the preceding code:

```
document.all["YourName"]          // Input box (not a collection)
document.all["Gender"]            // Collection of two elements
document.all["Gender"].length     // 2
document.all["Gender"].item(0)    // Male radio button
```

The subcollection follows the same rules as all other collections; in particular it exposes a *length* property and an *item* method. Its elements are in the same order as they are in the original collection.

When the *item* method returns a subcollection, you can pass a second parameter to select an element in the subcollection. For example, the Male radio button can be accessed this way:

```
document.all.item("Gender", 0)
```

VBScript and JavaScript each support a shortcut for accessing elements in a subcollection without using the *item* method. For example, the following code fragments both access the Male radio button:

```
' In VBScript, item is the default method.
document.all("Gender", 0)

// JavaScript uses array access.
document.all["Gender"][0]
```

Documents with duplicate *ids* are technically invalid, but nothing stops a developer from authoring them, and your scripts that access unknown documents in other frames or windows may encounter them. The following example code contains several elements with the *id test*:

```
<HTML>
    <HEAD>
        <TITLE>Duplicate IDs</TITLE>
    </HEAD>
    <BODY>
        <H1 ID="test">Header 1</H1>
```

(continued)

```
      <P ID="test">This is a paragraph.
      <P ID="test">This is another paragraph.
      <INPUT ID="test" NAME="foo">This is a named Input box.
   </BODY>
</HTML>
```

Duplicate *ids* are handled just like duplicate names. If a script looks up an element by an *id* and more than one element matches the *id*, all of the elements are returned as a collection. The following expressions access elements in the preceding code that have the *id test*:

```
document.all["test"].length              // 4
document.all.test.length                 // 4 (look up directly by id)
document.all.test.tags("P").length       // 2
document.all.test.item("test").length    // 4 (redundant code)
```

The Input box in the preceding code is an interesting element. It is part of the collection returned by *item("test")* and is exposed individually as *item("foo")*. The Input box can also be accessed through the collection of elements with *id test*:

```
document.all.test.item("foo").tagName    // INPUT
document.all.foo.tagName                 // Also INPUT
```

If an element's *name* and *id* attributes have the same value, it nonetheless appears only once in a collection of elements with that *name* or *id*. An element can exist only once in any collection.

Distinguishing Between a Collection and an Element

When your code accesses an element by its *name* or *id*, either a collection or an element may be returned. Therefore, your code might need to distinguish whether the returned object is an element or a collection. In JavaScript, the *length* property returns *null* for single elements and the numbers of elements for collections. The *length* property returns *null* for a single element because it does not actually exist on the object—JavaScript automatically adds the *length* property to the object with the default value of *null*.

The following code demonstrates how to check whether a collection or a single element is returned:

```
// Using length
if (null == document.all["Gender"].length) {
   // Single element
}
else {
   // Collection
}
```

NOTE: You cannot use *length* in VBScript to differentiate individual elements from collections. If you do, VBScript generates an error because the property does not exist on the element object.

Referencing Unknown Element Names

If the *item* method is called using a *name* or an *id* attribute that does not exist in the document or that has not loaded yet, the method returns a *null* object:

```
var el = document.all.item("foo");
if (null == el)
   alert("Please try again when the page is loaded.");
else {
   // Do something with the element named foo.
}
```

Directly Accessing Named Elements

In addition to being accessible through collections, some named elements are also properties of the document or the window. These elements are added to the document and the window purely for backward compatibility; the recommended way to access them is to use the *all* collection.

Elements of the following types are added directly to the document if they have a *name* or an *id* attribute: Form, IMG, and Applet. In addition, all elements with an *id* attribute except input elements in a form are added directly to the window, which allows you to access them without going through the document's *all* collection:

```
<H1 ID="myH1">Welcome to My Page</H1>
<FORM ID="form 1">
   <INPUT TYPE=TEXT ID="text1">
</FORM>
<SCRIPT LANGUAGE="JavaScript">
   // Access myH1 as a window property.
   alert(myH1.id);  // Output the id.
   // Access myH1 through the all collection.
   alert(document.all.myH1.id);
   // Input elements within a form are available through the form.
   alert(form1.text1.id);
</SCRIPT>
```

Built-In Collections

The document exposes a number of predefined collections, which all follow the set of rules introduced earlier in this chapter. These collections are provided for compatibility with older browsers. The following table lists the collections and the tags of the elements contained within them.

Collection	Tags	Description
all	All tags	Every element in the document, in source order.
anchors	<A NAME=...>	Bookmarks.
applets	<APPLET>; <OBJECT>	Embedded objects and Java applets.
forms	<FORM>	Forms.
frames	<IFRAME>	Inline frames.
images	<IMG>	Images.
links	<A HREF=...>; <AREA>	Links. If an Anchor element contains both a NAME and an HREF attribute, it will be exposed in both the *links* and the *anchors* collections.
scripts	<SCRIPT>	Scripts.

Rather than extend this list for arbitrary tags, collections expose the *tags* method for creating a new collection filtered by a specified tag. The *tags* method eliminates the need to clutter the object model with a collection for every element type and lets the developer determine which elements are interesting.

The *tags* Method

In addition to the *item* method, all document element collections expose a *tags* method. The *tags* method takes a parameter representing the tag as a string and returns a collection of all elements with that tag, as shown in the following code:

```
<HTML>
   <BODY>
      <H1>My Header</H1>
      <P>This is <STRONG>strong text</STRONG> and more
         <STRONG>strong</STRONG> text.</P>
      <H1>Another Header 1</H1>
   </BODY>
</HTML>
```

The following expressions use the *tags* method to create collections of elements from the preceding code:

```
document.all.tags("H1")          // Collection of both H1 elements
document.all.tags("STRONG")      // Collection of both Strong elements
document.all.tags("STRONG")[0]   // First Strong element
document.all.tags("P").length    // 1
```

Unlike the *item* method, the *tags* method always returns a collection, even if only a single element exists on the page. For example, calling the *tags* method on the Body element still returns a collection, even though only a single Body element can exist:

```
document.all.tags("BODY")      // A collection with one Body element
document.all.tags("BODY")[0]   // The first element in the collection
```

The *tags* method always returns a collection because it was designed with a single purpose, to filter a collection to a smaller collection. The *item* method returns the single element that matches the identifier—and where there are duplicate matches, a collection rather than an error is returned.

Empty Collections

If the *tags* method is called to query for a tag that does not exist in the document, an empty collection with zero elements is returned:

```
if (0 == document.all.tags("H1").length)
   alert("There are no H1 elements in this document.");
```

In order to ensure that even unknown elements can be queried and filtered for, the *tags* method does not return an error when passed to an invalid tag.

Custom Collections

Most of the document's built-in collections are the same as collections you can create using the *tags* method with the *all* collection. For example, the *forms* collection is the same as the collection created by calling the *tags* method and supplying *form* as the parameter. The following code creates a collection equivalent to the *forms* collection:

```
document.myforms = document.all.tags("form");
```

You can create custom collections and add them to the *document* object using a similar technique, as shown here:

```
// Create a tables collection on the document.
document.tables = document.all.tags("TABLE");
```

This technique relies on a language feature supported by JavaScript, so this code cannot run in VBScript and might not be capable of running under other languages. In VBScript, you must create a variable to hold the collection.

The preceding code demonstrates that multiple collections often refer to the same set of elements. Therefore, referencing an element in any of the collections is the same as referencing that element in the *all* collection. For example, the following code fragment returns *true* because the same object is being referenced through two different collections:

```
// Both expressions point to the same object.
document.forms[0] == document.all.tags("FORM")[0];
```

The *all* Collection in a Frameset Document

A document that contains a frameset also supports the *document* object and exposes the same *all* collection. The Frameset element replaces the Body element in the *all* collection because a document can contain traditional body contents or a frameset, but not both. All the Frameset and Frame elements in the document are exposed in source code order, as shown here, which is useful for determining the visual layout of the frames on the screen:

```
<HTML>
   <HEAD>
      <TITLE>Frameset Demo</TITLE>
   </HEAD>
   <FRAMESET ROWS="60, *">
      <FRAME SRC="a.htm">
      <FRAME SRC="b.htm">
   </FRAMESET>
</HTML>
```

The *all* collection for this document exposes the elements in the following order: HTML, Head, Title, Frameset, Frame, Frame.

In addition, all attributes of the Frameset and Frame elements are exposed through the *all* collection. Most of the attributes can be assigned a new value, but in some cases that value is not reevaluated—for example, the border of the frameset cannot be modified once the frameset is rendered. However, a frameset will update correctly if you change its *row* or *col* attribute, or if you change the *src* or *name* attribute of one of the frames.

Collections in frameset documents differ from those in other documents with respect to their inclusion of unrecognized elements. Only unrecognized elements that appear before the first <FRAMESET> tag are exposed in the object model. Once a <FRAMESET> tag is encountered, all elements other than Frameset and Frame are ignored and are not surfaced in the object model. Even NoFrames elements are ignored. If a NoFrames element appears before the Frameset element, it is exposed in the *all* collection, but the contents of the element are not available. This limitation may be removed by a future version of Internet Explorer.

The HTML Structure and Collections

This section focuses on how the document's collections are constructed while the document is parsed. HTML documents are supposed to satisfy the rules defined by the HTML DTD (document type definition). The HTML object model relies on these rules and some real-world exceptions to ensure that the document's structure is properly maintained. This section introduces the relationship between the DTD and the collections exposed on the document.

Building the *all* Collection

The *all* collection of elements correlates directly to the HTML document's tree. The following simple HTML document demonstrates this relationship:

```
<HTML>
   <HEAD>
      <TITLE>My Document</TITLE>
   </HEAD>
   <BODY>
      <H1>Welcome to My Page</H1>
      <P>This is an <STRONG>important document.</STRONG></P>
   </BODY>
</HTML>
```

Figure 7-1 displays the containment relationships between the elements in this document.

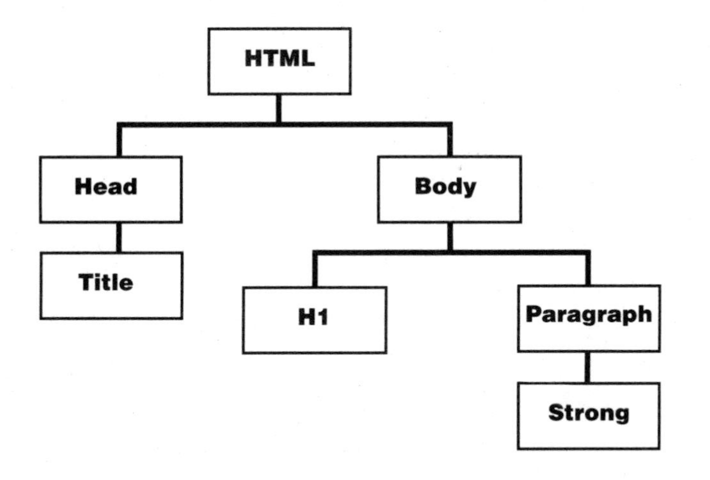

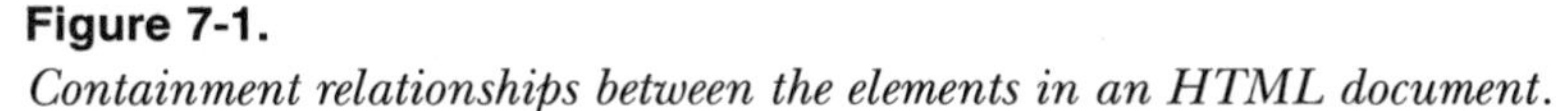

Figure 7-1.
Containment relationships between the elements in an HTML document.

The document's *all* collection, which contains every element in the document, represents this tree; it contains the elements in the tree in the order found in the source code. The parser creates the *all* collection by performing an operation known as a preorder traversal of the tree. In this example, the contents and order of the *all* collection are initially as follows: HTML, Head, Title, Body, H1, Paragraph, Strong.

The *all* collection always represents the current state of the document. You can change the elements in the *all* collection by dynamically manipulating the document's contents, but the *all* collection always maintains the order of the elements, even when scripts modify the contents. Dynamic contents manipulation is discussed in detail in Chapter 13, "Dynamic Contents."

Scope of Influence

The HTML tree contains information not immediately apparent from the *all* collection—namely, the scope of each element. The scope of an element is the set of elements it contains. For example, in the preceding document the Paragraph element contains the Strong element, so the Strong element is within the scope of the Paragraph element. You can determine the scope of an element by analyzing the *parentElement* and *children* properties of each element in the *all* collection, a process described in Chapter 8, "Scripts and Elements."

> NOTE: The *all* collection, as do all the element collections, represents the element as a single object. The elements, rather than individual begin and end tags, are sufficient for manipulating the document's structure. Because elements are represented rather than individual tags, fewer complexities are involved in understanding and working with the collections. The exception to this rule is for unrecognized tags. In this case, any unrecognized tag, whether a begin or an end tag, is added to the collection. Unrecognized tags have no scope of influence over any children. This limitation is discussed in greater detail in the section "Unrecognized Elements" later in this chapter.

Implied Elements

The DTD for HTML specifies that tags for the HTML, Head, Body, and TBody elements are optional in the HTML document because these elements can be inferred from the content, as shown here:

```
<TITLE>Welcome to My Document</TITLE>
<H1>Welcome to My Page</H1>
<P>This is an <STRONG>important document.</STRONG></P>
```

This document is equivalent to the preceding document. The trees, and therefore the contents of the *all* collections, are the same. The *all* collection always exposes the HTML, Head, and Body elements for every document, regardless of whether you explicitly authored them.

Differentiating the Head from the Body

In a document without <HEAD> and <BODY> tags, the split between head and body is determined by the rules of HTML as defined by the DTD. The Head element contains a specific set of elements that are different from the set in the Body element. Therefore, when the first Body element is encountered (for example, H1), the scope automatically changes from the head to the body.

The following code fragment represents the DTD for the head of the document. By examining this DTD, you can more clearly see the distinction between head and body:

```
<!ENTITY % head.misc "SCRIPT|STYLE|META|LINK"
   -- repeatable head elements -->
<!ENTITY % head.content "TITLE & ISINDEX? & BASE?">
<!ELEMENT HEAD O O  (%head.content) +(%head.misc)>
```

This code shows that there can be at most one IsIndex element and one Base element, that there must be exactly one Title element, and that there can be any number of elements specified by the *head.misc* entity. With two exceptions, the Style and Script elements, the entities available in the head are mutually exclusive from the entities available in the body. Therefore, it is quite easy for a parser to determine when the scope has switched from the head to the body.

The Style and Script elements are ambiguous cases because they can exist in both the head and the body. If a Style or Script element is encountered before any body contents, the element is considered contents of the head. This rule has no impact on the rendering or behavior of the document, but it is important to understand because it affects the scope of influence of the Head and Body elements.

Optional End Tags

A few elements in HTML do not require an end tag. For example, a <P> tag does not require a </P> to end its scope of influence. To determine when a Paragraph or other element ends, the DTD is used. When an element that cannot be contained within the current scope is encountered, the prior scope is considered to be terminated. As shown in the following example, if a <P> tag is followed by an <H2> tag, the Paragraph element ends with the <H2> tag because an H2 element cannot be a child of a Paragraph element.

```
<HTML>
   <H1>Scott's Home Page</H1>
   <P>Welcome to my page.<H2>New Cool Stuff</H2>
</HTML>
```

The tree in Figure 7-2 represents this HTML document. Notice that the H2 element is a child element of the Body element, not the Paragraph element.

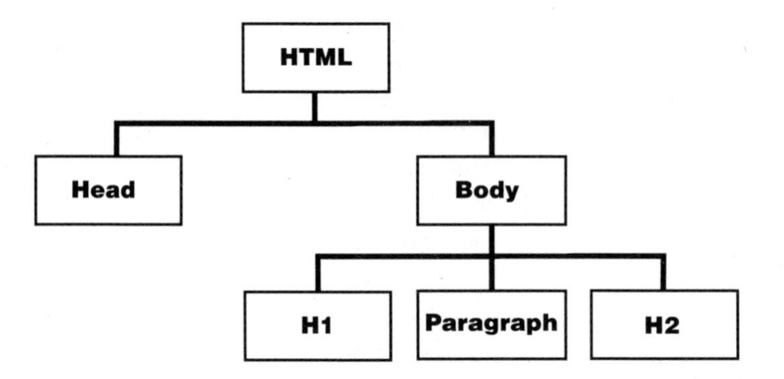

Figure 7-2.
Tree diagram of a document with an implied end tag.

In general, documents are more readable and maintainable when end tags are explicitly defined. Without end tags, anyone viewing the source must have knowledge of the HTML DTD to ascertain the relationship between various elements.

Unrecognized Elements

Parsing of unrecognized elements in the HTML document is an important consideration as HTML and browsers evolve. Imagine the introduction of an <H7> tag. New browsers will understand how to interpret <H7> as a block container tag, but down-level browsers will not recognize it. In accordance with the rules of HTML, the <H7> begin and end tags are ignored when the document is rendered by this hypothetical down-level browser because for unrecognized tags DTD information is unavailable to determine the rules and scope of the tag.

Because there is no DTD for unrecognized elements, the unrecognized begin and end tags are exposed in the *all* collection. Unlike the rules of HTML specifying that unrecognized elements should be ignored, the object model includes unrecognized tags, in order to provide complete information about the document to the developer.

The unrecognized end tag is also exposed because there is no way to accurately determine whether the element is a container. Even if a begin and end tag appear in sequence in the document, there are no assurances that their use would be in conformance with a DTD rule if one did exist for the element. For example, the element might not be defined in the DTD as a container element. Therefore, both unrecognized begin and end tags are always exposed as leaf nodes in the tree:

```
<HTML>
   <P>Welcome to my <FOO><B>cool</B> document.</FOO></P>
</HTML>
```

The tree in Figure 7-3 demonstrates how the internal parser represents this document with unrecognized elements.

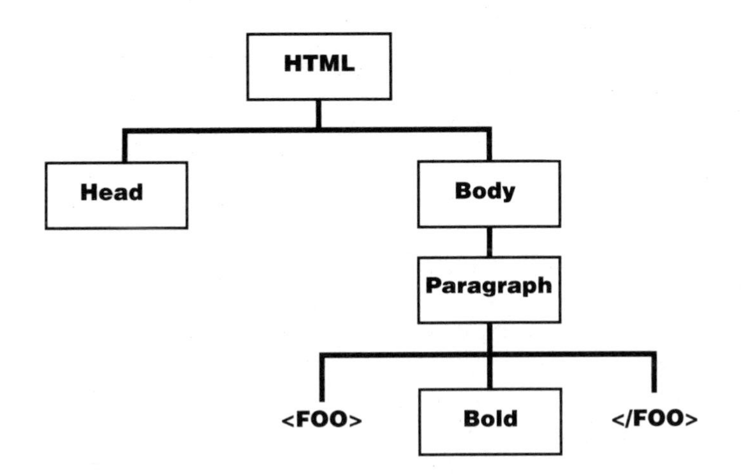

Figure 7-3.
Tree diagram of a document with unrecognized begin and end <FOO> tags.

The *all* collection in the preceding example contains the following elements: HTML, Head, Body, Paragraph, <FOO>, Bold, </FOO>. Notice that the Bold element is not considered a child of the Foo element, but rather a child of the Paragraph element. Because DTD information about Foo is unavailable, there is no way to reliably determine whether the Foo element is a container. For unrecognized elements, exposing both the begin and end tags allows the developer to calculate the scope of the element by manually walking through the *all* collection.

If in a future version of Internet Explorer Foo becomes a valid HTML element that can contain text, the document's tree will change. Figure 7-4 demonstrates this new tree.

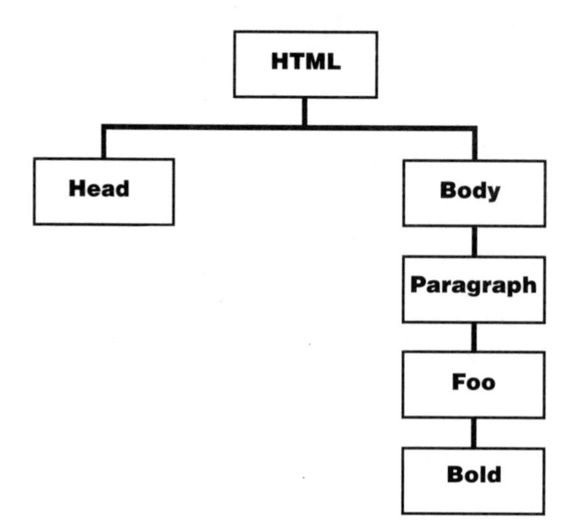

Figure 7-4.
Tree diagram that would result if the browser recognized <FOO> tags.

While the ordering will be consistent across implementations, the number of elements and the document's tree may vary depending on whether the Foo element is supported. This difference might cause problems if your code relies on ordinal positions of elements in the collection because the number of elements exposed can change from browser to browser. Instead, code that accesses a specific element should always use an ID or identify the element in a more explicit context.

All unrecognized end tags are also exposed in the object model because the object model makes no attempt to associate invalid begin and end tags and accepts them into the collection as specified in the document. Therefore, if a </BAR> end tag is floating in the middle of the document, it will be represented in the *all* collection, even if no <BAR> begin tag was ever encountered.

From the point of view of the DTD, all unrecognized begin and end tags are considered to have no contents. Any attributes and style sheet information found on an unrecognized tag will have no effect on the document's rendering but will be represented in the object model.

Unmatched End Tags

When an unmatched end tag that is recognized by the parser is encountered, HTML specifies that the end tag should be ignored. However, as with unrecognized tags, unmatched end tags are exposed in the *all* collection. In the following example, the </B> end tag is exposed in the object model:

```
<HTML>
   This is not bold.</B>
</HTML>
```

The end tag is exposed because the object model attempts to maintain an accurate representation of the document.

Overlapping Elements

Overlapping elements occur when a true containership hierarchy is not followed by the document. The following example demonstrates an overlap of Strong and EM elements:

```
<HTML>
   <BODY>
      <P>This is a <STRONG>demonstration of
         <EM>overlapping</STRONG> elements.</EM></P>
   </BODY>
</HTML>
```

Even though elements overlap, they do not affect the composition or ordering of the *all* collection. The *all* collection consists of the following elements in this order: HTML, Head, Body, Paragraph, Strong, EM. The tree for this document, shown in Figure 7-5, does not represent the overlapping of elements or the true scope of influence for each element.

Overlapping elements are actually invalid HTML. To achieve the desired behavior without using overlapping tags, you should create the document with a clean containership hierarchy:

```
<HTML>
   <BODY>
      <P>This is a <STRONG>demonstration of
         <EM>overlapping</EM></STRONG><EM> elements.</EM>
      </P>
   </BODY>
</HTML>
```

Overlapping elements have little effect on most collections, but an element's *children* collection may be inaccurate. The relationship between overlapping elements and the document's contents is a strong one, and is discussed in Chapter 13, "Dynamic Contents."

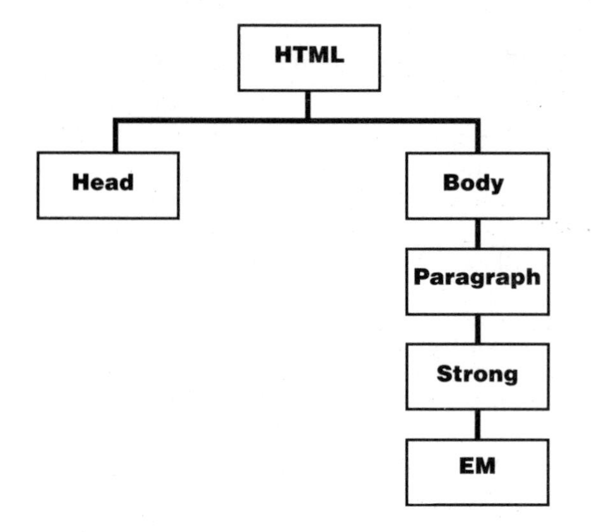

Figure 7-5.
Tree diagram of a document with overlapping elements.

Tagless Contents

Tagless contents—text that is not contained within any element—often occurs within the body:

```
<HTML>
   <BODY>
      These contents are without a tag.
      <P>These contents are within a Paragraph element.</P>
      These contents follow a Paragraph element without a tag.
   </BODY>
</HTML>
```

This HTML document would have only HTML, Head, Body, and Paragraph elements in its *all* collection. There is no element that represents text outside of containers. In strict HTML, this text is defined to be within a Paragraph element. However, a <P> tag cannot be synthesized in this case because explicitly defined paragraphs have a slightly different rendering scheme from implicit paragraphs.

Invalid HTML

Dynamic HTML is designed to work with valid HTML. Therefore, tags that are placed outside of their proper scope are usually parsed as unrecognized elements. This rule is not fixed, however, and in some cases the HTML may be cleaned up automatically during parsing. For example, imagine the following invalid definition of a table:

```
<HTML>
   <BODY>
      <TD>This is a table cell outside of a table.</TD>
   </BODY>
</HTML>
```

In this document, a table cell appears where it doesn't belong—namely, outside the scope of a table. When the document is parsed, the table cell is not recognized and is parsed as an unrecognized element. Therefore, both the begin and end tags are considered invalid by the parser. The *all* collection exposes the elements of this HTML document in the following order: HTML, Head, Body, <TD>, </TD>.

You should not write documents to rely on this behavior. Browsers may choose to clean up the HTML or may choose to not do any cleanup and ignore the invalidly scoped elements. The only way to ensure that the element collection is built consistently is to create valid HTML documents.

There are a couple of known exceptions for which the document's tree will not conform to the HTML DTD. These exceptions exist because they appear in a large number of documents on the Internet. The exceptions discussed here are by no means the only exceptions, but they are ones that occur commonly in HTML documents.

Lists

Lists are one of the few areas in which the HTML is not cleaned up by the parser. To ensure compatibility, the object model recognizes two cases of invalid HTML as valid markup:

- LI elements can exist outside of UL and OL list containers.
- A list container can directly contain other list containers.

The first exception was allowed in Netscape Navigator 2.0 for creating bulleted items that are not indented; the second exception came about through the common, illegal practice of nesting lists.

When the first exception occurs, Netscape Navigator 2.0, whose implementation was followed by Internet Explorer 3.0, renders the list item without indenting it. Even though the DTD for LI elements prohibits them from existing outside of lists, the DTD used to create the tree, shown in the following code, is lax and will not automatically wrap these LI elements.

```
<HTML>
   <BODY>
      <LI>This is an LI element outside of a list.</LI>
   </BODY>
</HTML>
```

The *all* collection for this document is ordered as follows: HTML, Head, Body, LI.

The second exception, in which nested lists are used entirely for increasing the amount of indentation for bullets, is shown here:

```
<HTML>
   <BODY>
      <UL>
         <UL>
            <LI>This is a deeply indented bulleted list item.</LI>
         </UL>
      </UL>
   </BODY>
</HTML>
```

This HTML violates the DTD because UL elements can only contain LI elements, not other ULs. When this situation is encountered, no cleanup occurs. The ordering for the *all* collection for this document is as follows: HTML, Head, Body, UL, UL, LI.

Form Elements in Tables

Another common practice is to use forms in tables (outside of cells) to create a form that spans multiple rows or cells, as shown here:

```
<HTML>
   <HEAD>
      <TITLE>Forms in Tables</TITLE>
   </HEAD>
   <BODY>
      <TABLE>
         <FORM NAME="Form1">
            <TR><TD>Form1-related fields</TD></TR>
            <TR><TD>More Form1-related fields</TD></TR>
         </FORM>
         <FORM NAME="Form2">
            <TR><TD>Form2-related fields</TD></TR>
         </FORM>
      </TABLE>
   </BODY>
</HTML>
```

In this document, the forms will be maintained with the correct scope inside the table.

The tree for this document is represented by Figure 7-6.

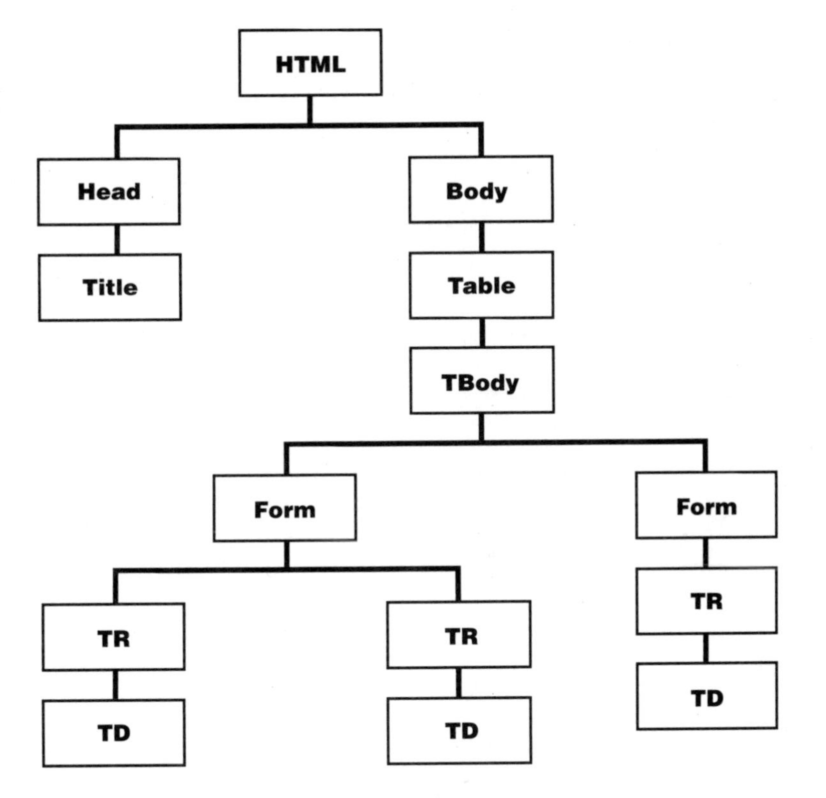

Figure 7-6.
Tree diagram for a document with Form elements inside a Table element.

There are probably other exceptions to the DTD. In general, invalid HTML may result in an unpredictable tree that may not be consistent in each browser release. Therefore, you should be careful to write HTML that corresponds to the DTD. Doing so not only makes the object model more consistent, but it also improves the likelihood that different browsers will render the document the same way.

// Create
var x = 10;
function foo() {
// This code is not
code
var y =
alert(
// output
// Call foo while
foo(
</SCRIPT>

CHAPTER EIGHT

Scripts and Elements

This chapter shows you how to program and manipulate the elements of an HTML document. All elements share a common set of information for identifying the element, accessing the attributes on the element, and defining the relationships between the element and other elements in the document. In addition, many elements provide custom properties, methods, and events, giving you increased control of your documents. A sampling of these elements is discussed in Chapter 9, "Scripting Individual Elements," and in Chapter 10, "Forms and Intrinsic Controls."

The following topics are covered in this chapter:

- **Identifying elements** This section shows you how to distinguish between the different elements in the document. HTML exposes a set of attributes that are useful for identifying and grouping elements, including the tag name itself and the ID, CLASS, and NAME attributes.
- **Accessing an element's attributes** All element objects encapsulate information about their attributes and even provide access to invalid attributes and values that may be specified on an element. This section shows you how to access and use this information.
- **Parsing information** Chapter 7, "Document Element Collections," described how the document's *all* collection is constructed and accessed. The *all* collection provides access to the individual elements, and each element exposes its relationships with other elements, including information about the parsing and rendering of the document. The parsing information represents the underlying HTML source, and the rendering information represents calculated information determined during the creation of the document. This section reviews the relationships between elements in the parsing tree and shows how these relationships are exposed by the individual elements.

- **Creating new elements** This section shows how elements can be added to the document using the *createElement* method. There are two techniques for controlling the document's structure: creating elements in memory, and modifying the HTML contents directly. Dynamic HTML currently supports the creation of elements in memory for only a few elements.
- **Customizing elements** This section demonstrates techniques for customizing existing elements and for creating new user-defined elements. Customization is similar to subclassing an element and takes advantage of Dynamic HTML's ability to expose unrecognized attributes to the scripting language. Custom elements can also be defined by accessing and using unrecognized elements in the object model. These user-defined elements can contain extra meta information about the document that can be accessed and manipulated through the object model.

Identifying Elements

When you write scripts and style sheets, you may want your code to apply to one particular element, to all elements of the same type, or to a heterogeneous set of elements that you specify. Element objects have several properties that make them easy to identify in these various ways. An object's *id* and *className* properties contain the values of the corresponding element's ID and CLASS attributes, respectively, and its *tagName* property contains the name of the element's tag. Your code can use the *id* property to reference a single element, the *tagName* property to reference all elements of the same type, or the *className* property to reference any set you define.

Elements that have a NAME attribute also have a *name* property that contains the attribute's value. You can use the *name* property to identify a single element or a group of related elements (such as radio buttons) in your code. But the *name* property isn't as widely applicable as the *id* property, for example, and the object model includes it mainly for backward compatibility.

Values of the *tagName* property are stored in all uppercase letters. The *id*, *name*, and *className* properties are case sensitive. The value *coolstuff*, for example, represents a different class than the value *cOOlStuff* in a case-sensitive language like JavaScript. Style sheets, however, are associated to elements without regard to capitalization.

The following table summarizes information about the four properties that identify elements.

Attribute	Property	Case-Sensitive?	Applicable Elements
(None)	*tagName*	Always uppercase	All, including comments
ID	*id*	Yes	All, except comments
CLASS	*className*	Yes	All, except comments
NAME	*name*	Yes	Anchor, Applet, Button, Form, IMG, Input, Map, Meta, Object, Select, and TextArea

Using properties to identify elements, you can write a single script that performs the same action for all the elements in whatever set you choose. The click event handler in the following sample code responds differently to mouse clicks on the element with an *id* value of *f123*, on elements in the class *coolstuff*, and on H1 elements. In each case, the handler changes the inline style of the element to alter the element's appearance.

```
<HTML>
   <HEAD>
      <TITLE>Identifying Elements</TITLE>
      <SCRIPT FOR="document" EVENT="onclick()" LANGUAGE="JavaScript">
         // The click event is fired on the document regardless of
         // where the user clicks.
         // The style property gives access to the inline style.
         var curElement = event.srcElement;
         if ("F123" == curElement.id.toUpperCase()) {
            // Toggle element color between red and blue.
            if ("red" == curElement.style.color)
               curElement.style.color = "blue";
            else
               curElement.style.color = "red";
         }
         if ("COOLSTUFF" == curElement.className.toUpperCase()) {
            // Make text bigger or smaller when clicked.
            if ("" == curElement.style.fontSize)
               curElement.style.fontSize = "150%";
            else
               curElement.style.fontSize = "";
         }
         if ("H1" == curElement.tagName) {
            // Toggle the header between centered and left-aligned.
            if ("center" == curElement.align)
               curElement.align = "";
```

(continued)

```
            else
               curElement.align = "center";
         }
      </SCRIPT>
   </HEAD>
   <BODY>
      <P ID="f123" STYLE="color:red">
         This paragraph has a unique ID.</P>
      <H1>Clicking on an H1 element changes its alignment.</H1>
      <P>This paragraph contains
         <STRONG CLASS="coolstuff">cool stuff.</STRONG>
      </P>
      <H1 CLASS="coolstuff">
         This header is also cool stuff.
      </H1>
   </BODY>
</HTML>
```

In the preceding code, the *className* and *id* values are converted to uppercase before making comparisons; these values are thus treated on a case-insensitive basis.

Accessing an Element's Attributes

Every element object exposes its attributes, style, and contents to scripting languages. This information is obtained from the underlying source code for the document. This section shows how attributes are exposed. Chapter 11, "Dynamic Styles," discusses accessing an element's style, and Chapter 13, "Dynamic Contents," discusses accessing an element's contents.

Data Types

In HTML, an attribute always takes one of the following data types: number, string, string from a predefined list, or compact value. (Compact values are values that are *true* or *false*.) The DTD (document type definition) specifies the data type for each attribute.

In the Dynamic HTML object model, each attribute is exposed as a property. Such a property has one of the following four data types:

- 32-bit integer for number values
- Boolean for compact values
- String for arbitrary or defined strings
- Function pointer for event attributes

The script in the following HTML document uses the four data types:

```
<HTML>
   <HEAD>
      <TITLE>Programming Attributes--Data Types</TITLE>
   </HEAD>
   <BODY>
      <INPUT TYPE=TEXT SIZE=35 ID="txt1" DISABLED>
      <H1 ALIGN="Left" ID="hd1" ONCLICK="alert('Clicked!')">
         This is a left-aligned header.
      </H1>
      <SCRIPT LANGUAGE="JavaScript">
         alert(document.all.txt1.disabled); // Boolean true
         alert(document.all.hd1.align);     // String left
         alert(document.all.txt1.size);     // 32-bit integer 35
         alert(document.all.hd1.onclick);   // Function pointer
      </SCRIPT>
   </BODY>
</HTML>
```

A property is exposed for every defined attribute in HTML, even if the attribute is not explicitly defined in the document. For example, the Input element in the preceding code does not have the VALUE attribute specified, but in the object model all Input elements always expose the *value* property. The value of a property corresponding to an unspecified attribute depends on its data type. String properties contain empty strings; number properties contain the default values for the corresponding attributes; compact properties contain *false;* and function pointers contain *null.*

An event attribute contains code that executes as the result of a specified action. When the code string is parsed, a *function* object is created. Rather than expose the string defining the function, a property representing such an event contains a pointer to the function.

If you try to assign a value of one data type to a property of another, the results will vary depending on the scripting language. Either the value will be coerced into the property's data type or an error will occur. For example, if you assign a number to a string property in JavaScript, the interpreter will translate the number into its string representation before making the assignment. If the language supports explicit casting from one type to another, you should explicitly cast values to ensure predictable results. The *parseInt* function in JavaScript, for example, changes a string representation of a number into an actual number:

```
document.myText.size = parseInt("100");  // 100
```

Naming Conventions

While HTML allows attributes to be defined insensitive of case, JavaScript is case sensitive. To simplify programming with case-sensitive languages, the object model defines all properties using a consistent naming convention, which allows you to determine the property name for any existing attribute without having to look it up in a reference.

Following this naming convention, all properties—not just properties representing attributes—have names beginning in lowercase; each appended keyword begins with a capital letter—for example, *tagName*. Because most attributes consist of a single keyword, the corresponding properties are generally all lowercase.

For each attribute, the corresponding property has the same name as the attribute, except in two cases: the *className* property represents the CLASS attribute, and the *htmlFor* property represents the FOR attribute (used with Label and Script elements). These exceptions are necessary because *for* and *class* are reserved words in many programming languages.

Access to Original Values

Because HTML is text based, there are times when an attribute might contain a value that is not compatible with the data type of the exposed property. For example, the SIZE attribute represents the integer size of a text box. However, if the HTML source contains a string rather than a number, the *size* property still returns the default size because the data type for the value is predetermined. The Dynamic HTML object model is designed to ensure that even invalid attributes and values are accessible to scripts. All elements expose the following methods to provide access to the untouched value from the original document.

- *getAttribute(propertyName [, options])*
- *setAttribute(propertyName, Value [, options])*
- *removeAttribute(propertyName [, options])*

The *getAttribute* method takes the property name as a string and returns the value as it appears in the source code. If the source file sets the SIZE attribute to the string *big*, for example, the *size* property returns the default size *20*. But *getAttribute("size")* returns the string *big* because the *getAttribute* method always returns the untouched value from the source code.

The *setAttribute* method lets the developer control the reverse operation, whereby a string can be inserted into the HTML stream, even if the property value is a number. For example, *setAttribute("size", "small")* puts the string value *small* into the SIZE attribute. The *size* property on the element still returns *20.*

The *removeAttribute* method is used to remove an attribute from the object.

The three attribute methods expose an *options* parameter that controls how the lookup is performed. Currently, the parameter controls only case sensitivity. With the default *options* value of *false,* the lookup is case insensitive. With an *options* value of *true,* the lookup is case sensitive, using the internal capitalization of the attribute for known attributes and the capitalization defined in the source code for unrecognized attributes.

In general, case-sensitive lookups are not necessary and the attribute methods can be invoked without the optional flag. For multiple properties that are capitalized differently, the property that is returned is the first match found in the properties list. The main purpose of the *options* parameter is to locate a property when the same property name exists multiple times with different capitalizations.

> NOTE: While the designers of the object model were careful to avoid collisions between common reserved words, there may be cases in which an existing attribute collides with a reserved word in the programming language. If this occurs, the three attribute methods can be used to access any property value on the element instead of accessing the attribute directly using the exposed property.

Enumerated Data Types

Many other object models expose value lists as enumerated data types. Usually, the enumerated data type is an integer or other number and a variety of constants are defined to represent its allowed values. To ensure language neutrality, integer-based enumeration is not used in the Dynamic HTML object model. Instead, all value lists are exposed as string values. For example, the ALIGN attribute stores a string that is supposed to be one of the three string values: *left, right,* and *center.*

An attribute can be assigned a string capitalized in any manner, and it will be properly evaluated. For example, the ALIGN attribute in HTML or the corresponding *align* property can be assigned the value *left* or *LeFT,* or any other combination of uppercase and lowercase. However, when you retrieve the value, it is always returned all lowercase.

Enumerated string values are converted to lowercase at parse time or assignment time; the original case of these values is not accessible. The *getAttribute, setAttribute,* and *removeAttribute* methods will not respect the original capitalization of the enumerated strings and will return them lowercased.

Unrecognized Attributes

Chapter 7, "Document Element Collections," demonstrated how unrecognized elements are handled in the object model. Dynamic HTML also accurately represents unrecognized attributes on any element. The attribute methods provide access to attributes specified in the document that are not recognized by Microsoft Internet Explorer 4.0. Using these methods, unrecognized attributes can be added and removed from any element. With JavaScript, this access is taken one step further—all unrecognized attributes are also exposed as properties of the element, as shown here:

```
<H1 ID=myH1 badAttribute=Test>
```

JavaScript can access a property named *badAttribute* on this H1 object. This property is accessed in the same manner as any other property on the element:

```
alert(document.all.myH1.badAttribute)                 // Test
alert(document.all.myH1.getAttribute("badAttribute")) // Test
```

Unrecognized attributes are exposed as properties with the same capitalization they have in the original document. For recognized attributes, the capitalization of the attribute in the document has no relation to its capitalization in the object model. To perform case-insensitive lookups, the attribute methods should be used. In general, these methods should be used instead of accessing unrecognized attributes directly. This technique also eliminates the potential for problems caused by typographical errors in the capitalization of attribute names. In the section "Customizing Existing Elements" later in this chapter, techniques are demonstrated for intelligently using unrecognized attributes.

Parsing Information

Every element exposes information about itself and its relationship to other elements. The exposed information falls into two categories: parsing information and rendering information. The parsing information relates directly to the attributes, styles, and contents defined by the document. The rendering information represents the information calculated by the browser before displaying the element.

The parsing information includes the identifying properties discussed earlier, all the specified known and unknown HTML attributes, the inline style sheet, and the element's relationship to other elements as defined by the document. The inline style sheet is parsing information, not rendering information, because it is defined explicitly in the document's source, rather than calculated at render time.

The rendering information is information that is calculated by the browser during the composition of the document. Rendering information includes the position and size of the element in relation to its rendering context—that is, who drew the element, which rendering context the element belongs to, and the positions of any scrollbars. Rendering contexts and the resulting rendering tree are discussed in detail in Chapter 12, "Dynamic Positioning." The remainder of this section focuses on accessing and using the parsing tree.

Determining HTML Containership

A couple of techniques are available for determining what elements are contained within other elements. As mentioned, the parent element of an element can be determined using the *parentElement* property. The child elements contained within an element are enumerated by a *children* collection and an *all* collection on the element. The *children* collection represents the immediate child elements, while the *all* collection represents all the contained elements.

Accessing Child Elements

The *all* collection on the document represents all the HTML elements contained by the document. This containership concept is carried through to every element object. Every element object also exposes an *all* collection that represents all the elements contained within that element. In addition, a *children* collection is exposed representing the elements that are immediate children of the current element. These collections work in the same manner as the document element collections introduced in Chapter 7, "Document Element Collections." Using these collections, you can create a highly customized collection. Here are a few examples:

```
// All the H1 elements that are children of the body
document.body.children.tags("H1")
// All LI elements in the third UL element on the page
document.all.tags("UL")[2].children.tags("LI")
// All Paragraph elements contained anywhere within the first DIV
// element, even in a nested DIV or Table element
document.all.tags("DIV")[0].all.tags("P")
```

Determining Whether One Element Is Contained Within Another

As mentioned in Chapter 3, "Dynamic HTML Event Model," every element exposes a *contains* method that can be used to quickly determine whether another element is within its scope. The *contains* method takes an element and returns a value of *true* if the element is a child element, a child of a child, and so forth.

The *contains* method was introduced to simplify writing *onmouseover* and *onmouseout* event handlers. Code in Chapter 3, "Dynamic HTML Event Model," demonstrates how to use the *contains* method to check whether the mouse cursor has entered or exited the element on which the event fired and hasn't only entered or exited a child element.

The *sourceIndex* Property

All elements expose a read-only 32-bit integer *sourceIndex* property that contains the element's ordinal position in the document's *all* collection. This position is also the position of the element in the parsing tree if the tree were flattened into a list. The *sourceIndex* property can be used to determine the relative location of an element and its relationship to other elements in the document.

Do not rely on the *sourceIndex* property to return the same value; the indexing can change if more elements are created for the document in the future. For example, do not expect two elements' *sourceIndex* values to always be a fixed distance apart. If you use the *sourceIndex* property, make comparisons by generically locating an element in a loop.

Constructing a Parsing Tree

One of the best ways to understand the containment relationships in an HTML document is to construct the parsing tree using the document's *all* collection. The following document contains code that automatically outputs a nested table representing the containership hierarchy of each element in the document. This code fragment can be placed in any document to get a quick tree view.

```
<HTML>
   <HEAD>
      <TITLE>Tree Builder</TITLE>
      <SCRIPT LANGUAGE="JavaScript">
         function buildTree() {
            var intParents = 0;
            var intIndent = 0;
            // strStruct stores the HTML string that
            // will represent the document.
            var strStruct = "<HTML><TITLE>Document Tree</TITLE>" +
               "<BODY><TABLE BORDER CELLPADDING=5><TR>";
            var elParent;
            // Walk through every element in the document.
            for (var intLoop = 0; intLoop < document.all.length;
                  intLoop++) {
               elParent = document.all[intLoop];
               // Determine depth of the element.
```

```
                while (elParent.tagName != "HTML") {
                    intParents++;
                    elParent = elParent.parentElement;
                }
                // Nest or close nesting based on new depth.
                if (intParents > intIndent)
                    strStruct +=
                        "<TABLE BORDER WIDTH=100% CELLPADDING=5><TR>";
                else if (intParents < intIndent) {
                    for (var intClose = intParents;
                            intClose < intIndent; intClose++)
                        strStruct += "</TABLE>";
                }
                intIndent = intParents;
                intParents = 0;
                strStruct += "<TD>" +
                    document.all[intLoop].tagName;
            }
            // Close any remaining scopes.
            for (var intClose = intParents; intClose < intIndent;
                    intClose++)
                strStruct += "</TD></TR></TABLE>";
            strStruct += "</BODY></HTML>";
                // Output the new document in a new window.
            var w = window.open("", "tree");
            w.document.open();
            w.document.write(strStruct);
            w.document.close();
        }
        window.onload = buildTree;
    </SCRIPT>
  </HEAD>
  <BODY>
    <H1>Tree Builder</H1>
    <UL>
        <LI>Test Item 1
            <UL>
                <LI>Subitem 1
                <LI>Subitem 2
            </UL>
        </LI>
        <LI>Test Item 2</LI>
    </UL>
    <DIV>
        <P>This is <EM>cool.</EM></P>
    </DIV>
  </BODY>
</HTML>
```

This code constructs the tree by enumerating the document's *all* collection and calculating the depth of each element using the *parentElement* property. This routine could be rewritten recursively using the *children* collection on each element.

Figure 8-1 shows the containership hierarchy generated by this code. The nested tables show what elements are scoped within what other elements.

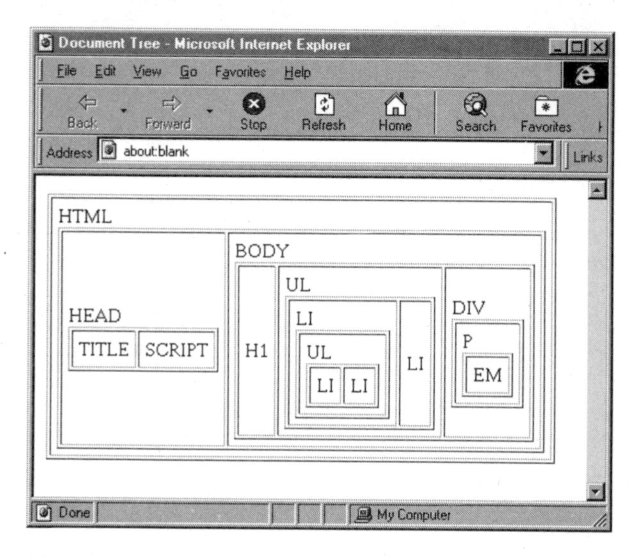

Figure 8-1.
The containership hierarchy for an HTML document.

The *document* Property

Each element exposes a *document* property that represents the document the element belongs to. This property allows generic scripts to determine what document—and from the document, what window—an arbitrary element originated from. For example, the following expression references the window containing the element:

```
myElement.document.parentWindow  // The window for an element.
```

Creating New Elements

Elements can be added to the document using one of two techniques: creating a new element in memory and associating it with the document, or directly modifying the underlying HTML contents. The direct modification of the underlying HTML contents is discussed in Chapter 13, "Dynamic Contents." This section demonstrates the first technique, creating elements in memory.

Some elements can be created by using the *createElement* method on the document or by using the *new* operator on the window. Both methods perform the same action and return a new element object. The *createElement* method is a language-independent mechanism for constructing elements; the *new* operator is provided for compatibility with Netscape Navigator. The newly created element object is not maintained in memory and is not associated with the document until it is explicitly added to the document. The following code demonstrates using both techniques to create an IMG element:

```
var img = new Image();
var img = document.createElement("IMG");
```

Internet Explorer 4.0 allows the creation of only three elements in this fashion: IMG, Option, and Area.

You can dynamically add new Option and Area elements to list boxes and image maps, respectively. The construction of images is currently limited to allowing images to preload into the cache. The IMG element itself cannot be added to the document. Instead, because the construction forces an image to download into the cache, simply assigning the URL of the image to the *src* attribute of an existing image causes the new image to display, as shown here:

```
var img = new Image();
img.src = "cool.gif";  // Download the image in the background.
document.all.myImage.src = "cool.gif";  // Use downloaded image.
```

New Option and Area elements can be added to the document. The Select element exposes an *options* collection of the Option elements it contains, and the Map element exposes an *areas* collection of the Area elements it contains. These collections allow additional Option or Area elements to be dynamically added or removed.

The technique for adding and removing these elements plus examples of how to take advantage of preloading images are discussed in the next two chapters. All other contents in the document's Body element can be modified by directly changing the HTML, as discussed in Chapter 13, "Dynamic Contents."

Customizing Elements

Dynamic HTML exposes all information about the document, including unrecognized elements and attributes. This feature can be used to create user-defined behavior based on custom elements and attributes. For example, you can write code that causes any UL element that is specified with the custom *outline* attribute to be expandable and collapsible. And you can define a new tag for defining constants and other behaviors in the document.

The benefit of these techniques is that code becomes much more generalized. No longer must a content author understand scripting to add complex behavior to elements. Developers can now write their code more intelligently and document how the content author can use this new functionality that custom attributes and elements offer.

Element Default Actions

All elements in the Body element of the document expose a *click* method. Scripts can use the *click* method to simulate a user clicking the element. The method fires the *onclick* event on the element, and then invokes any action the element takes by default when clicked. Because the *onclick* event is fired prior to the default action occurring, the developer can override the default action in an *onclick* event handler.

Customizing Existing Elements

Because the object model exposes unrecognized attributes and their values, extra information can be easily attached to the element and manipulated using scripts. By adding unrecognized attributes, you can provide existing elements with additional behavior. For example, you can add an *outline* attribute to a list element to specify that the list can be expanded and collapsed. The code checks whether the user has clicked in a list that has the *outline* attribute defined and performs the appropriate action.

Using unrecognized attributes is a powerful way to simulate subclassing of an element. The behavior of the element can be completely customized and even overridden by using unrecognized attributes with event bubbling.

Determining the Existence of an Attribute

Custom attributes can be used to modify an element's behavior just by the attribute's presence. Code can check an element to see whether it has the attribute and perform an action if it does:

```
<IMG ID="image1" SRC="img1.gif" dragEnabled>
<H1 ID="header1">Test</H1>
<SCRIPT LANGUAGE="JavaScript">
   alert(document.all.image1.getAttribute("dragEnabled") == null);
      // false
   alert(document.all.header1.getAttribute("dragEnabled") == null);
      // true
</SCRIPT>
```

This example demonstrates adding custom attributes and simply checking for their existence. Code in Chapter 12, "Dynamic Positioning," extends this example by enabling any element with the *dragEnabled* attribute to be dragged around the document.

A custom attribute used in this way differs from a compact value in an important respect. The custom attribute signals a behavior just by its presence, unlike a compact value, which signals a behavior by having the value *true.* To turn off the drag ability of an element in the preceding example, code must remove the *dragEnabled* attribute using *removeAttribute,* not simply change its value to *false.*

User-Defined Elements

Because unrecognized elements are exposed in the object model, you can add elements to the document that contain meta information or other processing information in a well-defined structured manner. For example, an unrecognized element such as *<LASTEDITBY name="Scott Isaacs">,* containing the name of the person who last edited the document, can be added to the document. This element can now be referenced through code:

```
// First instance of the LastEditBy element
document.all.tags("LASTEDITBY")[0].getAttribute("name")
```

All attributes of unrecognized elements and recognized elements can also be accessed in the object model. This technique can be used to define new behavior for a document, without modifying the scripts. For example, if a constant requires frequent changing by a nondeveloper, supplying it in an element or as an unknown attribute on an existing tag may be an appropriate approach. Or you could use a custom Sequence element to define a sequence of presentation effects to perform on the document.

This technique is extremely powerful for adding behavior to the document, but be careful when you are using invalid HTML to store information. In the future, if a custom-defined element becomes a valid element in HTML, there is potential for the page to no longer function properly.

HTML-Based Constants

By taking advantage of Dynamic HTML's ability to expose unrecognized elements, you can declare constants using HTML rather than within the code. The advantage to this approach is that constants can be edited without the need to modify or understand scripting.

The following code uses an unrecognized element, HTMLConstant, to store any necessary constants. HTMLConstant supports three attributes: *id, value,* and *type.* The *id* and *value* attributes are required; they specify the name of the constant and the default value. The *type* attribute is optional because all constants default to strings. If an integer or a floating constant is required, the *type* attribute must be specified.

```
<HTML>
   <HEAD>
      <TITLE>HTML-Based Constants</TITLE>
      <HTMLCONSTANT id="startPosition" value="3" type="integer">
      <HTMLCONSTANT id="endPosition" value="2.02" type="float">
      <HTMLCONSTANT id="defaultUser" value="Scott" type="string">

      <SCRIPT LANGUAGE="JavaScript">
         function setupConstants() {
            // Get all constants.
            var Constants = document.all.tags("HTMLCONSTANT");
            document._Constants = new Object();
            for (var intLoop = 0; intLoop < Constants.length;
                  intLoop++) {
               var temp = Constants[intLoop];
               // Determine data type.
               if ("integer" == temp.type)
                  document._Constants[temp.id] = parseInt(temp.value);
               else if ("float" == temp.type)
                  document._Constants[temp.id] =
                     parseFloat(temp.value);
               else
                  // String is default.
                  document._Constants[temp.id] = temp.value;
            }
         }
      </SCRIPT>
   </HEAD>
   <BODY ONLOAD="setupConstants()">
      <H1>HTML-Based Constants</H1>
   </BODY>
</HTML>
```

All constants are exposed on a subobject on the document, *_Constants*. Constants can be referenced as follows:

document._Constants.*constantID*

In the preceding document, constants are not available until the document is loaded because the *onload* event triggers the initialization of constants, allowing constants to be declared anywhere within the document. If access to the constants is required before the document is loaded, this function should be called during the parsing of the page. All constants must be defined before the script's location in the source.

Custom Content Containers

As demonstrated earlier, unrecognized tags can be used to add more contextual information to the document. This technique works well for creating contentless elements. Contentless elements do not have an end tag; they contain all their relevant information in attributes (similar to the IMG element).

The object model is not highly suited for creating custom content containers because of the way the elements are handled in the parsing tree. Unrecognized tags cannot have any children and therefore cannot have any text associated with them. Managing and associating contents with an unrecognized tag, while possible, is extremely difficult. This difficulty is not so much a shortcoming in the object model as a shortcoming in the design of HTML. There is no precise way to specify that an unrecognized element is a container and that an end tag should exist. Furthermore, the contents of the container will be rendered by any and all browsers because the element will not be recognized and therefore cannot have a style associated with it.

Although it is beyond the scope of this book, there is a markup language, called XML (Extensible Markup Language), that is designed for handling user-extensible elements. XML uses a syntax based on SGML and similar to HTML that can describe whether the element is a container or an empty element. For more information about XML, see the World Wide Web Consortium (W3C) Web site (www.w3.org) or Microsoft's Web site (www.microsoft.com).

<SCRIPT LANGUAGE="JavaSc
// Create property x
var x = 10;
function foo() {
// This code is not
code
var y =
alert(
// output
// Call foo while lo
foo();
window.foo(); // the
</SCRIPT>

CHAPTER NINE

Scripting Individual Elements

Chapter 8, "Scripts and Elements," introduced scripting elements in Dynamic HTML. While every element in an HTML document is accessible to scripts, this chapter focuses on techniques for programming a few of the elements that appear most commonly in scripts. Chapter 10, "Forms and Intrinsic Controls," describes techniques for programming elements in forms.

The following topics are covered in this chapter:

- **Programming the Body and Frameset elements** HTML defines two types of documents: documents with Body elements for displaying contents, and documents with Frameset elements for dividing the screen into frames for loading other documents. This section introduces techniques for manipulating these elements.
- **Programming the Anchor element** Anchor elements serve a dual purpose in HTML: as links that navigate to new pages, and as bookmarks that act as destinations. This section discusses how to manipulate both types of Anchor elements and how to add custom behavior to them.
- **Programming the Link element** The Link element is used to define relationships between documents. Microsoft Internet Explorer 4.0 supports the Link element for specifying linked style sheets. This section shows you how to define and take advantage of custom relationships between documents.
- **Programming the IMG and Map elements** Dynamic HTML exposes a rich object model for manipulating images and image maps. New images can be loaded in the background so that they can be displayed instantly, and image maps can be dynamically modified and scaled.

- **Programming the Marquee element** The Marquee element is currently an Internet Explorer–specific feature used to automatically scroll a block of text. The Marquee element can be customized and manipulated using the Dynamic HTML object model.
- **Programming the Object element** The Object element is used to embed custom contents, including ActiveX controls and Java applets, in the HTML document. The custom contents can expose a customized object model alongside that of the Object element. This section shows you how to access this object model.
- **Programming the Table element** Tables are used for two purposes: displaying tabular data in a gridlike format, and creating a sophisticated layout. This section discusses the relationship between the underlying HTML for the table and the object model representation.

Programming the Body and Frameset Elements

An HTML document can contain either of two types of contents: body contents or a frameset definition. The first Body or Frameset element appearing in the document defines the document's type. A similar object model is exposed for the document in both cases.

The *body* Property

The *document* object exposes a *body* property that represents the root of the document's contents. The name of this property is ambiguous because the *body* property can represent either a Frameset or a Body element, depending on the document type. As explained in Chapter 7, "Document Element Collections," every document has a Body or Frameset element, regardless of whether it is explicitly declared. If a document's frameset nests other Frameset elements, the *body* property represents the outermost Frameset element in the document.

The Body or Frameset element is also contained in the document's *all* collection. Thus, the *body* property can be accessed directly from the document as follows:

```
// Returns "BODY" or "FRAMESET" depending on the type of document
document.body.tagName;
```

Or it can be accessed through the *all* collection:

```
// For documents with a Body element
document.all.tags("Body").item(0).tagName;        // Returns "BODY"
```

```
/* Displays "true"; demonstrates that the two elements are the
   same */
alert(document.all.tags("Body").item(0) == document.body);

// For documents with a Frameset element
document.all.tags("Frameset").item(0).tagName;    // Returns "FRAMESET"
/* Displays "true"; demonstrates that the two elements are the
   same */
alert(document.all.tags("Frameset").item(0) == document.body);
```

In the preceding code, the *tags* method returns a collection consisting of the Body or the Frameset elements. If the document has a Body element, the HTML DTD (document type definition) limits it to a single Body element, and the parser ignores any extra ones. If the document has a Frameset element, it can have multiple Frameset elements; the *tags* method returns all of them, beginning with the outermost one. In either case, the first element in the collection returned by the *tags* method is the element contained in the *body* property. The code uses *item* to access this element.

Availability of the *body* Property

The object model is constructed and exposed simultaneously during the parsing of the document. Before the parser encounters the body or frameset of the document, the *body* property is not available, and therefore the *body* property returns *null*. The following code illustrates the availability of the *body* property:

```
<HTML>
   <SCRIPT LANGUAGE="JavaScript">
      alert(document.body == null);     // true--precedes <BODY> tag
   </SCRIPT>
   <BODY>
      <SCRIPT LANGUAGE="JavaScript">
         alert(document.body == null); // false--follows <BODY> tag
      </SCRIPT>
   </BODY>
</HTML>
```

For documents with body contents, the <BODY> tag does not have to appear explicitly in the document to be accessible. Instead, the Body element is implicitly created once the document contains an element—or simply some text—that must be a part of the body. The elements that make up body contents are defined by the HTML DTD. Chapter 1, "Overview of HTML and CSS," explains how to read a DTD, and more information about how the document is parsed is provided in Chapter 7, "Document Element Collections."

Distinguishing Between Body and Frameset Contents

You can use the *tagName* property to determine whether a document contains a body or a frameset. The following code displays an alert box reporting its document type—in this case, a frameset:

```
<HTML>
   <HEAD>
      <TITLE>Frameset Exposed as the Body</TITLE>
   </HEAD>
   <FRAMESET ROWS="100%" ONLOAD="alert(document.body.tagName);">
      <FRAME SRC="foo.htm">
   </FRAMESET>
</HTML>
```

Checking the length of the *frames* collection on the window is not an accurate way to determine whether a document is a frameset. A document with a Body element may contain IFrame elements, which would be included in the *frames* collection.

Client Window and Document Size

The width and height of the client window are exposed as properties of the Body and Frame elements. The *physical size* of the document is the size of the client area— that is, the amount of space the document occupies on the screen. The *logical size* of the document is the size of the contents. For document contents that are larger than the window, scrollbars are usually displayed. Figure 9-1 illustrates the properties that represent the physical and logical size of the document, and the subsequent sections describe them. Other elements in the document can expose the same properties for determining their size. The special relationship these properties share with other elements in the document is discussed in Chapter 12, "Dynamic Positioning."

Physical Size

The physical width and height of the document (frameset or body type) are exposed through the *offsetWidth* and *offsetHeight* properties of the Frameset or Body element. The physical width and height measure the area of the currently visible window including the scrollbars. The *clientWidth* and *clientHeight* properties are exposed to determine the size of the client area—the physical size as defined by the *offsetWidth* and *offsetHeight* properties less the size of the scrollbars and surrounding borders. These properties are read-only and cannot be used to change the size of the window.

In Figure 9-1, no horizontal scrollbar is displayed, so the *offsetHeight* and *clientHeight* properties would be the same if the border was set to *0*. However,

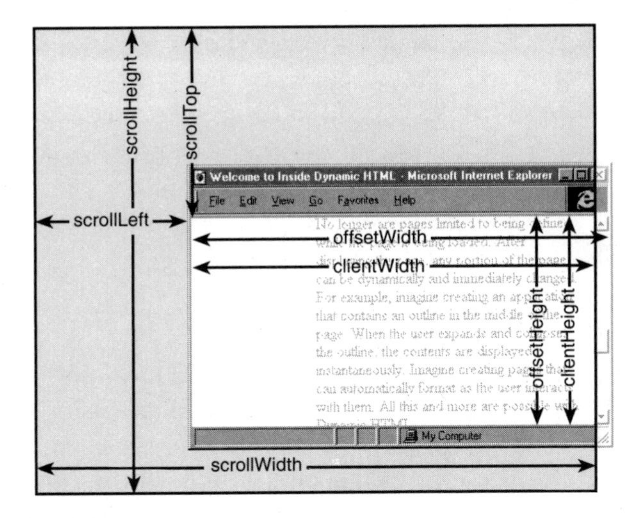

Figure 9-1.
Properties for determining the window and document size.

a vertical scrollbar is displayed, so the *offsetWidth* and *clientWidth* properties represent distinct values.

Logical Size

The Body element exposes four properties for determining the logical size of the document and the position of the user's view into the document: *scrollWidth*, *scrollHeight*, *scrollTop*, and *scrollLeft*. The logical size of the document represents the total height and width of the document, not the size of the browser window that provides a view into the document. These properties are not available or necessary on frameset documents because the logical size of the frameset is equivalent to its physical size.

The *scrollWidth* and *scrollHeight* properties represent the logical size of the document in pixels. These properties are read-only and are calculated by the browser based on the document contents. You can change the *scrollWidth* and *scrollHeight* properties by dynamically adding or removing elements or by resizing the window. Resizing the window usually affects both properties because the contents rewrap to the new width.

The *scrollTop* and *scrollLeft* properties represent the scroll offsets of the logical document. They represent the point in the document that is displayed in the upper-left corner of the window. When the horizontal and vertical scrollbars are scrolled all the way to the left and top edges of the document, *scrollLeft* and *scrollTop* both equal *0*. These properties are read/write and can be modified to immediately scroll the document to a particular pixel position.

If you need to set *scrollLeft* and *scrollTop* at the same time, the *scroll* method on the window is a more convenient mechanism because it takes both new coordinates, horizontal and vertical, as arguments.

As a group, these properties provide information for determining the visible portion of the screen. The currently viewable area of the document can be easily calculated using the size properties, as shown here:

```
upperLeftX = document.body.scrollLeft;
upperLeftY = document.body.scrollTop;
lowerRightX = upperLeftX + document.body.clientWidth;
lowerRightY = upperLeftY + document.body.clientHeight;
```

The scrolling-related properties are also exposed on any other scrolling element. For example, you can give a Div element scrollbars using the CSS (Cascading Style Sheets) *overflow 3* property, and the TextArea element displays scrollbars by default. When these elements have scrollbars, they expose the scrolling-related properties for determining the scrolled regions of their contents. The TextArea element is discussed in detail in Chapter 10, "Forms and Intrinsic Controls," and the CSS *overflow* property is discussed in Chapter 12, "Dynamic Positioning."

Window Events

The Body and Frameset elements expose attributes corresponding to all window-level events. For example, the following code in a document with a Body element specifies an ONLOAD event handler for the window:

```
<BODY ONLOAD="doThis();">
```

The code for a frameset document is similar:

```
<FRAMESET ONLOAD="doThis();" ROWS="*">
```

Even when you use the <BODY> or <FRAMESET> tag to specify the handler for a window event, the event is scoped to the *window* object, not to the *body* object. This distinction is important when you use the *this* pointer in the event handler. In a body-level event handler, *this* points to the *body* object; in a window event handler, *this* points to the *window* object, even if you specify the handler in the <BODY> tag. The following code illustrates how *this* pointers work for a window event (*onload*) and a body event (*onclick*):

```
<BODY ONLOAD="alert(this == document.body);  // false"
   ONCLICK="alert(this == document.body);    // true">
</BODY>
```

Furthermore, for window events, the *srcElement* property of the *event* object contains *null.*

While a document can have multiple framesets, it can have only one handler for each window event. If several Frameset elements in the document define handlers for an event, only the last handler's code is executed. In the following example, only the second *onload* event handler executes, displaying the alert *b*. The event does not fire until the entire document is loaded.

```
<HTML>
   <HEAD>
      <TITLE>Frameset onload Event</TITLE>
   </HEAD>
   <FRAMESET ONLOAD="alert('a');" ROWS="100, *">
      <FRAMESET ONLOAD="alert('b');" COLS="*,*">
         <FRAME SRC="a.htm">
         <FRAME SRC="b.htm">
      </FRAMESET>
      <FRAME SRC="c.htm">
   </FRAMESET>
</HTML>
```

Because you can define only one handler per window event, you cannot specify a handler on a Frame or nested Frameset element that works only for that particular element. To protect against this behavior possibly changing in the future, window event handlers should be specified only on the first Frameset element.

The *onresize* Event

The *onresize* event is fired whenever the size of the physical window changes, not the size of the contents within the body or frameset document. Therefore, this event is actually a window event when defined on the Body element. The *onresize* event is also exposed on elements within the document that have a defined size. In those cases, the event fires only when the physical size of the element changes.

When a document is first loaded into a new window, the *onresize* event does not fire. Therefore, if code is being used to lay out the document based on the initial window size, the code should be called from the *onload* event.

Programming Body Contents

Documents that contain a Body element have a few additional features not available to frameset documents, including access to the HTML and textual contents contained within the body and an *onscroll* event that fires when the window is scrolled.

You can write scripts to manipulate the text in the Body element or any element in the body. The techniques are discussed in Chapter 13, "Dynamic Contents."

The *onscroll* Event

The *window* object exposes an *onscroll* event that fires whenever the window is scrolled either explicitly by the user or through code. This event occurs only in documents with Body elements and not in frameset documents because they do not display scrollbars.

Programming Frameset Contents

Because the frameset document is another type of HTML document, it supports the document object model. The frameset document exposes an *all* collection that provides direct access to all the elements in the document. Through the *all* collection, the individual attributes of each Frameset and Frame element can be accessed and in many cases dynamically modified.

While the number of frames in the frameset is static and cannot be modified without creating a new document, a number of the attributes of the Frameset element can be changed. For example, the ROWS and COLS attributes are read/write attributes, which allows you to change the layout of the frameset dynamically. This flexibility can be used to add custom behavior to a traditional frameset.

The following code creates a custom layout that allows the user to select from a set of pages. This example turns off the resizing capability of each frame and instead automatically expands the frame the user clicks on. This layout model requires a small amount of code behind the frameset and each document.

```
<HTML>
   <HEAD>
      <TITLE>Sliding Frames</TITLE>
      <SCRIPT LANGUAGE="JavaScript">
         var defSize = 25;
         if (f == _current) return; // check if already active
         _current = f;
         function display(f) {
            var newRows = "";
            // Get all the Frame elements.
            var elFrame = document.all.tags("FRAME");
            for (var intFrames = 0; intFrames < frames.length;
                  intFrames++) {
               var curF = frames[intFrames].document;
               if (curF.body == f.document.body) {
                  // Give selected frame all the space.
                  newRows += "*, ";
                  /* Make the header much bigger. */
                  curF.all.header.style.fontSize = "200%";
                  /* Turn on scrollbars for the active frame
                     by accessing the Frame element
```

```
                  elFrame[intFrames].scrolling = "yes";
               }
               else {
                  // Set to default size.
                  newRows += defSize.toString() + ", ";
                  // Reset header font size.
                  curF.all.header.style.fontSize = "";
                  // Turn off scrolling.
                  elFrame[intFrames].scrolling = "no";
               }
            }
            document.body.rows = newRows;
         }
      </SCRIPT>
   </HEAD>
   <FRAMESET ROWS="*, 25, 25">
      <FRAME SRC="home.htm" NORESIZE>
      <FRAME SRC="news.htm" NORESIZE SCROLLING="No">
      <FRAME SRC="info.htm" NORESIZE SCROLLING="No">
   </FRAMESET>
</HTML>
```

Figure 9-2 demonstrates this code in action. When the user clicks on the News or Information heading, the other frames automatically shrink and the selected frame expands to take up the remaining view.

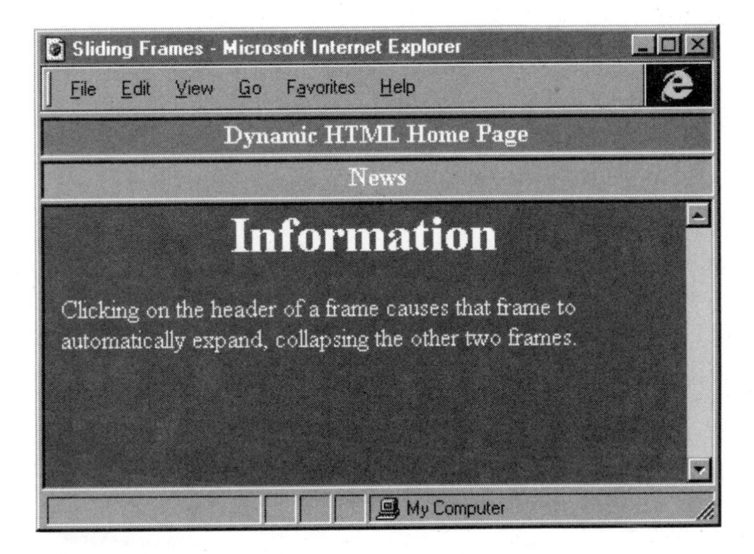

Figure 9-2.
An example of automatically sliding frames.

In each document in the frameset, the *onfocus* event handler must call the *display* routine. The *parent* property on the document must be referenced to call the function:

```
<!-- The onfocus event must be defined for each document in the
     frameset. -->
<BODY ONFOCUS="parent.display(this);">
```

Also in each document in the frameset, the ID of the first paragraph must have the value *header*. The text in this paragraph will be enlarged when the document has the focus.

This example demonstrates modifying the attributes of individual frames. The Frame element in the *all* collection of the document is different from the contents of the window's *frames* collection. The *frames* collection on the window returns the window instance created based on the document's source. The Frame element in the *all* collection represents the frame as defined by the HTML source and is used to create the window. Modifying the Frame element can modify the window and its contents—for example, scrollbars can be manually turned on and off. Scrollbars have been turned off in our example so that they do not clutter the collapsed heading view of the document.

Programming the Anchor Element

The HTML Anchor element serves a dual purpose: to specify links for navigating to URLs and to specify bookmarks within the document. An Anchor element acts as a link if its HREF attribute is defined, and it acts as a bookmark if its NAME attribute is defined:

```
<A HREF="http://www.insideDHTML.com#Chapter2"><!-- Link --></A>
<A NAME="Chapter2"><!-- Bookmark --></A>
```

The document's *all* collection references all of the Anchor elements. The document has two additional collections that separately reference the links and the bookmarks. Links are exposed through the *links* collection, and bookmarks are exposed through the *anchors* collection. A single Anchor element can appear in both collections if both a NAME and an HREF attribute are specified.

Both the *href* and the *name* properties can be changed through code, so the anchor object can dynamically switch collections. For example, if an anchor with an empty *href* is assigned a string, it is automatically added to the *links* collection and is also automatically rendered as a link on the screen. Regardless of the type of anchor and the collections it is in, the anchor object exposes the same set of properties, methods, and events.

NOTE: From here on, anchors specified as <A NAME=> are referred to as bookmarks and anchors specified as <A HREF=> are referred to as links to disambiguate the two types of anchors. These links are different from the Link element discussed in the section "Programming the Link Element" later in this chapter. The <LINK> tag defines the Link element.

The *href* Property

The anchor object has a number of properties that contain portions of the URL exposed by the *href* property. The *protocol, hostname, port, pathname, search,* and *hash* properties reference the individual parts of the URL, and the *host* property contains both host name and port information. These properties, which also belong to the *location* object, are described in Chapter 4, "The Browser Window."

Anchors and the Base HREF

An interesting relationship exists between relatively specified HREF values and the object model. A relative HREF is a URL that does not start explicitly with // (for example, *href="goHere.htm"*). All relative HREFs are prefixed with a default location. Unless otherwise specified, the default location is the location of the current document. You can use the Base element to change the default location. For relative URLs assigned to attributes, the default location is added when the document is parsed. For relative URLs assigned to properties by scripts, the default location is not added until the URL is referenced. The following code illustrates these points:

```
<HTML>
   <HEAD>
      <TITLE>Base HREF Demo</TITLE>
      <BASE HREF="http://scotti/">
   </HEAD>
   <BODY>
      <A HREF="page1.htm">page 1</A>
      <A HREF="http://ji/page2.htm">page 2</A>
      <SCRIPT LANGUAGE="JavaScript">
         alert(document.links[0].href); // http://scotti/page1.htm
         alert(document.links[1].href); // http://ji/page2.htm
         document.links[0].href = "newpage.htm";
         alert(document.links[0].href); // newpage.htm
      </SCRIPT>
   </BODY>
</HTML>
```

Script-Specified HREF Attribute

The HREF attribute of an Anchor element may be alternatively specified as a line of code to execute rather than as a URL. This technique is useful when a frame is to contain a short string because it reduces the number of necessary round-trips with the server. For example, when the user clicks on the following anchor, a simple document that displays the string *Hello, world!* is created:

```
<A HREF="JavaScript:'Hello, world!'">
```

The *protocol* is the language name followed by a colon, and the *pathname* is the rest of the string. The *href* property itself contains the entire string with appropriate escape sequences (such as *%20* for each space).

Script-specified HREF attributes execute after the *onclick* event stops firing. Also, since the HREF attribute is not an event, the *event* object is not available at the time the script-specified HREF executes.

NOTE: Take care when using VBScript for script-specified HREF attributes. Netscape Navigator recognizes only the JavaScript language and will display a navigation error if VBScript is specified.

Events on the Anchor Element

The Anchor element supports a set of standard events that indicate when the user clicks on, moves the mouse over, or types in an anchor. The events that can originate with the Anchor element depend on whether the anchor is a link or a bookmark. If the Anchor element cannot act as a source for the event, it will never be defined as *srcElement* if the event bubbles.

Event	Source
onblur	Link anchors
onclick	All anchors
ondblclick	All anchors
onfocus	Link anchors
onkeydown	Link anchors
onkeypress	Link anchors
onkeyup	Link anchors
onmousedown	All anchors
onmousemove	All anchors
onmouseout	All anchors
onmouseover	All anchors
onmouseup	All anchors

However, through event bubbling, the Anchor element can receive the event from a child event (such as an image in the anchor) even if it does not explicitly support it. The preceding table lists the events for which each type of anchor can act as the source. All events can be defined as attributes on the element, through the <SCRIPT FOR= EVENT= > syntax or through properties of the Anchor element. To be a source for focus and keyboard events, an element must be able to receive the focus. Anchors that are links can receive the focus; bookmarks cannot.

The default result of clicking on a link is a jump to the anchor. This action can be overridden to customize how a page handles a link. The following code cancels the default action of a specific link:

```
<A HREF="foo.htm#100" ONCLICK="event.returnValue = false;">
```

If you want compatibility with other browsers, return the value directly:

```
<A HREF="foo.htm#100" ONCLICK="return false;">
```

More generically, anchors can be overridden at the document level by handling the document's *onclick* event, as shown in the following code. This technique works because the standard events, except *onblur* and *onfocus*, bubble up the document's hierarchy chain.

```
<SCRIPT FOR="document" EVENT="onclick()" LANGUAGE="JavaScript">
   // Event object contains global information for the event handler.
   if ("A" == event.srcElement.tagName) {
      event.returnValue = false;
      // Write custom handler code for the anchor.
   }
</SCRIPT>
```

The event sequence defines the *ondblclick* event to follow the *onclick* event. The only way to determine whether a link received a double click is to override the default action of the single click because the event sequence is fixed. There is no way to write an event handler for a link that performs a default action for a click event and a different action for the double click because the link already navigates to the targeted link before the *ondblclick* event fires. Therefore, the usefulness of an *ondblclick* event on a link is fairly limited, and most interactions with anchors are accomplished using the *onclick* event.

Customizing Links to Target Multiple Frames

One technique for adding custom behavior to an anchor is to define a few new attributes on the Anchor element. This technique for simulating subclassing was introduced in Chapter 8, "Scripts and Elements." This section demonstrates how to augment the traditional behavior of anchors. The simple example presented here implements the basics for a much-requested feature of HTML and framesets—the ability to target multiple frames with a single anchor. This example demonstrates how authors can add their own functionality to a page, without having to wait for the browser to add the support.

The following code adds two user-defined attributes to the Anchor element: *mhref* and *mtarget*. Both attributes take a semicolon-delimited list of values—for *mhref*, a list of URLs, and for *mtarget*, a list of destinations for these URLs. When the user clicks on an anchor, the code first checks whether the anchor has these special attributes and, if it does, the code overrides the default behavior of following a single link with the custom linking code.

```
<HTML>
   <HEAD>
      <TITLE>Targeting Multiple Frames</TITLE>
      <SCRIPT LANGUAGE="JavaScript">
         function checkElementTree(el, strTag) {
            /* This simple function walks up the tree from the element
               el and looks for any element with the tag strTag.
               The first matching element found is returned. */
            while ("HTML" != el.tagName) {
               if (strTag == el.tagName)
                  return el;
               el = el.parentElement;
            }
            return null;
         }

         function multiJump() {
            // Find the anchor.
            var el = checkElementTree(event.srcElement, "A");
            if (null != el) { // Found an anchor.
               // Check whether it is a multitarget anchor.
               if ((null != el.getAttribute("mhref")) &&
                     (null != el.getAttribute("mtarget"))) {
                  event.returnValue = false;
                  var mhref = new Array();
                  var mtarget = new Array();
                  // Parse attributes into arrays.
                  mhref = el.getAttribute("mhref").split("; ");
                  mtarget =
                     el.getAttribute("mtarget").split("; ");
                  /* Be sure there are an equal number
                     of targets and URLs. */
                  if (mtarget.length == mhref.length)
```

```
                  for (var intLoop = 0; intLoop < mtarget.length;
                        intLoop++)
                     if (null != parent[mtarget[intLoop]])
                        parent[mtarget[intLoop]].location.href =
                           mhref[intLoop];
               }
            }
         }
      </SCRIPT>
   </HEAD>
   <BODY ONCLICK="multiJump();">
      <A HREF="#"
            mhref="http://www.microsoft.com; http://www.netscape.com"
            mtarget="left; right">
         Browser Web sites
      </A>
   </BODY>
</HTML>
```

This code works only for frames that are siblings to the frame containing it. To make this code work for frames that exist anywhere in the frameset hierarchy, you must write code that simulates the searching algorithm used by the browser to search the hierarchy of windows.

Subclassing elements with user-defined attributes is one of the most powerful ways to take advantage of Dynamic HTML. It lets you easily customize elements, without having to hard-code the customizations into HTML or the scripting language. Custom attributes can be defined for identifying new behavior, and the code can look for these identifiers and process the elements accordingly.

Pseudo-Classes for Anchors

Style sheets provide a technique for defining styles for the three states of a link: visited, not visited, and active. These states can each have a different style, which you set using pseudo-classes in CSS. Pseudo-classes provide a technique for improving user interactivity without requiring any code. See Chapter 1, "Overview of HTML and CSS," or the CSS specification at the W3C Web site for more information about pseudo-classes and the CSS language.

Beyond using the pseudo-class, no property is currently exposed to the scripting language for directly determining whether a link has been visited. Therefore, there is no simple way to conditionally script links based on whether they have been visited.

Removing Anchors

Simply assigning an empty string to either the *href* or the *name* property does not remove an Anchor element from the document. However, this technique will remove the element from the *links* or *anchors* collection, respectively. (The element will always remain in the *all* collection.)

An Anchor element and its contents can be completely removed from the document by using the *outerHTML* or the *outerText* property. To remove the influence of the anchor but leave the contents, the *TextRange* object can be used. The following code demonstrates how to manipulate *TextRange.* Don't worry if you do not understand this code. The *TextRange* object and its methods are discussed in detail in Chapter 14, "User Selection and Editing Operations."

```
<SCRIPT LANGUAGE="JavaScript">
   function removeAnchor(aElement) {
      // The anchor to remove is passed as an argument.
      // Create a TextRange object.
      var tr = aElement.parentTextEdit.createTextRange();
      // Locate the Anchor element in the TextRange.
      tr.moveToElementText(aElement);
      // Execute a command to remove the Anchor element.
      tr.execCommand("Unlink", false);
   }
</SCRIPT>
```

Programming the Link Element

The previous section showed you how to program an Anchor element that is either a bookmark or a link. HTML also provides a Link element that can be used to define relationships between different types of documents. This section focuses on a technique for defining relationships between documents using the Link element and the REL and HREF attributes, which can be accessed from scripts.

At the time of this writing, Internet Explorer uses link relationships for style sheets. However, by writing some simple scripts, you can use the REL attribute to define other relationships. Defining relationships not only can make your Web site more manageable, but it also can make the Web site accessible to tools that analyze Web sites.

The following example demonstrates how to create a navigation bar that reads each document's Link element to ascertain the next and previous documents. A navigation bar is useful when a sequence of documents is being presented. The navigation bar and contents panes are defined through a simple frameset. Whenever a new document is loaded, the document calls a function on the frameset to update the navigation buttons based on the new document's links.

Figure 9-3 shows the navigation bar in action. The availability of the buttons in the top pane and their destination when clicked are defined by Link relationships.

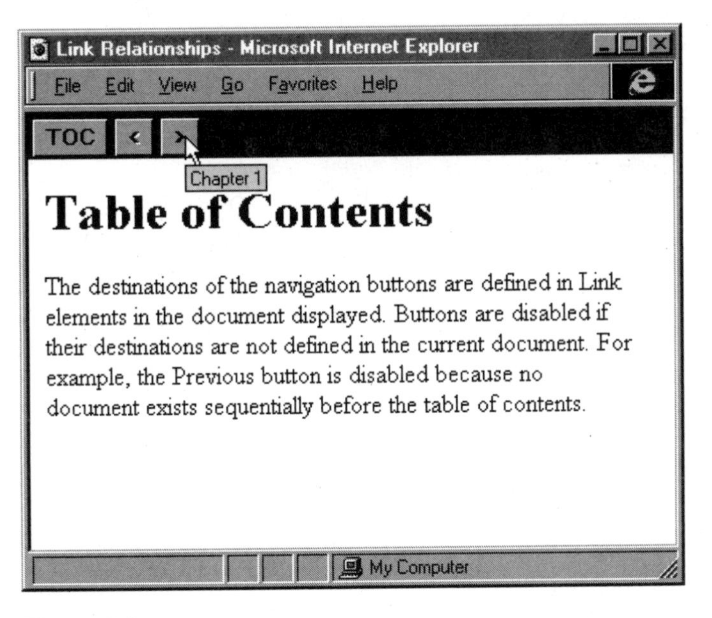

Figure 9-3.
A navigation bar based on Link elements.

The links.htm Document

The links.htm document, shown in the following code, defines the frameset and contains the core code for managing the relationship between the links on the page and the navigation bar. Each document displayed in the contents frame must call the *setupLinks* function after it loads in order to update the navigation bar of the navigation pane. When the page unloads, the *clearLinks* method must be called in order to disable all the relationship buttons, thereby ensuring that the links are appropriate if the user navigates to a page that does not define any relationships.

```
<HTML>
   <HEAD>
      <TITLE>Link Relationships</TITLE>
      <SCRIPT LANGUAGE="JavaScript">
         function setButton(b, dis, title, href) {
            b.disabled = dis;
            b.title = title;
            b.href = href;
         }

         function clearLinks() {
            var navDoc = window.navigation.document.all;
            // Initialize buttons by disabling them
            // and removing their titles.
            with (navDoc) {
               setButton(previous, true, "", "");
               setButton(next, true, "", "");
            }
         }

         function setupLinks(doc) {
            // The calling document needs to be passed in.
            // Get all the Link elements.
            var links = doc.all.tags("LINK");
            var navDoc = navigation.document.all;
            clearLinks();
            for (var intLink = 0; intLink < links.length; intLink++) {
               var el = links[intLink];
               if ("previous" == el.rel) {
                  /* If a previous relationship is defined, update
                     the buttons. */
                  setButton(navDoc.previous, false, el.title,
                     el.href);
               }
               if ("next" == el.rel) {
                  /* If a next relationship is defined, update
                     the buttons. */
                  setButton(navDoc.next, false, el.title, el.href);
               }
            }
         }
      </SCRIPT>
   </HEAD>
   <FRAMESET ROWS="28, *" BORDER=0>
      <FRAME SRC="navigate.htm" NAME="navigation" SCROLLING=NO>
      <FRAME SRC="contents.htm" NAME="contents">
   </FRAMESET>
</HTML>
```

The navigate.htm Document

This code creates the navigation bar:

```
<HTML>
   <HEAD>
      <TITLE>Navigation Bar</TITLE>
      <STYLE TYPE="text/css">
         body {margin-top:2pt; margin-left:2pt; background:gray}
         input {font-weight:bold}
      </STYLE>
   </HEAD>
   <BODY>
      <INPUT TYPE=BUTTON VALUE="TOC" TITLE="Table of Contents"
         ONCLICK="top.contents.location = 'contents.htm';">
      <INPUT TYPE=BUTTON ID="previous" VALUE=" < "
         ONCLICK="parent.contents.location = this.href;">
      <INPUT TYPE=BUTTON ID="next" VALUE=" > "
         ONCLICK="parent.contents.location = this.href;">
   </BODY>
</HTML>
```

> NOTE: The buttons in this example are drawn with extra spaces between them because carriage returns separate their tags in the code. To close the gap between the buttons, remove the carriage returns and all spaces between the Input elements.

The contents.htm Document

The following code is a sample contents file that defines a link relationship to the next document in the sequence. When this document loads, it must call the *setupLinks* function to update the available links, and when it unloads it must call *clearLinks*.

```
<HTML>
   <HEAD>
      <TITLE>Contents</TITLE>
      <!-- Only a next relationship is defined. The Previous button
           will be disabled for this document. -->
      <LINK REL="next" HREF="chapter1.htm" TITLE="Chapter 1">
   </HEAD>
   <BODY ONLOAD="parent.setupLinks(window.document);"
         ONUNLOAD="parent.clearLinks();">
      <H1>Table of Contents</H1>
   </BODY>
</HTML>
```

This example demonstrates two simple relationships, but it can be easily extended with more relationships to provide an enhanced toolbar in the navigation pane.

Programming the IMG and Map Elements

Images and image maps are fully programmable in Internet Explorer 4.0. You can now change the SRC attribute and size of an image and modify, add, and remove Area elements from an image map. The object model also allows new images to be asynchronously downloaded in the background while the user interacts with the page. This section presents techniques for downloading images and for manipulating the IMG element and associated image maps.

Image Animation

One common technique for animating images is to change the image as the mouse enters and exits the element. In Internet Explorer 4.0, this task is trivial—you use the *onmouseover* and *onmouseout* events on the IMG element itself:

```
<IMG SRC="start.gif"
   ONMOUSEOVER="this.src = 'over.gif';"
   ONMOUSEOUT="this.src = 'start.gif';">
```

Netscape Navigator will ignore this code because it does not currently support *onmouseover* and *onmouseout* events on the IMG element. Netscape Navigator does support these events on the Anchor element, however. Therefore, with a little forethought it is possible to re-create the preceding scenario in a more compatible way. By wrapping the IMG element in an Anchor element, both Netscape Navigator 3.0 or later and Internet Explorer 4.0 will properly change the image:

```
<A HREF=""
      ONMOUSEOVER="document.myImage.src = 'over.gif';"
      ONMOUSEOUT="document.myImage.src = 'start.gif';">
   <IMG BORDER=0 NAME="myImage" SRC="start.gif">
</A>
```

The *BORDER=0* attribute must be added so that the default anchor border is not drawn around the image. And while this technique does provide similar support in both Netscape Navigator and Internet Explorer, there is still one key difference. Because no size is supplied to the image, in Internet Explorer the container of the image is automatically resized to match the image and the surrounding contents are reflowed. In Netscape Navigator, the size of the image is fixed when the first image is loaded, so the next image is scaled to fit. To work around this discrepancy, either ensure that the images are the same size or provide *width* and *height* attributes on the IMG element.

While the preceding code works, a noticeable delay might occur when the second image is initially downloaded. Dynamic HTML supports the ability to preload an image behind the page so that it is immediately available for use.

Image Sequencing

Timer events can be used instead of user-generated events to change an image. Dynamic HTML makes it simple to create an image sequencer that rotates images after a specified amount of time. Images can be preloaded using a special image constructor, and the IMG element's SRC attribute can be dynamically changed.

The following code shows the application of this technique, a client-side billboard that cycles through images after a specified amount of time. This scenario uses unrecognized elements to define the list of advertisements. The advantages of this model are that new ads can be added and outdated ads can be removed without having to modify any code. Another technique used in this example is to preload the images before assigning the SRC attribute to ensure a smooth transition from image to image. An error recovery mechanism is included to skip an image if it fails to download.

```
<HTML>
   <HEAD>
      <TITLE>Ad Sequencing</TITLE>
      <!-- More ads can be added simply by extending this list. -->
      <ADLIST src="ad1.gif" duration=3000>
      <ADLIST src="ad2.gif" duration=5000>
      <ADLIST src="ad3.gif">
      <ADLIST src="ad4.gif" duration=1000>
      <SCRIPT LANGUAGE="JavaScript">
         var adSet = document.all.tags("ADLIST");
         adSet.current = 0;
         var nextImage = document.createElement("IMG");

         function preLoad() {
            // Get next image.
            // If an error occurs, skip to the next image.
            /* Always set up image event handlers before assigning the
               SRC attribute to ensure that no events are missed. */
            nextImage.onerror = preLoad;
```

(continued)

```
            nextImage.src =
               adSet[adSet.current].getAttribute("src");
            // The duration attribute specifies how long the image is
            // displayed.
            nextImage.duration =
               adSet[adSet.current].getAttribute("duration");
            if (null == nextImage.duration)  // If not specified, use
               nextImage.duration = 2000;    // default 2 seconds.
            if (++adSet.current == adSet.length)
               adSet.current = 0;            // Start over.
         }

         function skipImage() {
            // Check whether next image has been downloaded.
            if (nextImage.complete) {
               document.all.ad.src = nextImage.src;
               var duration = nextImage.duration;
               preLoad();
               window.tm = setTimeout('skipImage()', duration);
            }
            else  // Quickly iterate until image is available.
               window.tm = setTimeout('skipImage()', 10);
         }
         preLoad();
      </SCRIPT>
   </HEAD>
   <BODY ONLOAD="window.tm = setTimeout('skipImage()', 1);"
         ONUNLOAD="clearTimeout(window.tm);">
      <IMG ID="ad" SRC="ad4.gif" STYLE="border:2px solid navy">
   </BODY>
</HTML>
```

Internet Explorer 4.0 also supports the construction of new images for background downloading using the *new* operator in addition to the *createElement* method. This operator is supported for compatibility with Netscape Navigator's JavaScript implementation. The *new* operator is a language-dependent technique for creating new elements. For example, in the preceding code, the line

```
nextImage = document.createElement("IMG");
```

can also be written as

```
nextImage = new Image();
```

However, because Netscape Navigator does not expose custom elements to scripts, the code for sequencing advertisements requires further modifications in order to run in Netscape Navigator: the information about the ad graphics needs to be stored by the script, most likely in an array, rather than in custom AdList elements.

Image Maps

Image maps specify different click regions on an image. The most common use for image maps is to create visual navigation maps. When the user clicks in a particular area of the image, the default action is to navigate the user to a specified page. Using the event model, you can override the default action with an alternative action.

Defining an Image Map

HTML provides two types of image maps: server-side and client-side. A server-side image map is specified simply by adding an ISMAP attribute to the image and creating an image map file on the server. When the user clicks on the image, the *xy*-coordinates are submitted to the server. The server-side image map has two inherent disadvantages: it generally requires a server round-trip, and it is not easily accessible because the click regions are not known to the browser or to scripts.

Client-side image maps use the Map element and have the advantage of not requiring a round-trip to the server. They also allow browsers to intelligently map and outline the click regions of the image. The Map element contains a set of Area elements that define the coordinates for each click region.

Map elements must be named in order to be associated with an image. Once the Map element is named, any number of images can be associated with it through the images' USEMAP attribute. The value for USEMAP must be specified as a link reference. For example, the following code associates an image with an image map named *diagram*:

```
<IMG SRC="diagram.gif" USEMAP="#diagram">
```

Client-side image maps and their syntax are demonstrated in the following examples. However, the complete syntax for defining a server-side or client-side image map is beyond the scope of this book. For details about image map syntax, refer to an HTML reference book or the Microsoft Web site (www.microsoft.com).

Image Maps and Events

You can place an image map anywhere in the document, independent of the image the map is associated with. Because multiple images can share a single image map, the Dynamic HTML object model maintains a special relationship between the image and its image map when firing events.

When an event is fired on an image map, the Area element receives the event, followed by the Map element, followed by the IMG element the user clicked on. After the image receives the event, the event continues to bubble up through the image's parent elements. Thus, a single image map and events can be shared, or depending on the circumstances, the image itself can override or add its own behavior to the image map. Elements that contain the image map in the HTML source may never receive the events that originate in the image map.

Accessing the Image Map

An IMG element's *useMap* property contains the name of the associated image map, prefixed with a # character. By removing the leading # character from the *useMap* property, you can access the image map. The *useMap* property is read/write, so it allows image maps to be dynamically associated with the image. The following code demonstrates a simple function for obtaining the associated image map from an IMG element:

```
function getMap(elImage) {
   // Be sure that a map is specified for the image.
   if (null != elImage.useMap) {
      // Remove the leading # from the bookmark.
      var strMap = elImage.useMap.substring(1);
      // Return the element with the specified name.
      return document.all[strMap];
   }
   else
      return null;
}
```

A useful application of dynamically changing an image map is to provide a different level of granularity in a complex image or geographic map. Figure 9-4 shows how a set of items—in this case, cities and states—can be made more manageable by letting the user first define a subset of items of interest. This filtering technique becomes even more powerful when used to distinguish between multiple overlapping regions.

Because the cities in this image overlap the states, the user might find it difficult to make a selection. By allowing the user to decide between cities and states, selection becomes much simpler. This filtering is easily implemented by toggling between two image maps for the image, depending on the user's selection, as shown in the following code.

Figure 9-4.
An image that can use two different image maps.

```
<HTML>
   <HEAD>
      <TITLE>Switching Image Maps</TITLE>
      <SCRIPT LANGUAGE="JavaScript">
         function setMap(mapName) {
            document.all.mapImage.useMap = mapName;
         }
      </SCRIPT>
   </HEAD>
   <BODY>
      <P>Select From:<BR>
         <INPUT TYPE=RADIO NAME="feature" ID="States" Value="#States"
            ONCLICK="setMap(this.value);" CHECKED>
         <LABEL FOR="States">States</LABEL><BR>
         <INPUT TYPE=RADIO NAME="feature" ID="Cities" Value="#Cities"
            ONCLICK="setMap(this.value);">
```

(continued)

```
        <LABEL FOR="Cities">Cities</LABEL></P>
      <P><IMG ID="mapImage" SRC="places.gif" BORDER=0
        WIDTH=197 HEIGHT=448 USEMAP="#States"></P>
      <MAP NAME="Cities">
        <AREA SHAPE="POLYGON" HREF="la.htm"
          COORDS="108, 408, 164, 407, 165, 388, 111, 387,          ¬
            109, 361, 86, 361, 73, 394, 94, 411">
        <AREA SHAPE="POLYGON" HREF="sanfran.htm"
          COORDS="12, 301, 58, 275, 75, 305, 80, 301, 87, 314,     ¬
            92, 326, 119, 329, 121, 340, 45, 341, 44, 328,         ¬
            9, 328">
        <AREA SHAPE="POLYGON" HREF="portland.htm"
          COORDS="34, 120, 47, 120, 49, 115, 68, 115, 69, 123,     ¬
            86, 127, 86, 131, 140, 131, 137, 144, 86, 145,         ¬
            91, 162, 22, 160, 22, 148, 26, 144">
        <AREA SHAPE="POLYGON" HREF="seattle.htm"
          COORDS="73, 86, 93, 84, 92, 73, 125, 73, 123, 59,        ¬
            92, 57, 87, 43, 93, 22, 82, 2, 71, 21, 79, 45">
      </MAP>
      <MAP NAME="States">
        <AREA SHAPE="POLYGON" HREF="california.htm"
          COORDS="14, 204, 18, 200, 83, 209, 79, 278, 166, 386,    ¬
            171, 403, 167, 409, 166, 419, 163, 423, 164, 430,      ¬
            166, 436, 161, 439, 115, 438, 112, 433, 110, 420,      ¬
            97, 409, 92, 401, 82, 399, 77, 392, 56, 385, 54        ¬
            369, 46, 357, 46, 352, 34, 338, 39, 327, 35, 322,      ¬
            32, 309, 34, 297, 25, 297, 24, 288, 14, 273, 15,       ¬
            255, 9, 235, 12, 224, 12, 221, 16, 216">
        <AREA SHAPE="POLYGON" HREF="oregon.htm"
          COORDS="16, 199, 136, 216, 140, 178, 143, 171,           ¬
            138, 164, 153, 132, 147, 122, 103, 120, 80, 123,       ¬
            72, 121, 55, 121, 51, 109, 37, 105, 22, 163,           ¬
            23, 166, 18, 173, 14, 189">
        <AREA SHAPE="POLYGON" HREF="washington.htm"
          COORDS="33, 50, 64, 64, 57, 74, 57, 86, 63, 81,          ¬
            70, 65, 66, 41, 152, 55, 147, 123, 100, 119,           ¬
            86, 124, 74, 120, 56, 119, 51, 108, 40, 104,           ¬
            36, 99, 43, 93, 37, 87, 41, 84, 36, 80">
      </MAP>
    </BODY>
  </HTML>
```

NOTE: The coordinate lists in the Area elements cannot be broken onto multiple lines or the code will not run correctly. The lists are broken in the preceding code in order to fit them on the page; artificial line break symbols (¬) indicate line breaks that shouldn't appear in the actual code.

Accessing Area Elements

Dynamic HTML exposes the Area elements through the following collections:

- The *links* collection on the document
- The *all* collection on the document
- The *areas* collection on the Map element containing the Area elements

Scripts can access the attributes of the Area element in any of these three ways in order to dynamically modify them. The Area element has an HREF attribute that contains a URL, and it exposes the same properties containing parts of that URL that the *location* and *anchor* objects expose. The *areas* collection provides the extra functionality of allowing new Area elements to be added and removed from the image map.

Dynamically modifying the coordinates and shapes within an image map is supported, but it is usually easier and more maintainable to define multiple image maps in the document and switch between them. The exception is when you can calculate the new click regions from the old by a simple transformation. For example, if an image can be scaled, it is easier to scale both the image and the image map. If a *zoom* function is supported on an image, any associated image map also needs to be zoomed with the image:

```
<HTML>
   <HEAD>
      <TITLE>Dynamically Scaling Image Maps</TITLE>
      <SCRIPT LANGUAGE="JavaScript">
         function getMap(elImage) {
            // Be sure that a map is specified for the image.
            if (null != elImage.useMap) {
               // Remove the leading # from the bookmark.
               var strMap = elImage.useMap.substring(1);
               // Return the element with the specified name.
               return document.all[strMap];
            }
            else
               return null;
         }

         function zoomImage(elImage, amount) {
            // Expand the image the specified amount.
            var elMap = getMap(elImage);
            elImage.width *= amount;
```

(continued)

```
            elImage.height *= amount;
            // If an image map is available, scale it too.
            if (null != elMap) {
               for (var intLoop = 0; intLoop < elMap.areas.length;
                     intLoop++) {
                  var elArea = elMap.areas[intLoop];
                  // Break the coordinates string into an array.
                  var coords = elArea.coords.split(",");
                  var scaledCoords = "";
                  // Rebuild the new scaled string.
                  for (coord in coords) {
                     scaledCoords += (coords[coord] * amount) + ",";
                  }

                  // Put the scaled coordinates back into the map.
                  elArea.coords = scaledCoords;
               }
            }
         }

         function swapButtons(b1, b2) {
            // Swap the enabled/disabled buttons.
            document.all[b1].disabled = true;
            document.all[b2].disabled = false;
         }
      </SCRIPT>
   </HEAD>
   <BODY>
      <P>
         <INPUT TYPE=BUTTON VALUE="Zoom In"
            ONCLICK="zoomImage(document.all.img1, 2);
               swapButtons('zoomin', 'zoomout');"
            ID="zoomin">
         <INPUT TYPE=BUTTON VALUE="Zoom Out"
            ONCLICK="zoomImage(document.all.img1, .5);
               swapButtons('zoomout', 'zoomin');"
            ID="zoomout" DISABLED>
      </P>
      <P>
         <IMG SRC="img001.gif" WIDTH=200 HEIGHT=200
            ID="img1" USEMAP="#map1">
         <MAP NAME="map1">
            <AREA SHAPE="POLYGON"
               COORDS="92, 140, 126, 114, 155, 139, 124, 163"
               HREF="home.htm">
            <AREA SHAPE="CIRCLE" COORDS="30, 105, 30" HREF="cool.htm">
```

```
            <AREA SHAPE="RECT" COORDS="62, 28, 200, 79"
               HREF="dhtml.htm">
         </MAP>
      </P>
   </BODY>
</HTML>
```

Adding and Removing Area Elements

Using the *areas* collection, Dynamic HTML supports the ability to dynamically add and remove Area elements from an image map. The technique for creating a new Area element is the same as for creating a new image. The primary difference is that this new Area element can be added directly to an existing map's *areas* collection, whereas a new image object cannot be added to the document.

The *areas* collection exposes *add* and *remove* methods. The *add* method takes an Area element created with the *createElement* method and adds it to the *areas* collection. The *remove* method is used to remove an existing Area element from the image map. The following example is a simple image map editor written entirely in HTML:

```
<HTML>
   <HEAD>
      <TITLE>Image Map Editor</TITLE>
      <SCRIPT LANGUAGE="JavaScript">
         var curFocus = null;

         function areaFocus() {
            // Track the last Area element selected.
            if ("AREA" == event.srcElement.tagName)
               curFocus = event.srcElement;
         }

         function removeArea() {
            // Remove an Area element.
            var coll = document.all.dynaMap.areas;
            if (null != curFocus) // Make sure one is selected.
               // Loop over Area elements and find the one selected.
               for (var intLoop = 0; intLoop < coll.length; intLoop++)
                  if (curFocus == coll[intLoop]) {
                     document.all.dynaMap.areas.remove(intLoop);
                     return;
                  }
            alert("No Area element is selected.");
         }
```

(continued)

```
            function addArea(f) {
               /* Be sure that coordinates are specified. This code does
                  not perform any extra validation for the coordinates. */
               if ("" != f.coordinates.value) {
                  var elArea = document.createElement("AREA");
                  elArea.coords = f.coordinates.value;
                  // Determine shape selected.
                  for (var intLoop = 0; intLoop < f.shape.length;
                        intLoop++)
                     if (f.shape[intLoop].checked)
                        elArea.shape = f.shape[intLoop].id;
                  document.all.dynaMap.areas.add(elArea);
               }
               else
                  alert("You need to enter a Coords value.");
               event.returnValue = false;
            }
         </SCRIPT>
      </HEAD>
      <BODY>
         <H1>Image Map Editor</H1>
         <H2>Select a Shape</H2>
         <FORM NAME="area">
            <!-- The ID is used to determine the shape attribute. -->
            <P>
               <INPUT TYPE=RADIO NAME="shape" ID="rect" CHECKED>
               <LABEL FOR="rect">Rect</LABEL>
            <BR>
               <INPUT TYPE=RADIO NAME="shape" ID="polygon">
               <LABEL FOR="polygon">Polygon</LABEL>
            <BR>
               <INPUT TYPE=RADIO NAME="shape" ID="circle">
               <LABEL FOR="circle">Circle</LABEL>
            </P>
            <P>
               <LABEL FOR="coords">Coords</LABEL>
               <INPUT TYPE=TEXT ID="coords" NAME="coordinates">
            </P>
            <P>
               <INPUT TYPE=SUBMIT VALUE="Add Area"
                  ONCLICK="addArea(this.form)">
               <INPUT TYPE=BUTTON VALUE="Remove Area"
                  ONCLICK="removeArea()">
            </P>
         </FORM>
         <IMG SRC="img001.gif" WIDTH=200 HEIGHT=200 USEMAP="#dynaMap">
```

```
      <MAP NAME="dynaMap" ONCLICK="areaFocus()">
      </MAP>
   </BODY>
</HTML>
```

Programming the Marquee Element

Internet Explorer 3.0 supported a simple Marquee element for scrolling text horizontally. In Internet Explorer 4.0, the Marquee element was enhanced with a complete object model plus the ability to support and render any HTML code. This new Marquee control can even contain controls, which respond appropriately to mouse clicks and keyboard input as they move by. Other enhancements include the ability to scroll in any direction—left, right, up, or down.

A marquee can display one of three behaviors: *alternate*, *scroll*, and *slide*. In *alternate* mode, the marquee's contents move back and forth or up and down, always remaining on the screen. In *scroll* and *slide* modes, the contents move in one direction. They may appear from the right marquee border, for example, and move left across the screen. In *scroll* mode, the motion does not repeat until after all of the contents have scrolled onto and off the marquee. In *slide* mode, the motion repeats sooner, after the last of the contents have scrolled onto the marquee. With any of these three behaviors, you can specify a finite number of repetitions or allow the marquee to continue animating until the user jumps to another page.

Marquee Animation Properties

The marquee attributes are exposed as properties that can be dynamically modified. For some of these properties, assigning a new value while the marquee is running causes the marquee to restart its animation; with others, it does not. The following table describes the attributes and how changing them affects the marquee.

Attribute/Property	Restarts Marquee?	Description
behavior	Yes	Specifies the *alternate, scroll,* or *slide* behavior for the marquee. The default value is *scroll.*
direction	No	Specifies the direction of motion. All four directions are supported: *left, right, up,* and *down.* The default value is *right.*

(continued)

Attribute/Property	Restarts Marquee?	Description
height	Yes	Specifies the physical height of the marquee.
loop	Yes	Specifies the number of times for the animation to repeat. The default value is *infinite*.
scrollAmount	No	Specifies the number of pixels to move each time the contents are redrawn. The default value is *6*.
scrollDelay	No	Specifies the number of milliseconds between times the contents are redrawn. The default value is *85*.
trueSpeed	No	Specifies whether the marquee should catch up with any skipped cycles. The default value is *false*, which causes the marquee to act as it does in Internet Explorer 3.0.
width	Yes	Specifies the physical width of the marquee.

Marquee Events

The Marquee element supports all the standard mouse and keyboard events. All elements contained within the marquee also continue to fire their respective events. The following table describes the events that the marquee exposes during the animation.

Event	Description
onstart	The marquee is about to begin scrolling. For a marquee in *scroll* or *slide* mode, this event fires each time a new animation sequence is about to be initiated. For a marquee in *alternate* mode, this event fires once at the beginning of the animation.
onbounce	The marquee animation has reached the end and will reverse itself. This event fires when the Marquee's *behavior* property is set to *alternate*.
onfinish	The marquee has finished scrolling.

Marquee Methods

The Marquee element exposes two methods for starting and stopping the animation: *start* and *stop*. These methods can be used to manually control the scrolling of a marquee.

Using the *stop* and *start* methods, the following code allows the user to stop and start a marquee by holding down and releasing the mouse button over the marquee. By stopping the marquee, the user can read its contents more easily. The marquee's *title* attribute is displayed as a ToolTip when the mouse is held over the Marquee element.

```
<HTML>
   <HEAD>
      <TITLE>Marquee stop and start Methods</TITLE>
   </HEAD>
   <BODY>
      <MARQUEE TITLE="Hold down the mouse button to stop the marquee."
            ONMOUSEDOWN="this.stop();"
            ONMOUSEUP="this.start();">
         <H1>Test Marquee</H1>
         <P>Clicking the mouse button and holding it down
            stops the marquee from scrolling.</P>
         <INPUT TYPE=BUTTON VALUE="Demo Button"
            ONCLICK="alert('clicked');">
      </MARQUEE>
   </BODY>
</HTML>
```

Programming the Object Element

The Object element allows you to include controls and applets that extend the browser. For example, you can create objects to embed graphs or even other documents directly into the document. An object may have its own properties, methods, and events, which the Object element exposes to scripts in the same way that it exposes its own members.

Handling Property Conflicts

A conflict can occur between the object's members and the members of a generic Object element. For example, if the object exposes an *id* property, it will collide with the *id* property exposed on the Object element. When this conflict occurs, referencing the *id* property references the element's version, not the object's. For referencing the object's version of the *id* property, all object elements expose an *object* property. This property returns access to the embedded object's members, as shown in the following code.

```
document.all.myObject.id          // HTML element's id property
document.all.myObject.object.id   // Embedded object's id property
```

Alternative HTML

The Object element can contain HTML code that is displayed in browsers that do not support the Object element. The down-level contents are exposed as an *altHTML* property of the Object element in HTML.

The *altHTML* property can be used to provide contents to the user if the object fails to install. If the object fails to install, the alternative contents replace the object on the page. In the following code, the value of the Object element's *altHTML* property is the Paragraph element (the <P> and </P> tags and the text between):

```
<OBJECT CLASSID="java:myClass">
   <PARAM NAME="color" VALUE="red">
   <P>
      Either your browser does not support the Object element or an
      error occurred while downloading the object.
   </P>
</OBJECT>
```

Object Events

An object can fire its own custom events. You can bind a handler to such an event using the <SCRIPT FOR= EVENT= > syntax or a language-dependent mechanism, but not using an attribute in the element's tag. The Object element exposes attributes for only those events that are predefined, not for events that the embedded object may fire.

Objects that expose standard events such as mouse and keyboard events can also take part in event bubbling. The object itself fires its standard event, followed by the browser firing the event on every parent element. Generic event handlers for standard events can test whether they originated in an object.

Programming the Table Element

Tables are used in HTML for displaying tabular data and to provide greater control over the layout and position of elements in the document. Tables consist of rows; each row contains any number of cells. Dynamic HTML exposes a custom object model on tables that provides easy access to the underlying rows and cells within the table.

Tables were greatly enhanced in Internet Explorer 3.0 to support features that are now included in HTML 4.0. The THead, TBody, and TFoot elements were added to define the header, body, and footer sections of the table, and the Col and ColGroup elements provide greater control over columns. When used appropriately, these elements can improve the performance of the table, especially by defining the widths of the columns and providing more control over the rendering of borders. The Table element exposes a powerful object model for dynamically manipulating tables.

The *table* Object

Every Table element exposes rich information about its contents. The *table* object provides access to the three different sections of the table: THead, TBody, and TFoot. A table can have only one THead and TFoot but any number of TBody elements. Therefore, the object model exposes a single *tHead* and *tFoot* property and a *tBodies* collection. If a table does not explicitly define any sections, an implicit TBody element is created and added to the *tBodies* collection.

If the table happens to contain multiple THead or TFoot sections, the properties reference the first section encountered, and all remaining sections are exposed by the *tBodies* collection.

The *table* object exposes methods for creating and deleting THead, TFoot, and Caption elements. (There is currently no method to insert additional TBody elements into the table.) These methods are listed in the following table.

Method	Description
createTHead(), *createTFoot()*, *createCaption()*	Creates and returns the specified section if one does not exist. If the section already exists, rather than create another, the method returns the existing section.
deleteTHead(), *deleteTFoot()*, *deleteCaption()*	Deletes the specified section and its rows from the table if the section exists.
insertRow([index])	Inserts a row into the table before the specified *index*. The row is added to the same section as the row currently specified by the *index*. If no *index* is specified, the row is added to the end of the table in the same section as the existing last row. This method returns the row that was inserted.
deleteRow(index)	Deletes the row at the specified *index* from the table.

The *table* object also exposes a *rows* collection. This *rows* collection represents every row in the table, independent of what section contains them.

To determine what section contains a row, you can examine the *parentElement* property of the individual row. In addition, each section exposes a *rows* collection that represents the rows contained in that section.

The *rows* and *cells* Collections

The *table* object exposes the relationships between the table's rows and cells. As mentioned, the *rows* collection on the *table* object contains every TR element in the table, and the *rows* collections on the *tHead, tBody,* and *tFoot* objects contain the TR elements in their respective sections. Each row subsequently exposes a *cells* collection that references the TD or TH elements within the row. The *rows* and *cells* collections expose the same *tags* and *item* methods that are available on the other element collections. You can use an element's *id* property to look it up directly in a *rows* or *cells* collection.

Programming the *rows* Collection

The *rows* collection on the *table* object ignores whether a row is in the head, body, or foot of the table, but the TR element's relationship to its parent element is still maintained:

```
<TABLE ID="myTable">
   <THEAD>
      <TR ID="header"><TH>City</TH><TH>State</TH></TR>
   </THEAD>
   <TBODY>
      <TR><TD>Issaquah</TD><TD>Washington</TD></TR>
      <TR><TD>Seattle</TD><TD>Washington</TD></TR>
   </TBODY>
</TABLE>
```

In this example, the *rows* collection of *myTable* contains the three rows in the table. The *parentElement* property of an individual row can be examined to determine whether the row is inside a TBody or a THead element:

```
document.all.myTable.rows.length                       // 3
document.all.myTable.THead.rows.length                 // 1
document.all.myTable.rows[0].parentElement.tagName     // THEAD
document.all.myTable.rows[1].parentElement.tagName     // TBODY
```

You can easily determine any row's position in the table. Three of the row's properties represent the row's zero-based index in the entire document, in the table, and in a section. The *sourceIndex* property represents the element's location in the document. This property, which all elements expose, is described in Chapter 8, "Scripts and Elements." The *rowIndex* property represents the index of the row in the entire table, and the *sectionRowIndex* property represents the index of the row in its section. In the previous example, the row containing *Seattle* has a *rowIndex* value of *2* and a *sectionRowIndex* of *1*. (Its *sourceIndex* value depends on where the table appears in the document.)

Each row also provides access to its cells through a *cells* collection. The *insertCell* and *deleteCell* methods add and remove cells in the row. These methods work in the same manner as the *insertRow* and *deleteRow* methods. The *insertCell* method takes an optional parameter, the index of the cell before which the new cell is to be inserted, and returns the inserted cell. The *deleteCell* method takes the index of the cell to delete. The following code shows how to access and manipulate cells in the previous table:

```
document.all.myTable.rows[0].cells.length  // 2 cells
document.all.header.cells.length    // 2 cells, accessed through the ID
document.all.header.deleteCell(0); // Delete first cell in header row.
```

Each cell has a *sourceIndex* and a *cellIndex* property. The *cellIndex* property represents the index of the cell in the row.

The ROWSPAN and COLSPAN Attributes

The *rows* collections correspond to the HTML structure that defines the table. Therefore, even if a cell spans multiple rows, it is exposed only on the row that defines the cell. The following code demonstrates this relationship by flattening out access to a table that has a number of cells spanning multiple columns and rows:

```
<HTML>
   <HEAD>
      <TITLE>HTML Rows and Cells</TITLE>
   </HEAD>
   <BODY>
      <TABLE BORDER ID="tbl1">
         <CAPTION>Sample Table</CAPTION>
         <TR><TD ROWSPAN=3>0, 0</TD>
            <TD COLSPAN=2>0, 1</TD><TD>0, 2</TD></TR>
         <TR><TD>1, 0</TD><TD ROWSPAN=2 COLSPAN=2>1, 1</TD></TR>
         <TR><TD>2, 0</TD></TR>
      </TABLE>
      <SCRIPT LANGUAGE="JavaScript">
         // Output information about the table above.
         document.write("<H2>Table Information</H2>");
         with (document.all.tbl1) {
            for (var intRows=0; intRows < rows.length; intRows++)
               document.write("Row " + intRows + " has " +
                  rows[intRows].cells.length + " cell(s).<BR>");
```

(continued)

```
            document.write("<P>Here is the same table without " +
               "any cells spanning multiple rows or columns:");
            document.write("<TABLE BORDER>");
            for (var intRows = 0; intRows < rows.length; intRows++) {
               document.write("<TR>");
               for (var intCells = 0;
                     intCells < rows[intRows].cells.length;
                     intCells++)
                  document.write("<TD>" + intRows + "," + intCells +
                     "</TD>");
               document.write("</TR>");
            }
            document.write("</TABLE>");
         }
      </SCRIPT>
   </BODY>
</HTML>
```

Figure 9-5 displays the HTML representation of this table. The rows and cells are defined by the underlying source, independent of how the table is actually rendered. The numbers in a cell represent the index of its row in the *rows* collection, followed by the index of its cells in the *cells* collection. The second table provides a view of the table with the ROWSPAN and COLSPAN attributes removed. The corresponding cells have the same indexes in both tables.

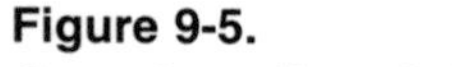

Figure 9-5.
Spanning cells and the collections that contain them.

You can modify the *colSpan* and *rowSpan* properties to dynamically change the table's layout. Changing these properties does not cause the *rows* or *cells* collections to change. The only way to affect the collections is to explicitly add or remove sections, rows, or cells from the table using the insert and delete methods.

The *onresize* Event

The table exposes an *onresize* event that is fired whenever the table is resized. This event fires when any cell changes in size. A script can change the size of a cell by changing its *height* or *width* property or by changing its contents. No matter how many cells may change in size due to a single action, the *onresize* event is fired only once on the table itself.

Global Style Sheets

In general, CSS is not inherited by the contents of a table cell. This fact follows from historical practice with regard to HTML formatting elements. For example, specifying a Font element around a table does not cause that font to be used by the table contents. When style sheets were introduced, this rule needed to be carried forward to ensure that existing pages did not break. Therefore, when style sheets are required on a table, they should be specified on the table or table cells directly to ensure that they are applied to the contents.

Creating a Calendar

The following code example demonstrates how to manipulate a table using the *rows* and *cells* collections. A script generates most of the document using the *document.write* method.

```
<HTML>
   <HEAD>
      <TITLE>Calendar</TITLE>
      <STYLE TYPE="text/css">
         .today {color:navy; font-weight:bold}
         .days {font-weight:bold}
      </STYLE>
      <SCRIPT LANGUAGE="JavaScript">
         // Initialize arrays.
         var months = new Array("January", "February", "March",
            "April", "May", "June", "July", "August", "September",
            "October", "November", "December");
         var daysInMonth = new Array(31, 28, 31, 30, 31, 30, 31, 31,
            30, 31, 30, 31);
```

(continued)

```
var days = new Array("Sunday", "Monday", "Tuesday",
   "Wednesday", "Thursday", "Friday", "Saturday");

function getDays(month, year) {
   // Test for leap year when February is selected.
   if (1 == month)
      return ((0 == year % 4) && (0 != (year % 100))) ||
         (0 == year % 400) ? 29 : 28;
   else
      return daysInMonth[month];
}

function getToday() {
   // Generate today's date.
   this.now = new Date();
   this.year = this.now.getYear() + 1900; // Relative
                                          // to 1900
   this.month = this.now.getMonth();
   this.day = this.now.getDate();
}

// Start with a calendar for today.
today = new getToday();

function newCalendar() {
   today = new getToday();
   var parseYear = parseInt(document.all.year
      [document.all.year.selectedIndex].text) - 1900;
   var newCal = new Date(parseYear,
      document.all.month.selectedIndex, 1);
   var day = -1;
   var startDay = newCal.getDay();
   var daily = 0;
   if ((today.year == newCal.getYear() + 1900) &&
         (today.month == newCal.getMonth()))
      day = today.day;
   // Cache the table's tBody element named dayList.
   var tableCal = document.all.calendar.tBodies.dayList;
   var intDaysInMonth =
      getDays(newCal.getMonth(), newCal.getYear() + 1900);
   for (var intWeek = 0; intWeek < tableCal.rows.length;
         intWeek++)
      for (var intDay = 0;
            intDay < tableCal.rows[intWeek].cells.length;
            intDay++) {
         var cell = tableCal.rows[intWeek].cells[intDay];
```

```
               // Start counting days.
               if ((intDay == startDay) && (0 == daily))
                  daily = 1;

               // Highlight the current day.
               cell.className = (day == daily) ? "today" : "";

               // Output the day number into the cell.
               if ((daily > 0) && (daily <= intDaysInMonth))
                  cell.innerText = daily++;
               else
                  cell.innerText = "";
            }
         }

         function getDate() {
            // This code executes when the user clicks on a day
            // in the calendar.
            if ("TD" == event.srcElement.tagName)
               // Test whether day is valid.
               if ("" != event.srcElement.innerText)
                  alert(event.srcElement.innerText);
         }
      </SCRIPT>
   </HEAD>
   <BODY ONLOAD="newCalendar()">
      <TABLE ID="calendar">
         <THEAD>
            <TR>
               <TD COLSPAN=7 ALIGN=CENTER>
                  <!-- Month combo box -->
                  <SELECT ID="month" ONCHANGE="newCalendar()">
                     <SCRIPT LANGUAGE="JavaScript">
                        // Output months into the document.
                        // Select current month.
                        for (var intLoop = 0; intLoop < months.length;
                              intLoop++)
                           document.write("<OPTION " +
                              (today.month == intLoop ?
                                 "Selected" : "") + ">" +
                              months[intLoop]);
                     </SCRIPT>
                  </SELECT>

                  <!-- Year combo box -->
                  <SELECT ID="year" ONCHANGE="newCalendar()">
                     <SCRIPT LANGUAGE="JavaScript">
```

(continued)

```
                        // Output years into the document.
                        // Select current year.
                        for (var intLoop = 1995; intLoop < 2000;
                              intLoop++)
                           document.write("<OPTION " +
                              (today.year == intLoop ?
                                 "Selected" : "") + ">" +
                              intLoop);
                     </SCRIPT>
                  </SELECT>
               </TD>
            </TR>
            <TR CLASS="days">
               <!-- Generate column for each day. -->
               <SCRIPT LANGUAGE="JavaScript">
                  // Output days.
                  for (var intLoop = 0; intLoop < days.length;
                        intLoop++)
                     document.write("<TD>" + days[intLoop] + "</TD>");
               </SCRIPT>
            </TR>
         </THEAD>
         <TBODY ID="dayList" ALIGN=CENTER ONCLICK="getDate()">
            <!-- Generate grid for individual days. -->
            <SCRIPT LANGUAGE="JavaScript">
               for (var intWeeks = 0; intWeeks < 6; intWeeks++) {
                  document.write("<TR>");
                  for (var intDays = 0; intDays < days.length;
                        intDays++)
                     document.write("<TD></TD>");
                  document.write("</TR>");
               }
            </SCRIPT>
         </TBODY>
      </TABLE>
   </BODY>
</HTML>
```

The contents of the two combo boxes that provide the month and year lists are generated through script from internal arrays that track the months and days available to the calendar. The code also ensures that the current month and year are initially selected when the document loads. The table that defines the calendar is itself generated by a script that generates the 42 cells using two nested loops. Once the page is loaded, the *newCalendar* function is called and automatically walks through and fills in the cells of the table's *tBody* element with the current month's calendar.

Figure 9-6 shows the calendar example in action.

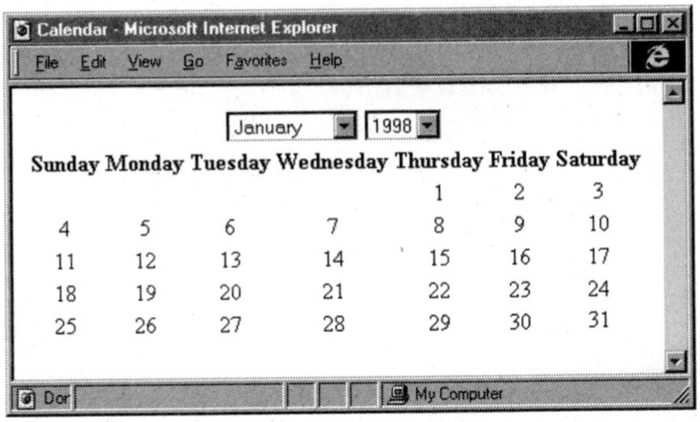

Figure 9-6.
A Dynamic HTML calendar.

This example also includes a simple click event handler that executes when the user clicks on any date in the calendar. Currently the handler does nothing more than display the date the user clicked, but it demonstrates how the calendar can be easily extended to be more interactive and useful to an application.

<SCRIPT LANGUAGE="JavaSc
// Create property x ar
var x = 10;
function foo() {
// This code is not
code
var y =
alert(
// output
// Call foo while lo
foo();
window.foo(); // the
</SCRIPT>

CHAPTER TEN

Forms and Intrinsic Controls

This chapter shows you how to script user interfaces that request and process input from the user. HTML supports both controls that can take user input and an element that provides a form model for grouping contents and submitting them back to the server. These controls are known as *intrinsic controls* because they are built into HTML. The functionality of the intrinsic controls is still fairly limited when compared to most forms and database packages. Validation and formatting are not yet directly supported, but you can easily add this behavior using the object model. This chapter presents techniques for manipulating forms and intrinsic controls within a document; it presents the intrinsic controls in functional categories and shows you how to extend HTML forms to be on a par with powerful forms packages.

The following topics are covered in this chapter:

- **HTML forms** Forms are used to group related input from the user and submit it back to the server. Forms are fully accessible to scripts and thus can also be used for client-side processing. This section provides an introduction to HTML forms and Input elements.
- **Programming text Input elements** Text Input elements create a text box for requesting information from the user. Four types of text boxes are defined by HTML: a single-line text box, a multiple-line text box, a password text box, and a filename text box. This section focuses on techniques for using events and the object model to validate and format the user's input.
- **Programming Select (list) elements** Select elements are used to provide the user with a defined list of options. Two styles of lists can be created using intrinsic controls: list boxes and combo boxes. For

both styles of lists, the programming model is the same. This section focuses on techniques for scripting lists and for dynamically adding and removing list items.

- **Programming lists using radio buttons and check boxes** An alternative way to allow the user to select from a list of elements is to provide a set of check boxes or radio buttons. Check boxes are useful for simple yes/no questions; radio buttons are used for selecting a single item from a list. This section discusses the benefits of using lists with buttons vs. using a list box style and provides scripting techniques.
- **Programming command button elements** Four types of command buttons can be created in HTML: plain-text buttons, rich HTML buttons, submit buttons, and reset buttons. Submit and reset buttons have a defined behavior when used in forms and also act as the Default and Cancel buttons. The Default button is indicated by an extra border and is the button that receives the click event when the user presses Enter; the Cancel button is clicked when the user presses Esc. The other types of command buttons' behavior must be defined through a script. This section shows you how to take advantage of command buttons.
- **Programming Label and Fieldset elements** Labels and fieldsets are a new addition to HTML and are necessary to create rich forms. The Label element is used to define the relationship between the Input element and some contents, and the Fieldset element is used to define the relationships among groups of controls.

HTML Forms

The Form element is used to logically group related intrinsic controls. These controls can optionally submit their values back to a server or be processed entirely on the client. When the contents of a form are submitted, the name and value of each input control within the form are enumerated and sent back to the server. The server then processes the information and usually returns a new page. The following HTML document demonstrates a form that requests information about the user:

```
<HTML>
   <HEAD>
      <TITLE>User Information</TITLE>
   </HEAD>
```

```
   <BODY>
      <FORM NAME="UserInfo">
         <LABEL FOR="USER">User Name: </LABEL>
         <INPUT TYPE=TEXT NAME="USER" VALUE="User Name" ID="USER">
         <LABEL FOR="ADDRESS">Address: </LABEL>
         <TEXTAREA ROWS=2 COLS=50 NAME="ADDRESS" ID="ADDRESS">
            Enter Address
         </TEXTAREA>
         <INPUT TYPE=SUBMIT VALUE="Submit Information">
      </FORM>
   </BODY>
</HTML>
```

This section focuses on how data is packaged for submission and how you can manipulate the Form element and intrinsic controls on the client. A discussion of the actual processing of the form on the server side is beyond the scope of this book.

Scoping Forms

Each form defines a separate scope for the elements within it. In addition, every element outside of a form shares its scope with the document. This scoping of Input elements is important because a single page can contain any number of forms, each of which operates independently. The Form element should not be contained within other Form elements, so the scope of an element should always be unambiguous to someone looking at your code.

Scoping separates the name spaces available to the elements. For example, if two forms both contain an element named User, the two elements will operate independently. This is especially important for radio button groups in which grouping is determined by each element's name. Radio buttons provide the easiest way to demonstrate the separation of scopes. For example, if two forms on the same page have a radio button group named State, the radio buttons will be mutually exclusive only within their respective forms. The following document defines two separate radio button groups that share the same name:

```
<HTML>
   <HEAD>
      <TITLE>Radio Button Scoping Demonstration</TITLE>
   </HEAD>
   <BODY>
      <!-- Radio buttons outside the form are scoped together. -->
      <INPUT TYPE=RADIO NAME="State" VALUE="NJ">NJ
```

(continued)

```
      <INPUT TYPE=RADIO NAME="State" VALUE="NY">NY
      <FORM STYLE="margin-left: 25pt">
         <!-- The two radio buttons are mutually exclusive
              and are independent of buttons outside this form. -->
         <INPUT TYPE=RADIO NAME="State" VALUE="WA">WA
         <INPUT TYPE=RADIO NAME="State" VALUE="CA">CA
      </FORM>
      <INPUT TYPE=RADIO NAME="State" VALUE="MA">MA
   </BODY>
</HTML>
```

In this example, all five radio buttons share the same name, State, but not the same scope. The first two radio buttons ("NJ", "NY") and the last radio button ("MA") are within the same global scope and are mutually exclusive. The two radio buttons inside the form ("WA", "CA") are in their own form scope and are mutually exclusive only of each other. Therefore, the user can select one value from within each radio button group.

Scripting the Form Element

Forms and the intrinsic controls within their scope have a rich programming model. Through the *form* object itself, you can submit and reset the form, as well as access and manipulate the individual controls.

The *forms* Collection

Forms in a document are exposed through the *all* collection and the *forms* collection. In addition, named forms have a special relationship with the document and can be accessed directly as properties of the document itself. The following code demonstrates a few of the ways to access Form elements using the object model. The comments show what will be displayed by the Alert dialog boxes.

```
<HTML>
   <HEAD>
      <TITLE>Forms in the Object Model</TITLE>
   </HEAD>
   <BODY>
      <FORM NAME="form1">
      </FORM>
      <FORM NAME="form2">
      </FORM>
      <SCRIPT LANGUAGE="JavaScript">
         alert(document.forms.length);         // 2
         alert(document.forms[0].name);        // form1
         alert(document.forms.form2.name);     // form2
```

```
            alert(document.form1.name);          // form1
            alert(document.all.form2.name);      // form2
            alert(document.forms["form1"].name); // form1
        </SCRIPT>
    </BODY>
</HTML>
```

The *elements* Collection

A special relationship is maintained between the form and its intrinsic controls. All the intrinsic controls contained within a form are exposed through properties of the *form* object as well as through an *elements* collection, which allows direct access to any intrinsic control that exists on a form. The *elements* collection of the *form* object works similarly to the *frames* collection of the *window* object, in which the collection is exposed simply to enhance code readability. As with the *frames* collection, the *elements* collection actually returns a reference to the *form* object. For example, the following two lines of code are the same:

```
document.forms[0].length // Number of elements on the first form
document.forms[0].elements.length
```

And the following three references are equivalent:

```
document.forms[0]
document.forms[0].elements
document.forms[0].elements.elements
```

The *elements* collection works like all other collections in the object model and provides access to the individual intrinsic controls on the form. The *elements* collection also contains all the images within the scope of the form.

The rules presented in Chapter 7, "Document Element Collections," can be used to access the contents of the *elements* collection of the *form* object. If any elements within a form share the same name, they are exposed as a subcollection. The *tags* and *item* methods are also available. For example, the following code can be used to quickly access all the Button elements in the first form and to access the third element in the collection:

```
// Return a collection of buttons in the first form.
document.forms[0].elements.tags("BUTTON")
// Access the third intrinsic control on the form.
document.forms[0].elements[2]
```

In addition, all the intrinsic controls on the form expose a *form* property that returns the form they belong to. This fact is useful if you need to access the parent form from a generic intrinsic control during an event handler, as shown in the following code.

```
<FORM NAME="User">
  <!-- Pass the current form to the event handler. The this
       property references the intrinsic control, and the form
       property references the form the control is scoped to. -->
  <INPUT TYPE=TEXT ONCHANGE="doClick(this.form);">
</FORM>
```

NOTE: If an intrinsic control is outside the scope of a form, the *form* property returns *null.*

Submitting a Form's Contents

As mentioned, forms can be used for client-side processing or to submit data back to the server. When a form is submitted to the server, the name and value of each of the form's controls are appended onto a single string and submitted to the server. The string is created as an escaped ampersand-delimited string of name-value pairs. All elements scoped within the form are enumerated, and the string is built by concatenating the name and value of all elements that have a name. For example, for the user information form at the beginning of this chapter, the submitted string would be the following:

```
?USER=SCOTT+ISAACS&ADDRESS=1+Somewhere+Street+WA
```

The submitted string is fully escaped, so spaces are represented by a plus sign (+).

Button Values

Buttons are submitted in a slightly different way from the standard text controls. The following table lists the rules for the different types of buttons.

Button Type	Description
Radio	Only the value of the selected button in a radio button group is submitted with the form. If no value is specified, the value defaults to *ON.*
Check box	Check boxes submit their name-value pairs only when they are checked. If no value is specified, the value defaults to *ON.*
Submit	More than one Submit button can be specified on a form. If the Submit button has a name, its name-value pair is submitted with the form.

Shared Element Names

The rules for determining what is submitted with a form are simple: the intrinsic control must have a name, and for buttons the button must be checked. Because only one radio button in a group can be checked at a time, only a single radio button value is submitted for each group. There is no restriction that the names in the submitted string be unique, however. For example, if multiple check boxes share the same name, the name-value pairs of all the checked check boxes with that name are submitted. And in multiple-select list boxes, a name-value pair is submitted for each selected item.

Submit command buttons also follow this rule. However, because only one command button can be selected at a time, only the Submit button that is selected is submitted. This technique can be useful for distinguishing between multiple Submit buttons on a single form. Most of the time, however, submitting a value for the Submit button is not necessary and a name need not be assigned to the button.

Disabled and Read-Only Elements

Elements can be disabled either through script or through HTML. Disabled elements cannot receive the focus, and they appear grayed in the Microsoft Internet Explorer window. Because a disabled element is not considered applicable to the current context of the form, its value is omitted during a form submission.

The contents of read-only elements cannot be edited. By default, buttons are read-only, and all other intrinsic controls are editable. Although there is no way to make a button editable, the other intrinsic controls can be made uneditable using the HTML *readOnly* attribute or the corresponding object model property. Unlike disabled elements, read-only elements are included in the form submission.

Object Values

Internet Explorer 4.0 supports submitting an Object element with the form if the object is given a name and has a default value that can be submitted. This allows applets or ActiveX controls to take part in the form's submission just as intrinsic controls do.

Where Do Form Submissions Go?

By default, the submitted string is sent back to the current URL. Two methods for submitting data are available: GET and POST. You specify which method to use by setting the *method* property of the form. The default is GET, which causes the submit string to be appended to the URL and then opened as though the resulting string were a new anchor. The submit method that should be used depends on the particular application being run on the server.

Instead of submitting the form back to the URL of the page, you can specify a custom location for the form using the *action* property of the form. The *action* property holds the URL of the server program that accepts the data sent by the form. This property can be dynamically changed through a script to conditionally submit data to different locations.

Where Do Form Results Return To?

While the *action* property defines the server destination for the data, the *target* property defines the client destination for any returned information. The *target* property works the same as the *target* property of the Anchor element and is used to specify what frame or window the contents are to be displayed in. This property can be used to create a clean user interface in which the entire screen is not constantly updated. For example, if two frames are displayed, one frame can request information from the user and the other frame can display the returned result.

Canceling a Form Submission

Scripts can be used to dynamically force a submission or to prevent a submission from occurring. You can prevent a form submission by returning *false* to the *onsubmit* event handler. To do so, either set the *returnValue* property of the *event* object to *false* or return *false* directly to the event. A common mistake when returning the value to the event handler is to return the value only to a line of code in the event handler rather than to the event handler itself, as shown here:

```
<HTML>
   <HEAD>
      <TITLE>Canceling Form Submission--Wrong Way</TITLE>
      <SCRIPT LANGUAGE="JavaScript">
         function doSubmit(f) {
            return false;
         }
      </SCRIPT>
   </HEAD>
   <BODY>
      <!-- The form's submission is NOT canceled. -->
      <FORM ONSUBMIT="doSubmit(this);">
         <INPUT TYPE=CHECKBOX NAME="Info">
         <INPUT TYPE=SUBMIT>
      </FORM>
   </BODY>
</HTML>
```

In this example, the form submission is not canceled even though *false* is returned by the called function because the return value is not subsequently returned to the *onsubmit* event handler.

The correct way to cancel the form submission is to return the value returned by the called function. Here is the correct way to define the <FORM> tag:

```
<FORM ONSUBMIT="return doSubmit(this);">
```

Now when the *onsubmit* event handler executes, the value returned by the function is correctly returned to the event handler.

Forcing a Form Submission

The *form* object exposes a *submit* method that results in the form's data being submitted. Calling the *submit* method does not fire an *onsubmit* event. Therefore, if validation is necessary, the *onsubmit*'s event handler must be manually invoked before the submit *method* is called, as shown in the following code. When you use this technique, the return value of the *onsubmit* event handler should always be checked.

```
<HTML>
   <HEAD>
      <TITLE>Manual Form Submission</TITLE>
      <SCRIPT LANGUAGE="JavaScript">
         function doSubmit(f) {
            // Write conditional code that determines
            // whether to submit.
            return f.Info.checked;
         }

         function manualSubmit(f) {
            var isSubmit = f.onsubmit();
            // Submit if no value or true is returned.
            if ((isSubmit) || (null==isSubmit))
               f.submit();  // Submit the form.
         }
      </SCRIPT>
   </HEAD>
   <BODY>
      <FORM ONSUBMIT="return doSubmit(this)
         // Must return the value of the event handler.">
         <INPUT TYPE=CHECKBOX NAME="Info">
         <INPUT TYPE=BUTTON ONCLICK="manualSubmit(this.form)"
            VALUE="Submit">
      </FORM>
   </BODY>
</HTML>
```

Resetting a Form's Contents

When a page is first loaded, the initial settings of the controls are cached in special default properties. For text controls, the default property is *defaultValue*; for command buttons or radio buttons, the default property is *defaultChecked*; and for the list controls, the default property for each item is *defaultSelected*. When the form is reset, the values from these properties are copied back into the values of the controls.

The Reset button provides a built-in way for a user to reset a form to the original values. The same action can be simulated on the form by calling the *reset* method on the form itself. Similar to the form's *submit* method, the *onreset* event is not fired when the *reset* method is invoked. The technique demonstrated in the preceding section for the *submit* method can also be used to force the *reset* method after first calling the *onreset* event handler.

Determining Whether to Use a Form Element

The Form element is generally required when the user is expected to submit results to the server. With Dynamic HTML, controls can be used solely for client-side interactions. In this case, the Form element is optional and the controls can be embedded directly on the page.

Using the Form element for client-side manipulation has no adverse effects and offers a number of benefits. Using a Form element provides Input element grouping within the *elements* collection and name space scoping for radio buttons. Also, with Netscape Navigator, controls are displayed and accessible from scripts only when they are contained within a form block. If compatibility with Netscape Navigator is required, the controls must always be contained within a Form element.

Hiding and Showing Intrinsic Controls

Dynamic HTML supports a special type of intrinsic control that is always hidden. Because this control cannot be accessed or manipulated by the user, it is used primarily as a placeholder for a calculated value that is to be submitted with the form. An Input element with its TYPE attribute set to HIDDEN cannot be made visible. Therefore, if you need to dynamically manipulate the visibility of a control, you should use a standard intrinsic control with its CSS (Cascading Style Sheets) *display* property set to *none* or its *visibility* property set to *hidden*. Later, by changing the *visibility* or *display* property, the control can be displayed. Like a HIDDEN Input element, invisible intrinsic controls are submitted with the form's contents. The following code makes an initially invisible control visible. If the intrinsic control was a HIDDEN Input element, the *display* property would have no effect on it.

```
<INPUT TYPE=TEXT STYLE="display:none" ID="myTextbox">
<SCRIPT LANGUAGE="JavaScript">
   // Make the text box visible.
   document.all.myTextbox.style.display = "";
</SCRIPT>
```

Using HIDDEN Input Elements

HIDDEN Input elements are useful mostly for submitting calculated data with a form. Another use of HIDDEN Input elements is to work around a shortcoming in Netscape Navigator that causes script variables to be reinitialized every time the window is resized—by storing the variables in hidden fields, you don't have to worry about the user resizing the window. A hidden field exposes the same object model as the text box without the events related to user interactions.

Interacting with Disabled Intrinsic Controls

Disabled elements appear grayed. However, if a disabled text box contains no contents, the user might not easily recognize that the element is disabled. By checking whether the user interacts with a disabled control using event bubbling, you can provide an explanation to users when they try to click on a disabled control.

Disabled elements do not themselves fire events. Instead, events are fired on the first parent element that is enabled. The following code demonstrates adding a special "disabledError" message to an intrinsic control and then generically testing for it:

```
<HTML>
   <HEAD>
      <TITLE>Disabled Demonstration</TITLE>
      <SCRIPT LANGUAGE="JavaScript">
         function checkControl() {
            /* If the user clicks on a disabled control, this code
               displays an error message if one exists. */
            var el = event.srcElement;
            if (el.disabled) {
               var msg = el.getAttribute("disabledError");
               if (null != msg)
                  alert(msg);
```

(continued)

```
                else
                    alert("You clicked on a disabled element.");
            }
        }
    </SCRIPT>
</HEAD>
<BODY ONCLICK="checkControl()">
    <INPUT TYPE=BUTTON DISABLED VALUE="Demo"
        disabledError = "This element is disabled because...">
</BODY>
</HTML>
```

> NOTE: Early HTML drafts proposed an ERROR attribute for the intrinsic controls. You should avoid adding a custom attribute named *error* to ensure that no conflict arises if this attribute becomes part of the HTML recommendation in the future.

Programming Text Input Elements

HTML supports the following four types of text controls for requesting input from the user:

- <INPUT TYPE=TEXT>
- <INPUT TYPE=PASSWORD>
- <INPUT TYPE=FILE>
- <TEXTAREA>...</TEXTAREA>

The TEXT Input element creates a single-line text box, and the TextArea element creates a multiple-line text box. The PASSWORD Input element is a special single-line text box in which the user's input is visually masked on the screen—each character the user types is displayed as an asterisk (*). The FILE Input element displays a text box and button with which the user can select a local file. When the form is submitted, the contents of the selected file are sent back to the server.

> NOTE: The TextArea element, as with any element that displays scrollbars in Dynamic HTML, exposes *scrollTop, scrollLeft, scrollWidth,* and *scrollHeight* properties. These properties provide full access to the size of the contents and the extent of the contents currently being viewed. For more information about these four properties, see Chapter 9, "Scripting Individual Elements."

The various text Input elements in HTML currently do not have built-in functionality for validating and formatting user input. Prior to scripting, such functionality had to be performed on the server, often creating unnecessary round-trips. By writing client-side scripts and using Dynamic HTML, you can format and validate input instantly on the client. This section focuses on techniques for testing user input.

Accessing the Control's Contents

The contents of the text Input elements are exposed through two techniques: the *value* or *innerText* property for direct access to the contents as a string, and the *createTextRange* method for rich access to the contents as characters, words, or sentences. The *innerText* property is an alias for the *value* property; the two can be used interchangeably. Text manipulation using the *TextRange* object is discussed in Chapter 14, "User Selection and Editing Operations." This chapter focuses on using the *value* property for manipulating the contents of the control.

The File Upload Element

The <INPUT TYPE=FILE> tag allows the contents of the file specified in the text box to be uploaded to the server. For security reasons, the File Upload element has a limited object model. The File Upload element is supported by Netscape Navigator 3.0 and later and by Internet Explorer 3.02 and later. Its *value* property is read-only and represents the filename and path, not the file's contents. Events are supported on the File Upload element, but their use is fairly limited since you cannot manipulate the user's input. When required, you can use the events and the *value* property to check that a file is selected.

Validating User Input

Validating user input prior to processing improves the usability of your Web site. This section presents four techniques that can be used with any text input from the user.

Validating While the User Types

Validation can be performed on each character the user types by tracking keyboard events: *keypress*, *keydown*, and *keyup*. The *keypress* event is the best event to use for tracking keyboard input because the default action of the *keypress* event is to process the typed character. Returning a value of *false* to this event prevents the character from being processed, so the character won't be appended to the user input. The following example demonstrates how to limit a text box to numeric input.

```
<HTML>
   <HEAD>
      <TITLE>Validating While the User Types</TITLE>
   </HEAD>
   <BODY>
      <LABEL FOR="age">Age</LABEL>
      <INPUT ID="age" TYPE=TEXT SIZE=3
         ONKEYPRESS="if ((event.keyCode < 48) ||
            (event.keyCode > 57)) event.returnValue = false;">
   </BODY>
</HTML>
```

This text box allows only ASCII values from 48 to 57, which represents the numerals 0 through 9 on the keyboard. Any other character typed by the user is ignored.

Validating When the User Exits the Control

Immediate validation is most useful for filtering user input. A more common approach is to validate the input at the time the user completes entering a new value. When an invalid value is entered, the user should be notified using at least one of the following two techniques:

- Modifying the appearance of an element to reflect invalid values
- Asking the user to correct an invalid value when he or she exits the field

Both techniques take advantage of the *onchange* event, which is fired at the time the user exits an input control after changing the value. The *onchange* event is fired on the element immediately prior to the *onblur* event. It can be used to validate the user's entry and then to display a dialog box or change the form's appearance based on the entry. Canceling the *onchange* event prevents the user from exiting the control when navigating within the page. If the user is navigating to a new page, canceling this event does not stop the navigation.

The following code demonstrates changing the style of an element based on the entered value. This technique is described in detail in Chapter 11, "Dynamic Styles." Dynamically changing the style is useful for providing the user with clear feedback.

```
<HTML>
   <HEAD>
      <TITLE>Validating When Exiting a Control--Technique 1</TITLE>
      <STYLE TYPE="text/css">
```

```
      .badValue {background:red; color:white}
    </STYLE>
    <SCRIPT LANGUAGE="JavaScript">
      function validateNumber() {
        // Get the source element.
        var el = event.srcElement;
        // Valid numbers
        var num = "0123456789";
        event.returnValue = true;
        /* Loop over contents. If any character is not a number,
          set the return value to false. */
        for (var intLoop = 0;
          intLoop < el.value.length; intLoop++)
          if (-1 == num.indexOf(el.value.charAt(intLoop)))
            event.returnValue=false;
        if (!event.returnValue)       // Bad value
          el.className = "badValue"; // Change class.
        else
          // Clear class to use default rendering.
          el.className="";
      }
    </SCRIPT>
  </HEAD>
  <BODY>
    <LABEL FOR="Age">Age:</LABEL>
    <INPUT ID="Age" TYPE=TEXT SIZE=3 TITLE="Enter your age"
      ONCHANGE="validateNumber();">
  </BODY>
</HTML>
```

Instead of changing the style of the element, you can warn the user with an Alert dialog box when an invalid value is entered. The following code demonstrates how to alert the user if he or she enters an invalid value in a State field. In addition, this code performs rudimentary formatting by making the user's input uppercase.

```
<HTML>
  <HEAD>
    <TITLE>Validating When Exiting a Control--Technique 2</TITLE>
    <SCRIPT LANGUAGE="JavaScript">
      function checkState(check) {
        var states = "ALAKAZARCACOCTDEDCFLGAHIIDILINIAKS";
        states += "KYLAMEMDMAMIMSMNMOMTNENMNVNHNJNMNY";
        states += "NCNDOHOKORPARISCSDTNTXUTVTVAWAWVWIWY";
```

(continued)

```
            // Include the following to test for Canadian provinces.
            /* Canadian provinces included only if
               a second parameter is supplied and is set to true. */
            if (arguments[1])
               states += "ABBCMBNBNFNSONPEPQSK";
            /* If the string is found in an even position, the state
               is valid. */
            return (0 == (states.indexOf(check) % 2));
         }
      </SCRIPT>
   </HEAD>
   <BODY>
      <LABEL FOR="state">State:</LABEL>
      <INPUT ID="state" TYPE=TEXT SIZE=2 MAXLENGTH=2
         ONCHANGE="this.value = this.value.toUpperCase();
            if (!checkState(this.value)){
               alert('Invalid State');
            return false;}">
   </BODY>
</HTML>
```

Validating When the User Submits the Form

You can use submit-time validation to determine whether related information is valid or to ensure that all required information is supplied. For example, if the user indicates that he or she is married, the spouse's name or other information might also be required. The following code demonstrates how to extend the intrinsic text box control with a *required* attribute to ensure that it is filled in by the user:

```
<HTML>
   <HEAD>
      <TITLE>Validating When the User Submits the Form</TITLE>
      <SCRIPT LANGUAGE="JavaScript">
         function isEmpty(str) {
            // Check whether string is empty.
            for (var intLoop = 0; intLoop < str.length; intLoop++)
               if (" " != str.charAt(intLoop))
                  return false;
            return true;
         }

         function checkRequired(f) {
            var strError = "";
            for (var intLoop = 0; intLoop<f.elements.length; intLoop++)
```

```
            if (null!=f.elements[intLoop].getAttribute("required"))
               if (isEmpty(f.elements[intLoop].value))
                  strError += "   " + f.elements[intLoop].name + "\n";
         if ("" != strError) {
            alert("Required data is missing:\n" + strError);
            return false;
         }
      }
   </SCRIPT>
</HEAD>
<BODY>
   <FORM NAME="demo" ONSUBMIT="return checkRequired(this);">
      User Name:
         <INPUT TYPE=TEXT NAME="User Name" required><BR>
      E-Mail Address:
         <INPUT TYPE=TEXT NAME="E-Mail Address" required><BR>
      Age (optional):
         <INPUT TYPE=TEXT NAME="Age"><BR>
      <INPUT TYPE=SUBMIT VALUE="Submit">
   </FORM>
</BODY>
</HTML>
```

Representing Required Information

An extension of the preceding example, demonstrated in the following code, is to initially display required fields with a different background color. As the user fills in those fields, the background color changes back to the default, which helps the user recognize which fields must be completed before submitting the form.

```
<HTML>
   <HEAD>
      <TITLE>Representing Required Information</TITLE>
      <STYLE TYPE="text/css">
         .required {background: red}
      </STYLE>
      <SCRIPT LANGUAGE="JavaScript">
         function isEmpty(str) {
            for (var intLoop = 0; intLoop<str.length; intLoop++)
               if (" " != str.charAt(intLoop))
                  return false;
            return true;
         }
```

(continued)

```
            function checkRequired(f) {
               for (var intLoop = 0;
                  intLoop<f.elements.length; intLoop++)
                  if ("required"==f.elements[intLoop].className) {
                     alert("All red fields are required.");
                     return false;
                  }
            }

            function fixUp(el) {
               el.className = isEmpty(el.value) ? "required" : "";
            }

            function checkChar(el) {
               if (32 != event.keyCode)
                  el.className = "";
            }
         </SCRIPT>
      </HEAD>
      <BODY>
         <FORM NAME="demo" ONSUBMIT="return checkRequired(this);">
            User Name:
               <INPUT TYPE=TEXT CLASS="required"
                  ONKEYPRESS="checkChar(this);"
                  ONCHANGE="fixUp(this);"><BR>
            E-Mail Address:
               <INPUT TYPE=TEXT CLASS="required"
                  ONKEYPRESS="checkChar(this);"
                  ONCHANGE="fixUp(this);"><BR>
            Age (optional):
               <INPUT TYPE=TEXT SIZE=3><BR>
            <INPUT TYPE=SUBMIT VALUE="Submit">
         </FORM>
      </BODY>
   </HTML>
```

In this example, the CLASS attribute is used instead of the user-defined *required* attribute to identify required fields.

Formatting User Input

Just as validation can improve the user's experience by warning of invalid input, formatting user input can make data more usable and readable. The same techniques used to validate data can also be used to format data. Formatting user input can be done while the user types or when the user exits the field. This section shows you how to extend the built-in input controls to add formatting information directly to an element using two custom attributes.

The following code demonstrates a minimal implementation that includes the number-validating routine used earlier plus some simple formatting code to change the style if the number is positive or negative. Although this example only changes the style, a formatter can also be written that customizes the value—for example, by adding digit separators or any other custom format.

```
<HTML>
   <HEAD>
      <TITLE>Formatting User Input</TITLE>
      <STYLE TYPE="text/css">
         .positive {color:green}
         .negative {color:red}
         .badValue {background:red; color:white}
      </STYLE>
      <SCRIPT LANGUAGE="JavaScript">
         function formatNumber() {
            with (event.srcElement)
               className =
                  parseInt(value) >= 0 ? "positive" : "negative";
         }

         function validateNumber() {
            // Get the source element.
            var el = event.srcElement;
            var num = "0123456789";  // Valid numbers
            event.returnValue = true;
            // Check first character for negative number.
            event.returnValue = ("-" == el.value.charAt(0)) ||
               (-1 != num.indexOf(el.value.charAt(0)));
            /* Loop over remaining contents. If any character
               is not a number, set the return value to false. */
            for (var intLoop = 1; intLoop < el.value.length;
                  intLoop++)
               if (-1 == num.indexOf(el.value.charAt(intLoop)))
                  event.returnValue = false;
            if (!event.returnValue)       // Bad value
               el.className = "badValue"; // Change class.
            else
               // Clear class to use default rendering.
               el.className = "";
         }

         function checkFormat() {
            event.returnValue = true;
            if (null != event.srcElement.validate)
```

(continued)

```
                    if ("number" == event.srcElement.validate)
                       validateNumber();  // Sets event.returnValue
                 if ((null != event.srcElement.getAttribute("format")) &&
                      (event.returnValue))
                    if ("number" ==
                          event.srcElement.getAttribute("format"))
                       formatNumber();
              }
           </SCRIPT>
        </HEAD>
        <BODY>
           <INPUT TYPE=TEXT ONCHANGE="checkFormat();" format="number"
              validate="number">
        </BODY>
     </HTML>
```

Using Password Input Controls

A Password field is a text box in which the entire user input is masked with asterisk (*) characters. This masking is useful when the user is typing sensitive information. For security, scripts running under Internet Explorer 4.0 cannot access the true value of the control. Instead, the *value* property always returns an * for each character the user types. The asterisks allow client-side code to verify that a password has been entered or that the password has a specific number of characters. Key-related events also always return * for all keypresses.

When using Password fields, you should use the POST method to submit the data. Otherwise, the password's value will be displayed as the *search* value in the form's submission. In either case, the value is not encrypted. Furthermore, Netscape Navigator currently exposes the real value entered, rather than asterisks, so Password fields should be used carefully in security-sensitive situations.

Programming List Elements

The Select element is used to present a list of options to the user. There are two styles of lists: combo boxes (drop-down lists) and list boxes. These two list styles are generally interchangeable, and their scripting model is identical. The only exception is that the list box style can be used to create a multiple-select list box, which lets the user select multiple list items. Figure 10-1 shows the three types of lists.

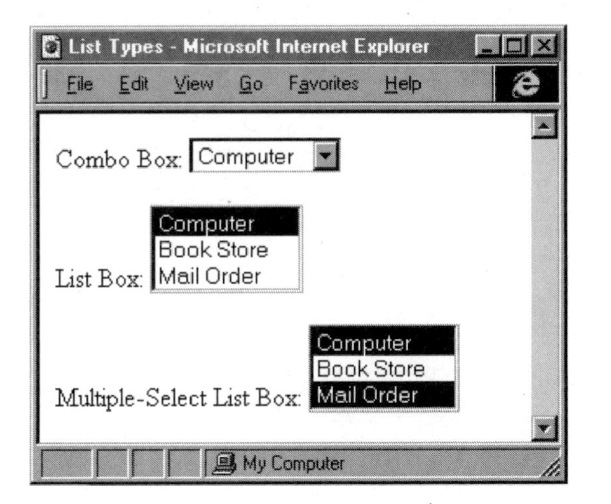

Figure 10-1.
The three types of lists available using the Select element.

Defining a List Box

You create a list box using the Select element. The Select element contains Option elements representing each list item. The three types of list boxes can be created as shown in the following code:

```
<HTML>
   <HEAD>
      <TITLE>List Types</TITLE>
   </HEAD>
   <BODY>
      <FORM NAME="lists">
         <SELECT NAME="combostore">
            <OPTION VALUE="Computer" SELECTED>Computer</OPTION>
            <OPTION VALUE="Bookstore">Book Store</OPTION>
            <OPTION VALUE="MailOrder">Mail Order</OPTION>
         </SELECT>
         <SELECT NAME="liststore" SIZE=3>
            <OPTION VALUE="Computer" SELECTED>Computer</OPTION>
            <OPTION VALUE="Bookstore">Book Store</OPTION>
            <OPTION VALUE="MailOrder">Mail Order</OPTION>
         </SELECT>
         <SELECT NAME="multistore" SIZE=3 MULTIPLE>
            <OPTION VALUE="Computer" SELECTED>Computer</OPTION>
            <OPTION VALUE="Bookstore">Book Store</OPTION>
            <OPTION VALUE="MailOrder" SELECTED>Mail Order</OPTION>
         </SELECT>
      </FORM>
   </BODY>
</HTML>
```

Specifying a SIZE attribute results in a list box instead of a combo box. The value of the SIZE attribute determines the number of rows displayed. To create a multiple-select list box, you specify the MULTIPLE attribute. When the MULTIPLE attribute is supplied without a SIZE attribute, a list box with a default size of four rows is automatically created.

Adding Styles to List Boxes

Limited style sheet support is provided for list boxes. The color and background color of each option can be modified using style sheets, which allows you to create visually interesting list boxes or even a color selector:

```
<HTML>
   <HEAD>
      <TITLE>Color Selector</TITLE>
   </HEAD>
   <BODY>
      <SELECT STYLE="width:75pt">
         <OPTION STYLE="background:red; color:white" VALUE="RED">
            Red
         </OPTION>
         <OPTION STYLE="background:navy; color:white" VALUE="NAVY">
            Navy
         </OPTION>
         <OPTION STYLE="background:black; color:white" VALUE="BLACK">
            Black
         </OPTION>
         <OPTION STYLE="background:white; color:black" VALUE="WHITE">
            White
         </OPTION>
      </SELECT>
   </BODY>
</HTML>
```

The style for selected items in the list in this example does not change, however.

Relating List Contents to the Submitted Value

The contents of an Option element are displayed on the screen, but this displayed value is not submitted back to the server. Instead, the *value* attribute is submitted and must also be specified in the <OPTION> tag. In general, when you are using a Select element inside a submittable form, each option should have a *value* attribute. For lists that are manipulated from script and are not displayed on a form, the *value* attribute can be used optionally or scripts can rely on the *text* property directly.

Scripting the List Contents

The *options* collection exposes the Option elements contained in a Select element. Each option in the collection exposes its attributes as well as the contents between the start and end tags of the Option element, which are exposed through the *text* property.

Option Elements

The Option elements in the document are an exception in the Dynamic HTML object model because they are not exposed in the document's *all* collection. Also, the Option element does not expose any extra events or properties beyond its standard sets of attributes and the *text* property. Instead, the Option element is exposed only through its parent Select element because the Select element owns all the interactions with the list, including events.

Adding and Removing List Elements

You can dynamically add items to or remove items from list boxes. This technique allows the list to be customized in response to user input. To add values to or remove values from a list box, you can use the technique introduced in Chapter 9, "Scripting Individual Elements," for adding and removing image map areas. This section presents a more appropriate alternative.

The *options* collection supports the ability to dynamically add or remove elements. Elements are created using the *createElement* method or through the *new* operator, as shown here:

```
var elOption = createElement("OPTION");
// or
var elOption = new Option;  // Netscape Navigator supports
                            // this method.
```

Options are then added to the list box using the *add* method on the *options* collection or removed using the *remove* method on the *options* collection. Options can also be added or removed by assigning an option directly to an array index or by setting an existing option to *null*. This technique is supported for Netscape Navigator compatibility. The following code compares using the two techniques on list items in a list box named *lb* on a form named *demo*:

```
var elOption = new Option();
// Add and remove using methods.
document.demo.lb.options.add(elOption, 0); // Add as first item.
document.demo.lb.options.remove(2);        // Remove third item.

// Add and remove using Netscape Navigator-compatible technique.
document.demo.lb.options[0] = elOption;    // Add as first item.
document.demo.lb.options[2] = null;        // Remove third item.
```

The following code demonstrates how to dynamically generate a list box that lists all the bookmarks on the page. When the user selects an item from the list, the document automatically scrolls the bookmark into view.

```
<HTML>
   <HEAD>
      <TITLE>Bookmark List</TITLE>
      <SCRIPT LANGUAGE="JavaScript">
         function addNew(text, value) {
            // Add a new option.
            var el = document.createElement("OPTION");
            el.text = text;
            el.value = value;
            document.all.bm.options.add(el);
         }

         function buildList() {
            /* When adding a new list item, the text is the contents
               of the anchor and the value is the name of the
               bookmark. The value is used to scroll the element into
               view. */
            for (var intLoop = 0; intLoop < document.anchors.length;
                  intLoop++)
               addNew(document.anchors[intLoop].innerText,
                     document.anchors[intLoop].name);
         }

         function scrollit(where) {
            // Scroll the specified bookmark into view.
            document.all[where.value].scrollIntoView();
            // Reset list box.
            where.value = null;
         }
      </SCRIPT>
   </HEAD>
   <BODY ONLOAD="buildList();">
      <LABEL FOR="bm">Bookmarks:
      <SELECT ID=bm STYLE="width:100pt" ONCHANGE="scrollit(this);">
      </SELECT>
      <H1><A NAME="Contents">Contents</A><H1>
      Table of Contents
      <H2><A NAME="Abstract">Abstract</A></H2>
      About this document
      <H2><A NAME="Chapter1">Chapter 1</A></H2>
      Chapter 1
```

```
      <H2><A NAME="Summary">Summary</A></H2>
      Summary contents
   </BODY>
</HTML>
```

Scripting Multiple-Select List Boxes

Multiple-select list boxes allow the user to select more than one item from a list. In a multiple-select list box, the *value* property returns only the first selected item. To determine all the selected items, the entire list of options must be enumerated using a script. The following function demonstrates how to build an array of selected items for any list box. (If you use this function with a single-select list box, the resulting array will contain only a single value.)

```
<SCRIPT LANGUAGE="JavaScript">
   function getSelected(opt) {
      var selected = new Array();
      var index = 0;
      for (var intLoop=0; intLoop < opt.length; intLoop++) {
         if (opt[intLoop].selected) {
            index = selected.length;
            selected[index] = new Object;
            selected[index].value = opt[intLoop].value;
            selected[index].index = intLoop;
         }
      }
      return selected;
   }
</SCRIPT>
```

Using Check Boxes for Small Lists

If the number of options is small, it might make more sense to use a set of check boxes instead of a multiple-select list box. By sharing the same name across each check box in the set, the check boxes will have the same submit behavior as the multiple-select list box. The preceding function can be rewritten as shown in the following code to determine which check boxes are selected. Rather than enumerating the *options* collection contained in the Select element, however, you must enumerate the Form elements with a given name. Instead of passing an *options* collection to the function, the collection of check boxes is used. Another distinction is that check boxes expose a *checked* property for determining whether they are selected, while the list box uses the *selected* property, so the conditional logic in the function tests for either *selected* or *checked.*

```
<HTML>
   <HEAD>
      <TITLE>Multiple-Select Check Boxes</TITLE>
      <SCRIPT LANGUAGE="JavaScript">
         function getSelected(opt) {
            var selected = new Array();
            var index = 0;
            for (var intLoop = 0; intLoop < opt.length; intLoop++) {
               if ((opt[intLoop].selected) ||
                   (opt[intLoop].checked)) {
                  index = selected.length;
                  selected[index] = new Object;
                  selected[index].value = opt[intLoop].value;
                  selected[index].index = intLoop;
               }
            }
            return selected;
         }

         function outputSelected(opt) {
            var sel = getSelected(opt);
            var strSel = "";
            for (var item in sel)
               strSel += sel[item].value + "\n";
            alert("Selected Items:\n" + strSel);
         }
      </SCRIPT>
   </HEAD>
   <BODY>
      <FORM NAME="ColorSelector">
         <INPUT TYPE=CHECKBOX NAME="color" VALUE="Red">Red
         <INPUT TYPE=CHECKBOX NAME="color" VALUE="Navy" CHECKED>Navy
         <INPUT TYPE=CHECKBOX NAME="color" VALUE="Black">Black
         <INPUT TYPE=CHECKBOX NAME="color" VALUE="White" CHECKED>White
         <INPUT TYPE=BUTTON VALUE="Selected Check Box Items"
            ONCLICK="outputSelected(this.form.color);">
         <P>
         <SELECT NAME="multistore" SIZE=3 MULTIPLE>
            <OPTION VALUE="Computer" SELECTED>Computer</OPTION>
            <OPTION VALUE="Bookstore">Book Store</OPTION>
            <OPTION VALUE="MailOrder" SELECTED>Mail Order</OPTION>
         </SELECT>
         <INPUT TYPE=BUTTON VALUE="Selected List Items"
            ONCLICK="outputSelected(this.form.multistore.options)">
      </FORM>
   </BODY>
</HTML>
```

Programming Lists Using Radio Buttons and Check Boxes

Radio buttons and check boxes are rendered similarly but serve distinct purposes. Radio buttons are used to represent a set of two or more mutually exclusive items. Check boxes are used to specify a decision with two or more independent choices.

Radio buttons are similar to the single-select list boxes introduced earlier in this chapter. Radio buttons can be used interchangeably with a single-select list, but they are most effective when a small number of options are available. For example, to specify a person's gender, a radio button group would be more effective than a single-select list box.

Radio buttons are more difficult to use than a list box if you are building the set of options dynamically. For this scenario, the list box is more appropriate because items in a list box can easily be manipulated as a group, whereas each radio button is actually a separate control that needs to be manipulated independently, and adding or removing radio buttons requires manipulating the contents of the document directly.

Radio Buttons

Radio buttons are exposed as a group similar to the options in a single-select list box. As mentioned, specifying the same name for buttons within the same scope creates a group. Mutual exclusion based on name is supported only for radio buttons. When the submission of a form with a radio button group occurs, of all the radio buttons in a group only the value for the selected radio button is submitted. Assigning the same name to any other type of control does not cause any special submission behavior. When multiple controls that are not radio buttons share the same name, all name-value pairs are appropriately submitted depending on the rules for each control—for example, named check boxes are submitted only if they are checked, and all named text boxes are submitted.

Supporting Custom List Values

Radio buttons are useful for providing a list of possible responses in a survey. Sometimes you might want to allow a user-entered value as a last resort if none of the list options are valid. The following code demonstrates a simple way to provide a text box for a custom response if the user's choice is not listed—the text control is enabled only when the user selects Other.

```
<HTML>
   <HEAD>
      <TITLE>Custom Entry</TITLE>
      <SCRIPT LANGUAGE="JavaScript">
         function checkRadio(f) {
            f.Custom.disabled = !f.Q1["Other"].checked;
            if ("Other" == event.srcElement.id)
               f.Custom.focus();
         }
      </SCRIPT>
   </HEAD>
   <BODY>
      <FORM NAME="Demo" ONCLICK="checkRadio(this);">
         <FIELDSET>
            <LEGEND>Where did you buy this book?</LEGEND>
            <P><INPUT ID="BStore" TYPE=RADIO NAME="Q1"
                  VALUE="Bookstore">
               <LABEL FOR="BStore"> Bookstore</LABEL>
            <P><INPUT ID="MOrder" TYPE=RADIO NAME="Q1"
                  VALUE="Mail Order">
               <LABEL FOR="MOrder"> Mail Order</LABEL>
            <P><INPUT ID="CStore" TYPE=RADIO NAME="Q1"
                  VALUE="Comp Store">
               <LABEL FOR="CStore"> Computer Store</LABEL>
            <P><INPUT ID="Other" TYPE=RADIO NAME="Q1">
               <LABEL FOR="Other"> Other: </LABEL>
               <INPUT ID="Custom" NAME="Other" TYPE=TEXT DISABLED>
         </FIELDSET>
      </FORM>
   </BODY>
</HTML>
```

This code works properly regardless of whether the user clicks on the label for Other or on the radio button itself because when a user clicks on the label the *onclick* event is first fired with *srcElement* as the label and then again with *srcElement* as the radio button. The *onclick* event handler also fires if the radio button is selected using the keyboard because the event is not tied to the mouse but rather to the operation of changing the value of the control. For this reason, a single *onclick* event handler for the radio button itself is sufficient to catch any potential change.

Check Boxes

Check boxes are useful for asking yes/no questions. In many cases, text boxes are used to specify other relevant information when necessary. By writing some simple code, you can make a check box enable or disable the relevant fields on a form. In the following code, if users request more information, they must enter their e-mail name and address. If they don't request additional information, the two fields are not used.

```
<HTML>
   <HEAD>
      <TITLE>Enabling Entry Fields</TITLE>
   </HEAD>
   <BODY>
      <FORM NAME="Info">
         <LABEL FOR=INFO>Send Info:</LABEL>
         <INPUT ID=INFO TYPE=CHECKBOX
            ONCLICK="this.form.email.disabled = !this.checked;
               this.form.snailMail.disabled = !this.checked;">
         <BR>
         <FIELDSET NAME="address">
            <LEGEND>Address Information</LEGEND>
            <LABEL FOR="email">E-mail Address</LABEL>
            <INPUT TYPE=TEXT NAME="email" DISABLED>
            <LABEL FOR="snailMail">Street Address:</LABEL>
            <TEXTAREA ROWS=3 COLS=40 NAME="snailMail"
               DISABLED></TEXTAREA>
         </FIELDSET>
      </FORM>
   </BODY>
</HTML>
```

NOTE: There is currently no technique you can use to override the default rendering for disabled controls.

The Indeterminate State

Check boxes support an indeterminate state, which allows a check box to represent three states: on, off, and unknown. For example, suppose you use a check box to indicate whether selected text is boldface. The unknown state would apply when the user selects some text that is part boldface and part not boldface. The unknown state can be set only through the object model, using the *indeterminate* property on the check box. The *indeterminate* property is a Boolean value—when this property is set to *true*, the check box is displayed in the indeterminate state.

The *checked* property of an indeterminate check box returns the value of the check box before it became indeterminate, even though an indeterminate check box always appears the same in the user interface. The check box is submitted depending on the *checked* property, regardless of whether the check box is indeterminate. Figure 10-2 shows the different check box states as displayed in Microsoft Windows:

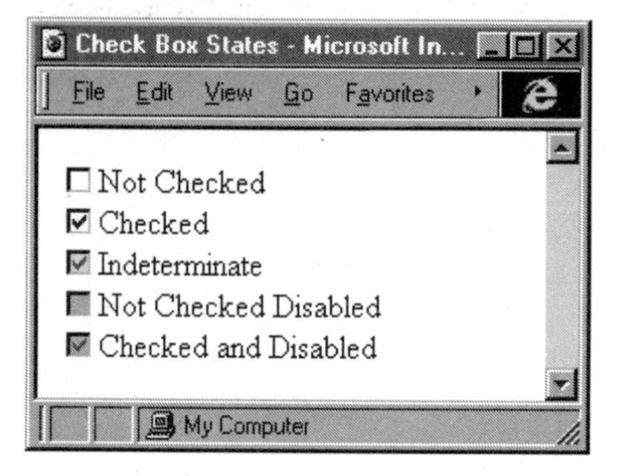

Figure 10-2.
The different check box states.

The indeterminate check box looks the same as the checked and disabled check box. The difference between the two is that you cannot click a disabled check box to change its value, but you can click an indeterminate check box.

The *onclick* Event

For radio buttons and check boxes, the *onclick* event has a slightly different behavior than it has for other elements. The *onclick* event fires prior to the execution of the default action, providing the Web author an opportunity to override it. For check boxes, the default action is to select or deselect the item, and for radio buttons the default action is to select the item. When the *onclick* event fires for these controls, the control's value already represents the new value of the element. Canceling the default action causes the value to revert to the previous value. This process is different from other elements, for which the state of the element does not change until after the event.

Programming Command Button Elements

Command buttons are created using either the standard Input element or the Button element. The Input element supports three types of command buttons: submit, reset, and plain-text buttons. The Button element is new in Internet Explorer 4.0 and provides the ability to create rich HTML buttons.

Defining Default and Cancel Buttons

The submit and reset buttons act as the Default and Cancel buttons within the context of a form or the scope of the document. The Default button is originally displayed with an extra border and signifies the default action that occurs if the user presses the Enter key. The Cancel button signifies the action that occurs if the user presses the Esc key.

Within the scope of a form, the submit and reset buttons are command buttons with the predefined behavior of submitting the form or resetting the contents of the form. Outside a form, these buttons act as standard command buttons, behaving as the Default or Cancel button. In all cases, invoking the Default or Cancel button behavior from the keyboard fires a *click* event on the appropriate button element.

Submit and reset buttons are defined using the TYPE attribute on the Input or Button element, as shown here:

```
<FORM NAME="User">
   <INPUT TYPE=TEXT NAME="User" VALUE="User Name">
   <INPUT TYPE=RESET VALUE="Reset the Form">
   <INPUT TYPE=SUBMIT VALUE="Submit the Form">
   <BUTTON TYPE=SUBMIT><EM>Submit</EM> the Form</BUTTON>
</FORM>
```

There can only be one Default and one Cancel button per form or document scope. When more than one Default or Cancel button is specified within a single scope (that is, more than one submit or reset button), the first button of each type specified in the HTML source is the one that will be used within that scope.

Button Events and Form Events

If you need code that executes for the submit or reset behavior of a form, you should write the code on the form's *onsubmit* and *onreset* events and not on the *onclick* event of the submit and reset buttons because there are cases in which the form can be submitted or reset without the buttons ever receiving an *onclick* event. For example, if the form has only one text box, a submit button, and a reset button, pressing Enter while the cursor is in the text box automatically submits the value, but the submit button does not receive an *onclick* event. Similarly, if the user presses Esc, the reset button does not receive the *onclick* event, but the *onreset* event is fired.

Creating Buttons Using the Button Element

You can create a button in HTML using <INPUT TYPE=BUTTON> or the more general <BUTTON>...</BUTTON> tags. The following code creates rich submit and reset buttons:

```
<FORM NAME="test">
   <BUTTON TYPE=SUBMIT>
      <H1>Submit this form.</H1>
   </BUTTON>
   <BUTTON TYPE=RESET>
      <H2>Reset this form.</H2>
   </BUTTON>
</FORM>
```

Because you can place HTML in the Button element, you can create interesting effects in a button. Although any HTML and style can be defined for the contents, the event model for the contents is limited compared to the rest of Dynamic HTML.

Button Events

As shown in the following code, the Button element supports rich HTML, but the elements within the button do not fire events. Therefore, event handlers cannot be written for any of the elements that exist within the button.

```
<!-- The event handlers defined in this button do not fire. -->
<BUTTON>
   <H1 ONCLICK="alert('clicked!');">Click Me!</H1>
   <H2 ONMOUSEOVER="this.style.color = 'red';">Turn red.</H2>
</BUTTON>
```

Instead, all events on items within the Button element are routed directly to the button itself.

Button Contents

The contents of the button are exposed differently depending on whether the button is defined using the <INPUT> tag or the <BUTTON> tag. The contents of a button created using the <INPUT> tag are exposed through the *value* and *innerText* properties, similar to the other Input types. The contents of a button created using the <BUTTON> tag are exposed through the *innerText* and *innerHTML* properties, but not through the *value* property. Like the TextArea element, a button created using a <BUTTON> tag also exposes richer access to the contents through the *createTextRange* method.

Programming Label and Fieldset Elements

Labels are used to associate HTML contents with an Input element, and fieldsets are used to group multiple controls. The Label and Fieldset elements are currently supported only by Internet Explorer 4.0.

The Fieldset element is useful for grouping different input controls within a single form—for example, to group the shipping address and the receiving address on a single form. The Fieldset element does not expose anything extra to the object model beyond the standard events and its attributes. However, with event bubbling Fieldset elements can be used to provide custom behavior to groups of controls.

Label elements are especially useful with check boxes and radio buttons. Before Label elements, when a radio button or check box was used, it had to be clicked on directly. Now a label associated with a button can also be used to select and deselect the button. The advantage to using Label elements is that they also provide a focus rectangle for the controls, making it clear what the purpose and contents of the control are and providing an extra click region that can be used to select the control. This feature can be added risk-free to any Web page, as down-level browsers ignore the Label element.

The Label Element and *onclick* Events

The Label element has an interesting effect on the event model. The default action of clicking on a Label element is that the associated control receives the focus. Therefore, when the user clicks on a Label element, the Label and all its parent elements receive the *onclick* event. If the default action is not overridden, the referenced control is given the focus. If the referenced control is a check box or radio button, the *onclick* event is then bubbled again from that control. This second bubbling is what allows clicking on the label for a radio button or check box to change the value.

Unless you need to distinguish between the user clicking on the label and the user clicking on the control itself, attach your event handler to the control, not the label.

<SCRIPT LANGUAGE="JavaSc
// Create property x
var x = 10;
function foo() {
// This code is not
code
var y =
alert(
// output
// Call foo while
foo();
window.foo(); // the
</SCRIPT>

PART III

DOCUMENT STYLE AND ANIMATION

<SCRIPT LANGUAGE="JavaSc
// Create propert
var x = 10;
function foo() {
// This code is not
code
var y =
alert(// output
// Call foo while
foo();
</SCRIPT>

C H A P T E R   E L E V E N

Dynamic Styles

Dynamic styles are an integral component of interactive Web pages. The document's appearance is defined using style sheets and HTML. Dynamic styles use the object model to modify the document's CSS (Cascading Style Sheets) in order to change the appearance of the document. The syntax for declaring a CSS was introduced in Chapter 1, "Overview of HTML and CSS." This chapter focuses on modifying style sheets using scripts in order to alter the document's appearance.

By applying dynamic styles, you can transform existing documents into more exciting documents without a loss of contents on down-level browsers. On a down-level browser, the document appears static, but when Dynamic HTML is supported the document comes to life. Because the easiest and most effective way to learn about dynamic styles is to study and review code samples, this chapter provides a large number of Plug and Play code modules. The purpose of these examples is to demonstrate how to apply various techniques for creating more interactive documents.

The following topics are covered in this chapter:

- **Dynamic styles and CSS** This section introduces the relationship between CSS and dynamic styles and compares the relationship between dynamic styles applied to CSS and procedural style sheet languages such as JavaScript Accessible Style Sheets (JASS) included in Netscape Navigator 4.0.
- **Style sheet properties** This section describes how style sheet properties are exposed by the object model. CSS properties do not always translate easily into object model properties because a single attribute may contain many properties. For example, the *background* attribute contains background color, image, and repeat information.

- **Inline styles** This section shows you how to program the inline style of an element, the simplest technique for adding dynamic styles. A *style* property that provides access to all the CSS-related properties is exposed on every element.
- **Changing the *class* attribute** A simple and elegant technique for creating dynamic styles is to write code that modifies the *class* or *id* attribute to associate an element with a different contextual rule. This section provides reusable examples that illustrate this technique.
- **Global style sheets** Changing the inline style and the *class* attribute are direct modifications of an element. The *document* object exposes a *styleSheets* collection that represents all the Style elements and linked style sheets in the document. This collection lets you modify the individual style sheets directly and thereby apply formatting to the entire document.
- **Techniques** This chapter concludes with three sections that describe techniques for taking advantage of the features introduced throughout the chapter. The section "Adaptive Layout Techniques" shows you how to make a document change in response to the environment. "Data Display Techniques" demonstrates hiding and showing data in response to the user. "Text Animation Techniques" shows you how to change styles in response to a timer.

  The samples demonstrating these techniques are included on the companion CD.

Dynamic Styles and CSS

CSS defines how particular elements within the document are to be rendered. The object model for manipulating the properties of the style sheet is based on the CSS recommendation. When an attribute or rule is modified through script, the static style sheet is updated and the page is immediately updated.

This dynamic style model is different from the JASS model supported by Netscape Navigator 4.0. JASS is a procedural model for defining a style sheet for the document at parse time rather than a programming model for manipulating a document's style. For example, JASS can be used to write conditional code that applies a different style sheet depending on the size of the screen during the loading of the document. JASS can't be used to change the style of an element in response to an event without reloading or requesting a new page from the server.

In Microsoft Internet Explorer 4.0, dynamic styles are not a procedural style sheet language, but they can accomplish all aspects of JASS and much more. Rather than define an alternative style sheet language, dynamic styles in Internet Explorer modify the document's CSS-defined style sheet by allowing you to define inline *style* properties on every element, enable and disable all global and linked style sheets, and add rules to and change rules on an existing style sheet.

Style Sheet Properties

Style sheets expose a number of properties that control the appearance of an element's contents. In the object model, these properties are exposed using a consistent naming convention. Most properties in CSS separate keywords using a hyphen (-) character. Because the hyphen is interpreted as an operator in most language constructs, it cannot be part of any CSS property names as exposed in the object model. Furthermore, for case-sensitive languages such as JavaScript, each CSS property is exposed consistent with other properties—that is, the first keyword is lowercased, and all subsequent keywords are capitalized. For example, the CSS *margin-top* property is exposed in the object model as *marginTop*.

NOTE: While this rule is simple and can be applied generally, one exception is necessary in order to avoid a keyword conflict with scripting languages. The CSS *float* property specifies whether an element should be aligned at the left or right edge with subsequent contents wrapping the element. Because float is a common data type in many languages, the CSS *float* property is exposed as *styleFloat* in the object model.

Compound Properties

Many style sheet properties are defined as compound properties. For example, the CSS *background* attribute contains information about the background image, URL, position, and so on. The following code shows the *background* attribute defined for the Body element:

```
body {background:red URL(cool.gif)}
```

These compound properties can be difficult to manipulate through script. To script the *background* property, a developer would have to parse the CSS property into its core components. This parsing is simplified in the CSS object model by decomposing compound CSS properties into multiple properties, each representing an aspect of the property. The following table lists the individual properties of the *background* property.

Property	Description
backgroundColor	String color name or RGB value
backgroundImage	URL to the background image
backgroundPosition	Position of the background image
backgroundRepeat	Whether the background image repeats horizontally, vertically, or both
backgroundScroll	Whether the background image scrolls with the document or acts as a static watermark

The *cssText* Property

The *cssText* property contains an element's style in the form of a string. Using this property, you can set an element's entire style or copy a style from one element to another. The following code gives paragraph *p2* the same style as *p1*. The section "Style Sheet Painter" later in this chapter provides a detailed example of defining and sharing style rules across an entire document.

```
<HTML>
   <HEAD>
      <TITLE>Sharing the cssText Property</TITLE>
   </HEAD>
   <BODY>
      <P ID="p1" STYLE="text-indent:.5in; color:red">
         This paragraph is red with a half-inch indent.
      </P>
      <P ID="p2">
         This paragraph has a default appearance. Click
         <INPUT TYPE=BUTTON VALUE="here"
            ONCLICK="document.all.p2.style.cssText =
               document.all.p1.style.cssText;">
         to make this paragraph look like the first paragraph.
      </P>
   </BODY>
</HTML>
```

Modifying Properties

Most of the style sheet properties supported by Internet Explorer 4.0 can be dynamically modified, but a few properties cannot be dynamically changed:

- The *display* property can only be switched between *none* and the default value. Therefore, elements cannot be switched between block and inline formats. Assigning a value other than *none* or the default value displays the document's contents using the default value.
- The *styleFloat* property is not fully dynamic on text elements such as Span and DIV. For text elements, the *styleFloat* property can only be changed from *left* to *right* or vice versa. If a text element was not originally floating to the left or to the right, it cannot be changed following the loading of the document. For input elements (Select, Button, Input, and so on), the *styleFloat* property can be dynamically modified between all the valid values.
- The *position* property is read-only and cannot be dynamically changed on any element.

Inline Styles

An inline style is assigned to an element using the STYLE attribute. The STYLE attribute lets you assign CSS properties directly to an instance of the element. For example, using the STYLE attribute, you can make a paragraph blue:

```
<P STYLE="color:blue">This is a blue paragraph.</P>
```

This technique improves on the existing HTML-based model for specifying text color. Prior to style sheets, the paragraph would be made blue using the Font element:

```
<P><FONT COLOR="Blue">This is a blue paragraph.</FONT></P>
```

The advantages of using the inline style over the stylistic HTML elements and attributes are as follows:

- Creates more compact HTML code
- Creates a smaller parsing tree, which leads to better performance
- Better separates the concepts of style and structure

Even inline styles are not in the true spirit of separating presentation from content. The true definition of separating presentation from content is to define all the styles outside the markup—for this, global or linked style sheets are more appropriate.

The inline style sheet does provide some conveniences for creating dynamic documents. For example, the style of an element can be quickly changed when the mouse moves over it:

```
<H1 ONMOUSEOVER="this.style.backgroundColor = 'yellow';"
      ONMOUSEOUT="this.style.backgroundColor = '';">
   This element turns yellow when the mouse moves over it.
</H1>
```

This code works by accessing the inline style for the H1 element and assigning a new value to the CSS *backgroundColor* property. The document's display is immediately updated to reflect the change to the style sheet. The inline style is represented on every element through the *style* property; *style* is an object-valued property through which scripts can access all the CSS properties.

Changing the *class* Attribute

Changing the inline style is useful, but it can be a burdensome technique when multiple property values need to be modified. A more effective way to change styles is to define styles for two or more classes in a global style sheet and dynamically change the *class* attribute of an element. The *class* attribute of an element is exposed through the *className* property. This property can be changed through script to associate a different style rule with the element. For example, the following code rewrites the simple *onmouseover* color change technique from the previous section to take advantage of global style sheets:

```
<HTML>
   <HEAD>
      <TITLE>Changing the class Attribute</TITLE>
      <!-- Create a global style sheet. -->
      <STYLE TYPE="text/css">
         .yellow {background:yellow; font-weight:bolder}
      </STYLE>
   </HEAD>
   <BODY>
      <H1 ONMOUSEOVER="this.className = 'yellow';"
          ONMOUSEOUT="this.className = '';">
```

```
         This element changes its class attribute
         when the mouse moves over it.
      </H1>
   </BODY>
</HTML>
```

In this example, when the mouse passes over the H1 element, the value of the CLASS attribute is changed to *yellow*. This causes the style specified for *yellow* to be immediately applied. In this case, the background becomes yellow and the text is made bold. The technique of changing class names offers two advantages: multiple parts of the style can be changed with a single line of code, and changing the style sheet rather than changing the code can modify the effect itself. This technique is extremely useful when you want a predefined effect, especially when the effect is to be shared across multiple elements.

You can make controls dynamic by using the same technique. Code in the following example changes the style sheet associated with a button in response to four mouse events: the mouse moving over and leaving the element and the left mouse button being clicked and being released.

```
<HTML>
   <HEAD>
      <TITLE>Animated Buttons</TITLE>
      <STYLE TYPE="text/css">
         .over {color:yellow; background:navy}
         .down {color:yellow; background:navy; font-style:italic}
      </STYLE>
   </HEAD>
   <BODY>
      <INPUT TYPE=BUTTON VALUE="Demo Button"
         ONMOUSEOVER="this.className = 'over';"
         ONMOUSEOUT="this.className = '';"
         ONMOUSEDOWN="this.className = 'down';"
         ONMOUSEUP="this.className = 'over';">
   </BODY>
</HTML>
```

This example can be extended for other events and other elements and can also be written generically by placing the event handlers in the Body element.

If you give the button in the previous example a new default style by assigning it a class name, you have to be careful to reassign that class name in response to the *onmouseout* event. Code in the next example automatically keeps track of elements' original class names. It demonstrates a reusable architecture for assigning different *onmouseover* effects to different elements, including nested elements, with only a small amount of code for each element.

```
<HTML>
   <HEAD>
      <TITLE>Exploding Effects</TITLE>
      <STYLE TYPE="text/css">
         .explode {color:red; letter-spacing:5px}
         .header {color:green}
         /* To add effects, simply define new rules and associate them
            with elements in the document. */
      </STYLE>
      <SCRIPT LANGUAGE="JavaScript">
         function walkStyles(src) {
            /* Walk up the tree; for every element with an effect
               property, swap the values of its effect and className
               properties. The tree walk is necessary to ensure that
               any nested effects are handled. */
            while ("HTML" != src.tagName) {
               if (null != src.getAttribute("effect", false)) {
                  var tempClass = src.className;
                  src.className = src.getAttribute("effect", false);
                  src.setAttribute("effect", tempClass, false);
               }
               src = src.parentElement;
            }
         }

         function setupEffect() {
            // Entering an element
            walkStyles(event.toElement);
         }

         function cleanupEffect() {
            // Exiting an element
            walkStyles(event.fromElement);
         }

         // Hook up event handlers.
         document.onmouseover = setupEffect;
         document.onmouseout  = cleanupEffect;
      </SCRIPT>
   </HEAD>
   <BODY>
      <H1 CLASS="header" effect="explode">
         This element will explode when the mouse moves over it.
      </H1>
   </BODY>
</HTML>
```

In the preceding code, the H1 element has a user-defined attribute named *effect* that contains a class name for use when the mouse is over the element. When the mouse is over the element, the *walkStyles* function swaps the values of the element's *className* and *effect* properties, thereby changing its style. When the mouse moves off the element, the same function swaps the values back.

You can add new elements with their own effects to this code quite easily. Simply define new classes in the style sheet and assign them to an element's built-in CLASS and custom *effect* attributes. The CLASS attribute specifies the default rendering of the element, and the *effect* attribute specifies the rendering of the element when the mouse moves over it.

The techniques sections at the end of this chapter use dynamic class changes to create interactive and fun Web pages. The code is similar to this example, allowing these techniques to be easily reused in existing Web pages.

Global Style Sheets

The previous two techniques involve changing the style of a single instance of an element at a time. By manipulating global style sheets, a script can change the style of many elements all at once. The global style sheet object model provides complete access to the global style sheets defined both within a document and in external files. Global style sheets contained within the page are associated with the document through the Style element; the Link element is used to associate an external style sheet file with the page. With the global style sheet object model, any style sheet can be completely customized, style sheets can be turned on and off, rules within the style sheet can be accessed and changed, and new rules can be added to quickly change the style of the entire document.

Dynamically modifying the global style sheet is an extremely powerful operation, but it can also be costly. Every time a new rule is added or removed or a style is changed in the global style sheet, the entire document is recalculated. Therefore, take care to minimize the number of operations you perform on the style sheet. When multiple changes to the document are necessary, an efficient technique is to define multiple style sheets and enable and disable them. This technique is introduced in the section "Providing a List of Alternative Style Sheets" later in this chapter.

The *styleSheets* Collection

The document exposes the set of style sheets associated with it through a *styleSheets* collection. The *styleSheets* collection contains all the global style sheets, whether they are contained in the document or linked from an external file. In the *styleSheets* collection, as in all other collections in Dynamic HTML, objects appear in the same order in which they appear in the document.

The *styleSheets* collection contains *styleSheet* objects, not element objects. There is a relationship between the *styleSheet* objects in the *styleSheets* collection and the *style* and *link* objects in the *all* collection. Each *styleSheet* object exposes an *owningElement* property that returns the *style* or *link* object that defined the style sheet. Each style and each Link element that associates a style exposes a *styleSheet* property that returns the *styleSheet* object.

Referencing a Style Sheet

All elements in the document support the ID attribute. The ID attribute in the Style and Link elements serves a dual purpose: it provides the index value to directly access the element through the *all* collection, and it provides the index value to directly access the *styleSheet* object in the *styleSheets* collection. It is important to recognize that in the *all* collection, a particular ID attribute references an actual *style* or *link* object, while in the *styleSheets* collection, it references the associated *styleSheet* object. The following example shows how to reference a *style* object and its associated *styleSheet* object using an ID, and how to reference each of those objects from the other:

```
<HTML>
   <HEAD>
      <TITLE>styleSheet Object vs. Style Element</TITLE>
      <STYLE ID="demo" TYPE="text/css">
         BODY {color:red}
      </STYLE>
      <SCRIPT LANGUAGE="JavaScript">
         // Return the style object.
         var styleElement = document.all["demo"];
         // Return a styleSheet object.
         var styleSheetObject = document.styleSheets["demo"];

         // Access each of these objects from the other.
         // Both alert boxes display true.
         alert(styleSheetObject.owningElement == styleElement);
         alert(styleElement.styleSheet == styleSheetObject);
```

```
    </SCRIPT>
  </HEAD>
  <BODY>
    Contents
  </BODY>
</HTML>
```

Providing a List of Alternative Style Sheets

The *styleSheets* collection can be used to enumerate all the style sheets in the document. Each style sheet can be individually enabled or disabled, turning on or off the application of the style sheet to the document. This technique enables a page to expose multiple styles for the user to select from; it can also be used to provide multiple views of the data.

Providing alternative style sheets has several advantages over dynamically modifying a single style sheet through code. Updating and maintaining alternative style sheets is easier than updating and maintaining scripts that modify a single style sheet. Also, code to switch between alternative style sheets is more efficient than code to modify a style sheet, especially if the code has to change a large number of styles. When you switch style sheets, the document is recalculated and displayed twice, once when the current style sheet is disabled and a second time when the new style sheet is enabled. In contrast, when you modify a single style sheet, the document is recalculated after each style is changed.

The DISABLED Attribute

The Style and Link elements support the DISABLED attribute, which initially disables a style sheet. You can use this attribute to control which style sheets are initially applied to the document. Scripts can later reset the Style and Link elements' corresponding *disabled* properties to change which style sheets are applied to the document. The examples that follow use this technique.

Providing Multiple Views

The following Web page allows the user to switch between different views of the same data. This technique is useful for providing several levels of detail at which to view the underlying data without requiring multiple pages to be downloaded. This example requires the user to explicitly choose between views. Your code can also change the view in response to other factors—for example, the size of the browser—as shown in the "Adaptive Layout Techniques" section later in this chapter.

```
<HTML>
   <HEAD>
      <TITLE>Multiple Views</TITLE>
      <STYLE ID="all" TYPE="text/css">
         #headOnly {display:none}
         #allText {color:red; cursor:default}
      </STYLE>
      <STYLE ID="headers" TYPE="text/css" DISABLED>
         #allText {display:none}
         #headOnly {color:navy; cursor:default}
         DIV {display:none}
      </STYLE>
   </HEAD>
   <BODY>
      <H1> Demonstration of Multiple Views</H1>
      <P ID="allText"
            ONCLICK="document.styleSheets['headers'].disabled = false;
               document.styleSheets['all'].disabled = true;">
         You are viewing an entirely expanded version of the
         document. Click on this paragraph to switch views.</P>
      <P ID="headOnly"
            ONCLICK="document.styleSheets['headers'].disabled = true;
               document.styleSheets['all'].disabled = false;">
         You are viewing only the headers of the document.
         Click on this paragraph to switch views.</P>
      <H2>Multiple Views</H2>
      <DIV>Using the CSS object model, you can provide multiple views
         of the data.
      </DIV>
      <H2>Swapping Data</H2>
      <DIV>You can also swap data displays. You can include
         predefined data in the document and selectively hide and
         display it.
      </DIV>
   </BODY>
</HTML>
```

Figure 11-1 demonstrates the two views of the document, with the two different style sheets applied. When the user clicks on the first paragraph, the style is automatically switched and different information is shown or hidden.

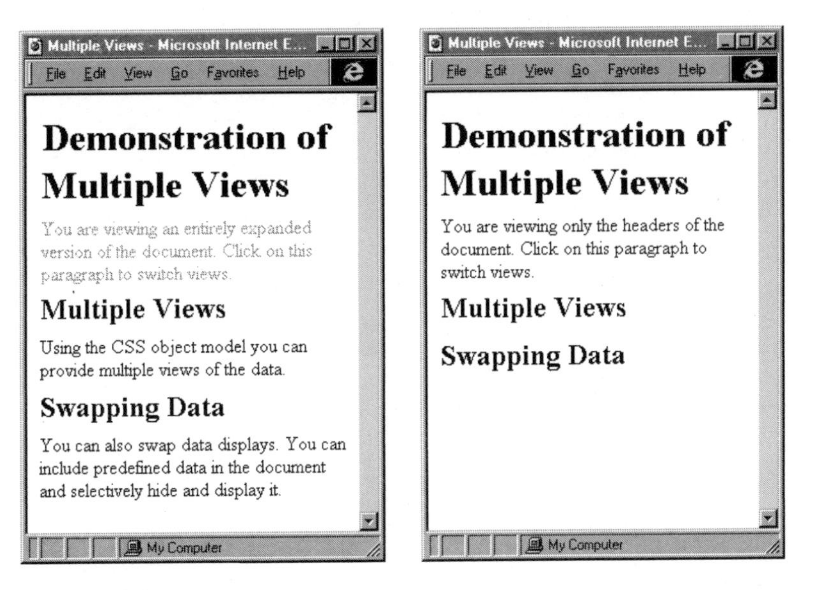

Figure 11-1.

Two views of a document obtained by alternating between style sheets contained within the document.

Selecting from Multiple Style Sheets

In the preceding example, the user clicks on a paragraph to change the display option. The following code takes an alternative approach; it provides a drop-down list from which the user can select a display option:

```
<HTML>
   <HEAD>
      <TITLE>Listing Style Sheets</TITLE>
      <STYLE ID="all" TITLE="Entire Document" TYPE="text/css">
         #headOnly {display:none}
         #allText {color:red; cursor:default}
      </STYLE>
      <STYLE ID="headers" TITLE="Headers Only" TYPE="text/css"
            DISABLED>
         #allText {display:none}
         #headOnly {color:navy; cursor:default}
         DIV {display:none}
      </STYLE>
      <SCRIPT LANGUAGE="JavaScript">
```

(continued)

```
      function selectSheet(s) {
         for (var intLoop = 0;
               intLoop < document.styleSheets.length; intLoop++)
            document.styleSheets[intLoop].disabled =
               (s.selectedIndex != intLoop);
      }
   </SCRIPT>
</HEAD>
<BODY>
   <H1>Listing Alternative Style Sheets</H1>
   <P>Select a View:
   <SELECT ONCHANGE="selectSheet(this);">
      <SCRIPT LANGUAGE="JavaScript">
         // Dynamically build list of options.
         for (var intLoop = 0;
               intLoop < document.styleSheets.length;
               intLoop++)
            document.write("<OPTION>" +
               document.styleSheets[intLoop].title);
      </SCRIPT>
   </SELECT>
   <P ID="allText">
      You are viewing an entirely expanded version of the document.
   </P>
   <P ID="headOnly">
      You are viewing only the headers of the document.
   </P>
   <H2>Multiple Views</H2>
   <DIV>Using the CSS object model, you can provide multiple views
      of the data.
   </DIV>
   <H2>Swapping Data</H2>
   <DIV>You can also swap data displays. You can include
      predefined data in the document and selectively hide and
      display it.
</BODY>
</HTML>
```

The drop-down list displays the TITLE attributes of the style sheets. TITLE attributes are available on all elements; they are used here to give the style sheets useful names. When the user selects an item from the list, the style sheet with the corresponding TITLE attribute is applied to the document.

Figure 11-2 shows the two available views for this document. Additional views can be added simply by defining additional style sheets.

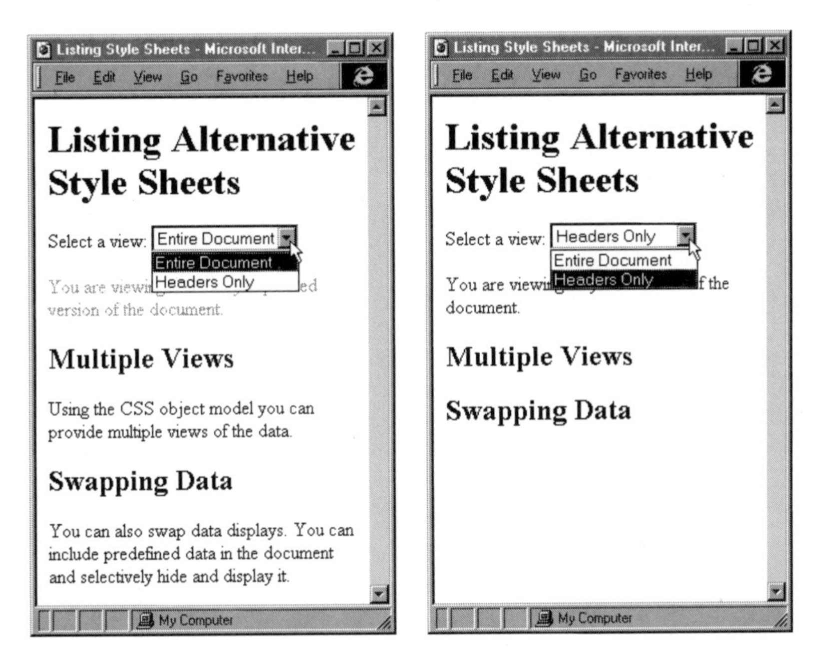

Figure 11-2.
Comparison of the two different views available for this document.

Randomly Applying Style Sheets

The previous example demonstrates a technique that lets the user manually select style sheets, but there is no requirement that this selection be done by the user. You can write code that automatically applies a random style sheet so that each visit to the page displays the same contents in a different way. This simple technique makes a Web site appear more interesting and dynamic without having to continually change the contents.

The section "Adaptive Layout Techniques" later in this chapter demonstrates a technique for changing the appearance of a page based on the user's environment. In general, any event—whether user initiated, the result of some action, or even the result of a timer—can be used to modify the appearance of the document.

Media-Dependent Style Sheets

HTML 4.0 defines a mechanism for associating different style sheets with different types of media. Internet Explorer 4.0 supports two types of media: *screen* and *print.* You can define different style sheets that apply to the document when it is displayed on screen or printed. The following code demonstrates how to define three style sheets, one for printing, one for viewing on screen, and one for all views of the document:

```
<STYLE TYPE="text/css" MEDIA="screen">
   /* Applies only when the document is viewed on screen */
   H1 {color:navy; text-align:center}
   P {margin-left:10pt}
</STYLE>
<STYLE TYPE="text/css" MEDIA="print">
   /* Applies only when the document is printed */
   H1 {color:black}
   P {margin-left:5pt}
</STYLE>
<STYLE TYPE="text/css" MEDIA="screen, print">
   /* Applies when the document is displayed  on screen or printed */
   H2 {font-size:12pt}
</STYLE>
```

If the *media* attribute is omitted, the style sheet applies to all views of the document. The *media* attribute is a property on the *styleSheet* object and on the Style and Link elements. You can dynamically change this property to switch the media the style sheet applies to. The next section contains sample code that can determine which style sheets are currently being applied to the on-screen view of the document.

The *styleSheet* Object's *cssText* Property

The section "The *cssText* Property" earlier in this chapter introduced the *cssText* property as a style property that is exposed on each element. In addition, each *styleSheet* object exposes a read-only *cssText* property, which represents the global style sheet formatted as text. This property is very useful for quickly viewing the style sheet associated with the page. The following code placed at the end of a document outputs all the style sheets that are currently applied to the document:

```
<SCRIPT LANGUAGE="JavaScript">
   var ss = document.styleSheets;
   document.write("<PRE>");
   for (var intLoop = 0; intLoop < ss.length; intLoop++)
      // Style sheet is for the screen and not disabled.
      if ((("" == ss[intLoop].media) ||
            (-1 != ss[intLoop].media.indexOf("screen"))) &&
            (!ss[intLoop].disabled))
         document.write(ss[intLoop].cssText);
   document.write("</PRE>");
</SCRIPT>
```

The *rules* Collection

Every style sheet exposes its collection of rules. A rule is the combination of the style declaration (for example, *color:red*) and its selector (for example, H1). Using this collection, you can access and dynamically change the declaration. The selector is read-only. If a new selector is necessary, you must remove the rule and add a new rule to the style sheet. Rules are added and removed through the *addRule* and *removeRule* methods on the *styleSheet* object.

Each rule in the *rules* collection represents a single selector and declaration, regardless of how it was defined in the style sheet. The following example demonstrates how a style sheet with grouped selectors is exposed by the *rules* collection:

```
<STYLE TYPE="text/css">
   H1, H2, P EM {color:green}
</STYLE>
<SCRIPT LANGUAGE="JavaScript">
   var rules = document.styleSheets[0].rules;
   for (var intLoop = 0; intLoop < rules.length; intLoop++)
      document.write("Rule: " + rules[intLoop].selectorText +
         ", Style: " + rules[intLoop].style.cssText + "<BR>");
</SCRIPT>
```

The preceding code outputs three separate rules because the grouping is separated in the object model so that the individual styles can be accessed and changed more easily. This code also demonstrates two of the three properties available on each rule. The *selectorText* is a read-only property that represents the selector portion of the rule. The *style* property works the same as the *style* property exposed on the individual elements; it allows the style for the selector to be modified.

Adding and Removing Rules

The *addRule* method adds a new rule to the style sheet; the *removeRule* method removes an existing rule from the style sheet. By default, new rules are added to the end of the style sheet, taking precedence over all rules defined earlier. Because each style sheet is merged independently, a new rule added to the first style sheet has higher precedence than all the rules in that sheet, but it has lower precedence than the rules in any style sheets that follow. Therefore, to ensure that the rule takes precedence over existing rules, you must add the rule to the last style sheet specified in the document, as shown here:

```
var intSS = document.styleSheets.length;
if (0 < intSS) // Be sure there is a style sheet to add the rule to.
   document.styleSheets[intSS - 1].addRule("H1",
      "color:red; font-size:18pt");
```

When you need more control over the position of the rule in the style sheet, you can add the rule to the *rules* collection at a specified position by supplying an index as the last parameter to the method. This code adds a rule to the beginning of the style sheet:

```
var intSS = document.styleSheets.length;
if (0 < intSS) // Be sure there is a style sheet to add the rule to.
   document.styleSheets[intSS - 1].addRule("H1",
      "color:red; font-size:18pt", 0); // Add before the first rule.
```

In all cases, the *addRule* method returns an index representing where the rule was added into the *rules* collection. In this example, where the index is explicitly defined, the *addRule* method returns *0*.

The *removeRule* method performs the reverse operation and returns the index of the rule removed. The following code demonstrates how to remove the first rule from the last style sheet:

```
var intSS = document.styleSheets.length;
if (0 < intSS) // Be sure there is a style sheet to remove
               // the rule from.
   document.styleSheets[intSS - 1].removeRule(0);
```

Linked Style Sheets and Rules

All style sheets expose a *readOnly* property, which indicates whether the style sheet can be modified. For linked style sheets, this property returns *true*. However, linked style sheets allow rules to be added and modified. Changing a linked style sheet affects only the currently displayed instance of the document. Adding a rule to a linked style sheet does not cause the other documents that share that style sheet to update with the same rule. There is currently no way, short of adding the rule to each document, to dynamically change a style sheet shared by multiple documents.

Imported Style Sheets

You can use the *@import* statement in your style sheet to import another style sheet. Through the object model, you can dynamically access, add, and remove imported style sheets.

The imports contained within a style sheet are exposed by the *imports* collection, each element of which is another *styleSheet* object. An imported style sheet can further import another style sheet. Therefore, to allow you to determine what style sheet the import is contained within, the *styleSheet* object exposes a *parentStyleSheet* property, which returns the *styleSheet* object that defined the import. For top-level style sheets, this property returns a value of *null*.

The *addImport* method on the *styleSheet* object takes a string value representing the URL. According to the CSS specification, imported style rules always exist at the beginning of the style sheet and therefore at the beginning of the cascading order. Thus, any rules in imported style sheets have lower precedence than the rules already in the style sheet. The following code imports a style sheet named *cool.css* into the first style sheet in the *styleSheets* collection:

```
document.styleSheets[0].addImport("URL('cool.css');");
```

Use the *removeImport* method to remove the import at the specified position in the *imports* collection. The following code removes the first import from the style sheet:

```
document.styleSheets[0].removeImport(0);
```

Adding New Style Sheets

Style sheets can be added to the document by using the *createStyleSheet* method on the document. By default, the *createStyleSheet* method adds a new style sheet to the end of the *styleSheets* collection. To add a new linked style sheet, supply a URL as the first argument; to specify where to insert the style sheet, supply an index as the second argument. If you need to create a nonlinked style sheet and insert it at a particular position in the *styleSheets* collection, pass *null* for the first argument.

Style Sheet Painter

The following example demonstrates how to dynamically modify the global style sheet of a document to quickly change the appearance of all elements of the same type. This demonstration uses a frameset in which the left frame contains a set of styles and the right frame contains contents to apply the styles to. The user selects a style from the left frame and then clicks on an element in the right frame; all elements of the same type as the one clicked on are immediately updated. The tag name of the element to which the style will be applied is displayed in the status bar. This example uses three files. The stylizer.htm file contains a frameset and most of the core code to transfer a style from the style frame to the contents frame. The styles.htm file contains a table of styles to choose from, and the contents.htm file contains the contents to apply the styles to.

This example uses the following techniques:

- Event handlers for the style and contents documents are written in the frameset.
- The style of a cell in the styles document's table is changed by changing its class name. A selected cell's inline style sheet specifies the colors and font size that are to be applied to elements clicked in the contents document. So the cell's border, which indicates that it is selected, cannot be part of its inline style; instead the border is defined in a global style sheet.
- The *addRule* method is used to add new rules to the contents document.
- The status bar is updated based on the position of the mouse.

Figure 11-3 shows the style painter application as defined by the code examples that follow.

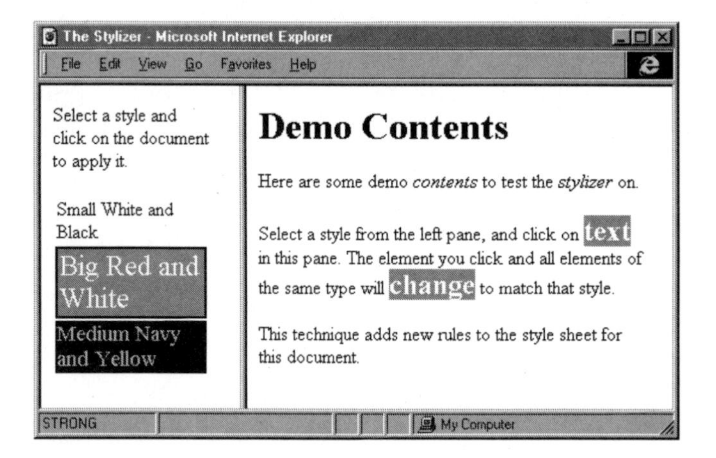

Figure 11-3.
The style painter application in action.

The stylizer.htm file The following frameset document divides the screen into two frames: the left pane displays a list of style options, and the right pane displays the document to apply the styles to. The code that handles communications between the two other documents is contained within this document.

```
<HTML>
   <HEAD>
      <TITLE>The Stylizer</TITLE>
      <SCRIPT LANGUAGE="JavaScript">
         window.curStyle = null;
         function selectStyle() {
            // Highlight the currently selected style cell.
            var el = this.parentWindow.event.srcElement;
            if ("TD" == el.tagName) {
               if (null != curStyle)
                  curStyle.className = "";
               curStyle = el;
               curStyle.className = "selected";
            }
         }

         function addStyle() {
            // Add a new rule to the document for the selected style.
            if (null != curStyle) {
               var srcWin = this.parentWindow;
               var tag = srcWin.event.srcElement.tagName;
               srcWin.document.styleSheets[0].addRule(tag,
                  curStyle.style.cssText);
            }
         }

         function hookupEvents() {
            /* Bind each frame's click events to the appropriate
               function in this document. */
            window.styles.document.onclick = selectStyle;
            window.content.document.onclick = addStyle;
         }
      </SCRIPT>
   </HEAD>
   <FRAMESET ONLOAD="hookupEvents();" COLS="170, *">
      <FRAME SRC="styles.htm" NAME="styles">
      <FRAME SRC="content.htm" NAME="content">
   </FRAMESET>
</HTML>
```

The styles.htm file The following document contains a table of styles that the user can select and apply to the contents document. Adding more table cells to the table can extend the list of styles.

```
<HTML>
   <HEAD>
      <TITLE>Style List</TITLE>
      <STYLE TYPE="text/css">
         /* This style is used to highlight the user's selection. */
         .selected {border:2px black solid}
      </STYLE>
   </HEAD>
   <BODY>
      <P>Select a style and click on the document to apply it.</P>
      <!-- A cell's inline style specifies the style that can be
           applied in the contents document when the cell is selected.
           The style is simply copied over. -->
      <TABLE>
         <TR>
            <TD STYLE="background:white; color:black; font-size:12pt">
               Small White and Black
            </TD>
         </TR><TR>
            <TD STYLE="background:red; color:white; font-size:18pt">
               Big Red and White
            </TD>
         </TR><TR>
            <TD STYLE="background:navy; color:yellow; font-size:14pt">
               Medium Navy and Yellow
            </TD>
         </TR>
      </TABLE>
   </BODY>
</HTML>
```

The content.htm file The following sample document contains contents to which the selected styles are applied. The small script in this document is used to display the tag name of the element to which the style is to be applied in the status bar.

```
<HTML>
   <HEAD>
      <TITLE>Demo Contents</TITLE>
      <SCRIPT LANGUAGE="JavaScript">
         function updateStatus() {
            /* Display the name of the element the mouse is over.
               This is the element type to which the new style will
               be applied. */
            window.defaultStatus = event.srcElement.tagName;
         }
      </SCRIPT>
```

```
      <STYLE TYPE="text/css">
         /* Style block to add rules to */
      </STYLE>
   </HEAD>
   <BODY ONMOUSEOVER="updateStatus();">
      <H1>Demo Contents</H1>
      <P>Here are some demo <EM>contents</EM> to test the
         <EM>stylizer</EM> on.</P>
      <P>Select a style from the left pane, and click on
         <STRONG>text</STRONG> in this pane. The element you click
         and all elements of the same type will
         <STRONG>change</STRONG> to match that style.
      <P>This technique adds new rules to the style sheet for
         this document.
   </BODY>
</HTML>
```

Style Sheet Events

A *styleSheet* object is not created and added to the *styleSheets* collection until the entire style sheet is loaded, including the complete downloading of any linked or imported style sheets. For tracking the status of a style sheet, the Style and Link elements expose an *onreadystatechange* and an *onload* event. The *readyState* property returns a string that represents the current state of the element. These events and the *readyState* property are similar to the members of the same names on the document and window.

While a style sheet is being parsed, its *readyState* value is *loading*. Once the entire style sheet has been loaded, *readyState* changes to *complete*. Immediately prior to *complete*, the *styleSheet* object is created and added to the *styleSheets* collection. The *onreadystatechange* or *onload* event can be used to track when the style sheet becomes available. The *onload* event always occurs immediately following the *onreadystatechange* event, firing when the style sheet reaches the *complete* state. The following document demonstrates the ordering sequence:

```
<HTML>
   <HEAD>
      <TITLE>Style Sheet Events</TITLE>
      <STYLE TYPE="text/css"
            ONREADYSTATECHANGE=
               "alert('readyState: ' + this.readyState);"
            ONLOAD="alert('load event');">
         H1 {color:red}
      </STYLE>
   </HEAD>
```

(continued)

```
    <BODY>
       <H1>Heading</H1>
    </BODY>
</HTML>
```

Alert boxes display the following messages in the order shown:

1. *readyState: loading*
2. *readyState: complete*
3. *load event*

The style sheet is loaded synchronously into the document; while the style sheet is being loaded, the rest of the document is not parsed or rendered. One use for the *onreadystatechange* and *onload* events is to provide the user with status bar notifications of the status of the document, as shown here:

```
<HTML>
   <HEAD>
      <TITLE>readyState of the Document</TITLE>
      <SCRIPT LANGUAGE="JavaScript">
         function updateStatus(msg) {
            window.defaultStatus = msg;
         }
      </SCRIPT>
      <!-- Provide an update of the downloading
           of the style sheet. -->
      <LINK REL="styleSheet" TYPE="text/css"
         HREF="dhtml.css" TITLE="Default Sheet"
         ONREADYSTATECHANGE="updateStatus('StyleSheet[' +
            this.title + ']: ' + this.readyState);">
      <SCRIPT LANGUAGE="JavaScript">
         // Let the user know the document is still parsing.
         updateStatus("Parsing: " + document.title);
      </SCRIPT>
   </HEAD>
   <BODY ONLOAD="updateStatus('');">
      <H1>Status Tracking</H1>
   </BODY>
</HTML>
```

If the style sheet fails to load because the server times out or the file does not exist, neither the *onload* or the final *onreadystatechange* event that signifies the download is complete is fired. Currently, no error is generated and no explicit error event is available to track whether the linked style sheet failed to download. One work-around to solve this problem is to set a flag in the *onload* event handler. If this flag is not set, an error must have occurred during downloading of the style sheet:

```
<HTML>
   <HEAD>
      <TITLE>Tracking Download Errors</TITLE>
      <LINK REL="styleSheet" TYPE="text/css" HREF="dhtml.css"
         TITLE="Default Styles" ID="ss1"
         ONLOAD="this.downloaded = true; // Success!">
      <SCRIPT LANGUAGE="JavaScript">
         /* If the property does not exist, an error occurred.
            The property would be added to the element, not to the
            styleSheet object. */
         if (null == document.all.ss1.downloaded)
            alert("Error downloading style sheet.");
      </SCRIPT>
   </HEAD>
   <BODY>
      <H1>Error Tracking</H1>
   </BODY>
</HTML>
```

Adaptive Layout Techniques

The CSS object model enables documents to adapt to the user's environment. Most of the examples in this chapter use dynamic styles to add effects or to allow the user to manually select alternative style sheets. The document's layout can also be changed based on the display resolution, window screen size, or other values intrinsic to the system. The following are a few high-level techniques you can use to create pages that adapt to the user's system:

- Declare an initial static style using style sheets. When appropriate, use the system settings for color and font values.
- Declare alternative style sheets for the different environments. Add script that establishes the initial style based on the environment.
- Bind to the *resize* event of the Body or other elements to dynamically change the enabled style sheets based on the size of the window.
- For more complex systems, construct rules dynamically, associate them with the document and change styles algorithmically.

The first three techniques are simple to add to a document. All the styles are declared using CSS, and scripting is used only to turn on and off the appropriate style sheet. Using the last technique, you can create pages that change in a much more procedural manner by directly manipulating the existing rules and adding new rules using the methods described earlier.

The following example uses the first three adaptive layout techniques. The document alternates between three main style sheets, depending on the window size. These three layout scenarios are merged with one of the two color schemes, based on the number of colors available. In addition, the navigation bar at the top of the window uses the color scheme of the system menus. All the style sheets are included within the document. Alternatively, they could have been defined as a linked style sheet and shared across an entire Web site.

Figure 11-4 shows two of the document's alternative layouts.

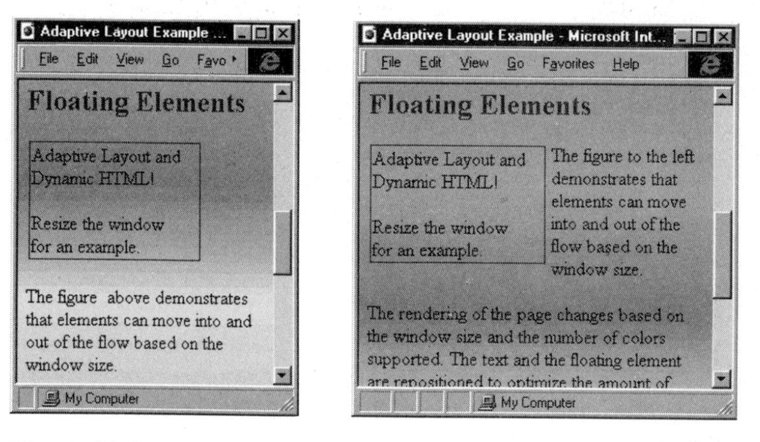

Figure 11-4.

Layouts of an adaptive document in narrow-width and medium-width windows.

Figure 11-4 displays part of the document in narrow-width and medium-width views. The most obvious difference between the views is the margins. The box appears above the text in the narrowest view and floats to the side of the text in the wider views, and the text changes to reflect the box's position.

Here is a full listing of the code for this example:

```
<HTML>
   <HEAD>
      <TITLE>Adaptive Layout Example</TITLE>
      <STYLE TYPE="text/css" ID="default">
         /* Default style sheet that is always applied to the
            document */
```

```
   /* Define the menu bar to match the built-in menus on
      the user's system. */
   .menu A.highlight {background:highlight; color:highlighttext}
   .menu {background:menu}
   .menu P {margin-left:5pt; margin-right:5pt}
   .menu A {color:menutext; text-decoration:none; font:menu}

   /* Define default margins. */
   body {margin-top:0pt; margin-left:0pt}
   .centerIndent {margin-left:5pt; margin-right:5pt}
   .leftIndent {margin-left:5pt; margin-right:5pt}
   .rightIndent {margin-left:5pt; margin-right:5pt}
   H1 {text-align:center}
   .outline {border:1pt solid gray; margin:2pt 2pt 2pt 2pt}
</STYLE>

<STYLE TYPE="text/css" ID="narrowScreen">
   /* Additional style rules for narrow screen;
      all contents for wide screens are hidden. */
   .wide {display:none}
</STYLE>

<STYLE TYPE="text/css" ID="midScreen">
   /* Rules for middle-size screen; hide narrow contents. */
   .narrow {display:none}
   .floatLeft {margin-left:0; width:150; float:left}
</STYLE>

<STYLE TYPE="text/css" ID="wideScreen">
   /* Nicest layout on the widest screen */
   .centerIndent {margin-left:15%; margin-right:15%}
   .leftIndent {margin-left:35%; margin-right:5%}
   .rightIndent {margin-left:5%; margin-right:35%}
   .floatLeft {margin-left:-154; width:150; float:left}
   .narrow {display:none}
</STYLE>

<STYLE TYPE="text/css" ID="4bit">
   /* Color depth of 4 or less */
   BODY {color:red; background:white}
</STYLE>

<STYLE TYPE="text/css" ID="8bit">
   /* Style sheets for 8 or more bits */
   BODY {background:URL(fancy.gif)}
```

(continued)

```
      H1 {color:purple}
      H2 {color:navy}
   </STYLE>

   <SCRIPT LANGUAGE="JavaScript">
      // Select the style sheet for the available color depth.
      var ss = document.styleSheets;

      ss["4bit"].disabled = (screen.colorDepth >= 8);
      ss["8bit"].disabled = !(ss["4bit"].disabled);

      function updateLayout() {
         // Change style sheet based on available screen width.
         var ss = document.styleSheets;
         ss["wideScreen"].disabled =
            (450 > document.body.offsetWidth);
         ss["midScreen"].disabled =
            (!ss["wideScreen"].disabled ||
               300 > document.body.offsetWidth);
         ss["narrowScreen"].disabled =
            !(ss["wideScreen"].disabled &&
               ss["midScreen"].disabled);
      }

      function highlight() {
         // Highlight the Anchor element in the menu.
         if ("A" == event.toElement.tagName)
            event.toElement.className = "highlight";
      }

      function cleanup() {
         // Clear the class.
         if ("A" == event.fromElement.tagName) {
            event.fromElement.className = "";
      }
   </SCRIPT>
</HEAD>
<BODY ONRESIZE="updateLayout();">
   <SCRIPT LANGUAGE="JavaScript">
      /* This call is in the body because updateLayout relies
         on the Body element being available. */
      updateLayout();
   </SCRIPT>

   <!-- Output a menu bar using the user's settings for menus. -->
   <DIV CLASS="menu" ONMOUSEOVER="highlight()"
         ONMOUSEOUT="cleanup()">
```

```
   <P><A HREF="home.htm">Home</A>   
      <A HREF="search.htm">Search</A>   
      <A HREF="about.htm">About</A></P>
</DIV>

<H1>Adaptive Layout</H1>
<DIV CLASS="centerIndent">
   This example demonstrates how to use dynamic styles to create
   a page that adapts to the surrounding environment. The menu
   bar uses the system settings for colors. For systems
   with poor color support, the document uses only black and
   white rather than colorful headers. The layout will change
   depending on the size of the window. The contents are
   also slightly modified when the environment changes.
</DIV>

<DIV CLASS="leftIndent">
   <H2>Floating Elements</H2>
   <TABLE ID="tleft" CLASS="floatLeft">
      <TR>
         <TD CLASS="outline" VALIGN="Top">
            Adaptive Layout and <BR>
            Dynamic HTML!
            <P>Resize the window<BR>
            for an example.
         </TD>
      </TR>
   </TABLE>

   <!-- The reference to the floating element is changed
        depending on the size of the screen. -->
   <P>The figure
      <SPAN CLASS="wide">to the left</SPAN>
      <SPAN CLASS="narrow">above</SPAN>
      demonstrates that elements can move into and out of the
      flow based on the window size.
   </P>
   <P>The rendering of the page changes based on the window size
      and the number of colors supported. The text and the
      floating element are repositioned to optimize the amount
      of real estate available on the screen.
   </P>
</DIV>
<DIV CLASS="rightIndent">
   <H2>Conditional Data</H2>
```

(continued)

```
          <P>
             Different data can be displayed in response to the
             environment.
          </P>
          <P CLASS="wide" STYLE="color:red">
             You are viewing a wider version of this document.
          </P>
          <P CLASS="narrow" STYLE="color:red">
             The document has a different style because your window is
             narrow.
          </P>
       </DIV>
       <DIV STYLE="display:none">
          <!-- This message is displayed only if the style sheet
               is not supported. -->
          This page is best viewed with a browser that supports CSS
          and Dynamic HTML.
       </DIV>
    </BODY>
</HTML>
```

This document independently adapts to the user's environment; it can be combined with user interactions that also change the display. When an adaptive layout document responds to user-initiated changes, the user-initiated styles should take precedence over the automatically applied styles. For example, if the user is explicitly hiding or showing data, the layout changes should respect the user's choices. The easiest way to give precedence to user-initiated styles is to put them in inline style sheets or the last global style sheet while using global style sheets for the adaptive layout styles.

Data Display Techniques

The adaptive layout technique changed the document automatically based on the user's environment. Data display techniques focus on the user interacting with the document to change the display of data. They allow the user to focus on the most important data on the page. For example, rather than present the user with a large document, you might initially display only headers and other relevant information. The user can then click on a header or other text to display or hide any related information, and by doing so will have a highly interactive experience. These techniques also adapt well to down-level browsers on which the document is displayed entirely expanded, without the extra interactivity.

Using Cursors to Highlight Contents

When you make a document dynamic, you turn various elements into click regions or give them other special behavior. In order to use these elements, the user has to know which ones they are. By displaying different cursors when the mouse is on different elements, you can help the user discover them.

By default, the mouse cursor over an informational element is an I-beam that indicates that the text is selectable. Over behavioral elements—for example, all links in the document—the cursor is a hand that indicates that the elements can be clicked.

Internet Explorer 4.0 provides the Web author control over the cursor through a new CSS *cursor* property. The *cursor* property allows the author to define the cursor to display when the mouse is on the element. For example, when you create a click region, a hand cursor or other pointer is more appropriate than an I-beam cursor. Chapter 1, "Overview of HTML and CSS," provides a table of all the types of cursors supported through the *cursor* property.

The following code demonstrates displaying a hand cursor when the mouse is on an H1 element:

```
<H1 STYLE="cursor:hand" ONCLICK="alert('clicked');"
      ONSELECTSTART="event.returnValue = false;">
   When on this header, the mouse pointer is a hand.
</H1>
```

The *onselectstart* event is handled to disable the initiation of text selection inside the header. Canceling this event by returning *false* prevents the user from starting a selection within the header; it does not prevent the text from being selected. Selections can start outside the header and be extended through the header contents. This behavior is the default behavior for links.

Hiding and Showing Data

The following example contains generic code that dynamically displays and hides existing data.

```
<HTML>
   <HEAD>
      <TITLE>Displaying and Hiding Data</TITLE>
      <STYLE TYPE="text/css">
         body {background:white}
         .expandable {color:blue; cursor:hand}
         .expanded {color:black; font-size:"12pt"}
         .collapsed {display:none}
      </STYLE>
```

(continued)

```
    <SCRIPT LANGUAGE="JavaScript">
      // Generic display code
      function outliner() {
        // Get child element.
        var child =
          document.all[event.srcElement.getAttribute("child",
            false)];
        // If child element exists, expand or collapse it.
        if (null != child)
          child.className = child.className == "collapsed" ?
            "expanded" : "collapsed";
      }
    </SCRIPT>
  </HEAD>
  <BODY ONCLICK="outliner();">
    <H1 CLASS="expandable" child="info">
      Click here for more information.
    </H1>
    <DIV ID="info" CLASS="collapsed">
      These contents are not displayed initially. Clicking on the
      header above displays them.
    </DIV>
  </BODY>
</HTML>
```

With this code, any element can act as the click source for displaying or hiding other information. To make an element act as a click source, assign it a class name of *expandable* and give it a custom attribute named *child.*

The *expandable* class defines the mouse pointer to be a hand when it is over an element of the class. The *expandable* class only standardizes the appearance of click sources, so using it is optional. You can modify the class to further standardize the appearance of expandable items.

The custom *child* attribute must contain the ID of the data that is to be displayed or hidden. Clicking on the expandable item causes the data's class name to be changed from *collapsed* to *expanded* or vice versa, depending on whether it is currently hidden or displayed. You should initialize the data's class name to *collapsed* or *expanded* to specify its initial appearance.

Expanding and Collapsing Outlines

The previous example demonstrates how to generically display and hide contents. The code can be extended to generically create an expanding and collapsing outline. The following scenario demonstrates how to subclass the list container

(UL or OL) elements to support outlining. When this code is on the page, lists on the page support expanding and collapsing.

```
<HTML>
   <HEAD>
      <TITLE>Expanding and Collapsing Outline</TITLE>
      <STYLE TYPE="text/css">
         /* Outline style sheet */
         UL {cursor:hand; color:navy}
         UL UL {display:none; margin-left:5pt}
         .leaf {cursor:text; color:black}
      </STYLE>
      <SCRIPT LANGUAGE="JavaScript">
         function checkParent(src, dest) {
            // Search for a specific parent of the current element.
            while (src != null) {
               if (src.tagName == dest)
                  return src;
               src = src.parentElement;
            }
            return null;
         }

         function outline() {
            // Expand or collapse if a list item is clicked.
            var open = event.srcElement;
            // Be sure the click was inside an LI element. This test
            // allows rich HTML inside lists.
            var el = checkParent(open, "LI");
            if (null != el) {
               var pos = 0;
               // Search for a nested list.
               for (pos = 0; pos < el.children.length; pos++)
                  if ("UL" == el.children[pos].tagName)
                     break;
               if (pos == el.children.length)
                  return;
            }
            else
               return;
            el = el.children[pos];
            if ("UL" == el.tagName) {
```

(continued)

```
                // Expand or collapse nested list.
                if ("" == el.style.display)
                   el.style.display = "block";
                else
                   el.style.display = "";
             }
             event.cancelBubble = true;
          }

          document.onclick = outline;
       </SCRIPT>
    </HEAD>
    <BODY>
       <UL>
          <LI>Item 1
             <UL>
                <LI CLASS="leaf">Subitem 1
                <LI>Subitem 2
                   <UL>
                      <LI CLASS="leaf">Subsubitem 1
                   </UL>
             </UL>
          </LI>
          <LI CLASS="leaf">Item 2
       </UL>
    </BODY>
</HTML>
```

Creating an Expandable Table of Contents

Combining an expanding and collapsing outline with the mouse effects introduced earlier in this chapter can create a highly interactive menu. The HTML used to create this document is the standard HTML for creating nested lists. Style sheets and code bring the standard HTML alive as an interactive outline. Because a standard list is used, this page degrades gracefully on browsers that do not support Dynamic HTML—for example, Internet Explorer 3.0 displays the document as a standard bulleted list.

The code for this example can be found on the companion CD. To create an expandable menu, follow these steps:

1. Create a bulleted list to represent the expandable items, but to make the list more user-friendly, replace the standard bullets with images. With Dynamic HTML, these images are changed to represent the expanded and collapsed state of each item. The two states

are defined using style sheets, as shown in the following code fragment. A special class, *open,* is specified to represent the expanded state. Because adding the *open* class gives the CSS style rule a higher precedence than the default case, the open.gif file is displayed.

```
/* GIFs of an open and a closed folder to use in
   place of the standard bullets */
UL.toc LI {list-style-image:url(close.gif)}
UL.toc LI.open {list-style-image:url(open.gif)}

/* Colors for highlighted menu options and for the selected
   link. */
UL.toc A:active, UL.toc A.select {color:white;
   background:blue}
UL.toc .over {color:red}  /* Highlight color */
```

2. Contain the child elements of all list items within a nested list for each item. The code for this example requires the nested UL to immediately follow the Anchor element representing the topic header, as shown in the following code fragment. Therefore, rich HTML cannot be used within the top-level link. If rich HTML is desired, the provided script can be extended to walk forward and skip over any of the extra elements.

```
<LI>
   <A HREF="ch1/overview.htm">Overview of HTML and CSS</A>
   <UL>
      <LI><A HREF="ch1/html40.htm" TITLE="HTML 4.0">
         HTML "4.0"</A></LI>
      <LI><A HREF="ch1/css.htm" TITLE="CSS Features">
         CSS Features</A></LI>
      <LI><A HREF="ch1/cssp.htm" TITLE="CSS Positioning">
         CSS Positioning</A></LI>
      <LI><A HREF="ch1/settings.htm" TITLE="System">
         System Settings</A></LI>
   </UL>
</LI>
```

3. Combine this layout with the appropriate script to create a completely expandable outline.

The complete document and the script necessary to create the expanding outline are shown in the following code. This example can be extended with more topics and children simply by adding more HTML—no extra code is necessary.

```
<HTML>
   <HEAD>
      <TITLE>Contents</TITLE>
      <STYLE TYPE="text/css">
         BODY {background:navy; color:white}

         UL.toc {cursor:hand}

         /* Set image for the bulleted list. */
         UL.toc LI {list-style-image:url(close.gif)}
         UL.toc LI.open {list-style-image:url(open.gif)}
         UL.toc UL {list-style:none}

         /* Hide the child elements by default. */
         UL.toc UL {display:none}
         /* Display the child elements. */
         UL.toc UL.expanded {display:block}

         UL.toc LI A {text-decoration:none; color:yellow;
            font-weight:bold}
         UL.toc LI UL A {color:white}
         UL.toc A:active, UL.toc A.select
            {color:white; background:blue}
         UL.toc .over {color:red}  /* Highlight color */
         UL.toc UL P {margin-top:0; margin-bottom:0}
      </STYLE>
      <STYLE TYPE="text/JavaScript">
         /* Technique to display the outline in Netscape
            Navigator 4.0. */
         /* Define an alternative style for "UL.toc UL". */
         contextual(classes.toc.UL, tags.UL).display = "block";
      </STYLE>
      <BASE TARGET="DEMO">
      <SCRIPT LANGUAGE="JavaScript">
         // Generic display code

         // This technique allows you to write generic code that
         // automatically causes related contents to be either
         // displayed or hidden.

         var curSelection = null;

         function setStyle(src, toClass) {
            // Format the element to the specified class.
            if (null != src)
               src.className = toClass;
         }
```

```
function mouseEnters() {
   // Be sure the element is not the current selection and
   // that it is an anchor.
   if ((curSelection != event.toElement) &&
         ("A" == event.toElement.tagName))
      setStyle(event.toElement,"over");
}

function mouseLeaves() {
   // Again, be sure the element is not the current selection
   // and that it is an anchor.
   if ((curSelection != event.fromElement) &&
         ("A" == event.fromElement.tagName))
      setStyle(event.fromElement, "");
}

function outliner() {
   var child = null, el = null;
   /* Assumes that the DIV containing the child
      elements immediately follows the heading anchor. */
   switch (event.srcElement.tagName) {
   case "A":
      el = event.srcElement.parentElement;
      child = document.all[event.srcElement.sourceIndex + 1];
      break;
   case "LI":
      el = event.srcElement;
      child = document.all[event.srcElement.sourceIndex + 2];
      break;
   }
   /* Be sure the child element exists and that it is the
      child LI. */
   if ((null != child) && ("UL" == child.tagName) &&
         ("LI" == child.parentElement.tagName)) {
      if ("" == child.className) {
         // Collapse the item.
         child.className = "expanded";
         el.className = "open";
      }
      else {
         // Expand the item.
         child.className = "";
         el.className = "closed";
      }
   }
```

(continued)

```
            if ("A" == event.srcElement.tagName) {
               if (null != curSelection)
                  setStyle(curSelection, "");
               // Save and highlight new selection.
               curSelection = event.srcElement;
               setStyle(curSelection, "select");
            }
         }
      </SCRIPT>
   </HEAD>
   <BODY>
      <UL CLASS="toc" ONCLICK="outliner();"
         ONSELECTSTART="return false;" ONMOUSEOVER="mouseEnters();"
         ONMOUSEOUT="mouseLeaves();">
         <LI>
            <A HREF="ch1/overview.htm">HTML and CSS Overview</A>
            <UL>
               <LI>
                  <A HREF="ch1/html40.htm" TITLE="HTML 4.0">
                     HTML "4.0"</A>
               </LI>
               <LI>
                  <A HREF="ch1/css.htm" TITLE="CSS Features">
                     CSS Features</A>
               </LI>
               <LI>
                  <A HREF="ch1/cssp.htm" TITLE="CSS Positioning">
                     CSS Positioning</A>
               </LI>
               <LI>
                  <A HREF="ch1/settings.htm"
                        TITLE="System Settings">
                     System Settings</A>
               </LI>
            </UL>
         </LI>

         <LI>
            <A HREF="ch2/overview.htm">
               Fundamentals of HTML Scripting</A>
            <UL>
               <LI>
                  <A HREF="ch2/langs.htm"
                        TITLE="Supported Languages">
                     Supported Languages</A>
               </LI>
```

```
              <LI>
                 <A HREF="ch2/guidelns.htm"
                       TITLE="Variable Naming Guidelines">
                    Naming Conventions</A>
              </LI>
           </UL>
        </LI>
        <!-- New options can be added simply by adding
              more list items. -->
     </UL>
  </BODY>
</HTML>
```

This example demonstrates how to write generic reusable code. The menu is completely encapsulated based on style sheets and scripts that are associated directly with the table of contents list. This example can be used in any document without modification to the document or this script.

While this page downgrades gracefully in browsers that do not support style sheets and with the style sheet support in Internet Explorer 3.0, it uses special code to display correctly in Netscape Navigator 4.0. As of that release, the *display:none* value is recognized and the child elements are not displayed. Because Netscape Navigator does not support dynamic style manipulation, the outline cannot be dynamically expanded to display the nested data. To display correctly in Netscape Navigator, this document uses the following JASS style sheet script. This style sheet is recognized only by Netscape Navigator 4.0 and is used to redisplay the hidden contents. The JASS style sheet follows the CSS-defined style sheet in the document.

```
<STYLE TYPE="text/JavaScript">
   /* Define an alternative style for "UL.toc UL". */
   contextual(classes.toc.UL, tags.UL).display = "block";
</STYLE>
```

This technique for defining a JASS style sheet is useful for tweaking the rendering between Internet Explorer 4.0 and Netscape Navigator 4.0. You can define other styles for use in Netscape Navigator using JASS; for more information, refer to the Netscape Web site (www.netscape.com).

Text Animation Techniques

Changing the style of an element in response to a timer can animate text. Scripts can modify one or more styles on every signal from a timer. The following two examples demonstrate changing the appearance of an element over time. These examples can be modified to change any CSS property of the element.

Modifying a document's appearance using a timer is useful for drawing attention to information on the document. The technique can be used in lieu of using large animated GIFs; animating text with a few lines of script always yields better performance than downloading GIFs that serve the same purpose.

As written, these samples will not work on down-level browsers, but you can easily add code to test what browser is running the page, and start and stop the timer only if the browser is Internet Explorer 4.0.

Elastic Text

The following simple demonstration changes the CSS *letter-spacing* property of an element in response to a timer. This technique can be used to add an interesting effect to headers or other contents.

```
<HTML>
   <HEAD>
      <TITLE>Elastic Text</TITLE>
      <SCRIPT LANGUAGE="JavaScript">
         // Array of sizes to cycle over
         var sizes = new Array("0px", "1px", "2px", "4px", "8px");
         sizes.pos = 0;

         function rubberBand() {
            var el = document.all.elastic;
            if (null == el.direction)
               el.direction = 1;
            else if ((sizes.pos > sizes.length - 2) ||
                  (0 == sizes.pos))
               el.direction *= -1;
            el.style.letterSpacing = sizes[sizes.pos += el.direction];
         }
      </SCRIPT>
   </HEAD>
   <BODY ONLOAD="window.tm = setInterval('rubberBand()', 100);"
         ONUNLOAD="clearInterval(window.tm);">
      <H1 ID="elastic" ALIGN="Center">This Is Elastic Text</H1>
   </BODY>
</HTML>
```

Pulsating Elements

The following code extends the previous example by modifying multiple elements on each tick of the timer and by using a new class to specify the alternative style:

```
<HTML>
   <HEAD>
      <TITLE>Pulsating Buttons</TITLE>
      <STYLE TYPE="text/css">
         .pulsate {letter-spacing:2; font-weight:bolder; color:blue}
      </STYLE>

      <SCRIPT LANGUAGE="JavaScript">
         function pulsate() {
            // Get all elements with the pulsate name or ID.
            var pEl = document.all.pulsate;
            if (null == pEl.length) // Only one element
               pEl.className = pEl.className == "pulsate" ?
                  "" : "pulsate";
            else  // Iterate over all pulsate elements.
               for (var i = 0; i < pEl.length; i++)
                  with (pEl[i])
                     className = className == "pulsate" ?
                        "" : "pulsate";
         }
      </SCRIPT>
   </HEAD>
   <BODY ONLOAD="window.tm = setInterval('pulsate()', 1500);"
         ONUNLOAD="clearInterval(window.tm);">
      <INPUT TYPE=BUTTON NAME="pulsate" VALUE="Click Me!">
      <INPUT TYPE=BUTTON NAME="pulsate" VALUE="Click Me Too!">
   </BODY>
</HTML>
```

// Create
var x = 10;
function foo() {
// This code is not
code
var y =
alert(
// output
// Call foo while
foo();
</SCRIPT>

CHAPTER TWELVE

Dynamic Positioning

CSS (Cascading Style Sheets) provides the syntax for specifying the precise positions of HTML elements. Dynamic positioning uses the object model to access and manipulate the positions of elements in the document through the CSS object model and through the rendered positions of the elements on the screen.

Precise control over positioning elements with HTML was pioneered in Microsoft Internet Explorer 3.0 using the HTML Layout control. The HTML Layout control was designed as an ActiveX control that interpreted an early version of the CSS positioning syntax. An ActiveX control was used rather than embedding the support directly into the browser to give the W3C (World Wide Web Consortium) more time to define and finalize a positioning syntax. In late 1996, a syntax was agreed upon in the W3C CSS Positioning (CSS-P) working draft. Scott Furman, a representative of Netscape, and I, as Microsoft's representative, cowrote the draft. Internet Explorer 4.0 and Netscape Navigator 4.0 both support the CSS-P working draft for positioning elements, so pages authored using CSS-P have a fair degree of interoperability between browsers. There are still some minor differences between browsers, however, in the exact rendering of an element's size and position.

The CSS-P working draft specifies the CSS syntax for defining the initial placement of elements on the page; it does not define the scripting model. The object model exposed in Netscape Navigator 4.0 for moving positioned elements is different from the model exposed in Internet Explorer 4.0. Netscape Navigator's model provides a subset of the functionality available in Internet Explorer.

The CSS-P working draft defines three types of positioning: static, absolute, and relative. Static positioning is the default and corresponds to the traditional way HTML documents are laid out. In absolute positioning, an element is taken out of the normal flow of the document and positioned according to the parent coordinate system. The absolutely positioned element has no effect on any of its surrounding elements in the document. In relative positioning, an element stays in the flow of the document and is positioned relative to its normal position in the flow. When the document is resized, a relatively positioned element may move and even change in shape as the document is reflowed. Absolutely and relatively positioned elements create coordinate systems for positioning any child elements they might have.

This chapter introduces the CSS-P properties and the scripting model for controlling the location of any element. The following topics are covered in this chapter:

- **CSS positioning** This section discusses the CSS enhancements for controlling the positions of elements. CSS positioning supports two new ways to position an element: relative, which positions an element relative to the element's normal location in the document's flow, and absolute, which moves the element outside the flow, where it can be positioned with precise accuracy. This section introduces the CSS positioning properties and the relationship between these two positioning models.
- **Scripting CSS positioning** CSS positioning properties can be dynamically manipulated through the Dynamic HTML object model. This section shows you how to animate text and graphics by using timers and how to respond to user events to enable drag-and-drop operations.
- **The rendering context** This section demonstrates the relationship between an element's position and its surrounding elements and introduces the rendering relationship between elements, which defines how an element's position is determined in the document.

CSS Positioning

The CSS-P working draft defines extensions to style sheets to provide increased positioning control over HTML elements. Absolute and relative positioning allow the Web author to precisely control the location and size of an element and to overlap elements. Combining these enhancements with scripting allows the animation of elements. This section provides a brief introduction to using the CSS positioning enhancements.

CSS Positioning Properties

The CSS-P working draft defines new CSS properties supported by both Internet Explorer 4.0 and Netscape Navigator 4.0. The following table lists these properties; the default value for each property is shown in boldface.

Property	Allowable Values	Applies To	Description
position	***static*** | *absolute* | *relative*	All elements	Specifies whether the element is positioned normally in the flow (*static*), relative to its normal position in the flow (*relative*), or outside the flow (*absolute*).
top, left	***auto*** | *<length>* | *<percentage>*	All elements with *position* set to *absolute* or *relative*	Define the top and left positions of the element relative to its parent rendering context.
width, height	***auto*** | *<length>* | *<percentage>*	All block elements, replaced elements (for example, IMG elements and intrinsic controls), and elements with *position* set to *absolute*	Define the width and height of the element. Percentages are relative to the parent rendering context.
clip	***auto*** | *rect(top right bottom left)*	All elements with *position* set to *absolute*	Defines the clipping region for the element.
z-index	***auto*** | *number*	All elements with *position* set to *absolute* or *relative*	Specifies an element's position overlapping or being overlapped by other elements.
visibility	***inherit*** | *visible* | *hidden*	All elements	Specifies whether the element is visible. A hidden element is not removed from the document's flow.
overflow	***visible*** | *hidden* | *auto* | *scroll*	All elements with *position* set to *absolute* and all block elements	Specifies whether scrollbars are displayed if the contents do not fit in the element.

Positioning Elements

Traditionally, most elements in HTML are positioned relative to previous elements in the flow of the document. One exception to this rule is the ability to align images and other objects and have text wrap around them. With the introduction of CSS positioning, elements can now be positioned on a fixed plane separate from the document's flow or offset from their traditional position in the document. CSS positioning allows elements to overlap and provides Web authors with more precise control over the layout than was previously possible.

As mentioned, the CSS *position* property takes one of three values: *static*, *absolute*, or *relative*. Static positioning, the default, has no effect on the traditional layout of the HTML document.

Relative positioning is used to offset an element from its normal position in the flow. Setting an element's *position* value to *relative* does not by itself change the layout, but if you also set the *top* or *left* property, the element is offset from its normal position in the flow. In the text in Figure 12-1, one word is relatively positioned with offsets of 10 pixels in both the *x* and *y* directions. Notice that the rest of the document is laid out just as it would be if the word wasn't offset. Relative positioning is especially useful when you are animating elements such as images near their normal positions in the document.

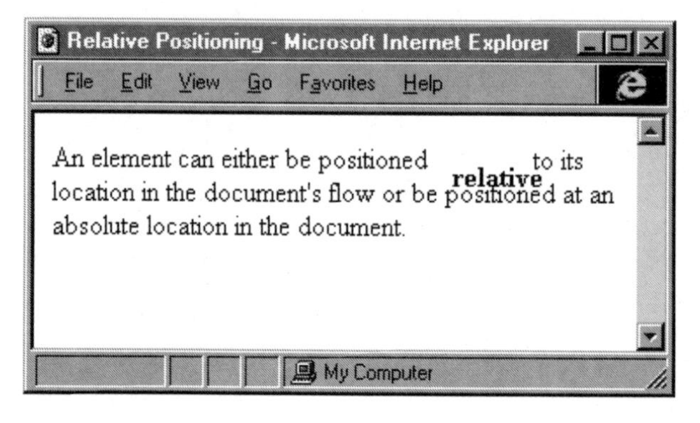

Figure 12-1.
A relatively positioned element.

Absolute positioning is used to specify a fixed location for the element outside the flow of the document. In the text in Figure 12-2, one word is absolutely positioned near the upper left corner. Notice that no space is set aside for this word in the flow.

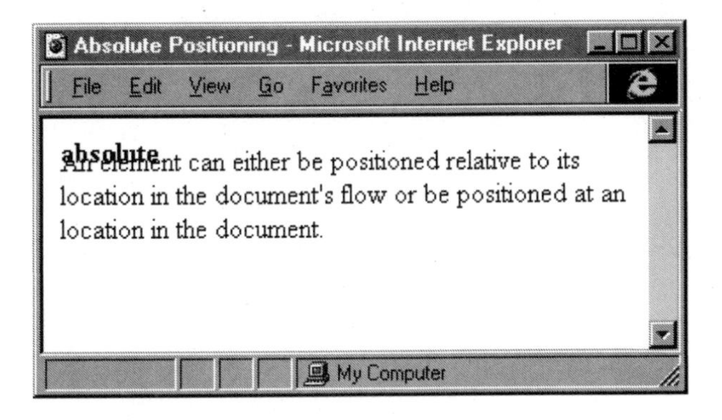

Figure 12-2.
An absolutely positioned element.

Because absolutely positioned elements are positioned outside the flow, the location of the element within the document's source becomes less important. The element should be placed in the source in a location that would provide reasonable results on down-level browsers that do not recognize the positioning enhancements and therefore display the image in the flow of the document.

In Internet Explorer 4.0, all elements in the body of the document support static and relative positioning. However, only the following elements support absolute positioning:

- Applet
- Button
- DIV
- Fieldset
- IFrame
- IMG
- Input
- Object
- Select
- Span
- Table
- TextArea

To absolutely position text, you should use a Span or DIV element. In general, the Span and DIV elements can be used interchangeably, but when you are deciding whether to use Span or DIV, consider the expected appearance of the element in down-level browsers. If the text requires a break before it and a break after it, a DIV element should be used; if the text can appear in the flow of the paragraph, a Span element should be used. The document should always be tested on all target platforms to ensure that it displays adequately.

Defining Coordinate Systems

Every element that is absolutely or relatively positioned must be positioned relative to another element or position in the document. The location from which the element is offset is called the *root* of the element's coordinate system. By default, relatively positioned elements have their root based on their normal flow position in the document. Therefore, if the document is reflowed, the root of the coordinate system as well as all child elements within that coordinate system will move.

Absolutely positioned elements are positioned with respect to some containing element's coordinate system. The upper left corner of the document defines the default coordinate system for all absolutely positioned elements. Whenever an element is relatively or absolutely positioned, a new coordinate system is defined for all elements it contains.

Size and Position Properties

When an element is positioned either absolutely or relatively, its *top* and *left* properties specify the offset of the element from the upper left corner of the coordinate system. The *width* and *height* properties define the physical width and height of the element as it is rendered on the screen. When you are using relative sizes, the *width* and *height* properties are interpreted relative to the size of the element defining the coordinate system. The *top, left, width,* and *height* properties can be specified as a percentage or in any of the units (for example, points, pixels, and ems) defined by CSS. Figure 12-3 shows the *top, left, width,* and *height* properties of two nested DIV elements.

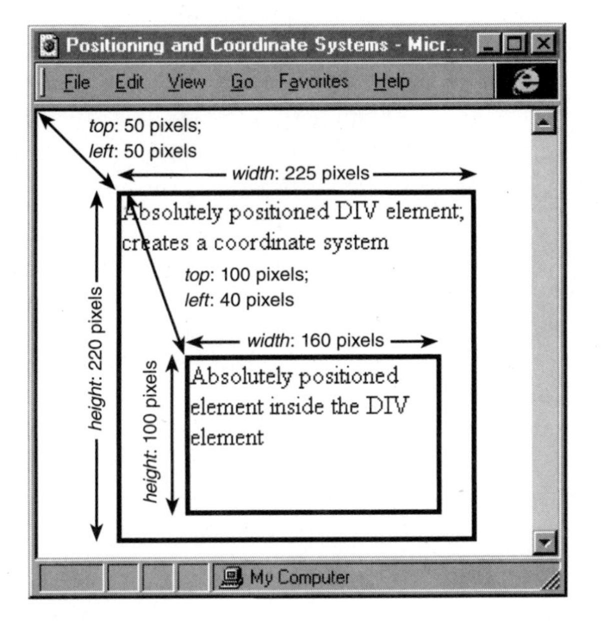

Figure 12-3.
Nested coordinate systems defining the roots for the positions and sizes of elements.

Automatic Sizing

For the *top* and *left* properties, the default *auto* value is the element's normal position in the flow. With *top* and *left* both set to *auto*, a relatively positioned element is displayed the same as a static element, and an absolutely positioned element is displayed outside the flow but anchored at the position it would have as a static element. If the *width* or *height* property is omitted, the element is automatically sized based on its contents.

The *visibility* Property

By default, an element is visible based on whether its parent element is visible. For example, hiding the Body element by setting the *visibility* property to *hidden* also hides all the contents in the document. You can override this inheritance by explicitly setting an element's *visibility* property to *hidden* or *visible*, rather than the default, *inherit.* When the *visibility* property is explicitly set, the element overrides any inherited value and is displayed or hidden appropriately.

The *z-index* Property

The *z-index* property defines the graphical z-order, or overlapping, of elements in relation to other elements. Every coordinate system defines a new z-ordering space for the rendered elements, thereby making the z-ordering hierarchical. For example, if a DIV element is absolutely positioned on top of the body's contents, the contents of the DIV element cannot appear behind the text in the body. All the elements within the DIV element can only be positioned relative to the DIV element's coordinate system.

By default, all elements that define a coordinate system, including the Body element, are positioned with a *z-index* of *0*. Other elements can be positioned behind the text by having a negative *z-index* value. Elements whose *z-index* values are not specified are implicitly assigned *z-index* values according to their order in the source document. Therefore, an element that is positioned later in the document is displayed above any elements positioned earlier.

Clipping Regions

Each absolutely positioned element has a clipping region associated with it. The purpose of this clipping region is to define the portion of the document available for displaying the element and its contents. Anything outside that portion is clipped, or not displayed, by the document.

The clipping region can be viewed in terms of an opaque piece of paper that covers the physical area of the absolutely positioned element. In this piece of paper is a rectangular hole that defines the visible area of the element. Everything not visible through the hole in the paper is clipped and becomes invisible.

Figure 12-4 illustrates how clipping regions work. The left side of the figure shows a page with no clipping performed. The larger rectangle is a DIV element. The smaller rectangle is contained in the DIV element but absolutely positioned outside the DIV element's borders. The right side of the figure shows the same page with clipping performed.

The default value of the *clip* property is *auto*, which causes the contents not to be clipped. You can set the *clip* property value to be a rectangle:

clip:rect(*top right bottom left*)

The *top*, *right*, *bottom*, and *left* settings define the clipping rectangle with respect to the absolutely positioned element's upper left corner. Each of the four settings can be specified with any valid CSS length or can be set to *auto* to prevent clipping in that direction. If the *top* and *left* settings are negative, elements above and to the left of the absolutely positioned element can be included within the clipping region.

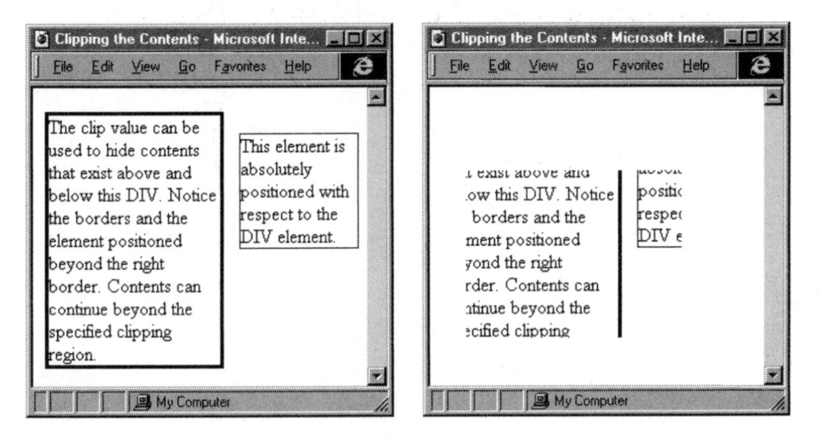

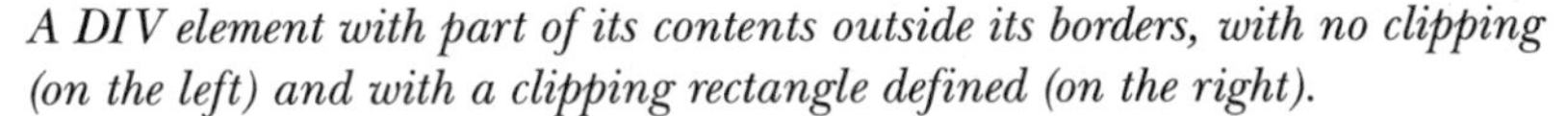

Figure 12-4.
A DIV element with part of its contents outside its borders, with no clipping (on the left) and with a clipping rectangle defined (on the right).

The *overflow* Property

The *overflow* property controls how any contents that extend beyond the physical size of the element are handled. The *overflow* property takes one of four values: *visible, hidden, auto,* and *scroll.* With *overflow* set to *visible,* all contents are displayed, even contents outside the specified *height* and *width* of the element. With *overflow* set to *hidden,* only the contents within the element's *height* and *width* are displayed; no contents flow beyond the specified boundaries.

The *auto* and *scroll* values are used for adding scrollbars if the contents are larger than the *height* and *width* of the element. Scrollbars can be added to any absolutely positioned element, to DIV elements with a defined height, and to any element that supports the CSS *float* property. The overflow value *scroll* always displays scrollbars, while the value *auto* displays them only when they are required.

The following document demonstrates how to create a scrolling sidebar:

```
<HTML>
   <HEAD>
      <TITLE>Scrolling Sidebar</TITLE>
   </HEAD>
```

(continued)

```
   <BODY>
      <DIV STYLE="overflow:scroll; float:left;
            width:120pt; height:120pt">
         <H1>Scrolling Sidebar</H1>
         <P>This text appears in a scrolling window that is floating
            to the left of the main contents.</P>
      </DIV>
      <P>These contents appear to the right of the scrolling DIV
         element.
   </BODY>
</HTML>
```

Figure 12-5 shows this document.

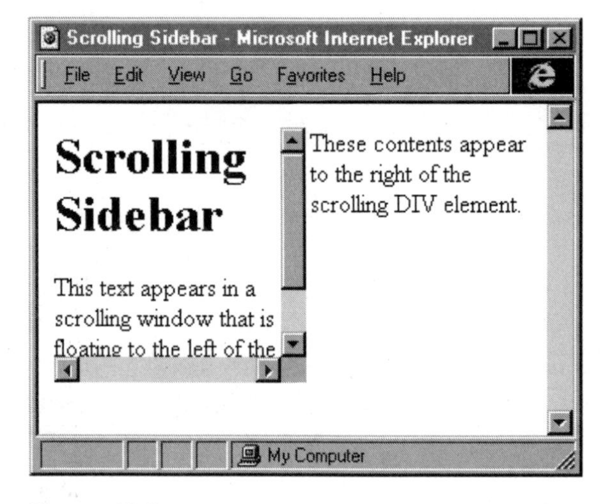

Figure 12-5.
A document with a scrolling sidebar.

When scrollbars are specified for an element, they automatically extend to include absolutely positioned child elements. This extension ensures that the user can reach all child elements that are absolutely positioned. You can create forms and complex layouts that are fully accessible. The exception to this feature is any element that is positioned negatively. Under no circumstances do the scrollbars extend into the negative coordinate space.

When scrollbars are displayed using the *overflow* property, clipping does not affect absolutely positioned child elements; the user can still scroll to them, and they will be visible. Instead, if the clipping region does not include the entire element with scrollbars, the element itself will be clipped. Figure 12-6 demonstrates this relationship. In the screenshot on the right, the absolutely positioned element is not visible because it is inside the DIV element with the scrollbars.

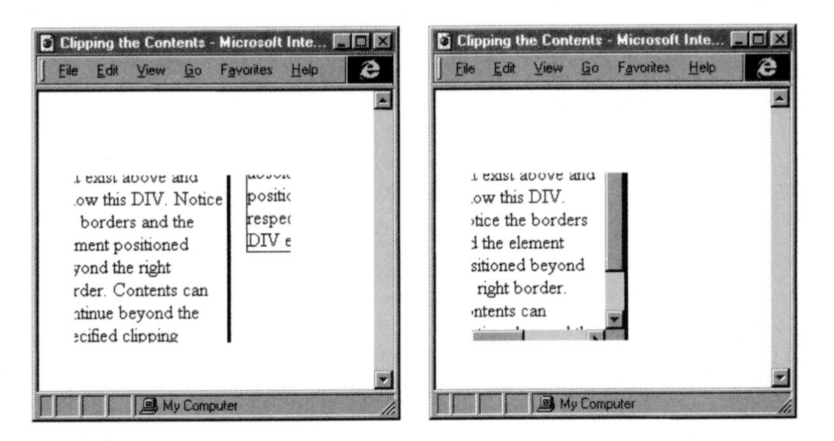

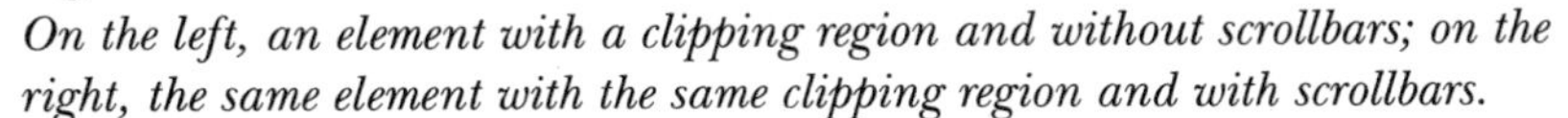

Figure 12-6.
On the left, an element with a clipping region and without scrollbars; on the right, the same element with the same clipping region and with scrollbars.

> NOTE: Relatively positioned elements have no effect on the scrollbar. Only the element's original space in the flow is used in the scrollbar calculation because the relatively positioned element's location in the document is technically its position in the flow and the offset is simply a manipulation of the rendering position. Furthermore, relatively positioned elements are most often used for animation. Including these elements in the scrollbar calculations would interfere with the animation effect. For example, you should be able to scroll text off the right edge of the screen; no scrollbar should appear that would allow the user to scroll the text back into view.

Scripting CSS Positioning

Any element predefined with absolute or relative positioning can be dynamically moved and resized through scripting. This technique allows positioned elements to be animated by repositioning, resizing, and dynamically changing the clipping region of the element. Manipulating an element's position and clipping region is done through the style sheet object models.

The CSS *position* property in Internet Explorer 4.0 is read-only. For a script to move an element, the element must be defined to have relative or absolute positioning when it is created, whether it is created from the source code or inserted using dynamic contents, the topic of Chapter 13, "Dynamic Contents." This rule holds true even if the style sheet is modified through the CSS object model after the element is rendered.

CSS Positioning Properties

Each CSS size or position property is exposed through a set of properties that make it more convenient and simpler to access and manipulate the element's size and location. Like the other CSS properties, *top*, *left*, *width*, and *height* are exposed through the *style* property on the element. These properties are strings and return the values and the specified units—for example, an element with a *top* value of 20 points returns *20pt*.

Manipulating this string can be fairly difficult, especially when your code is trying to reposition an element on the screen. Therefore, in addition to the string-value properties, four properties that represent just the specified value are exposed: *posTop*, *posLeft*, *posWidth*, and *posHeight*. If the *top* value is the string *20pt*, the *posTop* value is the number *20*; as a number, it can be manipulated more directly.

Because many measurements in the Dynamic HTML object model use pixels, four additional properties are exposed that return the size and position values converted to pixels: *pixelTop*, *pixelLeft*, *pixelWidth*, and *pixelHeight*. Assigning a value to one of these properties causes the value to be converted back to the originally specified units when it is exposed through the *pos** and string-value properties.

These twelve style sheet properties are determined when a document is parsed. In the section "The Rendering Context" later in this chapter, properties for accessing the rendered size and position of the element are explained. Together, these properties let you create completely custom layouts in which the script controls the entire rendering of the document.

Absolute Positioning

The following examples demonstrate how to manipulate absolutely positioned elements. Absolutely positioned elements are used to enable drag-and-drop operations and to position elements at fixed locations on the screen.

Static Logo

Using the CSS *background* property, you can fix the position of the background image to create a static logo that won't scroll with the window. For example, this code fixes an image in the lower right corner of the client window:

```
BODY {background:URL(logo.gif) fixed bottom right no-repeat}
```

Using CSS alone, you cannot fix elements other than background images so that they won't scroll with the window. However, using absolute positioning and a simple script you can add this behavior. This example creates static text that always sits in a fixed position relative to the upper left corner of the current window. The code for positioning the text tracks the *onscroll* events in order to move the element when the document is scrolled.

This example text logo is similar to the television logos that appear randomly throughout the broadcast of a show. Although this example displays the logo constantly, it can easily be revised to cause the logo to disappear and reappear after a scheduled amount of time by simply swapping the *display* property between *none* and *block* using a timer. (If an element's *display* property is set to *none* by a global style sheet, a script cannot change its value to an empty string to display the element. Instead, the script must explicitly set the *display* property to *block* or *inline,* as appropriate for the element.)

The following code is the simplest implementation of a text logo. It places the logo in the upper left corner of the screen, which requires only tracking the *scroll* event and does not require any calculations to determine the logo's position. To display the logo in any of the other corners, you must also track the *onresize* event. When the user resizes the page, the logo's position must be recalculated based on the new window size, and the width or height of the element itself must be taken into consideration.

```
<HTML>
   <HEAD>
      <TITLE>Static Logo</TITLE>
      <SCRIPT LANGUAGE="JavaScript">
         function resetLogo() {
            document.all.Logo.style.posTop = document.body.scrollTop;
            document.all.Logo.style.posLeft =
               document.body.scrollLeft;
         }
      </SCRIPT>
   </HEAD>
   <BODY ONSCROLL="resetLogo()">
      <DIV ID="Logo" SRC="logo.gif"
            STYLE="position:absolute; z-index:-1; top:0px; left:0px;
               color:gray">
         Inside DHTML
      </DIV>
      <P>Add HTML document here.</P>
   </BODY>
</HTML>
```

The logo works best with light-colored text; otherwise, it may obscure relevant contents on the page. The logo can be positioned either behind or on top of the contents by setting the *z-index* property: a –1 value positions the logo behind the contents; *1* (the default) positions the logo on top of the contents. The logo can fall either behind or on top of other elements depending on the other elements' *z-index* values.

Bouncing Ball

This example illustrates the relationship between the position properties and the size of the window. The following code is an extension of the static logo example—here an image moves around on the screen and bounces off the edges of the window:

```
<HTML>
   <HEAD>
      <TITLE>Bouncing Ball</TITLE>
      <SCRIPT LANGUAGE="JavaScript">
         var x = 0;
         var y = 0;
         var offsetx = 4;
         var offsety = 4;

         function bounceIt() {
            var el = document.all.bounce;
            x += offsetx;
            y += offsety;
            if ((x + el.offsetWidth >= document.body.clientWidth +
                     document.body.scrollLeft) ||
                  (x <= document.body.scrollLeft)) {
               offsetx = -offsetx;
               if (x <= document.body.scrollLeft)
                  x = document.body.scrollLeft;
               else
                  x = document.body.clientWidth - el.offsetWidth +
                     document.body.scrollLeft;
            }
            if ((y + el.offsetWidth >= document.body.clientHeight +
                     document.body.scrollTop) ||
                  (y <= document.body.scrollTop)) {
               offsety = -offsety;
               if (y <= document.body.scrollTop)
                  y = document.body.scrollTop;
               else
                  y = document.body.clientHeight - el.offsetHeight +
                     document.body.scrollTop;
```

```
            }
            el.style.posLeft = x;
            el.style.posTop = y;
         }
      </SCRIPT>
   </HEAD>
   <BODY ONLOAD="window.tm = setInterval('bounceIt()', 10);"
         ONUNLOAD="clearInterval(window.tm);">
      <IMG SRC="ball.gif" ID="bounce"
         STYLE="position:absolute; top:0; left:0; z-index:-1">
      <H1>Bouncing Ball</H1>
      <P>The ball bounces around and around under the text.</P>
      <P>This page works even if you resize
         or scroll the window.</P>
      <P>This page takes advantage of:
      <UL>
         <LI>Absolute positioning
         <LI>Moving elements based on the timer
         <LI>Z-indexing
         <LI>Client size and scrollbar position properties
      </UL>
   </BODY>
</HTML>
```

A timer controls the movement of the image on the screen. The image moves behind the text because its *z-index* value is lower. This example animates an image, but any HTML can be animated across the screen. For example, you can replace this image with a DIV element, supply the DIV element with a width, add some HTML contents, and animate it.

Wipe Effects

Scripting the CSS *clip* property lets you create interesting wipe effects. For a wipe-in effect, the contents of an element gradually appear on the screen, beginning with one edge and ending with the opposite edge. For a wipe-out effect, the contents disappear in the same manner. The following document provides a function for creating different vertical and horizontal wipe effects on an absolutely positioned element as well as buttons for testing the wipe effects:

```
<HTML>
   <HEAD>
      <TITLE>Wipe Effects</TITLE>
      <STYLE TYPE="text/css">
         BODY {text-align:center}
```

(continued)

```
      #wipe {position:absolute; top:200pt; left:40%;
         clip:rect(0 100% 100% 0); border:2pt navy solid;
         width:100pt; background:white}
      P {margin-top:0pt; margin-bottom:0pt}
      INPUT {width:100%}
   </STYLE>
   <SCRIPT LANGUAGE="JavaScript" ID="WipeEffects">
      function wipe(direction) {
         var el = document.all.wipe;
         /* The second argument is optional and specifies whether a
            wipe-in or wipe-out occurs. The default is a
            wipe-in. */
         var into = true;
         if (arguments[1] != null)
            into = arguments[1];

         if (null == el.init) {
            // Initialize effect.
            // All wipe information is stored in the element.
            el.init = true;
            el.clipTop = 0;
            el.clipRight = 0;
            el.clipBottom = 0;
            el.clipLeft = 0
            el.inc = 4;

            if (into)  // Set up wipe-in.
               switch (direction) {
               case "clipBottom":
                  el.clipRight = "100%";
                  el.size = el.offsetHeight;
                  break;
               case "clipRight":
                  el.clipBottom = "100%";
                  el.size = el.offsetWidth;
                  break;
               case "clipTop":
                  el.clipBottom = "100%";
                  el.clipRight = "100%";
                  el.clipTop = el.offsetHeight;
                  el.inc *= -1;
                  el.size = 0;
                  break;
               case "clipLeft":
                  el.clipBottom = "100%";
                  el.clipRight = "100%";
                  el.clipLeft = el.offsetWidth;
                  el.inc *= -1;
```

```
                el.size = 0;
                break;
             }
          else        // Set up wipe-out.
             switch (direction) {
             case "clipBottom":
                el.clipRight = "100%";
                el.clipBottom = el.offsetHeight;
                el.size = 0;
                el.inc *= -1;
                break;
             case "clipRight":
                el.clipBottom = "100%";
                el.clipRight = el.offsetWidth;
                el.size = 0;
                el.inc *= -1;
                break;
             case "clipTop":
                el.clipBottom = "100%";
                el.clipRight = "100%";
                el.clipHeight = el.offsetHeight;
                el.size = el.offsetHeight;
                break;
             case "clipLeft":
                el.clipBottom = "100%";
                el.clipRight = "100%";
                el.clipLeft = 0;
                el.size = el.offsetWidth;
                break;
             }
       }
       // Increment clip.
       el[direction] += el.inc;
       // Set clip.
       el.style.clip = "rect(" + el.clipTop + " " +
          el.clipRight + " " + el.clipBottom + " " +
          el.clipLeft + ")";
       // Check whether finished.
       if (((el.size >= el[direction]) && (el.inc > 0)) ||
             ((el[direction] >= 0) && (el.inc < 0)))
          setTimeout("wipe('" + direction + "', " + into + ")",
             10);
       else
          el.init = null;
    }
  </SCRIPT>
</HEAD>
```

(continued)

```
    <BODY>
      <H1>Wipe Effects</H1>
      <P STYLE="padding-bottom:5pt">
        <INPUT TYPE=BUTTON STYLE="width:260pt" VALUE="Display"
          ONCLICK=
            "document.all.wipe.style.clip='rect(0 100% 100% 0)'">
      <FIELDSET STYLE="width:130pt">
        <LEGEND>Wipe-In Effects</LEGEND>
        <P><INPUT TYPE=BUTTON VALUE="Wipe to Bottom"
          ONCLICK="wipe('clipBottom')">
        <P><INPUT TYPE=BUTTON VALUE="Wipe to Right"
          ONCLICK="wipe('clipRight')">
        <P><INPUT TYPE=BUTTON VALUE="Wipe to Top"
          ONCLICK="wipe('clipTop')">
        <P><INPUT TYPE=BUTTON VALUE="Wipe to Left"
          ONCLICK="wipe('clipLeft')">
      </FIELDSET>

      <FIELDSET STYLE="width:130pt">
        <LEGEND>Wipe-Out Effects</LEGEND>
        <P><INPUT TYPE=BUTTON VALUE="Wipe from Bottom"
          ONCLICK="wipe('clipBottom', false)">
        <P><INPUT TYPE=BUTTON VALUE="Wipe from Right"
          ONCLICK="wipe('clipRight', false)">
        <P><INPUT TYPE=BUTTON VALUE="Wipe from Top"
          ONCLICK="wipe('clipTop', false)">
        <P><INPUT TYPE=BUTTON VALUE="Wipe from Left"
          ONCLICK="wipe('clipLeft', false)">
      </FIELDSET>
      <DIV ID=wipe>
        <P>Home
        <P>News
        <P>Info
        <P>About
        <P>Demo
      </DIV>
    </BODY>
  </HTML>
```

Creating Pop-Up Menus

Using absolute positioning, you can create menus that are displayed when the user clicks on a keyword or an HTML-defined menu bar. You can extend the following code, which creates an expandable menu of URLs, for use in your own documents. The pop-up menus can be easily enhanced to slide into view using the wipe effects code in the preceding example.

```
<HTML>
   <HEAD>
      <TITLE>Pop-Up Menu</TITLE>
      <STYLE TYPE="text/css">
         /* Make the menu float to the left of the text. */
         #menu {float:left; width:50pt; background:lightgrey;
            border:2px white outset; cursor:default}
         /* Hide the pop-up menus initially. */
         #menu .popup {position:absolute; display:none;
            background:lightgrey; border:2px white outset;
            width:135pt; margin:2pt}
         #menu P {margin-top:0pt; margin-bottom:0pt}
         .over {color:navy; font-weight:bold}
      </STYLE>
      <SCRIPT LANGUAGE="JavaScript">
         var curPop = null;

         function clearCurrent() {
            // Hide the pop-up menu that is currently displayed.
            if (null != curPop)
               curPop.style.display = "";
            curPop = null;
         }

         function popup() {
            var el = event.srcElement;
            clearCurrent();
            // Display a new menu option.
            if (("P" == el.tagName) &&
                  ("menu" == el.parentElement.id)) {
               // Position and display the pop-up menu.
               var elpop = document.all[el.sourceIndex + 1];
               elpop.style.pixelLeft = document.all.menu.offsetLeft +
                  document.all.menu.offsetWidth - 7;
               elpop.style.pixelTop  = el.offsetTop +
                  document.all.menu.offsetTop;
               elpop.style.display = "block";
               curPop = elpop;
            }
            event.cancelBubble = true;
         }

         function highlight() {
            // Highlight the menu options.
            if (null != event.fromElement)
               if ((event.fromElement.tagName == "P") &&
```

(continued)

```
                    (event.fromElement.parentElement.id == "menu"))
                 event.fromElement.className = "";
           if (null != event.toElement)
              if ((event.toElement.tagName == "P") &&
                    (event.toElement.parentElement.id == "menu"))
                 event.toElement.className = "over";
        }
     </SCRIPT>
  </HEAD>
  <BODY ONCLICK="clearCurrent()">
     <H1>Menu Example</H1>
     <DIV ID="menu" ONCLICK="popup()" ONMOUSEOVER="highlight()"
           ONMOUSEOUT="highlight()">
        <P>Navigate
           <DIV CLASS="popup">
              <P><A HREF="home.htm">Home</A>
              <P><A HREF="insideDHTML.htm">Inside DHTML Information
                 </A>
              <P><A HREF="tip.htm">Tip of the Week</A>
           </DIV>
        <P>News
           <DIV CLASS="popup">
              <P><A HREF="headlines.htm">Headlines</A>
              <P><A HREF="internet.htm">Internet News</A>
              <P><A HREF="rumors.htm">Rumor Mill</A>
           </DIV>
     </DIV>
     <P>Click on a menu option in the box on the left.</P>
  </BODY>
</HTML>
```

Adding Drag Support

By combining absolute positioning with the mouse events, you can simulate the dragging and dropping of elements. A simple way to add drag-and-drop support is to write a script that looks for a *dragEnabled* attribute on any element. The script in the following code automatically handles dragging for all elements that have this attribute, including nested positioned elements, so the code doesn't have to be modified every time you add another element to drag. If the user holds down the mouse button on an element that has the *dragEnabled* attribute and then moves the mouse, the element will follow. An alternative technique is to use a special class name value instead of the *dragEnabled* attribute.

```
<HTML>
   <HEAD>
      <TITLE>Adding Drag Support</TITLE>
      <SCRIPT LANGUAGE="JavaScript">
         // This code allows any absolutely positioned element
         // with the custom attribute dragEnabled to be dragged.
         var elDragged = null  // Element to drag

         function doMouseMove() {
            // Check whether mouse button is down and whether
            // an element is being dragged.
            if ((1 == event.button) && (elDragged != null)) {
               // Move the element.
               // Save mouse's position in the document.
               var intTop = event.clientY + document.body.scrollTop;
               var intLeft = event.clientX + document.body.scrollLeft;
               // Determine what element the mouse is really over.
               var intLessTop  = 0;
               var intLessLeft = 0;
               var elCurrent = elDragged.offsetParent;
               while (elCurrent.offsetParent != null) {
                  intLessTop += elCurrent.offsetTop;
                  intLessLeft += elCurrent.offsetLeft;
                  elCurrent = elCurrent.offsetParent;
               }
               // Set new position.
               elDragged.style.pixelTop =
                  intTop - intLessTop - elDragged.y;
               elDragged.style.pixelLeft =
                  intLeft - intLessLeft - elDragged.x;
               event.returnValue = false;
            }
         }

         function checkDrag(elCheck) {
            // Check whether the mouse is over an element
            // that supports dragging.
            while (elCheck != null) {
               if (null != elCheck.getAttribute("dragEnabled"))
                  return elCheck;
               elCheck = elCheck.parentElement;
            }
            return null;
         }
```

(continued)

```
      function doMouseDown() {
         // Store element to be dragged.
         var elCurrent = checkDrag(event.srcElement);
         if (null != elCurrent) {
            elDragged = elCurrent;
            // Determine where the mouse is in the element.
            elDragged.x = event.offsetX;
            elDragged.y = event.offsetY;
            var op = event.srcElement;
            // Find real location with respect to element being
            // dragged.
            if ((elDragged != op.offsetParent) &&
                  (elDragged != event.srcElement)) {
               while (op != elDragged) {
                  elDragged.x += op.offsetLeft;
                  elDragged.y += op.offsetTop;
                  op = op.offsetParent;
               }
            }
         }
      }

      function doSelectTest() {
         // Don't start text selections in dragged elements.
         return (null == checkDrag(event.srcElement) &&
            (elDragged!=null));
      }

      // Hook up mouse event handlers.
      document.onmousedown = doMouseDown;
      document.onmousemove = doMouseMove;
      // Reset element when mouse button is released.
      document.onmouseup = new Function("elDragged = null;");
      document.ondragstart = doSelectTest;
      document.onselectstart = doSelectTest;
   </SCRIPT>
</HEAD>
<BODY>
   <H1>Dragging Positioned Elements</H1>
   <P>These contents are static and can't be dragged. The
      following image can be dragged even though it is behind
      this text.
   <IMG SRC="ball.gif" dragEnabled
      STYLE="position:absolute; top:10px; left:20px; cursor:hand;
         z-index:-1;">
   <DIV STYLE="position:absolute; top:150px; left:20px;
```

```
                border:2px navy solid; width:100; cursor:hand"
             dragEnabled>
          This text can be dragged.
       </DIV>
    </BODY>
</HTML>
```

To move an element, this code calculates the element's new position relative to the document based on the mouse's position relative to the document. The mouse's position is calculated by adding the *clientX* and *clientY* properties to the *scrollTop* and *scrollLeft* properties of the Body element. The element's position relative to the document is the sum of its offsets and the offsets of all of its offset parents relative to their respective rendering contexts. The offset properties are discussed in the section "The Rendering Context" later in this chapter.

Relative Positioning

Elements that are relatively positioned take up space in the normal flow of the document. These elements are positioned offset from their normal flow position. The primary function of this feature is to animate elements into their correct location in the document.

The following two examples demonstrate animating text onto the screen. The first example provides an introduction to animating text; the second example is more comprehensive and provides a set of functions for creating a sequence of presentation effects. An example in the section "Aligning Relatively Positioned Elements" later in this chapter demonstrates how to cause all relatively positioned elements to be animated from a single point on the screen.

Flying Text

In general, when you want text to fly in from beyond an edge of the screen, the text should be invisible initially and then appear after a reasonable amount of time. To create text that animates in from the edge of the screen, the best technique is to start with the text off screen at a distant negative coordinate and then set its initial position based on the state of the browser when the animation is about to begin.

Because Dynamic HTML does not specify a concrete size for the contents and because the user can scroll anywhere within the document, the initial position of the element is very important. The initial position of the element must take into account the physical size of the screen and the position of the scrollbars. The following code demonstrates how to make text fly in from the right edge of the screen. This example starts with the text somewhere in the negative coordinate space so that the user cannot reach the text using the scrollbars. At the time the animation is about to begin, the element is repositioned beyond the right edge of the screen. This way, regardless of where the user is in the document, the element always appears to animate onto the page without a long delay, and under no circumstances can the user accidentally view the element before the animation.

```
<HTML>
   <HEAD>
      <TITLE>Flying Text</TITLE>
      <STYLE TYPE="text/css">
         H1 {text-align:center}
         #tip {position:relative; left:-1000px}
      </STYLE>
      <SCRIPT LANGUAGE="JavaScript">
         function slideIn() {
            var el = document.all.tip;
            // Test whether element is off screen.
            if (-1000 == el.style.pixelLeft) {
               el.style.fontStyle = "italic";
               // Reposition element beyond right edge of screen.
               el.style.pixelLeft = document.body.offsetWidth +
                  document.body.scrollLeft;
            }
            if (20 <= el.style.pixelLeft) {
               el.style.pixelLeft -= 20;
               setTimeout("slideIn();", 50);
            }
            else {
               el.style.pixelLeft = 0;
               el.style.fontStyle = "";
            }
         }
      </SCRIPT>
   </HEAD>
   <BODY ONLOAD="slideIn();">
      <H1 ID="tip">Tip of the Week</H1>
      <P>Animating text from off screen
   </BODY>
</HTML>
```

Presentation Effects

By expanding on the preceding example, you can easily create presentation style effects that animate text onto the page. This example demonstrates how to add custom presentation behavior that can iterate through elements either automatically or through the user clicking the mouse. The sequencing is defined by taking advantage of Dynamic HTML's ability to expose unrecognized elements. A Sequence element defines a set of elements to animate and specifies whether they should animate automatically or in response to mouse clicks. Multiple sequences can be defined by specifying multiple Sequence elements.

The following document demonstrates two sequences—the first sequence occurs based on a timer, and then the second sequence occurs based on the user clicking the mouse:

```
<HTML>
   <HEAD>
      <SEQUENCE order="Text1, Text2, Text3, Text4, Text5" speed="20"
         type="auto" increments=15>
      <SEQUENCE order="Text6, Text7" speed="20" type="click"
         increments=15>
      <TITLE>Presentation Effects</TITLE>
      <SCRIPT LANGUAGE="JavaScript">
         var slideShow = new Object();

         function initSequence(s) {
            var sTemp = s.sequences[s.currentSequence];
            if (null != sTemp) {
               // Get list of element IDs to sequence.
               s.sequencer = new Array();
               s.sequencer = sTemp.getAttribute("order").split(", ");
               // Initialize sequence.
               for (var intLoop = 0; intLoop < s.sequencer.length;
                     intLoop++)
                  if (null != document.all[s.sequencer[intLoop]]) {
                     var el = document.all[s.sequencer[intLoop]];
                     el.initTop = el.style.posTop;
                     el.initLeft = el.style.posLeft;
                  }
               s.speed = (null == sTemp.getAttribute("speed")) ?
                  20 : sTemp.getAttribute("speed");
               s.type = ("auto" == sTemp.getAttribute("type"));
               s.increments =
                  (null == sTemp.getAttribute("increments")) ?
                     15 : sTemp.getAttribute("increments");
               s.inc = 0;
               s.position = -1;
            }
```

(continued)

```
      else {
         s.position = null;
         if (document.onclick == doFly)
            document.onclick = new Function();
      }
   }

   function nextSequence(s) {
      // If sequence is available, run it.
      if (null != s.position) {
         // s.position represents an element in a sequence.
         // Run until no more elements are found; then look for
         // next sequence.
         s.position++
         if (s.position < s.sequencer.length) {
            s.inc = 0;
            if (s.type)  // Runs on a timer
               window.setTimeout("doFly();", s.speed)
            else         // Runs on the click event
               document.onclick = doFly;
         }
         else {
            s.currentSequence++;
            initSequence(s);
            nextSequence(s);
         }
      }
      else  {
         s.position = null;
         if (document.onclick == doFly)
            document.onclick = null;
      }
   }

   function slide() {
      // Initialize sequencer--get all <SEQUENCE> tags.
      slideShow.sequences = document.all.tags("SEQUENCE");
      slideShow.sequencer = new Array();
      if (0 < slideShow.sequences.length) {
         slideShow.currentSequence = 0;
         initSequence(slideShow); // Initialize.
         nextSequence(slideShow); // Start first sequence.
      }
   }

   function doFly() {
      var dt, dl;
```

```
        var el =
           document.all[slideShow.sequencer[slideShow.position]];
        document.onclick = null;  // Stop click events
                                  // until complete.
        // Reposition the element.
        slideShow.inc++;
        dt = el.initTop / slideShow.increments;
        dl = el.initLeft / slideShow.increments;

        el.style.posTop = el.style.posTop - dt;
        el.style.posLeft = el.style.posLeft - dl;

        if (slideShow.inc < slideShow.increments)
           window.setTimeout("doFly();", slideShow.speed)
        else {
           el.style.top = 0;
           el.style.left = 0;
           nextSequence(slideShow);
        }
     }
   </SCRIPT>
   <STYLE TYPE="text/css">
      BODY {color:white}
      DIV {position:relative; width:100%; font-size:16pt;
         height:40px}
      H1 {text-align:center; font-size:18pt}
   </STYLE>
 </HEAD>
 <BODY BACKGROUND="img001.gif" ONLOAD="slide();">
   <H1>Inside Dynamic HTML</H1>
   <DIV ID="Text1" STYLE="top:0px; left:-350px">
      Overview of HTML and CSS</DIV>
   <DIV ID="Text2" STYLE="top:0px; left:-350px">
      Fundamentals of HTML Scripting</DIV>
   <DIV ID="Text3" STYLE="top:0px; left:-350px">
      Dynamic HTML Event Model</DIV>
   <DIV ID="Text4" STYLE="top:0px; left:-350px">
      Dynamic Styles</DIV>
   <DIV ID="Text5" STYLE="top:0px; left:-350px; color:yellow">
      Click to Continue</DIV>
   <DIV ID="Text6" STYLE="top:0px; left:-350px">
      Dynamic Contents</DIV>
   <DIV ID="Text7" STYLE="top:0px; left:-350px">
      Dynamic Presentations!</DIV>
 </BODY>
</HTML>
```

The custom <SEQUENCE> tag, which should be defined in the head of the document, supports the following attributes. The only required attribute is *order*; the other attributes will be provided with default values if they are omitted.

Attribute Name	Description
order	Defines the element IDs that should be sequenced. Each item must be explicitly separated using a comma followed by a space.
speed	Defines how fast the items are animated in. This same speed is used to determine the delay between elements that are autosequenced.
type	Specifies whether the sequence occurs automatically through the timer (*auto*, the default) or manually in response to clicks (*click*).
increments	Specifies how many intermediate positions each image will assume as it animates to its final position. More increments with faster speed can create a smoother animation.

The Rendering Context

While CSS positioning offers tremendous flexibility, it can often add a lot of complexity to the page. The preceding examples demonstrate using CSS positioning on elements that are positioned independently. One of the key advantages of HTML is its ability to automatically reflow contents depending on their size and the size of the window. If the Web author intends to position elements in response to the size of the window and contents, the author must write custom layout code with script rather than rely on HTML. In general, it is easier to author and maintain documents that use dynamic styles to take advantage of the automatic flow nature of HTML than to write custom layout code, and writing a custom layout manager can require a large amount of script.

Dynamic HTML exposes the information—complex as it is—necessary to create a powerful custom layout. For each element, this information includes offset information and the identity of the element from which the offsets are calculated. To write scripts that handle their own layout, you have to understand these offset relationships.

Rendering information—the size and position of each element in the body of a document—is recalculated by the browser each time the document is reflowed. Rendering information is therefore much more transient than parsing information, which includes the attributes, styles, and contents defined for the elements in the source document. The distinction between the values provided by the document and the rendering values calculated by the browser is important to understand.

For example, an element might be defined as having a *width* value of 20% and an unspecified *height*. The 20% value as well as its pixel equivalent are exposed through the *style* property. However, the *height* value is not exposed through the *style* property because it is not defined. When the browser renders the element, it calculates a height and exposes it as a separate property. In addition, the browser calculates and exposes the top and left positions of the element; these values are not always the same as the *top* and *left* values defined using CSS positioning.

Each element is drawn relative to another element, its *offset parent*. An element's offset parent provides the *rendering context* in which the element is drawn. The Body element is the topmost offset parent. For many elements, the Body element is the offset parent, and the browser calculates each element's position relative to the upper left corner of the document. But if an element is inside an absolutely positioned DIV element, for example, its position is calculated relative to the DIV element, which is its offset parent. An offset parent provides the context in which an element is rendered; specifically, it defines a root for the offsets that determine the element's position.

Every element exposes its rendering information. An element's *offsetParent* property contains a reference to the element defining its rendering context, and its *offsetTop* and *offsetLeft* properties contain its coordinates with respect to the origin defined by its *offsetParent*. In addition, rectangular elements generally expose *offsetWidth* and *offsetHeight* properties, which represent the element's size.

Only certain elements and elements of certain styles can define new rendering contexts and become offset parents for other elements. The following elements define new rendering contexts:

- Body element
- Elements with CSS *position* values of *absolute*
- Elements with CSS *position* values of *relative* (define new rendering contexts only for absolutely positioned elements they contain)

- Elements with CSS *float* values of *left* or *right*
- Elements given explicit *width* or *height* values
- Table, Caption, TR (table row), and TD and TH (table cell) elements
- Fieldset and Legend elements
- Marquee elements
- Map elements

Each element has a single offset parent, and it might define a rendering context for any number of child elements. In this regard, an element's offset parent is similar to its parent element in the parsing tree. But an element's offset parent is not required to be the same as its parent in the parsing tree; its *offsetParent* and *parentElement* properties can and often will reference different elements. A diagram showing the offset parents for all elements in the document is known as the rendering tree for the document.

Figure 12-7 shows both the parsing tree and the rendering tree for the following document.

```
<HTML>
   <HEAD>
      <TITLE>Parsing Tree vs. Rendering Tree</TITLE>
   </HEAD>
   <BODY>
      <P>The parsing tree represents the
         <EM>containership hierarchy</EM>
         defined by the contents of the HTML document.</P>
      <DIV ID=D1 STYLE="position:absolute; top:60; left:20">
         <P>The rendering tree represents the relationship between
            elements as they are rendered by the browser.</P>
         <DIV ID=D2 STYLE="height:80; width:100%; overflow:scroll">
            <P>This code creates a scrolling element. However, it does
               not define a new <EM>coordinate system</EM>. The
               following element is positioned based on the coordinate
               system of the absolutely positioned DIV.</P>
            <IMG STYLE="position:absolute; top:60; left:40"
               SRC="img1.gif">
         </DIV>
      </DIV>
   </BODY>
</HTML>
```

Parsing Tree

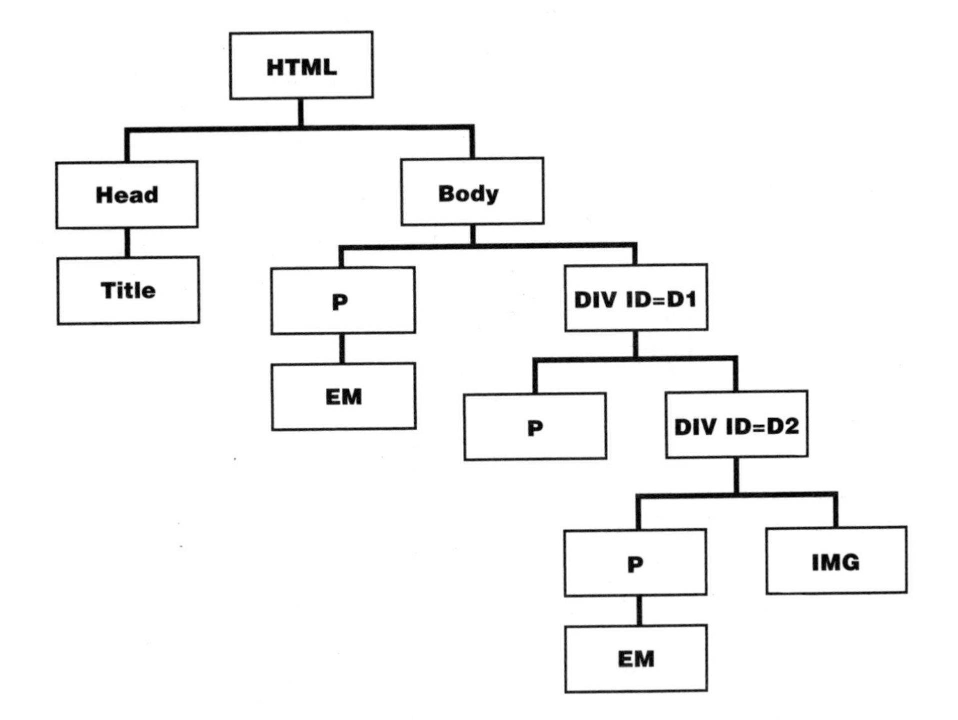

Rendering Tree

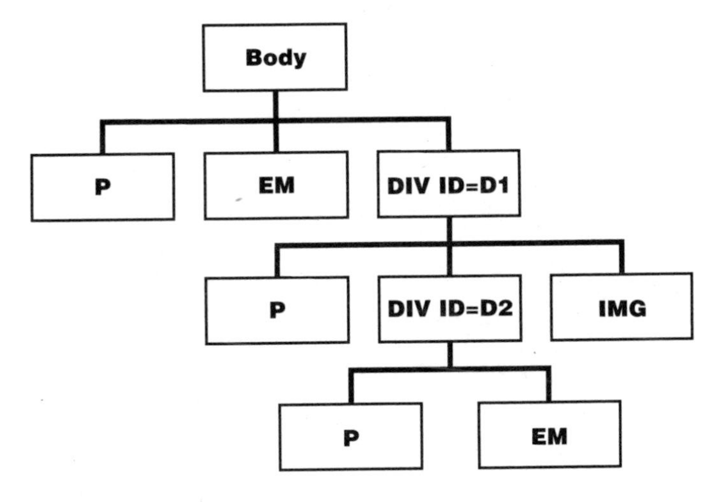

Figure 12-7.
Parsing tree and rendering tree for a document.

In this example, the Paragraph element, the EM element, and the first DIV element are all children of the Body element. The EM element becomes a rendering child of the body because its parent element, Paragraph, is not a constrained element according to the preceding list. The first DIV element, on the other hand, defines a new rendering context because it is absolutely positioned. Therefore, all elements within this DIV element are children of this rendering container unless another element creates a new rendering context within the DIV element.

The second DIV element, D2, also creates a new rendering context because it is a constrained container. This is where things seem to get tricky. When an element is positioned absolutely, it is taken out of the flow of the document and positioned relative to the nearest coordinate system. A constrained container does not necessarily define a new coordinate system. The scrolling DIV, D2, does not create a new coordinate system because no absolute or relative positioning is specified. Only elements with *position* values of *absolute* or *relative* create new coordinate systems. Therefore, the image inside D2 that is absolutely positioned is actually positioned relative to the first DIV, D1. This relationship is also maintained in the rendering relationship. D1 is the offset parent for D2.

A Rendering Context Demonstration

The relationship between an element and its rendering context is best understood by examining a sample HTML document. The following document, included on the companion CD, reports the offsets of any element on the page. The document also contains examples of several different ways in which a rendering context can be created. Clicking on any element in the document displays a list of offsets for each rendering context the element is contained within.

```
<HTML>
   <HEAD>
      <TITLE>Offset Demonstration</TITLE>
      <STYLE TYPE="text/css">
         BODY, TD, DIV, CAPTION, FIELDSET, LEGEND {cursor:default}
      </STYLE>
      <SCRIPT LANGUAGE="JavaScript">
         function doClick() {
            // Build a string of all the offsets, starting from the
            // clicked element.
            var el = event.srcElement;
            var offset = "Offsets\n";
            while (el != null) {
```

```
                offset += "\n" + el.tagName + ":  (" + el.offsetTop +
                   ", " + el.offsetLeft + ")";
                el = el.offsetParent;
             }
             alert(offset);
          }
          document.onclick = doClick;
       </SCRIPT>
    </HEAD>
    <BODY>
       <H1>Offset Demonstration</H1>
       <P>Click on an element to see its rendering context and offset
          relationship. This page helps demonstrate how an element
          becomes constrained and creates a new rendering context for
          the elements it contains.
       <P>This is a standard paragraph containing
          <EM>emphasized text</EM>.
       <TABLE BORDER>
          <CAPTION>Table <EM>Demo</EM></CAPTION>
          <TR><TD>Table Cell 1</TD>
             <TD>Table Cell <STRONG>2</STRONG></TD></TR>
          <TR><TD>Table Cell 3</TD><TD>Table Cell 4</TD></TR>
       </TABLE>
       <FIELDSET STYLE="width:200pt">
          <LEGEND>Fieldset <EM>Demo</EM></LEGEND>
          <P>This is a fieldset.
          <BUTTON><P>HTML <STRONG>Button</STRONG></BUTTON>
       </FIELDSET>
       <P STYLE="position:relative; top:50; left:160pt">This is a
          <EM>relatively</EM> positioned paragraph.</P>
       <DIV STYLE="overflow:auto; height:50pt; width:150pt
             border:1pt gray solid">
          <P>This DIV element has a constrained width and height and
             may display scrollbars if the contents <EM>do not</EM>
             fit.
       </DIV>
       <DIV STYLE="position:absolute; top:300pt; left:150pt;
             width:100pt; border:1pt gray solid">
          <DIV STYLE="position:absolute; top:0pt; left:120pt;
                width:100pt; border:1pt gray solid">
             <P>This is an absolutely positioned DIV element within
                another absolutely positioned DIV element.
          </DIV>
          <P>This is an absolutely positioned DIV element.</P>
       </DIV>
    </BODY>
 </HTML>
```

The Offset Properties of Relatively Positioned Elements

A relatively positioned element's *top* and *left* style properties represent its offsets from its normal position in the flow, but its *offsetTop* and *offsetLeft* properties represent its position with respect to its offset parent. Figure 12-8 demonstrates the relationship between these style properties and rendered position properties.

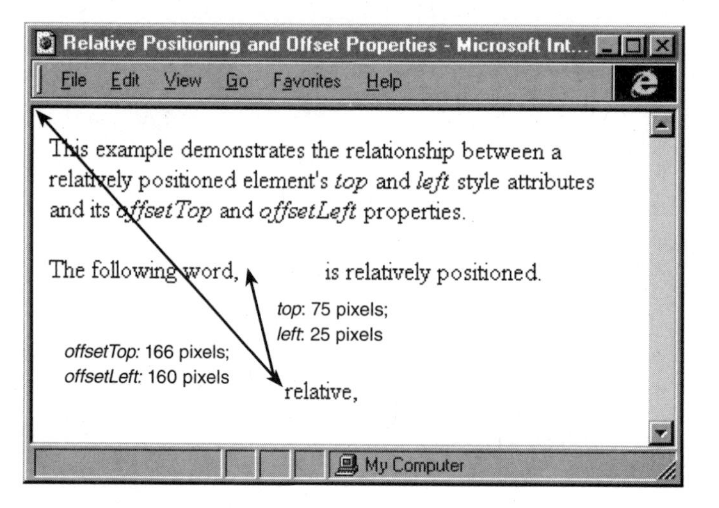

Figure 12-8.
A relatively positioned element's top *and* left *style properties and its* offsetTop *and* offsetLeft *properties.*

The offset properties are purely rendering properties that represent the calculated positions of an element in the document.

Determining Whether an Element Is in View

The following function can determine whether the upper left corner of an element is currently visible on the screen. This function returns *false* if the element's upper left corner is not visible, even if the element is partially on screen. The function works this way so that it can can be applied to any element on the page.

```
function onScreen(e) {
   // Test whether the supplied element is visible.
   var rp = e.offsetParent;
   if (rp == null)
      return false;
```

```
   var pleft = e.offsetLeft;
   var ptop = e.offsetTop;
   while (true) {
      if (!((pleft >= rp.scrollLeft) &&
            (pleft <= rp.scrollLeft + rp.clientWidth) &&
            (ptop >= rp.scrollTop) &&
            (ptop <= rp.scrollTop + rp.clientHeight)))
         return false;
      pleft += rp.offsetLeft - rp.scrollLeft ;
      ptop += rp.offsetTop - rp.scrollTop;
      rp = rp.offsetParent;
      if (rp == null)
         return true;
   }
}
```

This code can be easily enhanced to test whether an intrinsic control or a constrained element is visible by factoring in the width and height of the element, but this technique will not work for nonrectangular elements because they do not expose *offsetWidth* and *offsetHeight* properties.

Scrolling to an Element

Any element in the body of a document can be brought into view using the *scrollIntoView* method. The *scrollIntoView* method supports a single optional parameter that specifies whether the element should appear as the first or last line in the window. Omitting the parameter or supplying the value *true* scrolls the element to the first line; a value of *false* scrolls the element to the last line. For example, the following code scrolls the first H1 element in the document into view:

```
// Scroll element to the first line.
document.all.tags("H1").item(0).scrollIntoView()
// Scroll element to the last line.
document.all.tags("H1").item(0).scrollIntoView(false)
```

Identifying an Element at a Specified Position

The *document* object exposes the *elementFromPoint* method for identifying an element at a particular *xy*-coordinate position on the screen. This method takes an *xy*-pixel position relative to the window's client area and returns the element object at that position. The *elementFromPoint* method is useful for determining what element the mouse is on during an event handler. For example, the following code places the tag name of the element the mouse is on in a text box:

```
<HTML>
   <HEAD>
      <TITLE>Where Is the Mouse?</TITLE>
      <SCRIPT FOR="document" EVENT="onmousemove()"
            LANGUAGE="JavaScript">
         document.all.txtCurrent.value =
            document.elementFromPoint(event.x, event.y).tagName;
      </SCRIPT>
   </HEAD>
   <BODY>
      <H1>This Is a <EM>Header.</EM></H1>
      <P>Current Element: <INPUT TYPE=TEXT ID="txtCurrent" SIZE=20>
      </P>
   </BODY>
</HTML>
```

The Map Element

The Map element defines a special rendering context. Because a Map element can be shared by multiple images, it is considered outside any rendering context. Therefore, the Map element returns *null* for the *offsetParent* property and *0* for the *offsetTop* and *offsetLeft* properties. The Area elements within the Map element return values for their *offsetTop* and *offsetLeft* properties relative to the upper left corner of the containing Map element and return the Map element as the offset parent. Therefore, to determine the position of an Area element on the screen, you must take into account the particular image's offsets.

Aligning Relatively Positioned Elements

Aligning elements horizontally or vertically can range from trivial, requiring no code, to somewhat complex, requiring a fair amount of code. With two absolutely positioned elements within the same coordinate system, aligning the elements is as simple as providing the same *top* or *left* property. Because relatively positioned elements are offset from their position in the flow, aligning relatively positioned elements requires a few lines of code.

The following document demonstrates how to first stack all relatively positioned elements on top of each other and then animate them back to their normal positions in the document. The code that aligns the elements is contained in the *alignElements* function. This function takes any relatively positioned element and stacks it on top of the element with an ID of *src.* Alternatively, a fixed point on the screen can be used instead of another element.

```
<HTML>
   <HEAD>
      <TITLE>Animating from a Single Point</TITLE>
      <STYLE TYPE="text/css">
         .fly {position:relative; color:navy; visibility:hidden}
      </STYLE>
      <SCRIPT LANGUAGE="JavaScript">
         function alignElements(el) {
            /* Position the passed-in relatively positioned
               element that is in the same coordinate system
               on top of the element whose ID is src. */
            el.style.pixelTop
               = document.all.src.offsetTop - el.offsetTop;
            el.style.pixelLeft
               = document.all.src.offsetLeft - el.offsetLeft;
            el.style.visibility = "visible";
         }

         function moveIn(el) {
            // If the element is not at its position in the flow,
            // move it closer.
            var moved = false;
            if (el.style.pixelTop < 0) {
               el.style.pixelTop += 8;
               if (el.style.pixelTop > 0)
                  el.style.pixelTop = 0;
               moved = true;
            }
            else {
               if (el.style.pixelTop > 0)  {
                  el.style.pixelTop -= 8;
                  if (el.style.pixelTop < 0)
                     el.style.pixelTop = 0;
                  moved = true;
               }
            }
            if (el.style.pixelLeft < 0) {
               el.style.pixelLeft += 8;
               if (el.style.pixelLeft > 0)
                  el.style.pixelLeft = 0;
               moved = true;
            }
```

(continued)

```
            else {
               if (el.style.pixelTop > 0) {
                  el.style.pixelLeft -= 8;
                  if (el.style.pixelLeft < 0)
                     el.style.pixelLeft = 0;
                  moved = true;
               }
            }
            /* The move variable reflects whether the element has
               moved. If the element has already reached its position
               in the flow, this function returns false. */
            return moved;
         }

         function flyInTogether() {
            var more = false;
            // Animate into place all elements with class name fly.
            for (var intLoop = 0; intLoop < document.all.length;
                  intLoop++) {
               if ("fly" == document.all[intLoop].className)
                  more = moveIn(document.all[intLoop]) || more;
            }
            // Keep running until all elements reach their locations
            // in the flow.
            if (more)
               setTimeout("flyInTogether()", 10);
         }

         function setup() {
            // Align all elements that are going to be animated.
            for (var intLoop = 0; intLoop < document.all.length;
                  intLoop++) {
               if ("fly" == document.all[intLoop].className)
                  alignElements(document.all[intLoop]);
            }
            flyInTogether();
         }

         window.onload = setup;
      </SCRIPT>
   </HEAD>
   <BODY>
      <H1 ID=src>Animate from a Single Point</H1>
      <UL>
         <LI CLASS="fly"><P>Create animated documents.</P>
         <LI CLASS="fly"><P>All elements start together
            at a single point.</P>
```

```
         <LI CLASS="fly"><P>This example works using relative
            positioning.</P>
         <LI CLASS="fly"><P>First align the elements, and then fly
            them into place.</P>
         <LI CLASS="fly"><P>Once the elements are in place, this is
            a standard HTML document!</P>
         <LI CLASS="fly"><P>Simply supplying a special class name
            animates an element.</P>
      </UL>
      <P STYLE="text-align:center">Not all text must be animated!
   </BODY>
</HTML>
```

<SCRIPT LANGUAGE="JavaSc
// Create propert
var x = 10;
unction foo() {
// This code is no
code
var y =
alert(
output
// Call foo while l
foo();
foo(); // th
</SCRIPT>

P A R T   I V

DOCUMENT CONTENTS AND DATA BINDING

<SCRIPT LANGUAGE="JavaSc
// Create property x
var x = 10.;
function foo() {
// This code is not
// The code
var y
alert(
// output
// Call foo while lo
foo();
window.foo(); // the
</SCRIPT>

C H A P T E R   T H I R T E E N

Dynamic Contents

The term *dynamic contents* refers to the ability to access and change a portion of a document's contents without requiring the downloading or construction of an entirely new page. A good example is a ticking clock that is automatically updated in the HTML of the document. Once per second, the clock in the document is updated with a new time—without having to generate a new document.

Dynamic HTML provides direct access to the contents of a document, all the way down to the individual characters. This access enables any portion of the document to be quickly and immediately updated. Once the document is updated, surrounding contents may reflow, depending on the size and position of the new contents. Reflowing the document also often occurs with dynamic styles when the size or display of an element is changed. Dynamic contents extends this model to changing the text and HTML on the page.

Because the most effective route to understanding how to dynamically manipulate the document's contents is to review code, this chapter focuses on code samples to demonstrate the different techniques. The following topics are covered in this chapter:

- **Contents manipulation** This section briefly introduces three contents manipulation techniques supported by Dynamic HTML.
- **Dynamic contents properties** The contents of an element are exposed through four properties and two methods. These properties provide the easiest and most direct way to access and change the document's contents. This section discusses how to use the properties to change an element's contents, as well as how these properties interact with the document.
- **Dynamic contents and *document.write*** The *document.write* method allows contents to be inserted into a page while the page is being loaded; dynamic contents allows the manipulation of contents after

the page has been loaded. This section explores techniques for combining these features to create interactive documents.

Contents Manipulation

Dynamic HTML exposes the following three techniques for manipulating the contents of a document. The first technique is used to generate contents while a page is loading, and the other two techniques are used to manipulate the document after the page has finished loading.

- Writing contents into the stream during the loading of a page
- Manipulating the contents using properties and methods exposed on all elements in the body of the document
- Programming the *TextRange* object, which exposes an object model for the document's text

The first technique uses the *write* and *writeln* methods of the *document* object. These methods can insert contents into the current document as it is being downloaded, and they can construct new documents, but they cannot change contents that have already been parsed. Chapter 6, "The HTML Document," discussed the document's *write* methods. The *write* and *writeln* methods are supported in Netscape Navigator version 2.0 and later and Microsoft Internet Explorer 3.0.

The latter two techniques constitute dynamic contents and are new with Internet Explorer 4.0. All elements in the document's body provide direct access to the contained contents of any element by using four properties and two methods. This chapter introduces these members, which are the simplest way of accessing and changing the contents of the document.

The *TextRange* object exposes a custom text-based object model that provides arbitrary access to the underlying contents, giving you more control over the document at the expense of predictability. This technique allows you to manipulate contents as you would using a text editor. While many manipulations are possible through the text-based model, it is not as precise as a true top-down tree approach and has a number of limitations. Chapter 14, "User Selection and Editing Operations," reviews the *TextRange* object model's strengths and weaknesses.

Dynamic Contents Properties

The Body element and all elements contained within it expose four properties for accessing and modifying the HTML contents: *innerHTML*, *innerText*, *outerHTML*, and *outerText*. An element's *innerHTML* property exposes its contents, including the HTML markup for any child elements. The *innerText* property exposes the contained text without any HTML tags. Assigning a new value to one of an element's inner properties replaces the contents of the element. The *outerHTML* and *outerText* properties resemble the *innerHTML* and *innerText* properties, but they reference the entire element rather than just its contents. Assigning a value to one of an element's outer properties replaces the entire element. In the following example, clicking a button replaces the button with the boldface text *Blown Away!*:

```
<HTML>
   <HEAD>
      <TITLE>Disappearing Button</TITLE>
   </HEAD>
   <BODY>
      <INPUT TYPE=BUTTON VALUE="Blow me away!"
         ONCLICK="this.outerHTML = '<B>Blown Away!</B>'">
   </BODY>
</HTML>
```

One limitation of these properties is that they can reference an element or its contents only in their entirety; they cannot reference just a portion of the contents. To use these properties to change the third character or word within an element, for example, you would have to reconstruct the string and reinsert it. The *TextRange* object provides an alternative technique that allows any portion of the document to be manipulated directly.

The dynamic contents properties use fairly strict rules for determining what HTML is valid. These rules are stricter than the rules used to originally parse the page, but not as rigid as the HTML DTD (document type definition). If you assign invalid HTML to one of these properties, an error can occur and the new contents might not be inserted. While the properties accept some invalid HTML, you should always supply syntactically valid HTML to ensure predictable results.

In addition to these properties, every element in the body of a document also exposes two methods for inserting contents before or after the begin or end tag: *insertAdjacentHTML* and *insertAdjacentText*. These two methods are useful for quickly inserting new paragraphs or list items into the document.

Figure 13-1 illustrates all the ways the contents of an element can be manipulated.

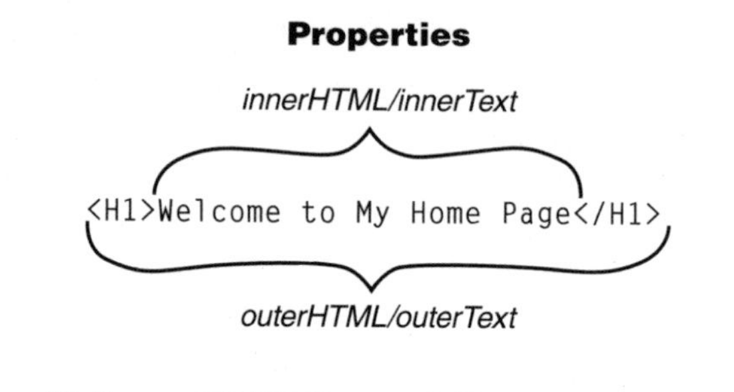

***InsertAdjacentHTML/InsertAdjacentText* Methods**

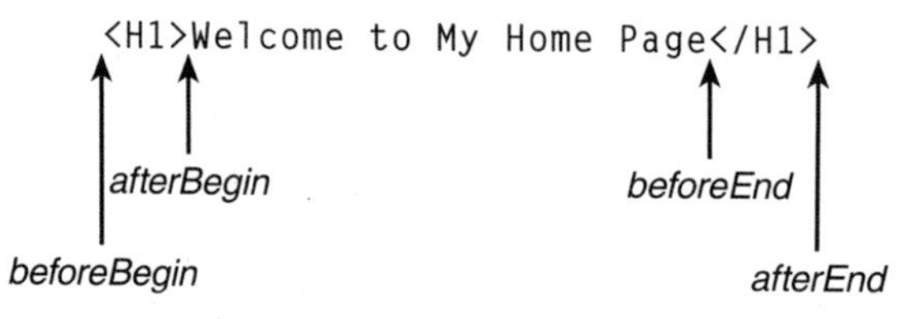

Figure 13-1.
All the places HTML and text can be accessed and modified.

HTML vs. Text Properties

The primary distinction between the *innerHTML* and *outerHTML* properties on the one hand and the *innerText* and *outerText* properties on the other hand is that the HTML properties expose the entire markup while the text properties expose the contents without the markup. Consider the following HTML fragment:

```
<H1>Welcome to <EM>Scott's</EM> Home Page</H1>
```

For the H1 element in this fragment, the following table lists the values of each of the four properties.

Property	Value
innerText	*Welcome to Scott's Home Page*
innerHTML	*Welcome to <EM>Scott's</EM> Home Page*
outerText	*Welcome to Scott's Home Page*
outerHTML	*<H1>Welcome to <EM>Scott's</EM> Home Page</H1>*

The *innerText* and *outerText* properties always return the same value but behave differently when you assign new values to them. Assigning a value to the *innerText* property replaces only the contents of the H1 element with new contents. Assigning a value to the *outerText* property replaces the H1 element and its contents with the new text. For example, assigning the value *Thank you for visiting* to each of these properties has different results: When you assign this value to the *innerText* property, the resulting HTML is *<H1>Thank you for visiting</H1>*. If you use the *outerText* property instead, the resulting HTML is *Thank you for visiting*; the <H1> tags are removed.

The markup in the values of the *innerHTML* and *outerHTML* properties does not necessarily match the markup in the source code. Instead, extraneous spaces are cleaned up and the attributes may be reordered. When you assign values to the HTML-related properties, be sure to use proper escape sequences for any entities. The < and > angle brackets are interpreted as tag delimiters; if the angle brackets are to be included in the contents and not parsed as HTML, they must be specified as entities by using *<* and *>*. When you assign values to the text properties, these brackets are automatically converted to their escape sequence equivalents.

Nonbreaking Spaces

Nonbreaking spaces (spaces at which line breaks are prohibited) and ordinary spaces are considered separate characters in the object model, where they are represented by the ASCII values 160 and 32, respectively. Comparing the two characters yields the value *false*, as in this example:

```
<SPAN ID="s1"> </SPAN>
document.all.s1.innerText == " "  // false; not a space
```

To check whether a nonbreaking space is an element's contents, either check the ASCII value directly or compare the HTML property to the entity itself, as shown here:

```
document.all.s1.innerHTML == " " // true
```

Any specified entity that matches a built-in entity value is converted to the built-in name. The nonbreaking space entity can also be specified as * * instead of using its keyword identifier. Dynamic HTML recognizes that this value is a nonbreaking space and converts it to * *.

Using the Dynamic Contents Properties

The easiest way to learn the differences between the dynamic contents properties on an element is through examples. The following sections present two examples: the first is a review of the ticking clock example in Chapter 4, "The

Browser Window," and the second is a tic-tac-toe game that demonstrates dynamically retrieving contents and assigning contents into a document.

A Ticking Clock

The ticking clock example in Chapter 4 uses the *innerText* property to update the time. A Span element with the ID *clock* contains the text with the current time. Every second, a script calls a function named *buildTime* to create a string with the current time, and then outputs the string into the Span element with ID *clock* using this statement:

```
document.all.clock.innerText = buildTime();
```

Tic-Tac-Toe

The tic-tac-toe example creates an interactive game using dynamic contents. A table provides the layout for the game board. Every time the user clicks in a cell, the cell's contents are replaced with an *X* or an *O* using the *innerText* property. The size of the game board can be dynamically changed by inserting a new table in the place of the existing one using the *outerHTML* property.

```
<HTML>
   <HEAD>
      <TITLE>Tic-Tac-Toe</TITLE>
      <STYLE TYPE="text/css">
         TD {font-weight:bold}
         #board TD {width:50px; height:50px; text-align:center;
            font-size:18pt; cursor:hand}
         .X {color:blue}
         .O {color:red}
         .draw {color:green}
      </STYLE>
      <SCRIPT LANGUAGE="JavaScript">
         function TicTac() {
            // Object for tracking the game
            this.lastMove = true;
            this.inProcess = true;
            this.scores = new Object();
            this.scores.xScore = 0;
            this.scores.oScore = 0;
            this.scores.draws = 0;
            this.size = 3;
            this.drawBoard = initBoard;
         }

         function buildTable() {
            // Build the HTML table to be inserted into the document.
```

```
   var tb = "<TABLE BORDER ID=board
      ONCLICK='doBoardClick();'>";
   for (var intRow = 0; intRow < game.size; intRow++) {
      tb += "<TR>";
      for (var intCell = 0; intCell < game.size; intCell++)
         tb += "<TD> </TD>";
      tb += "</TR>";
   }
   tb += "</TABLE>";
   return tb;
}

function initBoard() {
   document.all.board.outerHTML = buildTable();
   game.inProcess = true;
   game.lastMove = true;
}

function checkWinner(xCount, oCount) {
   // Process results of the scan for a winner.
   if (game.size == xCount) {
      alert("X Wins!");
      game.scores.xScore++;
      return false;
   }
   if (game.size == oCount) {
      alert("O Wins!");
      game.scores.oScore++;
      return false;
   }
   return true;
}

function checkGame() {
   // Tests all the directions for a winner.
   var xCount = 0, oCount = 0, total = 0;
   var el = document.all.board;
   // Check horizontal direction.
   for (var intRows = 0; intRows < el.rows.length;
         intRows++) {
      xCount = 0, oCount = 0;
      for (var intCells = 0;
            intCells < el.rows[intRows].cells.length;
            intCells++) {
         var strCell = el.rows[intRows].cells[intCells];
         if ("X" == strCell.innerText)
```

(continued)

```
            xCount++;
         if ("O" == strCell.innerText)
            oCount++;
      }
      game.inProcess = checkWinner(xCount, oCount);
      if (!game.inProcess)
         return;
      total += xCount + oCount;
   }
   // Check vertical direction.
   for (var intCells = 0; intCells < el.rows.length;
         intCells++)  {
      xCount = 0, oCount = 0;
      for (var intRows = 0;
            intRows < el.rows[intCells].cells.length;
            intRows++) {
         var strCell = el.rows[intRows].cells[intCells];
         if ("X" == strCell.innerText)
            xCount++;
         if ("O" == strCell.innerText)
            oCount++;
      }
      game.inProcess = checkWinner(xCount, oCount);
      if (!game.inProcess) return;
   }

   // Check diagonal (upper left to lower right).
   xCount = 0, oCount = 0;
   for (var intRows = 0; intRows < el.rows.length;
         intRows++) {
      var strCell = el.rows[intRows].cells[intRows];
      if ("X" == strCell.innerText)
         xCount++;
      if ("O" == strCell.innerText)
         oCount++;
   }
   game.inProcess = checkWinner(xCount, oCount);
   if (!game.inProcess) return;

   // Check diagonal (lower left to upper right).
   xCount = 0, oCount = 0;
   for (var intRows = 0; intRows < el.rows.length;
         intRows++) {
      var strCell =
         el.rows[game.size - intRows - 1].cells[intRows];
      if ("X" == strCell.innerText)
         xCount++;
```

```
         if ("O" == strCell.innerText)
            oCount++;
      }
      game.inProcess = checkWinner(xCount, oCount);
      if (!game.inProcess)
         return;
      if (total == game.size * game.size) {
         alert("draw");
         game.inProcess = false;
         game.scores.draws++;
         return
      }
   }

   function updateScore() {
      // Output new score.
      for (scores in game.scores)
         document.all[scores].innerText = game.scores[scores];
   }

   function doBoardClick() {
      if (game.inProcess) {
         if ("TD" == event.srcElement.tagName) {
            var strCell = event.srcElement;
            // Check whether the cell is available.
            if (" " == strCell.innerHTML) {
               strCell.innerText = (game.lastMove ? "X" : "O");
               event.srcElement.className =
                  game.lastMove ? "X" : "O";
               game.lastMove = !game.lastMove;
            }
         }
         checkGame();
         if (!game.inProcess)
            updateScore();
      }
   }

   // Manages the game variables
   var game = new TicTac;
</SCRIPT>
<SCRIPT FOR="size" EVENT="onclick()" LANGUAGE="JavaScript">
   // Shared event handler for the board-sizing radio buttons
   game.size = parseInt(this.value);
   game.drawBoard();
</SCRIPT>
```

(continued)

```
   </HEAD>
   <BODY>
      <H1>Tic-Tac-Toe</H1>
      <P><INPUT TYPE=BUTTON VALUE="New Game"
            ONCLICK="game.drawBoard();">
      <P><INPUT NAME=size TYPE=RADIO VALUE="3" ID="x3" checked>
         <LABEL FOR="x3">3 x 3</LABEL><BR>
         <INPUT NAME=size TYPE=RADIO VALUE="4" ID="x4">
         <LABEL FOR="x4">4 x 4</LABEL><BR>
         <INPUT NAME=size TYPE=RADIO VALUE="5" ID="x5">
         <LABEL FOR="x5">5 x 5</LABEL>
      <P>
      <SCRIPT LANGUAGE="JavaScript">
         document.write(buildTable());
      </SCRIPT>
      <TABLE>
         <TR class=x><TD>X Wins:</TD><TD ID=xScore>0</TD></TR>
         <TR class=o><TD>O Wins:</TD><TD ID=oScore>0</TD></TR>
         <TR class=draw><TD>Draws:</TD><TD ID=draws>0</TD></TR>
      </TABLE>
   </BODY>
</HTML>
```

Figure 13-2 shows the Tic-Tac-Toe program in action.

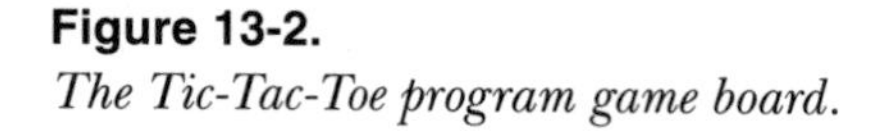

Figure 13-2.
The Tic-Tac-Toe program game board.

Using the Adjacent Methods

An element's *insertAdjacentHTML* and *insertAdjacentText* methods insert HTML and text before or after the start tag, or before or after the end tag. Both methods take two arguments: the first argument represents where the contents are being inserted, and the second argument represents the actual contents.

The four valid values for the first argument represent each of the four insertion locations: *beforeBegin*, *afterBegin*, *beforeEnd*, and *afterEnd*, where *Begin* represents the begin tag and *End* represents the end tag. These methods are useful for insertions that do not affect any of the existing contents.

Generating Footnotes

This example demonstrates how to add pop-up footnotes to a page. The following code works by locating all elements that are specified as footnotes and inserting footnote numbers in the document. The author designates a footnote by adding a Span element with the class name *footnote*. The style sheet defines these Span elements as invisible. An alert containing the footnote text is displayed when the user clicks on the inserted footnote number.

```
<HTML>
   <HEAD>
      <TITLE>Dynamic Footnotes</TITLE>
      <STYLE TYPE="text/css">
         SPAN {display:none}
         SUP.FNID {color:blue; cursor:hand}
      </STYLE>
      <SCRIPT LANGUAGE="JavaScript">
         function setupFootnotes() {
            // Get a collection of all the Span elements.
            var spans = document.all.tags("SPAN");
            for (var i = 0; i < spans.length; i++) {
               var el = spans[i];
               // If element is a footnote, process it.
               if ("footnote" == el.className) {
                  // Add a superscripted footnote number.
                  el.insertAdjacentHTML("beforeBegin",
                     "<SUP CLASS=FNID>" + (i + 1) + " </SUP>");
                  // Link the footnote number to the Span element.
                  document.all[el.sourceIndex - 1].linkFN = el;
               }
            }
         }
```

(continued)

```
         function displayFN() {
            // If the number is clicked on, display the footnote.
            if ("FNID" == event.srcElement.className)
               if (null != event.srcElement.linkFN)
                  alert(event.srcElement.linkFN.innerText);
         }

         window.onload = setupFootnotes;
         document.onclick = displayFN;
      </SCRIPT>
   </HEAD>
   <BODY>
      <H1>Dynamic Footnotes
         <SPAN CLASS="footnote">
            Copyright (C) 1997 by Scott Isaacs.
         </SPAN>
      </H1>
      <P>Dynamic HTML is a "powerful way of creating Web pages"
         <SPAN CLASS="footnote">Scott Isaacs, "Inside Dynamic HTML."
         </SPAN>
         and "Soon Dynamic HTML will be used in most applications."
         <SPAN CLASS="footnote">
            Joe-Cool Developer, "The Future of the Web."
         </SPAN>
      <P>This page automatically generates and numbers the footnotes
         at load time. The footnotes are stored as hidden contents on
         the page.</P>
   </BODY>
</HTML>
```

You can display footnotes in ToolTips rather than in alert boxes by setting the TITLE attribute of each footnote number to the text of the footnote. Another alternative would be to display each footnote within the text when the user clicks the footnote number; for this technique, customize the *displayFN* function to change the *display* style attribute for the footnote text.

Creating Custom HTML List Boxes

This example uses HTML elements to simulate two list boxes whose items can be selected and copied between the lists. A single custom list box can also be used without the copying functionality to provide a rich selection list.

In the following code, two list boxes are created using scrolling DIV elements. Each item in the list boxes is a standard list item in a bulleted list. When the user clicks on an item to select it, the background color changes. When the user double-clicks on the item or clicks one of the arrow buttons, the item is removed from one list and inserted at the end of the other list using the *insertAdjacentHTML* method.

```
<HTML>
   <HEAD>
      <TITLE>Custom HTML List Boxes</TITLE>
      <STYLE TYPE="text/css">
         .list {cursor:hand; overflow:auto; height:75pt; width:150pt;
            border:1pt black solid}
         .list UL {list-style-type:none; margin-left:2pt;
            margin-top:0pt; margin-bottom:0pt}
         .list UL LI {margin-top:0pt; margin-bottom:0pt}
         .list UL LI.selected {background:navy; color:white}
      </STYLE>
      <SCRIPT LANGUAGE="JavaScript">
         function checkParent(src, tag) {
            while ("HTML" != src.tagName) {
               if (tag == src.tagName)
                  return src;
               src = src.parentElement;
            }
            return null;
         }

         function selectItem(list) {
            var el = checkParent(event.srcElement, "LI");
            if ("LI" == el.tagName) {
               if (null != list.selected)
                  list.selected.className = "";
               if (list.selected != el) {
                  el.className = "selected";
                  list.selected = el;
               }
               else
                  list.selected = null;
            }
         }

         function copy(src, dest) {
            var elSrc = document.all[src];
            var elDest = document.all[dest];
            if (elSrc.selected != null) {
               elSrc.selected.className = "";
```

(continued)

```
               elDest.insertAdjacentHTML("beforeEnd",
                  elSrc.selected.outerHTML);
               elSrc.selected.outerHTML = "";
               elSrc.selected = null; // reset  selection
            }
         }
      </SCRIPT>
   </HEAD>
   <BODY>
      <H1>Custom HTML List Boxes</H1>
      <P>The bulleted lists simulate rich HTML selection lists.</P>
      <TABLE>
         <TR>
            <TD>
               <DIV CLASS="list">
                  <UL ID="src" ONCLICK="selectItem(this);"
                        ONDBLCLICK="copy('src', 'dest');">
                     <LI>Scott's <EM>Home</EM> Page</LI>
                     <LI>Parents' Home Page</LI>
                     <LI><IMG SRC="foo.gif"></LI>
                     <LI>Inside Dynamic HTML Home Page</LI>
                     <LI>Microsoft Home Page</LI>
                     <LI>Item 6</LI>
                     <LI>Item 7</LI>
                  </UL>
               </DIV>
            </TD><TD>
               <P><INPUT TYPE=BUTTON VALUE="-->"
                  ONCLICK="copy('src', 'dest');">
               <P><INPUT TYPE=BUTTON VALUE="<--"
                  ONCLICK="copy('dest', 'src');">
            </TD><TD>
               <DIV class="list">
                  <UL ID="dest" ONCLICK="selectItem(this);"
                     ONDBLCLICK="copy('dest','src');">
                  </UL>
               </DIV>
            </TD>
         </TR>
      </TABLE>
   </BODY>
</HTML>
```

Figure 13-3 illustrates these custom list boxes.

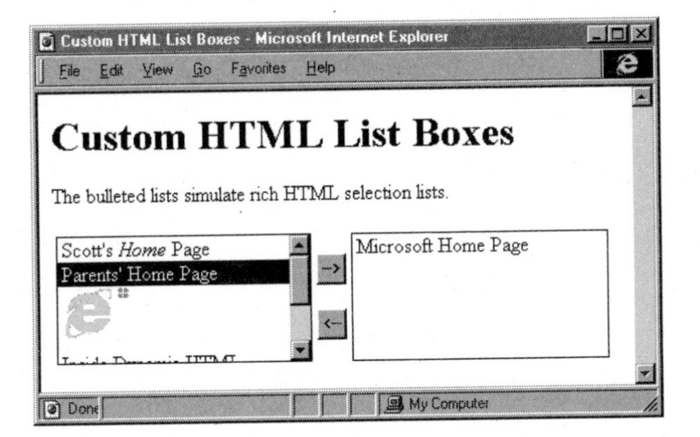

Figure 13-3.
Two list boxes created from existing HTML elements.

Accessing the Contents

The contents of a document cannot be accessed or manipulated until the document is completely loaded. Therefore, be careful when a script or an event handler attempts to access and manipulate the contents. If the code might execute before the page is loaded, the code should first test the *readyState* property of the document:

```
if ("complete" == document.readyState) {
   // Manipulate the contents.
}
else {
   // Display a warning or perform alternative action.
}
```

Image Error Handling

The next example demonstrates how to queue document changes until the page is entirely loaded. This example replaces any images that fail to download with error messages and the images' titles. The trick here is to ensure that the document is loaded before accessing the contents because an image might fail and fire the *onerror* event before the page is completely loaded.

The following code builds a collection of all the images that failed before the page entirely loaded. Once the page is loaded, each image in the queue of bad images is replaced with the appropriate text. Any future errors are handled immediately.

```
<HTML>
   <HEAD>
      <TITLE>Image Error Handling</TITLE>
      <STYLE TYPE="text/css">
         SPAN.error {background:yellow; font-weight:bold}
      </STYLE>
      <SCRIPT LANGUAGE="JavaScript">
         var Errors = new Array();
         Errors[0] = 0;

         function badImage(el) {
            if (document.readyState != "complete") {
               Errors[0]++;
               Errors[Errors[0]] = el;
            }
            else  // The document is loaded; output error directly.
               el.outerHTML =
                  "<SPAN CLASS='error'>Error Loading Image: " +
                     el.title + "</SPAN>";
         }

         function reviewErrors() {
            for (var i = 1; i <= Errors[0]; i++)
               Errors[i].outerHTML =
                  "<SPAN CLASS='error'>Error Loading Image: " +
                     Errors[i].title + "</SPAN>";
         }

         window.onload = reviewErrors;
      </SCRIPT>
   </HEAD>
   <BODY>
      <P><IMG SRC="bad.gif" ONERROR="badImage(this);"
         TITLE="Cool Picture">
      <P><A HREF="http://www.insideDHTML.com">
         <IMG SRC="bad.gif" ONERROR="badImage(this);"
            TITLE="Inside Dynamic HTML Web Site"></A>
   </BODY>
</HTML>
```

This code also works if an anchor wraps the image. The new text that replaces the image is rendered within the anchor and properly jumps to the page when the user clicks on the element. This code can be expanded to output a message after an *onabort* event.

If replacing the image with text is considered too extreme, you can easily modify the *title* attribute by adding a message that says an error has occurred.

(The *title* attribute in Internet Explorer 4.0 is displayed as a ToolTip.) This modification can be accomplished without all the hard work of creating the error queue because attributes of elements can be modified before the page is loaded. The following code demonstrates this feature added in line for an image; it works without any other code:

```
<IMG SRC="bad.gif" TITLE="Cool Picture"
   ONERROR="this.title = 'Error Loading: ' + this.title";>
```

Dynamic Contents and *document.write*

The dynamic contents model is a powerful tool for manipulating a loaded document, but it does not completely eliminate the need for the *document.write* method. In fact, these two features complement each other extremely well. In the following examples, dynamic contents techniques are used to locate specific text that is then output into a new window using the *document.write* method. The first scenario creates a banner frame when the document is contained within a frameset, and the second scenario demonstrates two techniques for indexing a page.

Creating a Header Bar

Web authors have long desired a feature whereby an HTML page can supply a banner to be displayed in a header bar above it. In earlier browsers, this feature could only be simulated by creating a frameset that loads two files at a time, one file for the document and another file for its banner. Using two files per document adds complexity, as the files need to be synchronized. The following code simplifies matters by including the banner in the document's contents. If the page is loaded outside a frameset, the code displays the banner inside the document, so no document fidelity is lost.

```
<HTML>
   <HEAD>
      <TITLE>Banner Document</TITLE>
      <STYLE TYPE="text/css">
         DIV#bannerContents {display:none}
      </STYLE>
      <SCRIPT LANGUAGE="JavaScript">
         function outputBanner() {
            if (null != parent.frames[0]) {
               parent.frames[0].document.open();
               parent.frames[0].document.write(
                  document.all.bannerContents.outerHTML);
```

(continued)

```
                parent.frames[0].document.close();
             }
             else  // Not in a frameset; turn on the banner.
                document.all.bannerContents.style.display = "block";
          }

          window.onload = outputBanner;
       </SCRIPT>
    </HEAD>
    <BODY>
       <DIV ID=bannerContents>
          <H1>Inside Dynamic HTML</H1>
       </DIV>
       <P><EM>Inside Dynamic HTML</EM> teaches the Web developer
          how to create interactive and live Web pages.</P>
    </BODY>
 </HTML>
```

The contents of the banner DIV can be any HTML, including scripts. The entire contents will be copied to the other frame.

To complete this example, the following frameset document contains code that automatically sizes the frameset once the banner is loaded. This code changes the dimensions of the rows by assigning the *scrollHeight* property of the banner to the height of the frame so that the banner frame is appropriately sized.

```
<HTML>
   <HEAD>
      <TITLE>Banner Frameset</TITLE>
      <SCRIPT LANGUAGE="JavaScript">
         function fixup() {
            // Auto-size banner frame.
            document.all.FS.rows =
               window.frames.Banner.document.body.scrollHeight +
               ", *";
         }

         window.onload = fixup;
      </SCRIPT>
   </HEAD>
   <FRAMESET ROWS="100, *" ID="FS" FRAMEBORDER=0>
      <FRAME NAME="Banner" SCROLLING=NO NORESIZE>
      <FRAME SRC="Banner.htm">
   </FRAMESET>
</HTML>
```

This frameset code sizes the header bar for the first document that loads, but it doesn't automatically resize the header bar when the user navigates to another page that has a different size banner. You can add code to such other pages to call the parent window's *fixup* function to resize the header bar.

Enhanced Indexes and Tables of Contents

The most common use of framesets is to display a list of document options in one frame and the selected document in another frame. The following examples demonstrate more interesting uses of framesets. The first example automatically generates an anchor index, and the second example automatically generates a table of contents. The index or table of contents is best displayed in a sibling frame.

The first example includes custom code to determine where to display the index. If the document is loaded inside a frameset and a sibling frame has the ID *menu*, the document displays the index in that frame. Otherwise, the document opens a new window to display the index. The second example includes similar code to determine where to display the table of contents.

Link and Bookmark Indexes

The following quick indexer example creates an index window containing copies of all the document's Anchor elements. The code uses each anchor's *innerHTML* property to copy its contents so that images can be appropriately rendered in the index window.

```
<HTML>
   <HEAD>
      <TITLE>Auto Indexing</TITLE>
      <SCRIPT LANGUAGE="JavaScript">
         function setupIndex() {
            // Open new window.
            var winIndex = null;

            /* If in a frameset and a menu frame exists, output to
               that frame; otherwise, output to a new window. */
            if (window.parent != self)
               if (null != parent.menu)
                  winIndex = parent.menu;
            if (null == winIndex)
               winIndex = window.open("", "Index",
                  "width=300; height=500");
            // Start writing index document.
            winIndex.document.open();
```

(continued)

```
winIndex.document.write("<HTML>");
winIndex.document.write("<TITLE>Index</TITLE>");

// Determine the base HREF and base target.
var baseHREF = null;
var baseTarget = null;
// Check whether any <BASE> tags are present in
// the document.
var base = document.all.tags("BASE");
for (var i = 0; i < base.length; i++) {
   // Retrieve the base HREF and target if specified.
   if (null != base[i].href)
      baseHREF = base[i].href;
   if (null != base[i].target)
      baseTarget = base[i].target;
}

// Set up window name to act as target if no base exists.
if ((null == baseTarget) || ("" == baseTarget)) {
   if ("" == window.name)
      window.name = "outputhere";
   baseTarget = window.name;
}

// If base HREF doesn't exist, set to current path.
if ((null == baseHREF) || ("" == baseHREF)) {
   baseHREF = location.protocol + location.pathname;
}

// Output base into window.
winIndex.document.writeln("<BASE TARGET=" +
   "'" + baseTarget + "'" + "HREF='" + baseHREF + "'>");
winIndex.document.writeln("<H1>Links</H1>");
// innerHTML is used so that images and rich HTML
// are automatically retrieved.
// Enumerate all Anchor elements; skip image maps.
for (var i = 0; i < document.links.length; i++) {
   var el = document.links[i];
   if ("A" == el.tagName) {
      var hText = el.outerHTML;
      winIndex.document.writeln("<P>" + hText);
   }
}

winIndex.document.writeln("<H1>Bookmarks</H1>");
// Enumerate all bookmarks.
for (var i = 0; i < document.anchors.length; i++) {
```

```
               var el = document.anchors[i];
               if ("A" == el.tagName) {
                  var hText = el.innerHTML;
                  winIndex.document.writeln(
                     "<P><A HREF='#" + el.name + "'>" + hText +
                     "</A>");
               }
            }

            winIndex.document.close();
         }
         window.onload = setupIndex;
      </SCRIPT>
   </HEAD>
   <BODY>
      <H1><A NAME="top">Auto Indexing</A></H1>
      <H2><A NAME="links">Link Demonstrations</A></H2>
      <P>The following links will appear in the link index:</P>
      <P><A HREF="http://www.insideDHTML.com">Inside Dynamic HTML</A>
      <P><A HREF="http://www.microsoft.com">Microsoft's Web Site</A>
      <P>Images also work:
      <P><A HREF="http://www.insideDHTML.com"><IMG SRC="open.gif"></A>
      <P>Rich HTML anchors are automatically picked up:
      <P><A HREF="http://www.insideDHTML.com">Inside <EM>Dynamic</EM>
         HTML</A>
   </BODY>
</HTML>
```

Table of Contents

This example, which is similar to the link indexing code, automatically numbers all headers and creates links to them in a separate table of contents window. Letting Dynamic HTML number the headers eliminates the need to renumber them by hand every time you insert a new one. If the table of contents is in a separate window, the window closes when the user navigates away from the page.

```
<HTML>
   <HEAD>
      <TITLE>Manipulating Headings</TITLE>
      <SCRIPT LANGUAGE="JavaScript">
         // Variable for the table of contents window
         var winTOC = null;

         function setupHeaders() {
            var levels = new Object;
            var level = 0;
```

(continued)

```
if (window.parent != self)
   if (null != parent.menu)
      winTOC = parent.menu;
if (null == winTOC)
   winTOC = window.open("", "Index",
      "width=300; height=500");

winTOC.document.open();
winTOC.document.write("<HTML>");

winTOC.document.writeln("<TITLE>Contents</TITLE>");
// Write click event handler to scroll element into view.
winTOC.document.writeln("<SCRIPT> function gotoHeader()" +
   "{if (event.srcElement.linkTo != null)" +
   "event.srcElement.linkTo.scrollIntoView(true)} </" +
   "SCRIPT>");
winTOC.document.writeln("<BODY ONCLICK='gotoHeader()'" +
   "STYLE='cursor:hand'" +
   "onmouseover='if (event.srcElement.tagName ==" +
   "&quot;SPAN&quot;)" +
   "event.srcElement.style.textDecorationUnderline " +
   "= true' onmouseout = " +
   "'event.srcElement.style.textDecorationUnderline " +
   "= false'>");
winTOC.document.writeln("<H1>Contents</H1>");
var level = 0;

// Enumerate all elements for Heading elements.
for (var i = 0; i < document.all.length; i++) {
   var el = document.all[i];
   var char1 = el.tagName.substring(0, 1);
   var val2 = parseInt(el.tagName.substring(1, 2));
   if (("H" == char1) && (2 == el.tagName.length) &&
         (val2 > 0) && (val2 < 7)) {
      // Nest or unnest the list.
      if (val2 > level)
         for (; level < val2; level++) {
            if (levels[level] == null)
               levels[level] = 0;
            winTOC.document.writeln("<DL>");
         }
      else if (level > val2)
         for (; level > val2; level--) {
            levels[level - 1] = 0;
            winTOC.document.writeln("</DL>");
         }
      levels[level - 1]++;
      var hText = document.all[i].innerText;
```

```
                winTOC.document.writeln("<DT><SPAN>");
                var strNum = "";
                for (var iOut = 0; iOut < level; iOut++) {
                   winTOC.document.write(levels[iOut].toString() +
                      ".");
                   strNum += levels[iOut] + ".";
                }
                document.all[i].insertAdjacentText("afterBegin",
                   strNum + " ");
                winTOC.document.writeln(" " + hText + "</SPAN>");

                // Add a property with a reference to the header.
                winTOC.document.all[winTOC.document.all.length -
                   1].linkTo = el;
             }
          }
          winTOC.document.close();
       }

       window.onload = setupHeaders;
       // If outputting to a frame, remove this unload event
       // handler.
       window.onunload = new Function
          ("if (!winTOC.closed) winTOC.close()");
    </SCRIPT>
  </HEAD>
  <BODY ONLOAD="setupHeaders();">
    <H1>Dynamic HTML Auto-Numbering</H1>
    <P>All the headers are automatically numbered and
       a table of contents is generated.</P>
    <P>Below are sample headings to be numbered.
    <H2>Finds all the headers.</H2>
    <P>All done automatically!</P>
    <H2>Automatically fills in a heading number.</H2>
    <H1>Better Performance and Less Maintenance</H1>
    <H2>Just maintain the page.</H2>
    <H2>Don't worry about renumbering headings.</H2>
    <H3>Test header 3</H3>
    <H2>No need to maintain separate contents document.</H2>
  </BODY>
</HTML>
```

Inserting code from this document into any long Web page makes the page more interactive and easier to navigate. This example also demonstrates why proper nesting of headers is valuable. While the code can handle incorrectly nested headings, the results are more meaningful when the headers are properly ordered.

Figure 13-4 shows the Table of Contents application in action. The table of contents and numbered headers are automatically generated after the page is loaded.

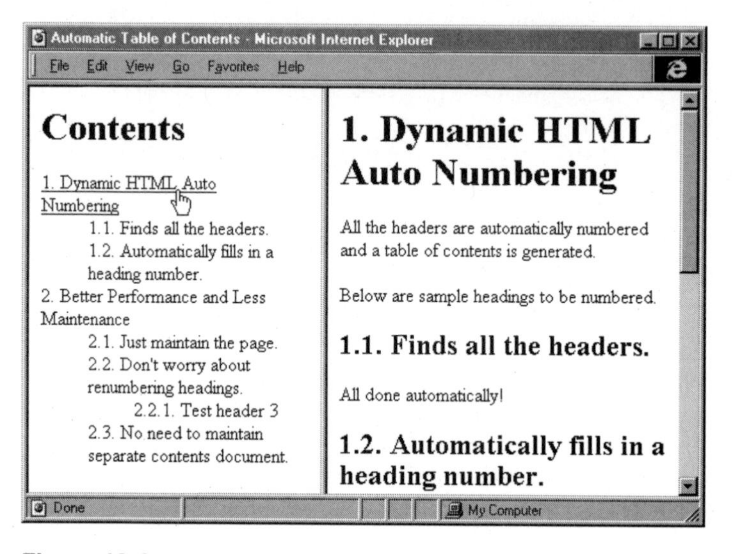

Figure 13-4.
A table of contents and numbered headers.

C H A P T E R   F O U R T E E N

User Selection and Editing Operations

This chapter introduces the *TextRange* object, which is used to access and manipulate the document's contents. Dynamic HTML defines an object model that can manipulate a document through script, similar to a text editor. The *TextRange* object represents the editing capabilities of the browser and exposes operations that constitute the editing model. Using the *TextRange* object, you can edit any text and you can access and manipulate the highlighted text that the user has selected on the screen.

The following topics are covered in this chapter:

- **Introducing the *TextRange* object** This section introduces the *TextRange* object, how it represents the text contents of the document, and its relationship to the document's structure. In addition, some of the limitations and ambiguities of the *TextRange* object are discussed.
- **Programming the *TextRange* object** This section shows you how to navigate and modify a document's contents using the *TextRange* object's properties and methods.
- **Accessing the user's selection** This section shows you how to access the user's selection, one of the primary uses of the *TextRange* object. Both plain text and HTML text selected by the user are accessible, and the user's current selection can be manipulated and changed.
- **Executing commands** Dynamic HTML exposes a set of editing-related methods that are exposed both on the document and on the *TextRange* object. This section shows you how to use these methods to query for information about the document and to manipulate

the appearance of the document. The methods that manipulate the document are used to indirectly modify the HTML in order to obtain desired effects—for example, to create an Anchor element from arbitrary text.

Introducing the *TextRange* Object

Up to now, you've seen how to modify a document directly by manipulating the individual elements or the style sheets. Just as global style sheets manipulate a document's style independent of its structure, the *TextRange* object manipulates the document's contents independent of both style and structure. This object is intended to complement the inner and outer element properties for manipulating document contents introduced in Chapter 13, "Dynamic Contents." These element properties offer more robust results and should generally be used instead of the *TextRange* object whenever possible.

The *TextRange* object provides access to the text as a long buffer of characters. For example, consider the text in this simple document:

```
<HTML>
   <BODY>
      <H1>Welcome</H1>
      <H2>Table of Contents</H2>
      <UL>
         <LI>Chapter 1</LI>
         <LI>Chapter 2</LI>
      </UL>
   </BODY>
</HTML>
```

Figure 14-1 shows the text for this document, positioned below the parsing tree. Characters belonging to a particular element in the tree are shown under that element's influence. For example, *Chapter 1* is influenced by the first LI element.

TextRange objects can be created only by special elements that are considered text edit owners. A text edit owner is an element that can create a *TextRange* object using the *createTextRange* method, thereby providing access to the underlying buffer. Currently only two types of HTML elements can act as text edit owners in Dynamic HTML: the Body element is the text edit owner for all the rendered contents, and the input elements, such as Input, Button, and TextArea, are text edit owners for their contents. For example, you can create a *TextRange* object for the preceding document by calling the *body* object's *createTextRange* method:

```
var tr = document.body.createTextRange();
```

Once a *TextRange* object is created, any of the contents within the object can be freely accessed.

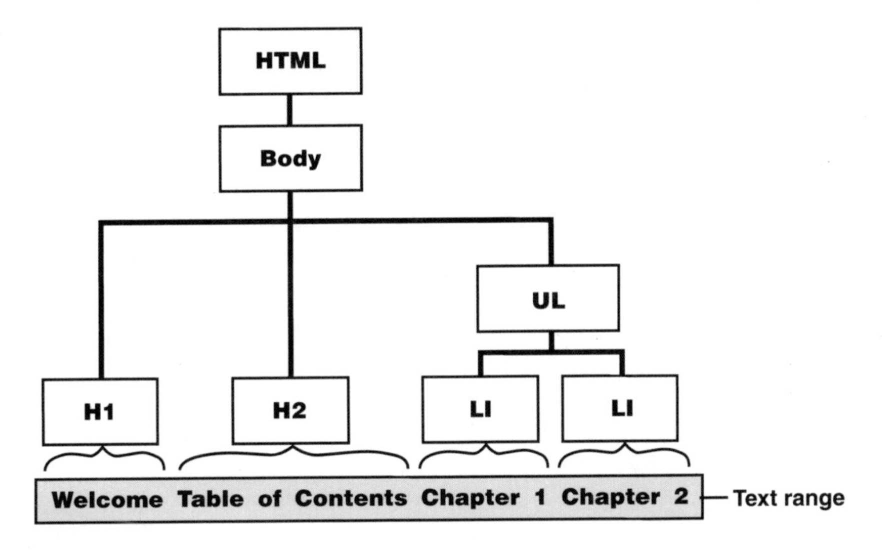

Figure 14-1.
Relationship between the TextRange *object and the document structure.*

Initially, all the text influenced by the text edit owner is spanned by the *TextRange* object. For example, the *TextRange* object in the preceding document spans all the text in the Body element. You can use a *TextRange* object's methods to reposition it to span different text. A *TextRange* object spans the text that is being manipulated or changed. A script can replace the spanned text just as a user can select old text and type in replacement text in a word processor. The section "Executing Commands" later in this chapter introduces methods for manipulating the appearance of the document that are similar to a user selecting a font or changing the style of text in a rich text editor.

The *TextRange* object is designed to be robust enough to automatically accept arbitrary HTML embedded in the document. When new text is inserted into a *TextRange* object, the HTML is also inserted into the document, just as if the user had chosen Paste from an Edit menu and inserted arbitrary text. These operations are powerful, but they are not intended to provide the developer with precise control over the document. Instead, the developer can use these operations to modify the document on a high level without being concerned about the specific HTML code that implements the modifications. The rules governing the HTML code that these operations generate are likely to change for the next release of Microsoft Internet Explorer. Therefore, the *TextRange* object should not be used when the result of an operation requires the HTML to have a particular shape. Instead, the inner and outer properties should be used.

Spanning Text

A *TextRange* object does not specify the text that it spans in terms of the ordinal indexes of the text range's start and end characters. Rather, it specifies the spanned text in a way that is more loosely bound to positions in the document and can survive state changes to the document. For example, if the *TextRange* object spans the entire contents of the document and the contents expand or shrink through another process, the *TextRange* object automatically reflects this change and continues to span the entire contents.

TextRange Limitations

The *TextRange* object currently is very closely tied to characters, which causes ambiguities between the *TextRange* object and the document structure. In many cases in HTML, a single character position cannot accurately represent how the character is influenced by the HTML, as shown here:

```
<P>This is <B><I>bold and italic</I> text.</B></P>
```

In the *TextRange* object, these contents are represented as *This is bold and italic text.* The parent of the letter *b* in the text buffer is the Italic element, and the parent of the Italic element is the Bold element. No character in the word *bold* or the preceding space has the Bold element as its immediate parent. Using the *TextRange* object, you cannot insert boldface but not italic text before the word *bold.* The *TextRange* object is currently based on a single insertion point that can exist either before the letter *b* (which makes the text boldface and italic) or in the space following the word *is* (which makes the text neither boldface nor italic). The *TextRange* object cannot insert text between the <B> and <I> tags. To insert text between the <B> and <I> tags, use the *insertAdjacentText* and *insertAdjacentHTML* methods, introduced in Chapter 13, "Dynamic Contents." These methods can insert text before or after any begin or end tag in the document's body.

Programming the *TextRange* Object

This section introduces the properties and methods available for manipulating the *TextRange* object. The methods allow scripts to manipulate the underlying text in much the same way as a person could edit it with a text editor, selecting text and typing or pasting new text into the document. Viewing the methods this way will help you understand how they work.

Creating a *TextRange* Object

As mentioned, a *TextRange* object is created by calling the *createTextRange* method on an element that is a text edit owner. Like the dynamic contents properties, the *TextRange* object is not available until after the entire document is parsed. During the parsing of the document, any attempt to create a *TextRange* object using the *createTextRange* method fails. Therefore, ensure that the document is entirely loaded before using any method that returns a *TextRange* object.

The *TextRange* object returned by the *createTextRange* method should almost always be assigned to a variable. Otherwise, the *TextRange* object created in memory is immediately destroyed. Here is the right way to create a *TextRange* object:

```
var tr = document.body.createTextRange();
```

And here is the wrong way:

```
document.body.createTextRange(); // This does nothing.
```

The only circumstance in which you don't have to assign a new *TextRange* object to a variable occurs when a sequence of operations can be performed in a single step—for example, when you replace the HTML that the *TextRange* object represents:

```
// Replace the entire body's HTML.
document.body.createTextRange().pasteHTML("<H1>New Document</H1>");
```

The *parentTextEdit* Property

Every element has a property named *parentTextEdit* that references the text edit owner responsible for the element's contents. Using this property can give your code compatibility with future versions of the object model. Currently the *parentTextEdit* properties for most elements in a document reference the Body element. Elements contained within a Button element are the only exceptions; their text edit owner is the Button element. However, future versions of the object model might support more elements as text edit owners. When you create a *TextRange* object for an element, use its *parentTextEdit* property to identify its text edit owner, and your code should still work if the text edit owner changes. The following code illustrates this technique:

```
// el represents an element object in the document.
var tr;
if (!el.isTextEdit)
   tr = el.parentTextEdit.createTextRange();
else
   tr = el.createTextRange();
```

Every element in the body of a document exposes the *isTextEdit* property, which indicates whether the element is a text edit owner. The preceding code uses the element *el* to create a *TextRange* object if *el* is a text edit owner; otherwise, the code uses the parent text edit owner of *el.* The following simple line of code demonstrates that the Body element is a text edit owner:

```
alert(document.body.isTextEdit);  // true; the Body element is a
                                   // text edit owner.
```

Representing the Document's Contents

The *TextRange* object has two properties, *text* and *htmlText,* that provide access to the document's unformatted and formatted text.

The *text* property represents the document's text without any of the HTML markup. This property is read/write and can be used to replace the unformatted contents. The *text* property is similar to the *outerText* property on the element objects in the way it exposes the document's contents and in the types of values that can be assigned to it.

The *htmlText* property represents the text together with the HTML markup. This property represents the HTML the same way the *outerHTML* property represents it, but unlike the *outerHTML* property, the *htmlText* property is read-only. To assign new HTML to the *TextRange* object, you must use the *pasteHTML* method instead. Assigning new HTML is handled by a separate method because it is not symmetric with reading the current HTML. A value you insert into a text range using the *pasteHTML* method might not match the value that is subsequently returned by the *htmlText* property; the *TextRange* object might modify or clean up the HTML you insert, and the HTML might even influence contents beyond the boundaries of the *TextRange* object.

The *pasteHTML* method is designed to insert valid HTML. When you call the *pasteHTML* method on a particular element, the fragment you paste will be within the span of that element, and it should be valid HTML within that span as defined by the DTD (document type definition). The browser will attempt to clean up any HTML that doesn't conform, and it can extend HTML beyond the boundaries originally spanned by the *TextRange* object. When the *pasteHTML* method returns, the *TextRange* object is updated to span the newly inserted text.

text vs. *htmlText*

The primary advantage of using the *text* property over *htmlText* and *pasteHTML* involves the handling of entities representing angle brackets. When you assign a value to a *text* property, the value is parsed as unformatted HTML, so any angle brackets are automatically replaced by the corresponding entities; for example, < is replaced by *<*. When you read a *text* property, entities are returned as their literal values.

When you insert new text in a text range using the *pasteHTML* method, the text is parsed as HTML, so any angle brackets are interpreted as parts of HTML tags. If you want to embed an angle bracket in the text, you must substitute the appropriate entity yourself. When you use the *htmlText* property to retrieve a text range, any angle brackets in the text appear as entities; for example, < is returned as *<*.

White Space

The *text* property of the *TextRange* object represents white space as it is rendered on the screen, not as it is represented in the underlying document. In most cases in HTML, extra white space is ignored. For example, if an HTML document uses three spaces between each word, the text will be displayed with only a single space between each word. In addition, carriage returns inside an HTML document are ignored; block tags determine line breaks.

The exception to these rules is in PRE and XMP elements. In these elements, the existing white space is preserved and any white space later inserted is maintained.

Floating End Tags

You cannot force an existing element in the document to end earlier by inserting a new end tag. For example, suppose a document has this Bold element:

```
<B>This is bold text.</B>
```

If you use a *TextRange* object to insert a new </B> end tag between the words *bold* and *text*, the new tag will not become the end tag for the Bold element.

The *pasteHTML* method does not insert a fragment literally into the tree. Instead, the fragment is validated against the DTD, which specifies that any extra end tags are ignored. So inserting the </B> tag will have no effect on the text or on the document tree.

Invalid Scope

Some HTML elements can validly appear only within the scope of other elements. For example, a TD element is supposed to be contained in a TR element inside a Table element. Chapter 7, "Document Element Collections," describes the parser's rules for handling elements in the source document that are not within their valid scope. Many of the same rules also apply to HTML that is inserted using a *TextRange* object. For example, the following code attempts to replace the document's body with a single TD element:

```
var tr = document.body.createTextRange();
tr.pasteHTML("<TD>Cell outside any table or row</TD>");
```

In this example, the contents are inserted into the document, but the surrounding <TD> tags are ignored because a valid table is not defined. This error handling is not guaranteed to be maintained from version to version of Dynamic HTML; therefore, to ensure predictable results, be careful to supply a proper HTML fragment.

Relating the *TextRange* Object to the Document's Structure

The *TextRange* object has a *parentElement* method that reports the relationship between the text range and the document's structure. This method returns the lowest element in the parsing tree that influences the entire range of text. As illustrated in Figure 14-1 on page 397, every character in the text range is influenced by a leaf node (a node with no children). When a *TextRange* object represents a character, its *parentElement* method returns the leaf node influencing the character. When a *TextRange* object represents a range of characters, its *parentElement* is the node that influences the entire range. When a *TextRange* object is first created on the Body element, it represents all of the text, so its *parentElement* is usually the Body element itself.

Positioning the *TextRange* Object

When a *TextRange* object is first created, it encompasses all of the text influenced by the text edit owner on which it was created. For example, calling the *createTextRange* method on the Body element returns a text range that contains all the contents of the body.

A set of *TextRange* object methods repositions the *TextRange* object to span different text. The underlying architecture for the *TextRange* object is not tied to the ordinal indexes of the characters it spans in the text buffer. You cannot directly manipulate the endpoints of a text range, assigning them new character indexes. Instead, the *TextRange* object move methods reposition the object in ways to facilitate operations on the text. They can position the *TextRange* object to span any character, word, sentence, text edit owner, element, or point on the screen. These methods do not cause any text to be moved around the document. The following list enumerates the methods available for positioning a *TextRange* object:

- *expand(unit)*
- *collapse(start)*
- *moveToElementText(element)*
- *move(unit, count)*
- *moveStart(unit, count)*
- *moveEnd(unit, count)*
- *moveToPoint(x, y)*
- *findText(string, count, flags)*

Two additional methods are available for repositioning the *TextRange* object: *setEndPoint* and *moveToBookmark*. The *setEndPoint* method complements the *compareEndPoints* method. These methods are discussed in the sections "Managing *TextRange* Objects" and "Manipulating Bookmarks" later in this chapter.

The *expand* and *collapse* Methods

The *expand* method expands a *TextRange* object to fully encompass a character, a word, a sentence, or the entire text of the text edit owner on which it was created. For example, if the *TextRange* object spans a portion of a word, calling its *expand* method with the parameter *word* causes it to span the entire word. The *expand* method returns a Boolean value indicating whether the method succeeded.

The *collapse* method performs the reverse operation, placing the *TextRange* object's begin and end markers together as an insertion point. An optional parameter determines whether the insertion point is placed at the beginning or end of the current range; the default value is *true*, which places the insertion point at the beginning.

The *moveToElementText* Method

The *moveToElementText* method positions the *TextRange* object to span the text influenced by an element. Consistent with the behavior of the *TextRange* object, there is no guarantee that assigning a value to the *TextRange* object positioned using *moveToElementText* will change only the element's contents. Instead, if you need to change the contents of an element directly, you should use the inner and outer properties, introduced in Chapter 13, "Dynamic Contents."

The *moveToElementText* method is useful for navigating through the document to perform subsequent manipulations such as analyzing the first word of each header. The *TextRange* object can be easily moved to an element and then repositioned to span just the first word of text in that element without having to parse any strings. The next section focuses on the move methods that can do this.

The *move*, *moveStart*, and *moveEnd* Methods

The *move*, *moveStart*, and *moveEnd* methods reposition the *TextRange* object by a specified amount. The *moveStart* and *moveEnd* methods reposition the begin and end markers of the *TextRange* object. The *move* method repositions the *TextRange* object's begin marker by the specified amount and collapses the object to an insertion point.

Each of the three methods takes the same two parameters. The first parameter specifies whether to move by word, character, or sentence or to the end of the text stream. The second parameter specifies how many units to move. The second parameter can be either a positive or a negative value, which indicates whether to move forward or backward. The first parameter can be any of the following string values:

Unit	Definition
character	Moves by the specified number of characters
word	Moves by the specified number of words
sentence	Moves by the specified number of sentences
textedit	Moves by the specified number of text edit elements

The *move*, *moveStart*, and *moveEnd* methods return the actual number of units that were moved. For example, if you were trying to move 200 words in a 100-word document, the *move* method would reposition the *TextRange* object to the last word in the document and return the number of words moved. To check whether an operation was successful, compare the return value with the number of units moved:

```
if (200 == tr.move("word", 200)) {
   // Success!
}
else {
   // Failed to move 200 words.
}
```

The *move* method positions the *TextRange* object as an insertion point between two characters. For example, calling the *move* method to move forward three words positions the *TextRange* object between the third and fourth words. In this case, the *text* property would return an empty string. Assigning a value to the *text* property or calling the *pasteHTML* method would insert the text into the document at that point.

The *moveStart* and *moveEnd* methods move the start and end character positions. For example, this technique can be used to expand a selection of four words to five words either by moving the start position backward or by moving the end position forward. The following code demonstrates how to obtain the first word of an element in the document:

```
function firstWord(myElement) {
   // Obtain a TextRange object.
   var tr = document.body.createTextRange();
   // Move the TextRange object.
   // myElement represents an element in the document.
   tr.moveToElementText(myElement);
   // Collapse the TextRange object to the beginning of the element.
   tr.collapse();
   if (tr.moveEnd("word", 1))
      return tr.text;
   else
      return "";
}
```

The following example demonstrates how to count the number of words in a document. This code can be easily changed to count other units by changing the first parameter in the *move* method.

```
function countWords() {
   var tr = document.body.createTextRange();
   var intCount = 0;
   // Collapse the TextRange object to the beginning of the document.
   tr.collapse(true);
   while (tr.move("word", 1))
      intCount++;
   return intCount - 1; // Loop moves past last word
}
```

When moving by word or character units, all elements that represent an object, including images, intrinsic controls, and so on, represent a single unit.

> NOTE: The ways these methods reposition the *TextRange* object can be compared with the ways certain keystrokes move the cursor or change text selection in popular word processors such as Microsoft Word. For example, the *move* method repositions the *TextRange* object as an insertion point the same way that the Right and Left arrow keys reposition the cursor in a word processor. Pressing an arrow key moves the cursor one character; holding down the Ctrl key and pressing an arrow key moves the cursor one word. The *moveStart* and *moveEnd* methods expand or contract the text spanned by a *TextRange* object the same way that keystrokes expand or contract selected text. Holding down the Shift key and pressing the Right or Left arrow key causes a selection to expand or contract one character in the specified direction. Holding down the Shift and Ctrl keys causes the selection to expand or contract a word at a time.

The *moveToPoint* Method

The *moveToPoint* method takes a point in the client area of the screen as an argument, determines what item in the document is rendered at that point on the screen, and places the *TextRange* object as an insertion point by that item. This method, when used in a mouse event handler to determine what text the mouse is on, offers finer granularity than the *srcElement* property, which returns the element the mouse pointer is in. The following mouse event handler code displays in the status bar the word the mouse is on:

```
function doMouseMove() {
   var tr = document.body.createTextRange();
   tr.moveToPoint(event.clientX, event.clientY);
   // Expand to the entire word under the mouse.
   tr.expand("word");
   window.status = tr.text;
}
document.onmousemove = doMouseMove;
```

The *findText* Method

The *findText* method locates a specified string in the document. The browser's Find dialog boxes use the *findText* method and can demonstrate the flexibility provided by this method.

The *findText* method takes three parameters. The first parameter is the string to locate in the document. The second parameter represents how many characters to search in the document; the value must be positive for a forward search and negative for a backward search. The third parameter specifies whether an entire word must match the string and whether a match must be case sensitive: pass *2* for full word matching, *4* for case-sensitive searching, and *6* for case-sensitive word matching.

Managing *TextRange* Objects

Methods are available to clone a *TextRange* object, to compare two *TextRange* objects, and to position one *TextRange* object relative to another one.

The *duplicate* Method

The *duplicate* method creates a copy of the *TextRange* object on which it is called. For example, the following code creates a copy of the *TextRange* object named *tr*:

```
var tr2 = tr.duplicate();
```

The *inRange* and *isEqual* Methods

The *inRange* method specifies whether the supplied text range is within the span of the *TextRange* object on which the method is called:

```
alert(tr2.inRange(tr)); // true; tr is within tr2.
```

The *isEqual* method compares two *TextRange* objects to see whether they span the same text. The method is necessary because two *TextRange* objects representing the same range of text can nonetheless be distinct objects, so comparing them directly as objects will not work. The following code demonstrates the right and wrong ways to see whether two objects span the same text:

```
// Set up example.
var tr = document.body.createTextRange();
var tr2 = tr.duplicate();
// Wrong way to compare text ranges:
alert(tr == tr2);        // false; these are two different objects.
// Right way to compare text ranges:
alert(tr.isEqual(tr2)); // true
```

The *compareEndPoints* and *setEndPoint* Methods

The *compareEndPoints* method compares two *TextRange* objects to see whether their start or end positions coincide. The *setEndPoint* method sets the start or end position of one *TextRange* object to the start or end position of another *TextRange* object. Both methods take two parameters. A start or end position of the *TextRange* object on which the method is called is compared with or set to a start or end position of the *TextRange* object specified by the second parameter. The first parameter can take any of the values in the following table, which specify what positions are to be used.

Value	Description
StartToStart	Sets or compares the start position of the current *TextRange* object to the start position of the *TextRange* object specified in the second parameter
StartToEnd	Sets or compares the start position of the current *TextRange* object to the end position of the *TextRange* object specified in the second parameter
EndToEnd	Sets or compares the end position of the current *TextRange* object to the end position of the *TextRange* object specified in the second parameter
EndToStart	Sets or compares the end position of the current *TextRange* object to the start position of the *TextRange* object specified in the second parameter

For example, the following function determines whether the *trDest* object continues where the *trSrc* object leaves off:

```
function continues(trSrc, trDest) {
   return trSrc.compareEndPoints("EndToStart", trDest);
}
```

Scrolling the Range into View

TextRange objects are manipulated entirely in memory. Changing the *text* and *htmlText* properties on the *TextRange* object does not cause the document to scroll. To scroll the text spanned by a *TextRange* object into view, use the same *scrollIntoView* method that all elements support. This method takes a single optional parameter that specifies whether to scroll the text in the *TextRange* object to the top of the screen (*true*) or to the bottom of the screen (*false*).

Manipulating Bookmarks

A bookmark represents a *TextRange* object's position in the text, similar to an HTML bookmark representing a position in a document. You can use a *TextRange* object's *getBookmark* method to save a record of the object's current position as a bookmark and its *moveToBookmark* method to return to a saved position.

The *getBookmark* method returns a bookmark as a string value. Like *TextRange*, a bookmark does not record start and end positions as character indexes. Rather, the bookmark is a string that contains the position information in an encoded form. The string is not meant to be manipulated directly and should be used only with *TextRange* methods.

The *moveToBookmark* method takes a bookmark string as a parameter and positions the *TextRange* object according to the bookmark. This method returns a Boolean value that indicates whether the operation is successful.

You could make one *TextRange* object's position match a second *TextRange* object's position by calling the first object's *moveToBookmark* method and passing it the bookmark returned by the second object's *getBookmark* method. However, a more direct way to copy a bookmark is to use the *duplicate* method.

Embedded Objects

Embedded objects are the HTML elements that represent intrinsic controls, Object elements, images, and so on. Each embedded object is represented by a space in the *TextRange* object. To determine whether a space in a *TextRange* object actually represents an embedded object, obtain another *TextRange* object that spans just the space and check the *parentElement* method.

To add an embedded object to the *TextRange* object, insert the appropriate HTML into the document using the *pasteHTML* method. Once the assignment is made and the HTML is parsed, the text in the *TextRange* object is automatically updated with a space to represent the newly instantiated embedded object.

Selecting the Text Range

The *TextRange* object exposes a *select* method that makes the text spanned by the object the user's current selection. When a *TextRange* object is selected, the text it spans is selected on the screen. Subsequently extending the *TextRange* object does not extend the selection unless you call the *select* method again.

Accessing the User's Selection

User selection is closely related to the *TextRange* object. The document's *selection* property references an object that exposes the current selection in the browser to scripts. This *selection* object also exposes a *type* property that returns the type of the selection: *None* for no selection and *Text* for a text-based selection. When text is selected on the screen, the selection object's *createRange* method returns a *TextRange* object that spans the selected text. Repositioning this *TextRange* object will not change what text is selected on the screen, but changes made to the text by the *TextRange* object will of course be reflected on the screen. To change the selection on the screen to match a *TextRange* object, you can call the *TextRange* object's *select* method. For example, the following code uses a *TextRange* object to extend the selection on the screen by one word:

```
if ("Text" == document.selection.type) {
   var tr = document.selection.createRange();
   // Move the end position to include one more word.
   tr.moveEnd("word", 1);
   // Reselect the range.
   tr.select();
}
else
   alert("No text is selected.");
```

Always test the type of the selection before you do any manipulating because the browser supports a second type of object, called a *ControlRange*, for selecting multiple controls. Because multiple controls are currently not selectable when you are browsing a document, the *ControlRange* object is not discussed here.

Executing Commands

The Dynamic HTML object model exposes a set of methods that allow user operations to be executed directly on a range or on the document. These operations correspond to different actions the user can perform on the text. For example, there are commands for making text boldface or not boldface, similar to a Bold toggle button in a text editor. These commands modify the underlying HTML to achieve the desired result. Currently all style manipulations occur by inserting the presentational HTML markup into the document. There are no guarantees that the commands will perform style manipulations this way in future releases of the browser. The only guarantee is that the commands will still create the same visible end results.

These commands enable a page to manipulate the document style and contents without worrying about the HTML structural rules. For example, when the Bold command is invoked, appropriate HTML is automatically generated. Commands are also available for performing other basic user operations, such as cutting and copying text, adding controls to a fixed region, and undoing the last operation.

TextRange objects and the *document* object expose a number of methods for executing and querying the status of commands. These methods fall into two categories: those that return the status of a command and those that execute a command. The six available methods for determining a command's status are shown here:

- *queryCommandSupported(cmdID)*
- *queryCommandEnabled(cmdID)*
- *queryCommandState(cmdID)*
- *queryCommandIndeterm(cmdID)*
- *queryCommandText(cmdID, text)*
- *queryCommandValue(cmdID)*

These methods are best understood in the context of a text editor's user interface. The *queryCommandSupported* and *queryCommandEnabled* methods return Boolean values reporting whether the specified command is supported by the object and whether it is currently available. If a command is disabled, executing the command has no effect on the document. The *queryCommandState* method indicates whether the specified command has been carried out on the object; for example, calling this method with the parameter *Bold* returns *true* if the object spans boldface text, *false* if not, and *null* if the method cannot determine the state. The *queryCommandIndeterm* method indicates whether the state of the command is available. For example, if a *TextRange* object spans both boldface text and plain text, this method returns *true* because the actual bold state is unavailable.

The *queryCommandText* and *queryCommandValue* methods provide further information about a command. The *queryCommandText* method returns a short menu string or a longer status bar string that describes the function. Because the texts of these strings may vary among browsers, you should not write code that relies on a particular string being returned. The *queryCommandValue* method returns the actual value of the command. For example, calling this method with the parameter *FontName* returns the name of the font.

None of the preceding methods have any effect on the document; they simply return information about the current state. To interact with the document, the following two methods are exposed:

- *execCommand(cmdID [, displayUI] [, value])*
- *execCommandShowHelp(cmdID)*

The *execCommand* method executes a command. The *cmdID* argument represents the command to invoke and is required. The optional *displayUI* parameter specifies whether to display or hide any corresponding user interface. By default, any associated user interface is not displayed. In some cases, bypassing the user interface would create a security concern, so the *displayUI* argument is ignored and the user interface is always displayed. For example, invoking the Print command will not print the document without first alerting the user. The *value* attribute supplies a value to the command. The *execCommandShowHelp* method displays the help file if one is supported for the specified command.

The following code, which analyzes a document in order to determine how many fonts are displayed, illustrates how the *queryCommandValue* method can be used:

```
<SCRIPT LANGUAGE="JavaScript">
   function walkDocument() {
      var fonts = new Array();
      var tr = document.body.createTextRange();
      tr.collapse();
      while (tr.moveEnd("character", 1)) {
         var val = tr.queryCommandValue("FontName");
         if (null == fonts[val]) {
            fonts[val] = true;
            fonts.length++
         }
         tr.collapse(false);
      }
      var settings = "Total Fonts: " + fonts.length + "\n";
      for (var font in fonts) {
         settings += "   " + font + "\n";
      }
      alert(settings);
   }
</SCRIPT>
```

The companion CD contains a list of all the available commands and the types of values they accept and return.

CHAPTER FIFTEEN

Data Binding with HTML

Until the arrival of data binding, accessing data via Web pages was slow. (And the Internet has become slower as traffic has increased—especially if you're limited to a 28.8-Kbps modem.) Pages that accessed data were slow to render. This was due, in large part, to servers not only supplying Web pages but also being tasked with accessing the database and merging the data with the page to create a complete HTML page for the client. Moreover, once that page was transmitted to the client there was no way for the client to differentiate between the data and the HTML that contained it. As a result, when users wanted to manipulate the data—for example, to sort it in a different order—they needed to make another request to the server. Such a request would result in the server accessing the same data again, formatting it differently, and transmitting the new page to the client. The server would once again transmit the same data embedded in the HTML page to the client. Some servers were also required to maintain client state to ensure that data was consistently displayed to the user. All these factors resulted in a user experience equivalent to mainframe terminals in terms of interactivity. Fortunately, all this has changed.

Enter data binding. Data binding is a feature of Dynamic HTML that solves many of these problems. Data binding maintains the distinction between the data and the HTML that displays it. Data is transmitted to the client asynchronously and rendered asynchronously as it arrives, much like a progressively rendered GIF. Because the client is able to differentiate the data, it can perform manipulations, such as sorting, on the client without a round-trip to the server. This autonomy reduces the number of server hits and the amount of data transmitted. Web pages built using data binding display data more quickly, remove the burden of formatting from the server, and provide a more interactive, responsive experience to the user by eliminating long waiting periods between pages.

The goal of this chapter is to give you enough information to build an HTML page using data binding as well as to provide a reference as you build data-bound pages. The following topics are covered in this chapter:

- **What is data binding?** Data binding is a concept introduced in Dynamic HTML. This section defines the term *binding* and introduces the concepts that will be explored in the remainder of this chapter.
- **Data-binding architecture** This section discusses the three components of the data-binding architecture: data source objects, HTML data-binding extensions, and the binding and repetition agent. Data source objects supply data to Web pages and encapsulate the functions of transmission, specification, manipulation, and script access. The HTML data-binding extensions are attributes that can be included on HTML elements. Elements that include data-binding attributes are called data consumers. The attributes specify the data source object that supplies data to the element. The binding and repetition agent recognizes data source objects and data consumers on a Web page and synchronizes data transfers between the HTML elements and the data source.
- **Data consumers: HTML elements** A large number of HTML elements support data binding. This section provides a list of these elements and explains how they are used to display and allow user interaction with the data supplied by a data source object. This section also provides examples that demonstrate how to bind each supported HTML element.
- **Building basic pages using data binding** This section discusses the three basic types of binding: current record binding, repeated table binding, and paged table binding. Current record binding displays data from the current record in bound elements. You can use a script to change which record in the data set is current. When a new record becomes current, the bound elements are updated to show data from that record. Repeated table binding allows the Web author to repeat a set of HTML elements, called a template, to build a table that displays all the rows in a data set. Paged table binding is similar to repeated table binding except that it allows the Web author to limit the number of records displayed in the table. The paged table can be thought of as a window into the data set. Using scripts, the Web author can then move this window around the data set to display additional data.

- **Writing scripts using data binding** As part of the data-binding functionality, a rich event model is provided to Web authors for writing applications. Events are provided for validation, record movement, and asynchronous data transmission. This section also describes the basics of accessing data from a data source object using ADO (ActiveX Data Objects).
- **Advanced features** This section gives a brief overview of a number of advanced features of data binding, including data updates, the *recordNumber* property, and object model access to the data-binding attributes. This section discusses how a Web page can be made into a client/server application by enabling data updates. The *recordNumber* property, available from every element in a repeated or paged table, allows the Web author to easily determine to which record from the data source object the element is bound. The remainder of the section discusses adding, deleting, and modifying data-binding attributes on elements using the Dynamic HTML object model.

What Is Data Binding?

Before we discuss the three components of the data binding architecture, let's explain what is meant by the term *binding*. Simply put, a binding expresses the relationship between the data supplied by a data source object and the HTML consumer of the data. This relationship is called a binding because the value of the *datem* (short for data item) is synchronized between the client and the server. When an HTML consumer—for example, an HTML text box—modifies a datem, the modified datem is saved back to the data source object. Conversely, if the data source object changes the data value, the modified datem is sent to the data consumer. Generalizing further, multiple consumers can be bound to the same datem, and all values of all consumers are synchronized to the value supplied by the data source object. Values in the data source object are bound to the values in one or more data consumers.

Two distinct styles of binding are available: *current record binding* and *repeated table binding*. Current record binding uses HTML elements to display data from a single record from the data set—the current record. A different record can then be made current, in which case—the elements are updated dynamically to display the data from that record. Repeated table binding lets you specify a set of bound elements, called a template, that is repeated once for each record in the data set. Web authors also have the option of limiting the number of records repeated in the table, a feature known as table paging. Table paging and the two binding styles will be discussed in detail in the section "Building Basic Pages Using Data Binding" later in this chapter.

Data-Binding Architecture

The data-binding architecture consists of three major components: data source objects, HTML data-binding extensions that define data consumers, and the binding and repetition agent. Data source objects supply data to the page, and HTML data consumers display the data and provide ways for the user to interact with the data. The binding and repetition agent provides support for the two styles of bindings. Additionally, the binding and repetition agent is responsible for synchronizing all bindings to a single datem when users modify the data on the page.

Data Source Objects

Data source objects provide an open architecture for supplying data to a Web page. Data source objects are inserted in a Web page using either an <APPLET> tag or an <OBJECT> tag, as shown here:

```
<OBJECT ID="stocklist" WIDTH="0" HEIGHT="0"
      CLASSID="clsid:333C7BC4-460F-11D0-BC04-0080C7055A83">
   <PARAM NAME="DataURL" VALUE="stockdata.txt">
   <PARAM NAME="FieldDelim" VALUE="|">
   <PARAM NAME="TextQualifier" VALUE="">
   <PARAM NAME="UseHeader" VALUE="true">
</OBJECT>
```

Once a data source object has been inserted on a page, data consumers can be defined to display the data and interact with the user.

Data source objects can be implemented in a variety of programming languages, including Java, Microsoft Visual Basic, and Microsoft Visual C++. Data source objects are responsible for four major functions of data access:

- Transporting data to and from the page—Data source objects must implement the mechanisms for retrieving data for an HTML page. Data source objects are solely responsible for transporting the data to the client and, optionally, transporting modifications of the data by the client back to the server. They can transport this information in any manner they see fit—using HTTP (hypertext transfer protocol), FTP (file transfer protocol), local file access, or connection-based database protocols. Dynamic HTML does not place any constraints on the transporting of data.

Most well-authored data source objects will support asynchronous data delivery—that is, the data source object will expose the data incrementally as it is transmitted to the client rather than waiting for the entire data set to be present before exposing the data. Because the Microsoft Internet Explorer 4.0 browser supports incremental display of bound data, use of a data source object that supports asynchronous delivery will result in the data being displayed and available for interaction with the user sooner, much like an interlaced GIF is displayed incrementally.

- Supplying the mechanism for specifying the data to be transferred—Because data source objects are responsible for the transfer of data, they are similarly responsible for the mechanism that specifies what data is to be transferred (accessed). Data source objects are free to use a query language of their choice, URLs, paths to files, other processes, other objects, or any other means of specifying data that is compatible with the protocol they utilize for accessing the data.
- Providing methods for manipulating the data on the client—Data source objects can support properties and methods for manipulating the data they supply. For example, the data source objects included with Internet Explorer 4.0 support properties and methods for sorting and filtering the data that they supply. When you set these properties or call these methods from a script, the data source object performs the manipulation and, through notification interfaces with the binding and repetition agent, informs the browser that the data has been modified. The browser in turn redisplays the bound data to reflect the current order (for sorting) or the new, reduced or expanded data set (for filtering).

  Data source objects can also support data updating. The data source object can allow the user to change the values of bound HTML elements on the Web page. The data source object transmits the changed data back to its source, usually a database or a Web server, where the changes will be saved. The RDS (Remote Data Service) is one such data source object. RDS is included with minimal configurations of Internet Explorer 4.0. More information about RDS can be obtained from the Microsoft Web site at www.microsoft.com/data.

  Sorting, filtering, and updating aren't the only manipulations supported by data source objects. A data source object can support any manipulation appropriate to the type of data it supplies. For example, a data source object that provides an amortization schedule for a loan might expose three properties: interest rate, loan amount, and duration. Whenever any of these properties are modified, the data source object would generate a different data set because a change to the values will change the amortization schedule for the loan.

- Providing an object model for script access to data (referred to as a data object model)—In general, data binding requires little or no script to build basic pages unless you need to perform validation, calculations, or data manipulations.

  Internet Explorer 4.0 provides the ADO object model for every data source object. However, data source objects can optionally expose their own additional object model in circumstances in which the data exposed does not lend itself to access using ADO. An example of a data source object that must expose its own data object model is the XML (Extensible Markup Language) data source object; see the Microsoft Web site at www.microsoft.com/standards/xml for more information.

HTML Data-Binding Extensions

Data from data source objects is displayed to the user using standard HTML elements. The key to these elements displaying the data is the inclusion of one or more of the HTML data-binding extensions.

> NOTE: The data-binding extensions have been proposed to the W3C (World Wide Web Consortium) for inclusion in the HTML standard.

The data-binding extensions are four new attributes that can be included on a wide variety of HTML elements. The attributes specify the data source object that supplies the data to the element, what column or field of the data source object to bind, whether the data is plain text or should be interpreted as HTML, and, for repeated tables, whether the table should display only a subset of the data supplied by the data source object. The following sections discuss these attributes in detail. For a complete listing of elements that support the data-binding attributes, see the section "Data Consumers: HTML Elements" later in this chapter.

OLE-DB Simple Provider

In general, a data source object will read its data into an in-memory cache on the client. The data source object must then have a way to expose the data in this cache to the browser. Data source objects do this by implementing either the OSP (OLE-DB Simple Provider) interface or directly through OLE-DB, which is a set of OLE interfaces for accessing data.

For the initial release, Internet Explorer 4.0 will support all data source objects implementing OSP. The RDS included with Internet Explorer 4.0 is the only supported OLE-DB provider for Internet Explorer 4.0. Support for arbitrary OLE-DB providers will be added in future releases, but this section will discuss only OSP.

OSP is an open specification and is compatible with both JavaBeans (the component model for Java) and OLE. OSP provides a simple interface for exposing data in the client-side cache. In most circumstances, the client-side cache can be viewed as an array or a set of tabular data—that is, a data set made up of rows, in which each row has the same number of columns. OSP provides access to this array of data one cell at a time. OSP supports the capability to add and delete rows; it also requires the data source object to fire notifications when cells are modified or when rows are added and deleted. These notifications are used by the Internet Explorer 4.0 binding and repetition agent to keep each bound element synchronized with the current record's data values. Data source objects that expose OSP can be implemented in Java, Microsoft Visual Basic 5.0, and Microsoft Visual C++ using MFC (Microsoft Foundation Classes) or, preferably, ATL (Application Transaction Language) 2.0.

The DATASRC Attribute

The DATASRC attribute indicates the data source object that supplies the data. DATASRC is set to #*<IDref>* where *<IDref>* is the ID of the data source object. Using the earlier example under "Data Source Objects," the DATASRC attribute pointing to the *stocklist* object would be expressed as follows:

```
DATASRC=#stocklist
```

In general, the DATASRC attribute is not used alone; it is combined with the DATAFLD attribute. However, there is one exception to this rule: repeated tables. Repeated tables use only the DATASRC attribute because the binding on a repeated table indicates only the source of repetition. Bound HTML elements inside the table display and interact with the actual data.

The DATAFLD Attribute

Data source objects expose their data as a tabular set consisting of multiple rows with a fixed number of columns. The data source object gives the columns names that can be referenced through the OSP interface. The definition of column names is the responsibility of the data source object. The DATAFLD attribute indicates the named column or field that is to be bound from the data source object.

In general, the DATAFLD attribute must be accompanied by DATASRC. However, for an element within a repeated table, DATASRC is omitted because it is inherited from the DATASRC attribute on the Table element. See the section "Repeated Table Binding" later in this chapter for more information.

The DATAFORMATAS Attribute

The DATAFORMATAS attribute specifies the format of the data supplied by a data source object. DATAFORMATAS can take one of three values: *NONE*, *TEXT*, and *HTML*. The default value is *NONE*. When *NONE* is specified (or when the attribute is not included), the data source object is asked for the native type required by the data consumer—almost always text for HTML elements. When *TEXT* is specified, the data source object is asked specifically for a text value, regardless of the underlying data type of the column. For example, if the data source object supplied a column of type integer, it would be required to convert those integers to strings when DATAFORMATAS was specified as *TEXT*.

Most important, when DATAFORMATAS has the value *HTML*, the data supplied by the data source object is interpreted as HTML rather than as plain text. The data is parsed, and any HTML elements within it are rendered as if they were present directly on the Web page. By setting DATAFORMATAS to *HTML*, you can store HTML in your data rather than storing it statically on your page.

The DATAPAGESIZE Attribute

The DATAPAGESIZE attribute is specific to a repeated table. It gives the Web author the flexibility to limit the length of a repeated table, and hence the overall length of a data-bound page. It takes positive integers as its value, and it must be used in conjunction with the DATASRC attribute.

If the DATAPAGESIZE attribute is not specified, the table's template is repeated for every record supplied by the data source object. Including DATA-PAGESIZE on a table limits the number of times the template is repeated to the value specified. The rows displayed in the table can then be scrolled using methods from the Dynamic HTML object model on the Table element.

Binding and Repetition Agent

The third component of the data-binding architecture is the binding and repetition agent—called the binding agent for short. The binding agent is a built-in component of Internet Explorer 4.0. It is responsible for interpreting the data-binding attributes and then actually supplying the data from a data source object to the data consumers. To achieve this, the binding agent performs a number of tasks. First the binding agent recognizes data source objects and data consumers included on a page or added dynamically to the page using the Dynamic HTML object model. The binding agent keeps track of what data source objects are available and to which columns of the data source object the data consumers are bound.

The binding agent also performs the appropriate processing as determined by the type of binding expressed. For current record binding, the binding agent supplies data from the current record to the data consumers. When a new record becomes current, the binding agent updates the data consumers with the data from the new current record. For repeated table bindings, the binding agent repeats the table's template for each record supplied by the data source object. Individual bound elements within the table are supplied values from the appropriate column for each record in the data source object.

Another function of the binding agent is to keep the data synchronized between data consumers and data source objects. This is actually a dual function. The binding agent monitors data source objects and detects changes to data by handling notifications; when data to which an HTML element is bound changes, the binding agent propagates the changes to the bound element. Likewise, when a user changes a bound element's value by interacting with the page, the binding agent propagates the change back to the data source object.

Last, the binding agent is responsible for firing script events for the data source objects and data consumers. Events are provided on data consumers to allow page authors to write scripts that validate user input or that respond to actions taken by the user, such as changing which record is current. More details on the available script events can be found in the section, "Writing Scripts Using Data Binding" later in this chapter.

Data Consumers: HTML Elements

Data binding uses standard HTML elements to present data to the user. These elements include HTML Form elements, basic HTML constructs such as Anchors and Images, more esoteric constructs such as Objects and Applets, simple containers for other HTML elements such as DIV and Span, and Tables for repeating items from a data set. This section provides a detailed explanation of each data consumer, beginning with the basic consumers and continuing to the more complex elements.

The DIV and Span Elements

DIV and Span are simple containers for text or for other HTML elements. Because DIV and Span are block elements (they have begin and end tags), binding them binds their contents. Both DIV and Span support the DATAFORMATAS attribute and can be bound to HTML data in the column of a data source object. Neither element can have its contents modified by the viewer of the page; therefore, the bindings to the DIV and Span are also read-only.

NOTE: Data can still be modified through the data object model. In this case, changes to the data from a script will be reflected in bound DIVs and Spans.

The following code demonstrates a bound DIV and a bound Span:

```
<DIV DATASRC=#stocklist DATAFLD="Symbol" DATAFORMATAS=TEXT></DIV>
<SPAN DATASRC=#stocklist DATAFLD="ChangeF" DATAFORMATAS=HTML></SPAN>
```

The Input Element

The types of Input elements supported by data binding are listed here:

- TYPE=TEXT—Data binding enables binding to the VALUE attribute of the text box and, in keeping with the text box's normal mode of operation, allows the user to edit the value. Changes made to the item are stored in the data source object. An example of how to bind a text box control is shown here:

  ```
  <INPUT TYPE=TEXT DATASRC=#stocklist DATAFLD="Shares">
  ```

- TYPE=RADIO—Data binding binds the VALUE attribute from a group of radio buttons having the same NAME attribute. The DATASRC and DATAFLD attributes must be included on all the radio buttons in the group. If the bound value from the data source does not match any of the values of the bound radio buttons, no radio buttons are selected. When the user selects a radio button, the corresponding value is stored in the data source object.

An example of a group of data-bound radio buttons is shown here:

```
<INPUT TYPE=RADIO VALUE=S DATASRC=#stocklist
   DATAFLD="Type">Short
<INPUT TYPE=RADIO VALUE=L DATASRC=#stocklist
   DATAFLD="Type">Long
```

- TYPE=CHECKBOX—The data-bound behavior of a check box differs significantly from its behavior within an HTML form. Data-bound check boxes bind a Boolean value, not the VALUE attribute of the check box. A data-bound check box always provides a value of *True* or *False*.

  An example of a data-bound check box is shown here:

```
<INPUT TYPE=CHECKBOX DATASRC=#stocklist DATAFLD="ExDiv">
```

- TYPE=HIDDEN—A data-bound hidden element is useful only in hybrid pages that use data binding in conjunction with a Submit button. A data-bound hidden element has its VALUE attribute bound. When an HTML form that contains a data-bound hidden element is submitted, the hidden element's value will be sent to the server.

  An example of a data-bound hidden element is shown here:

```
<INPUT TYPE=HIDDEN DATASRC=#stocklist DATAFLD="DateUpdated">
```

- TYPE=PASSWORD—Data-bound password fields have exactly the same data-binding behavior as data-bound text boxes. Their VALUE attribute is bound and the value typed by the user is stored in the data source object.

NOTE: The Input elements do not require an enclosing Form element when used for data binding. No Submit button is required either.

The TextArea Element

Data binding a TextArea element binds the complete text of the multiline text box to a single column.

An example of a data-bound TextArea element is shown here:

```
<TEXTAREA DATASRC=#stocklist DATAFLD="News">
```

The Marquee Element

As with the DIV and Span elements, binding to a Marquee element binds the contents of the element. You can optionally add the DATAFORMATAS=HTML attribute to indicate that the bound data is HTML. If you do so, the data will be parsed and rendered by the browser.

An example of a data-bound Marquee element is shown here:

```
<MARQUEE DATASRC=#stocklist DATAFLD="Last" DATAFORMATAS=HTML>
</MARQUEE>
```

The Select Element

A data-bound Select element allows the binding of a single selected value from a list. The VALUE attribute of the Option element corresponding to the selection is the value stored in the bound column of the data source object. When the value in the data source object does not correspond to any values specified on an Option element in the Select element, no values are selected. Data-bound Select elements can use either the drop-down list or the combo box user interface, depending on setting of the SIZE attribute. The MULTIPLE attribute is ignored on data-bound Select elements because it is not possible to bind an element to more than one value from a single column.

An example of a data-bound combo box is shown here:

```
<SELECT DATASRC=#stocklist DATAFLD="Type">
   <OPTION VALUE=L>Long
   <OPTION VALUE=S>Short
</SELECT>
```

A data-bound drop-down list would use the following Select element:

```
<SELECT SIZE=2 DATASRC=#stocklist DATAFLD="Type">
   <OPTION VALUE=L>Long
   <OPTION VALUE=S>Short
</SELECT>
```

Although the list of options for the Select element cannot be bound directly to a data source object, it is possible, through a script, to populate the options of the Select element from a data source object. The following code illustrates this technique:

```
<!-- Data source object to supply the Select element options -->
<OBJECT ID="selectlist" WIDTH="0" HEIGHT="0"
      CLASSID="clsid:333C7BC4-460F-11D0-BC04-0080C7055A83">
   <PARAM NAME="DataURL" VALUE="selectdata.txt">
   <PARAM NAME="UseHeader" VALUE="True">
</OBJECT>
```

```
<!-- List to be populated -->
<SELECT ID=typeselect>
</SELECT>

<SCRIPT FOR=window EVENT=onload() LANGUAGE="JavaScript">
   var i, newop;

   selectlist.recordset.MoveFirst();
   for (i = 1; i <= selectlist.recordset.AbsolutePosition; i++) {
      newop = document.createElement("option");
      newop.value = selectlist.recordset("value");
      newop.text = selectlist.recordset("display");
      typeselect.add(newop);
      selectlist.recordset.MoveNext();
   }
</SCRIPT>
```

The handler for the window *onload* event reads through the data from the data source object and adds an option for each record in the data to the Select element. The *MoveFirst* method and *AbsolutePosition* property are explained in the sections "Move Methods" and "The *recordNumber* Property," respectively, later in this chapter.

The IMG Element

Data binding supports binding the SRC attribute of the Img element. The value supplied by the binding should be a URL to the image file to be displayed. The URL can be either an absolute URL or a relative URL. When it is a relative URL, either the base URL for the document or the URL specified in a <BASE> tag is used to construct the full URL to retrieve the image file. The downloading of the image file proceeds as if the IMG element were statically defined within the document—that is, the image data is downloaded using the threads available to the browser.

An example of a data-bound IMG element is shown here:

```
<IMG DATASRC=#stocklist DATAFLD="Chart">
```

The Anchor Element

Like the IMG element, binding to the HREF attribute of an Anchor element is supported in Dynamic HTML. The bound value is expected to be either a relative or an absolute URL. The same rules apply to the URL of the Anchor element as apply to the Img element.

An example of a data-bound Anchor element is shown here:

```
<A DATASRC=#stocklist DATAFLD="Website">...</A>
```

You can include bound text for an Anchor element by using the anchor in combination with other elements, such as a Span element. Here the symbol for the stock in our example is used as a hyperlink to the company's Web site:

```
<A DATASRC=#stocklist DATAFLD="Website">
   <SPAN DATASRC=#stocklist DATAFLD="Symbol"></SPAN>
</A>
```

The Button Element

It is possible to bind the contents of the Button element by including the DATASRC and DATAFLD attributes on the element. The face of the button will display the bound text. The DATAFORMATAS attribute can also be included on the binding to display HTML on the face of the button.

An example of a data-bound Button element is shown here:

```
<BUTTON DATASRC=#stocklist DATAFLD="Chart" DATAFORMATAS=HTML></BUTTON>
```

The Label Element

Binding a Label element is similar to binding a Button element. The contents of the Label element are bound, and the binding can contain HTML. One word of caution: Label elements cannot be used within a repeated table. Because a Label element is associated with a control by setting its FOR attribute to the ID of the associated control, it is not possible to uniquely assign a Label element to a single control in a repeated table.

The Object and Applet Elements

You can also bind an arbitrary number of properties of ActiveX controls and Java applets. To bind a property of an Object or Applet element, you include the DATASRC and DATAFLD attributes on the <PARAM> tag that specifies the name of the property to bind. This example shows bindings to the foreground and background colors of the control or applet:

```
<APPLET CODE=myapplet.class>
   <PARAM NAME="backcolor" VALUE="green"
      DATASRC="#dsc1" DATAFLD="color">
   <PARAM NAME="forecolor" VALUE="yellow"
      DATASRC="#dsc1" DATAFLD="textcolor">
   ⋮
</APPLET>
```

To bind to Java applets, the Applet element must be implemented according to the JavaBeans specifications for properties—that is, there should be corresponding public *get* and *set* methods for the property specified by the NAME attribute of the <PARAM> tag. As with ActiveX controls, the Applet element is not required to implement property change notifications.

Object elements (ActiveX controls) work exactly the same way as Applet elements. An example of a data-bound Object element is shown here:

```
<OBJECT CLSID="...">
   <PARAM NAME="backcolor" VALUE="blue"
      DATASRC="#dsc1" DATAFLD="color">
   <PARAM NAME="forecolor" VALUE="white"
      DATASRC="#dsc1" DATAFLD="textcolor">
   ⋮
</OBJECT>
```

An ActiveX control must support a property whose name is specified by the NAME attribute of the <PARAM> tag. Most ActiveX controls fire notifications when the value of a property changes. However, data binding does not require the control to fire these notifications.

ActiveX controls can specify a default property for binding by setting the *DefaultBind* flag in the type information for the property. Data binding supports binding to this default property by setting the DATASRC and DATAFLD attributes directly on the Object element:

```
<OBJECT CLSID="..." DATASRC="#dsc1" DATAFLD="text">
   <PARAM NAME="backcolor" VALUE="blue"
      DATASRC="#dsc1" DATAFLD="color">
   <PARAM NAME="forecolor" VALUE="white"
      DATASRC="#dsc1" DATAFLD="textcolor">
   ⋮
</OBJECT>
```

Notice that you can mix default binding with any number of Param element bindings.

The Frame and IFrame Elements

You can bind the HREF attributes of both Frame and IFrame elements. In both cases, the bound data should supply a URL. The bindings differ in that IFrame elements can exist in any page. An IFrame element can be used like any other element that supports data binding simply by adding the DATASRC and DATAFLD attributes:

```
<IFRAME DATASRC=#stocklist DATAFLD="Website">
```

On the other hand, a Frame element must exist within a Frameset element and not within the body of an HTML document. To take advantage of Frame binding, the data source object must be placed within the Head element of the HTML document that contains the Frameset element:

```
<HTML>
   <HEAD>
      <OBJECT ID="stocklist" WIDTH="0" HEIGHT="0"
            CLASSID="clsid:333C7BC4-460F-11D0-BC04-0080C7055A83">
         <PARAM NAME="DataURL" VALUE="stockdata.txt">
         <PARAM NAME="FieldDelim" VALUE="|">
         <PARAM NAME="TextQualifier" VALUE="">
         <PARAM NAME="UseHeader" VALUE="true">
      </OBJECT>
   </HEAD>
   <FRAMESET>
      <FRAME DATASRC=#stocklist DATAFLD="Website">
   </FRAMESET>
</HTML>
```

Binding to the Frame element is useful when you want to enable the user to view a list of URLs in sequence. A current record binding is used with the Frame element, and as the current record is moved, the Frame element displays data from the new URL supplied by the data source object. Frame elements cannot be used within a repeated table.

The Table Element

The last supported data consumer is the Table element. The Table element is a special data consumer in that it is a container for other bindings rather than a binding itself. A binding on a Table element specifies that the contents of the table, excluding the THead and TFoot elements, is to be repeated over the data set specified by the DATASRC attribute:

```
<TABLE DATASRC=#stocklist>
   ⋮
</TABLE>
```

When the contents of the table are repeated, a bound element within the Table element takes its data from the current record and from subsequent records in the data source. For example, the following table displays a list of all the stock symbols—with their last quote, change, and volume—from a data source named *stocklist*:

```
<TABLE ID="stocktbl" DATASRC="#stocklist" BORDER=1>
   <THEAD>
```

```
      <TR ONCLICK="sort();">
         <TD CLASS=thd><DIV ID=Symbol>Symbol</DIV></TD>
         <TD CLASS=thd><DIV ID=Last>Last</DIV></TD>
         <TD CLASS=thd><DIV ID=Change>Change</DIV></TD>
         <TD CLASS=thd><DIV ID=Volume>Volume</DIV></TD>
      </TR>
   </THEAD>

   <TBODY>
      <TR>
         <TD><A DATAFLD="Website">
            <SPAN DATAFLD="Symbol"></SPAN></A>
         </TD>
         <TD ALIGN=right>
            <DIV DATAFLD="Last"></DIV>
         </TD>
         <TD ALIGN=right>
            <SPAN DATAFLD="ChangeF" DATAFORMATAS=HTML></SPAN>
         </TD>
         <TD ALIGN=right><DIV DATAFLD="Volume"></DIV></TD>
      </TR>
   </TBODY>
</TABLE>
```

Figure 15-1 shows the resulting table.

Repeated Table Data Binding - Microsoft Internet Expl...

File Edit View Go Favorites Help

Repeated Table

Symbol	Last	Change	Volume
aapl	19.19	1.69	4302800
amzn	29	0.25	299000
csco	79.81	0.25	5469200
ibm	104.75	-1.00	4000800
intc	93.63	1.81	21846700
msft	140.63	-0.75	7364100
nscp	37.63	0.94	1768800
orcl	54.88	0.44	4345400
sunw	45.06	-0.63	5014000
yhoo	55.25	-1.25	829600

My Computer

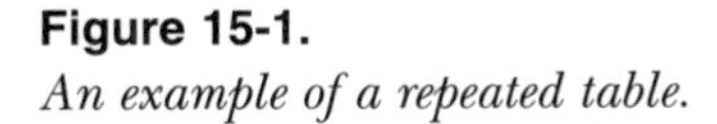

Figure 15-1.
An example of a repeated table.

Table 15-1 lists the data consumers, the data-binding attributes they support, and whether they support data updates.

Tag	Bound Attribute	DATA-SRC	DATA-FLD	DATA-FORMATAS	DATA-PAGESIZE	Data Updates
<DIV>	Contents	✔	✔	✔		
<SPAN>	Contents	✔	✔	✔		
<INPUT TYPE=TEXT>	VALUE	✔	✔			✔
<INPUT TYPE=RADIO>	VALUE	✔	✔			✔
<INPUT TYPE=CHECKBOX>	Boolean corresponding to checked state	✔	✔			✔
<INPUT TYPE=HIDDEN>	VALUE	✔	✔			
<INPUT TYPE=PASSWORD>	VALUE	✔	✔			✔
<TEXTAREA>	Contents	✔	✔			✔
<MARQUEE>	Contents	✔	✔	✔		
<SELECT>	Selected item	✔	✔			✔
<IMG>	SRC	✔	✔			
<A>	HREF	✔	✔			
<BUTTON>	Contents	✔	✔	✔		
<LABEL>	Contents	✔	✔	✔		
<OBJECT> or <APPLET>	Default property	✔	✔			✔
<PARAM>	Property of object or applet	✔	✔			✔
<FRAME>	HREF	✔	✔			
<IFRAME>	HREF	✔	✔			
<TABLE>	Repetition	✔			✔	

Table 15-1.
Summary of data consumers.

Notice in the Table element example that the data-bound elements within the Table element do not specify the DATASRC attribute. Because the Table element is repeated, elements in the table inherit the DATASRC attribute value—namely, *#stocklist*—from the repeated table.

You can include multiple TBody elements and multiple rows with any combination of ROWSPAN and COLSPAN attributes. When you are creating a repeated table, you should construct the table to display and format the data for a single record from the data source object. The entire contents of the table will then be repeated for each record in the data set. It is possible to limit the number of records repeated in a Table element. See the section "Paged Tables" later in this chapter for details.

Building Basic Pages Using Data Binding

Now that you understand the role of data source objects, the attributes used to specify a binding, and the HTML elements that can be bound, let's apply this information to building three basic pages using data binding.

Current Record Binding

Think of the current record as an index or a pointer to some record in the data source. The values from the columns in this record are displayed in the bound elements. A different record can be made current by incrementing or decrementing the index or pointer. When a new record becomes current, the bound elements are dynamically changed to reflect the data from the new record.

The following code demonstrates how to specify a current record binding:

```
<BODY TOPMARGIN=0 LEFTMARGIN=40 BGCOLOR="#FFFFFF">
   <FONT FACE="verdana,arial,helvetica" SIZE=2>
   <H2>Current Record Binding</H2>
   ⋮
   <P>Stock:
      <A DATASRC=#stocklist DATAFLD="Website">
         <SPAN DATASRC=#stocklist DATAFLD="CompanyName"></SPAN>
          (<SPAN DATASRC=#stocklist DATAFLD="Symbol"></SPAN>)
      </A>
   <P>Last: <SPAN DATASRC=#stocklist DATAFLD="Last"></SPAN>
   <P>Change:
      <SPAN DATASRC=#stocklist DATAFLD="ChangeF" DATAFORMATAS=HTML>
      </SPAN>
```

(continued)

```
    <P>Chart: <IMG ALIGN=top DATASRC=#stocklist DATAFLD="Chart">
    <HR>
    <INPUT TYPE=BUTTON VALUE=" |< "
       ONCLICK="stocklist.recordset.MoveFirst();">
     
    <INPUT TYPE=BUTTON VALUE=" < "
       ONCLICK="stocklist.recordset.MovePrevious();">
     
    <INPUT TYPE=BUTTON VALUE=" > "
       ONCLICK="stocklist.recordset.MoveNext();">
     
    <INPUT TYPE=BUTTON VALUE=" >| "
       ONCLICK="stocklist.recordset.MoveLast();">
</BODY>
```

For current record binding, every bound element contains both the DATASRC and DATAFLD attributes.

Figure 15-2 shows how the current record binding example is displayed.

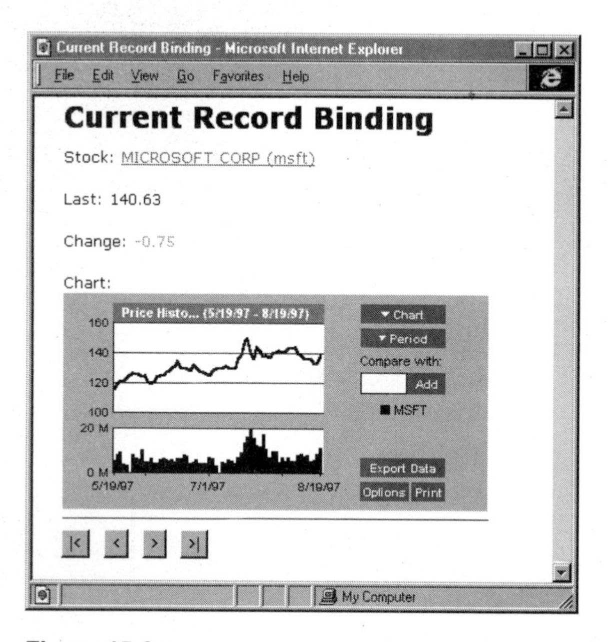

Figure 15-2.
A page using current record binding.

Notice the four HTML button controls included in this example. These controls provide user interface elements to control which record is current in the data source. Clicking the buttons sets the first, previous, next, or last record as the current record. This technique is discussed in detail in the section "Move Methods" later in this chapter.

Repeated Table Binding

The following code demonstrates how to create a simple repeated table. This example builds on the earlier stock table example with a few modifications. Here the Symbol column contains both the stock symbol and a bound Anchor element linking to each company's Web site. The data has been divided between two table rows, and a small chart has been added to each item in the table to show that stock's performance over the last six months. The cell containing the chart spans the two rows of each item.

```
<TABLE ID="stocktbl" DATASRC="#stocklist" BORDER=1>
   <THEAD>
      <TR ONCLICK="sort();">
         <TD CLASS=thd ROWSPAN=2><DIV ID=Symbol>Symbol</DIV></TD>
         <TD CLASS=thd><DIV ID=Last>Last</DIV></TD>
         <TD CLASS=thd><DIV ID=Change>Change</DIV></TD>
         <TD ROWSPAN=2>Chart</TD>
      </TR>
      <TR ONCLICK="sort();">
         <TD CLASS=thd><DIV ID=Volume>Volume</DIV></TD>
         <TD CLASS=thd><DIV ID=Type>Type</DIV></TD>
      </TR>
   </THEAD>

   <TBODY>
      <TR>
         <TD ALIGN=left ROWSPAN=2>
            <A DATAFLD="Website"><SPAN DATAFLD="Symbol"></SPAN></A>
         </TD>
         <TD ALIGN=right>
            <DIV DATAFLD="Last"></DIV>
         </TD>
         <TD ALIGN=right>
            <SPAN DATAFLD="ChangeF" DATAFORMATAS=HTML></SPAN>
         </TD>
         <TD ALIGN=left ROWSPAN=2>
            <IMG DATAFLD="Chart">
         </TD>
      </TR>
      <TR>
         <TD ALIGN=right>
            <DIV DATAFLD="Volume"></DIV>
         </TD>
```

(continued)

```
            <TD ALIGN=center>
               <SELECT DATAFLD="Type">
                  <OPTION VALUE=L>Long
                  <OPTION VALUE=S>Short
               </SELECT>
            </TD>
         </TR>
      </TBODY>
   </TABLE>
```

A few of the concepts illustrated here may not be obvious. First, you can use multiple bindings in a single cell of a table; the first cell contains an Anchor and a Span element, each of which are bound to different fields. Remember that the Table element is simply a container for repetition; the specification of the template can include any element or control with or without data binding, as long as the template obeys the rules of HTML.

Figure 15-3 shows the revised stock table.

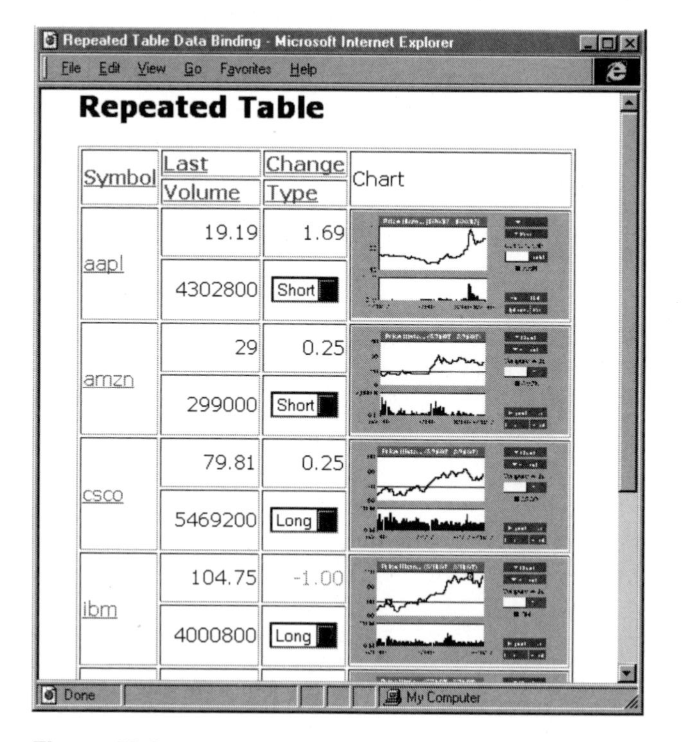

Figure 15-3.
Basic repeated table binding.

Note also that this example uses the TDC (Tabular Data Control) as its data source. The TDC is a data source object included with the minimal configuration of Internet Explorer 4.0. It uses a URL to retrieve data in a delimited text format. The data set used in the examples in this section has the fields shown in the following table.

Field	Data Type
Symbol	text
Last	float
Change	float
ChangeF	text
Volume	int
%Change	float
DateUpdated	text
High	float
Low	float
Open	float
Close	float
52WeekHigh	float
52WeekLow	float
PERatio	float
CompanyName	text
Shares	int
Website	text
Chart	text
Type	text
ExDiv	text

Paged Table Binding

In the preceding example, the table was repeated for each and every record in the data set. This repetition can result in large tables that are neither pleasing to view nor efficient to display. To solve this problem, the concept of *table paging* was introduced. Table paging allows the Web author to specify the exact number of records to be displayed in a repeated table at a given time. This technique lets the Web author limit how large the page will become as a result of repeating the table's template. It also allows the Web author to constrain the table to a specific region of the page and to place other page elements around the table without having to worry about elements below the table being moved out of view.

To enable table paging, the DATAPAGESIZE attribute is specified on a repeated table. DATAPAGESIZE takes an integer argument that defines the number of records from the data set, and correspondingly the number of instances of the table template, to repeat in the table at any one time. (Display of partial templates is not supported.)

Building on the preceding example, the only change necessary to enable table paging is to include the DATAPAGESIZE attribute on the Table element:

```
<TABLE ID="stocktbl" DATASRC="#stocklist" DATAPAGESIZE=4 BORDER=1>
  ⋮
</TABLE>
```

This code displays the data from four records in the table at a time.

Figure 15-4 shows the stock table example with table paging enabled.

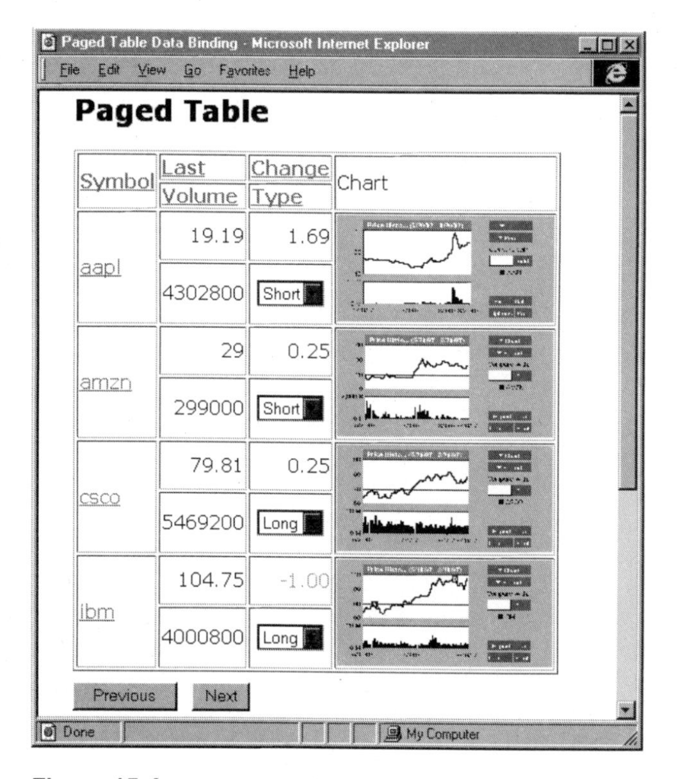

Figure 15-4.
Basic paged table binding.

But how can the user view the remainder of the data? Two methods are exposed on a paged, repeated table to show additional records from the data set: *nextPage*, which displays the next page of data in the table, and *previousPage*, which displays the previous page of data. Using these methods, the Web author can include HTML elements that invoke scripts to display additional pages of data. The Next and Previous buttons, shown in Figure 15-4, call the *nextPage* and *previousPage* methods on the repeated table. These buttons are defined as follows:

```
<INPUT TYPE=BUTTON VALUE=" Previous "
   ONCLICK="stocktbl.previousPage();">
<INPUT TYPE=BUTTON VALUE=" Next "
   ONCLICK="stocktbl.nextPage();">
```

Boundary conditions are worth noting. If *nextPage* is invoked when there is less than a page of records remaining in the data set, the table displays only the remaining records. Thereafter, *nextPage* fails silently. If *previousPage* is invoked when the current record is less than a page of records from the first record in the data set, a full page of records beginning with the first record is shown. Thereafter, *previousPage* fails silently. Finally, when records are dynamically added or deleted, the data displayed will be adjusted accordingly. In that case, the record displayed at the top of the table remains at the top unless it is deleted.

Writing Scripts Using Data Binding

The preceding section showed you how to write bindings using HTML. In this section, you'll learn how to combine script code with data binding to create actual data-access applications that can run in Internet Explorer 4.0. The discussion begins by introducing ADO (ActiveX Data Objects) and then proceeds to the events provided by Internet Explorer 4.0 on data-bound elements and data source objects.

ADO-Recordset Version

The current record-binding example presented earlier in this chapter used HTML button controls to move the current record pointer forward and backward. The script used for the *onclick* event was *stocklist.recordset.MoveNext()*. This code references the *recordset* object from the data source object *stocklist* and then invokes the *MoveNext* method on the *recordset* object.

The *recordset* object in this case is ADO-Recordset version, referred to here as ADOR, which includes only the *recordset* and *field* objects from the full version of ADO provided with various other Microsoft products, such as Active

Server Pages. Internet Explorer 4.0 supplies ADOR to all data source objects on a Web page. As shown in the preceding example, the *recordset* object is accessible from the *recordset* property of the data source object.

You can access the data in an ADOR recordset using scripts. Through scripts you can change which record is current and perform calculations, validation, or any other function that requires access to the data. The data used in the ADOR recordset need not be bound to any HTML elements on the page. You can use the ADOR recordset solely for programmatic access to data from a data source object.

The specifics of using ADOR are beyond the scope of this chapter. However, the following sections touch on two key areas of functionality commonly used by Web pages: move methods and *field* objects.

Move Methods

The move methods allow you to change which record is current, thereby changing the values displayed in any bound elements. The methods used to move the current record pointer are: *Move, MoveNext, MovePrevious, MoveFirst,* and *MoveLast.* The *Move* method takes an argument to move the current record pointer to the specified position in the recordset. The functions of the other move methods are self-explanatory.

ADOR allows you to move the current record pointer before the first record in the data set (BOF, or beginning of file) or after the last record in the data set (EOF, or end of file). Because these positions have no data associated with them, moving to these positions will result in all bindings on the page having null values, which usually means nothing is displayed. This problem can be avoided by checking the current position in the recordset prior to moving the pointer. The following code checks whether the current record is the last record in the recordset prior to advancing the current record pointer:

```
<SCRIPT LANGUAGE="JavaScript" FOR=NextButton EVENT=onclick>
   if (stocklist.recordset.AbsolutePosition <
       stocklist.recordset.RecordCount)
      stocklist.recordset.MoveNext();
   else
      alert("Already at last record.");
</SCRIPT>
```

NOTE: The current record position can also be changed by setting the *AbsolutePosition* property on the recordset.

The *fields* Collection/The *field* Object

The *fields* collection provides a set of *field* objects for a recordset. A *field* object corresponds directly to a single column of data. The *field* object is used to read data values from the column for the current record of the recordset. For example, the data for the current record in a column named Last could be obtained using the following lines of code, all of which return the same value:

```
stocklist.recordset.Fields("Last").value
stocklist.recordset.Fields("Last")
stocklist.recordset("Last")
```

Assigning a value to the *Value* property of the *field* object modifies the value. The following code sets the last stock price in the current record to *103.0*:

```
stocklist.recordset("Last") = 103.0;
```

Again, any of the three equivalent forms could be used to write this statement.

For more details about ADOR, consult the Internet Client SDK (Software Development Kit), available from the Microsoft Web site at www.microsoft.com/msdn/sdk/inetsdk.

Script Events

Internet Explorer 4.0 provides a rich event set to enable Web authors to write scripts in response to user actions on data-bound pages. The event set can be divided into two categories. One category of events fires on data-consuming elements. These events (*onbeforeupdate, onafterupdate,* and *onerrorupdate*) provide for validation of user input. The second category of events (*onrowexit, onrowenter, ondatasetchanged, ondataavailable,* and *ondatasetcomplete*) fires on data source objects to enable validation and processing when a new record becomes current or in response to data being asynchronously transmitted to the client. An additional event, *onbeforeunload,* is not specific to data binding but is particularly useful in data-binding applications. The following sections describe these events in greater detail.

> NOTE: As with all events in the Dynamic HTML object model, the events described in this section bubble up the containment hierarchy. Handlers for them can be written at any level of the hierarchy. If multiple data source objects are present on the page, the Web author can include a single handler for any event in a common container to process the event.

The *onbeforeupdate* Event

The *onbeforeupdate* event fires on HTML elements that support data updating. (See Table 15-1 earlier in this chapter for a list of data consumers that support updating.) The *onbeforeupdate* event fires when the user moves the focus from an element whose value has been updated and before the updated data is transmitted to the data source object by the binding agent. The previous value of the data can be obtained from the data source object using the ADOR recordset. The *onbeforeupdate* event can be used by the Web author to perform validation. If the Web author cancels the event, the focus remains on the element and the data is not transmitted to the data source object.

The following code demonstrates a handler for the *onbeforeupdate* event. In this example, the value in the HTML text box is verified to be in the range 5 through 15. If the value is outside the range, an error message is displayed and the event is canceled.

```
<SCRIPT LANGUAGE="JavaScript" FOR=textbox1 EVENT=onbeforeupdate>
   if (textbox1.value < 5 || textbox1.value > 15)
   {
      alert("Number must be in the range 5 through 15.");
      returnValue = false;
   }
</SCRIPT>
```

The *onafterupdate* Event

The *onafterupdate* event is also fired on HTML elements that support updating; however, it fires immediately after the data is transmitted from the element to the data source object. The *onafterupdate* event is not fired if the *onbeforeupdate* event is canceled, and *onafterupdate* itself is not cancelable.

One use of *onafterupdate* is for updating the value of a calculated amount. For example, suppose the user is filling out an order form, has selected an item, and is now selecting the quantity. When the quantity is entered, you want to calculate the line item total based on the price of the item and the quantity requested. You can accomplish this in the handler for the *onafterupdate* event of the text box in which the quantity is entered:

```
<SCRIPT LANGUAGE="JavaScript" FOR=quant_tbox EVENT=onafterupdate>
   line_total.value = quant_tbox.value * item_price.value;
</SCRIPT>
```

The *onerrorupdate* Event

The *onbeforeupdate* and *onafterupdate* events span the transfer of data from the HTML element to the data source object. But these two events don't cover the rare case in which the transfer of the data fails. In this case, the *onerrorupdate* event fires.

The *onerrorupdate* and *onafterupdate* events are mutually exclusive—that is, *onafterupdate* fires only if the data transfer succeeds, and *onerrorupdate* fires only when the data transfer fails. The *onerrorupdate* event provides the Web author with an opportunity to display a sensible error message to the user when the data transfer fails.

> NOTE: A data transfer occurs when the binding and repetition agent notices that the value in a bound element has changed. But the binding and repetition agent might not notice the change in value immediately after the change takes place. For example, if a bound value is changed through a script, the binding and repetition agent won't notice the change until the current record pointer is moved or the page is unloaded.
>
> Additionally, because an object or applet is not required to fire notifications when the value of one of its bound properties changes, the binding and repetition agent automatically transfers data from an object or applet when the current record pointer is moved or the page is unloaded, even if the value has not changed.

The *onrowexit* Event

The *onrowexit* event is the first of the set of events that fire on the data source object. Recall that each data source object has one record that is the current record. A different record can be made current by using the move methods in ADOR. The *onrowexit* event fires on the data source object to signify that the current record pointer is about to be moved.

A number of steps must take place before *onrowexit* is fired. First the current record pointer must be requested to move, generally by the execution of a move method on the ADOR recordset. Once the request is received, the binding agent examines each bound HTML element to determine whether any data items from the current record have been modified. It does this by comparing the value in the element to the value in the column of the data source object. If the columns differ, the binding agent fires the *onbeforeupdate* event on that element. If the event is canceled, the sequence is terminated and the current record pointer remains unmoved. If *onbeforeupdate* is not canceled, the *onafterupdate* event is fired on the element. This process is repeated for each bound HTML element. After all elements have been synchronized, the *onrowexit* event is fired on the data source object.

The *onrowexit* event is cancelable. When the Web author cancels the event, the current record pointer remains in place. The *onrowexit* event is useful for performing record-level validation or for recalculating columns of the data source object that are not bound but are based on the values in other columns.

The following example shows an *onrowexit* handler:

```
<SCRIPT LANGUAGE="JavaScript">
   function myrowexit() {
      if (stocklist.recordset("Last") * stocklist.recordset("Shares")
            > my_cash_balance) {
         alert("Purchase exceeds cash position in your account.");
         returnValue = false;
      }
   }
</SCRIPT>
```

The *onrowenter* Event

As its name implies, the *onrowenter* event fires immediately after the current record pointer has been moved. When it fires, all data from the new current record will be present in the HTML elements bound to the data source object.

The *onrowenter* event is not cancelable because the data from the new current record is already displayed to the user. The *onrowenter* event is useful for calculating fields based on the data elements in a row. The following example demonstrates how to use *onrowenter*:

```
<SCRIPT LANGUAGE="JavaScript">
   function myrowenter() {
      total_value.text =
         stocklist.recordset("Price") * stocklist.recordset("Shares");
   }
</SCRIPT>
```

The *ondatasetchanged* Event

Web authors need to know when the data source object is ready to supply data, and the *ondatasetchanged* event is the first of three events available to help. The *ondatasetchanged* event fires on the data source object as soon as data is available, signifying that the ADOR recordset can now be obtained from the data source object. The *ondatasetchanged* event is not cancelable.

In addition to firing when an HTML page is initially displayed, *ondatasetchanged* fires when data source objects perform data manipulations. This manipulation can be in response to a reordering of the data set caused by sorting or to a change in the underlying structure of the data set (number of rows or columns, or column names) caused by filtering.

The *ondataavailable* Event

Web authors can be notified when more data from a data source object has arrived by handling the *ondataavailable* event. The *ondataavailable* event fires when data from a data source object has been received by the browser; *ondataavailable* is not cancelable.

The data source object determines the firing frequency of *ondataavailable.* For performance reasons, most data source objects don't fire *ondataavailable* for each record displayed. Instead, data source objects will collect a number of rows as a block and fire *ondataavailable* for the block of rows. The *ondataavailable* event does not, however, indicate the number of rows available nor does it indicate their position within the data set. This information must be determined directly from the ADOR recordset.

The *ondataavailable* event can be used to calculate a running total of records as they are received or to perform script operations as data arrives in the browser:

```
<SCRIPT LANGUAGE="JavaScript">
   var count;
   function myondataavailable() {
      total_stocks.value = stocklist.recordset.RecordCount;
   }
</SCRIPT>
```

The *ondatasetcomplete* Event

Rounding out the set of asynchronous events is the *ondatasetcomplete* event. Probably the most useful asynchronous event, *ondatasetcomplete* notifies the Web author that asynchronous transmission is complete and the entire data set is available.

The *ondatasetcomplete* event sets the *reason* property on the *event* object to inform the Web author of the status of the transmission. The following table lists the three possible values for the *reason* property.

Value	Description
0	Transmission was completed without error.
1	User aborted the transmission. Generally, this interruption occurs when the user clicks the Stop button on the page.
2	Transmission generated an error. This is the catchall case for transmission failures of all sorts, including the inability to contact the host or a dropped connection.

The *onbeforeunload* Event

The *onbeforeunload* event is not specific to data binding, but handling it can be useful for avoiding data loss on data-bound pages. Some data source objects can cache updates to the data they supply on the client until a method is invoked on the object to save the updated values to the server. Because these values can be cached, the user can attempt to navigate away from the page prior to saving the updated values. The *onbeforeunload* event can be used to prompt the user to cancel the navigation, avoiding the loss of the changes.

The operation of the *onbeforeunload* event is somewhat different from the other events discussed so far. The *onbeforeunload* event fires in response to a request from the user to navigate to a new page—for example, when the user clicks on a hyperlink, clicks the Back or Forward button, or types a new URL in the address bar. The *onbeforeunload* event fires on the *window* object prior to the *unload* event on a page. When the event fires, the Web author can set the *returnValue* property on the *event* object to a string value, which will be displayed to the user along with a standard message from the browser explaining that the user has the option to cancel the requested navigation. Generally, Web authors will return a message instructing the user that continuing with the navigation will result in the cached changes being discarded. If the user chooses to cancel the navigation, the page remains visible and the user can interact with it as if the hyperlink or other navigation method was never invoked. If the user continues the navigation, the page is unloaded and the changes to the data are discarded.

Canceling the *unload* Event Requires User Interaction

Shouldn't the author be able to simply cancel the *unload* event without prompting the user? The answer to this question is centered in operating system security issues. If the Web author were able to cancel the *unload* event, it would be possible to create a page that would never unload—that is, the *unload* event would always cancel the navigation. The only way for the user to navigate away from the page would be to kill the browser process, which is a violation of basic operating system integrity because the user should be in control of his or her local machine and processes at all times. Although *onbeforeunload* can be canceled, it is the user who chooses to cancel the *unload* event, not the Web author. The Web author only has the ability to provide the user with an informational message.

Advanced Features

Now that you've learned the basics, you're ready for some of the advanced features of data binding that enable the construction of more sophisticated, application-like pages.

Data Update

A data source object can enable the user to update the data it supplies. When the user updates the data in an element bound to the data source object, the binding agent will store the modified value in the data source object. The data source object can then save these changed values in the underlying data source.

Generally, data source objects support data updates by allowing the user to modify data values stored within the local cache. The data source object can then choose when to update the data in the underlying data source: data can be updated immediately or in batch mode. Changes to a single cell, to a single row, or to the entire data set can be cached. Which mode the data source object operates in will be based largely on whether a connection to the underlying data source is maintained. When the entire data set is cached, data source objects usually expose a method that Web authors can call in order to save the cached data.

RDS is an example of a data source object that provides the ability to update data. RDS works in conjunction with a server-side component that enables access to ODBC (Online Database Connectivity) data sources. RDS stores the entire data set (the result of a SQL query) in a local in-memory cache. In addition to storing the data, RDS stores concurrency information to resolve conflicts when multiple users modify the same data values simultaneously. Data changed by a user is sent with this concurrency information to a server component that performs the update to the database. RDS can be used to build sophisticated client/server applications using HTML and scripts.

> NOTE: Examples of applications written using RDS can be found on the Microsoft Web site at www.microsoft.com/data. The server component can be obtained free at the same URL. The client component of RDS is an integral part of the Internet Explorer 4.0 browser and is installed with the minimal configuration of the browser.

The *recordNumber* Property

The *recordNumber* property is available on all elements that are part of the template of a repeated table. Recall that when repeated table binding is used, the contents of the table are used as a template and repeated once for each record in the data set. Each instance of the repetition is called a *template instance.* For each element in a template instance (including elements that are not data bound, such as the <TR> and <TD> tags), *recordNumber* provides the record number from the data set that generated the element.

The *recordNumber* property corresponds directly to the *AbsolutePosition* property of the ADOR recordset. By using *recordNumber* to set *AbsolutePosition* on the recordset, the Web author can access additional data elements from the same column of the data set. You need to set the *AbsolutePosition* property because ADOR allows access only to fields in the current record.

The *recordNumber* property is not a bookmark; *recordNumber* changes as a result of rows being inserted or deleted from the local client cache. Using ADOR, however, the Web author can obtain a bookmark for the column by using the *recordNumber* property:

```
<SCRIPT LANGUAGE="JavaScript">
   var clone_rs = stocklist.recordset.clone();
   clone_rs.AbsolutePosition = textbox1.recordNumber;
   var bkmk = clone_rs.Bookmark;
</SCRIPT>
```

This bookmark always refers to the same record in the recordset, regardless of whether rows are inserted and deleted.

The *recordNumber* property can also be used to assist with navigating a collection of elements in a repeated table. You can uniquely name an element in HTML by including an ID attribute in the element's tag. When you name an element in the template of a repeated table, however, the result is a collection of elements with the same ID because the template is repeated for each record of the data set. The *recordNumber* property can be used in conjunction with a script to display details for the record corresponding to the selected element. For example, say that instead of viewing all of your stock data at once you want to view detailed data when you click on a particular stock. You can include selector buttons in the table to select a stock and then set the current record to the selected stock to display the detailed data using the following HTML:

```
<BODY TOPMARGIN=0 LEFTMARGIN=40 BGCOLOR="#FFFFFF">
   <FONT FACE="verdana,arial,helvetica" SIZE=2>
   <H2>Record Number</H2>
   ⋮
   <TABLE>
      <TR>
         <TD VALIGN=top>
            <TABLE ID="stocktbl" DATASRC="#stocklist" BORDER=1>
               <THEAD>
```

```
            <TR ONCLICK="sort();">
               <TD> 
               <TD CLASS=thd><DIV ID=Symbol>Symbol</DIV></TD>
               <TD CLASS=thd><DIV ID=Last>Shares</DIV></TD>
               <TD CLASS=thd><DIV ID=Volume>Volume</DIV></TD>
            </TR>
         </THEAD>
         <TBODY>
            <TR>
               <TD>
                  <BUTTON CLASS=sb ONCLICK="setrn(this);">
                     <B>show</B>
                  </BUTTON>
               </TD>
               <TD><A DATASRC="Website"><SPAN DATAFLD="Symbol">
                  </SPAN></A>
               </TD>
               <TD ALIGN=right><DIV DATAFLD="Shares"></DIV></TD>
               <TD ALIGN=right>
                  <SPAN DATAFLD="Volume" DATAFORMATAS=HTML>
                  </SPAN>
               </TD>
            </TR>
         </TBODY>
      </TABLE>
   </TD>
   <TD VALIGN=top>
      <B>Company Name:</B>
         <SPAN DATASRC="#stocklist" DATAFLD="CompanyName">
         </SPAN>
      <BR>
      <B>Last Updated:</B>
         <SPAN DATASRC="#stocklist" DATAFLD="DateUpdated">
         </SPAN>
      <BR>
      <B>Open:</B>
         <SPAN DATASRC="#stocklist" DATAFLD="Open">
         </SPAN>
      <BR>
      <B>High:</B>
         <SPAN DATASRC="#stocklist" DATAFLD="High">
         </SPAN>
      <BR>
      <B>Low:</B>
         <SPAN DATASRC="#stocklist" DATAFLD="Low">
         </SPAN>
```

(continued)

```
                <BR>
                <B>PE Ratio:</B>
                   <SPAN DATASRC="#stocklist" DATAFLD="PERatio">
                   </SPAN>
                <BR>
                <B>Chart:</B>
                <IMG ALIGN=top DATASRC="#stocklist" DATAFLD="Chart">
                </SPAN>
          </TR>
       </TABLE>
       :
       <SCRIPT LANGUAGE="JavaScript">
          function setrn(button) {
             stocklist.recordset.AbsolutePosition = button.recordNumber;
          }
       </SCRIPT>
    </BODY>
```

Figure 15-5 shows how the details are displayed next to the table.

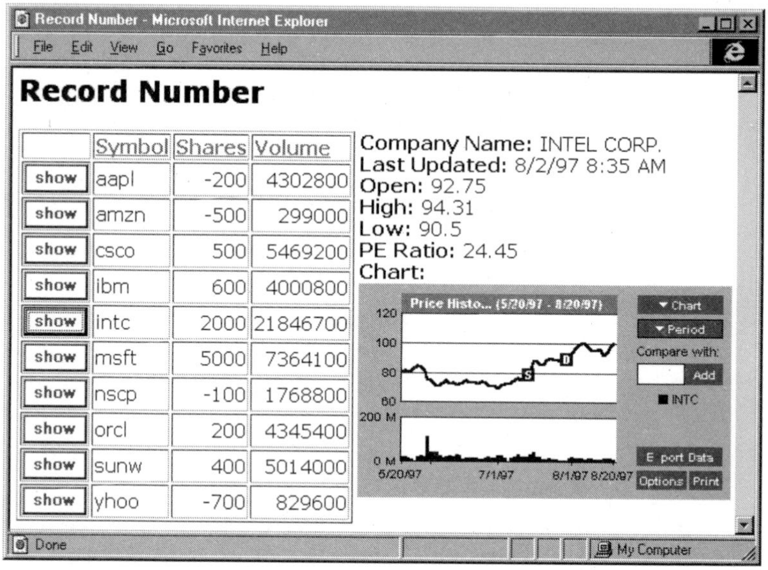

Figure 15-5.
Using the recordNumber *property to display details from a single record in a repeated table.*

Modifying Binding Attributes

Dynamic HTML exposes properties that correspond to the attributes and styles on the tags for HTML elements. The data-binding attributes are no exception. The Web author has the full capability to add, delete, and modify the data-binding properties on HTML elements after the page has been rendered. Moreover, using Dynamic HTML the Web author can also add data source objects to and delete data source objects from the page.

The one caveat to this correspondence is that the DATASRC, DATAFLD, and DATAFORMATAS attributes cannot be modified on elements within a repeated table. You can get around this limitation by changing the table to a standard HTML table. First remove the DATASRC attribute from the table. The table reduces to a nonrepeated state and includes only the template. The elements within the template, although not bound, can then be modified. DATASRC can then be added back to the table to reinstate the repetition. Using the multimedia extensions of Internet Explorer 4.0, the Web author can also suspend redisplay of the table so that this series of steps occurs without multiple redraws.

> NOTE: Additional information about data binding can be obtained from the Internet Explorer 4.0 section of the Microsoft Web site at www.microsoft.com. Examples can also be found at the same location.

<SCRIPT LANGUAGE="JavaSc
// Create property x
var x = 10;
unction foo() {
// This code is not
code
var y =
alert(
// output
// Call foo while lo
foo();
window.foo(); // th
</SCRIPT>

INDEX

SPECIAL CHARACTERS

A

C

D

E

G

H

J

K

L

M

P

Q

R

S

T

U

V

W

X

Z

Scott Isaacs

Scott Isaacs is a Microsoft program manager working on Internet Explorer. He has worked on the design of Dynamic HTML from the beginning and frequently presents the technology at industry conferences. Scott also represents Microsoft on working groups of the World Wide Web Consortium (W3C) for standardizing HTML, CSS, and the document object model. Independently, Scott maintains a Web site, www.insideDHTML.com, that covers the latest Dynamic HTML developments.

The manuscript for this book was prepared and submitted to Microsoft Press in electronic form. Text files were prepared using Microsoft Word 97. Pages were composed by Microsoft Press using Adobe PageMaker 6.5 for Windows, with text in New Baskerville and display type in Helvetica bold. Composed pages were delivered to the printer as electronic prepress files.

Cover Graphic Designer
Tim Girvin Design

Cover Illustrator
Glenn Mitsui

Interior Graphic Designer
Pamela Hidaka

Interior Graphic Artist
Joel Panchot

Principal Compositor
Elizabeth Hansford

Principal Proofreader
Roger LeBlanc

Indexer
Liz Cunningham

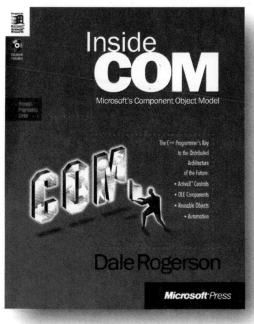

Register Today!

Return this
Inside Dynamic HTML
registration card for
a Microsoft Press® catalog

U.S. and Canada addresses only. Fill in information below and mail postage-free. Please mail only the bottom half of this page.

1-57231-686-1A ***INSIDE DYNAMIC HTML*** ***Owner Registration Card***

NAME

INSTITUTION OR COMPANY NAME

ADDRESS

CITY STATE ZIP

Microsoft® Press
Quality Computer Books